The Universe Natural History Series

THE LIFE OF REPTILES
VOLUME II

The Universe Natural History Series

Editor: Richard Carrington
Associate Editors:
Dr L. Harrison Matthews
Professor J. Z. Young

The Life of Reptiles

Volume II

ANGUS BELLAIRS

UNIVERSE BOOKS

NEW YORK CITY

Published in the United States of America in 1970
by UNIVERSE BOOKS
381 Park Avenue South, New York City, 10016

Copyright © 1970 by Angus Bellairs

Library of Congress Catalog Card Number: 70–99976
SBN 87663–113–8

Printed in Great Britain

Contents

Acknowledgments for Photographs

The author and publishers wish to thank the following for providing photographs for this volume: Dr C. M. Bogert, plates 45, 73, 77; Prof. A. S. Breathnach and Dr S. V. Bryant, plates 40–44; Dr H. R. Bustard, plates 46, 47, 49, 58, 59, 60, 64, 78; Dr H. B. Cott, plates 62, 63 (63 taken by Dr P. H. Greenwood); Dr H. J. Gamble, plate 50; Dr R. Gaymer, plate 74; Mr B. Hughes, plate 48; Dr P. F. A. Maderson, plate 71; Popper Photos, jacket photo; Dr P. C. H. Pritchard, plates 56, 57; Dr L. R. Robinson, plate 51; Sally Anne Thompson, plate 75; Dr A. Vinegar, plate 61.

List of Plates

Chapter 7

The Skin

Skin structure and function

THE SKIN is an organ with many functions. It acts as a barrier between the tissues of the animal and the outside world, defending them from the attacks of predators, the wear and tear of the surroundings and other unfavourable physical conditions. When furnished with appendages such as horns and spines it enhances the creature's powers of offence or defence. By virtue of its colour it is important in concealment, or alternatively, may render an animal frighteningly conspicuous to its foes or attractive to its mates. Because of its frictional resistance it can be important in locomotion. It is well supplied with nerves, at least in some places, and therefore has a sensory function. Indeed there is hardly any activity in which the skin is not either directly or indirectly involved, and the emergence of a science of comparative dermatology would be a happy event in the growth of modern biology.

Structure and evolution

The skin of reptiles is characteristically dry and scaly, and is poorly supplied with glands. As in other vertebrate animals it consists of two main layers, an outer one or epidermis which is derived from the ectoderm of the embryo, and an inner one, the dermis, which originates from mesoderm. The scales are formed mainly from the epidermis, although the dermis also participates in their composition. Although these scales may look as if they were separate structures superimposed on the skin, they are in fact a series of localised thickenings or folds in a continuous sheet of tissue; all the various layers of the skin pass without interruption from one scale to the next, although they are thinned out in the regions between the scales (figure 90 B, p. 288).

Scales have a definite pattern and arrangement which is usually fairly constant within any particular species. Since they can often be precisely described and numbered they provide very useful recognition characters for the taxonomist, especially in the distinction between closely related species and subspecies. Counting of scale rows and close study of scale patterns is therefore of great importance in systematic work. The scutes of the chelonian shell have a similar utility.

Since scale variations often have a hereditary basis their occurrence in a population may suggest that new races or subspecies are being evolved. Sometimes they are correlated with geographical distribution. Klauber [240] has shown that in certain parts of California snakes which inhabit desert areas tend to have larger numbers of ventral scales than members of the same species which live along the coast. It is possible that these differences may sometimes be due to the direct effects of environment rather than heredity, for it has been shown that the offspring of snakes kept at lower temperatures during pregnancy may have fewer rows of body scales than those kept warmer; some of the scales on the head show a similar reduction.

Generally speaking, the scales on the head of reptiles are bigger and fewer in number than those elsewhere. They are often called plates or shields and have individual names such as nasal, parietal and supra-ocular (figure 89). In some lizards such as geckos, however, and in certain snakes such as the oriental water snakes *(Acrochordus)* and many vipers, some or all of the scales on the head are quite small and resemble those on the body. In some chelonians such as the soft-shelled freshwater terrapins *(Trionyx)* the scales over the head are ill-defined, and the skin shows only a faint indication of regional thickenings.

The appearance of the scales over the body and legs varies enormously. They may be raised up into rough horny scutes, as along the back in crocodiles and in a few lizards such as the caiman lizards *(Dracaena)* of South America. They may be spiny, as in many desert lizards, or flattened like the stones of a tesselated pavement, as in lizards of the subfamily Gerrhosaurinae, or small and granular, as in most geckos and certain water snakes. In the majority of lizards and snakes they are elongated and the back of each scale overlaps the front of the one behind it. Scales of this imbricating type often have knobs or keels on their outer surfaces which may help to stiffen them. The thinner skin between such scales is much folded and forms a kind of hinge which allows for distension, as, for example, when a snake has swallowed a large meal. In many lizards, such as monitors, gerrhosaurs and the big limbless glass lizard *Ophisaurus,* there is a well-developed fold in the skin running down each flank which may serve a similar purpose.

In the majority of snakes the under-surface of the body is covered by a single row of wide ventral scales called gastrosteges which are important in locomotion (p. 108). The presence of these big scales is characteristic of snakes and distinguishes most of them from legless lizards, in which the belly scales are always small and comparable in appearance to those on the back and flanks. In the boid snakes, however, the ventrals do not extend across the width of the body (figure 89 F), while in many of the primitive burrowing snakes (figure 40, p. 114) such as *Typhlops* and *Cylindrophis,* and in most marine and some freshwater snakes, the ventrals are little, if any, larger than those elsewhere. The anal or cloacal shield, which lies just in front of the vent, and the scales beneath the tail or subcaudals, are paired in many snakes (figure 89 E). It is interesting that the normally unpaired ventral scales arise as paired structures in the embryo, fusing in the midline shortly before the time of hatching or birth. The ventral scales of snakes have a fairly constant position in relation to the internal organs such as the thyroid, liver and kidneys, in a particular species. Counting down the scale row can then be a useful guide to surgical operations necessary in experimental work [67].

The body scales of reptiles show evidence of the segmental pattern which all vertebrates possess during embryonic life. Thus, in a typical snake such as a boa or a member of one of the advanced groups (Caenophidia) each of the wide ventral scales or each pair of subcaudals corresponds with a single segment of the body; hence the number of ventrals and subcaudal pairs conforms with the numbers of vertebrae in the body and tail. In some primitive snakes and in many lizards there are two transverse rows of scales to each segment, and in certain geckos the number may be as high as eight or even more [88, 434].

The microscopic structure of the reptilian skin is very interesting and is only now beginning to receive the study it deserves. As in other vertebrates the main outer layer or epidermis can be subdivided into a number of fairly distinct layers or regions (figures 90, 91; Plates 40–43). Its outermost region is called the horny layer or stratum corneum and is thicker on the outer surface of the scale than on the

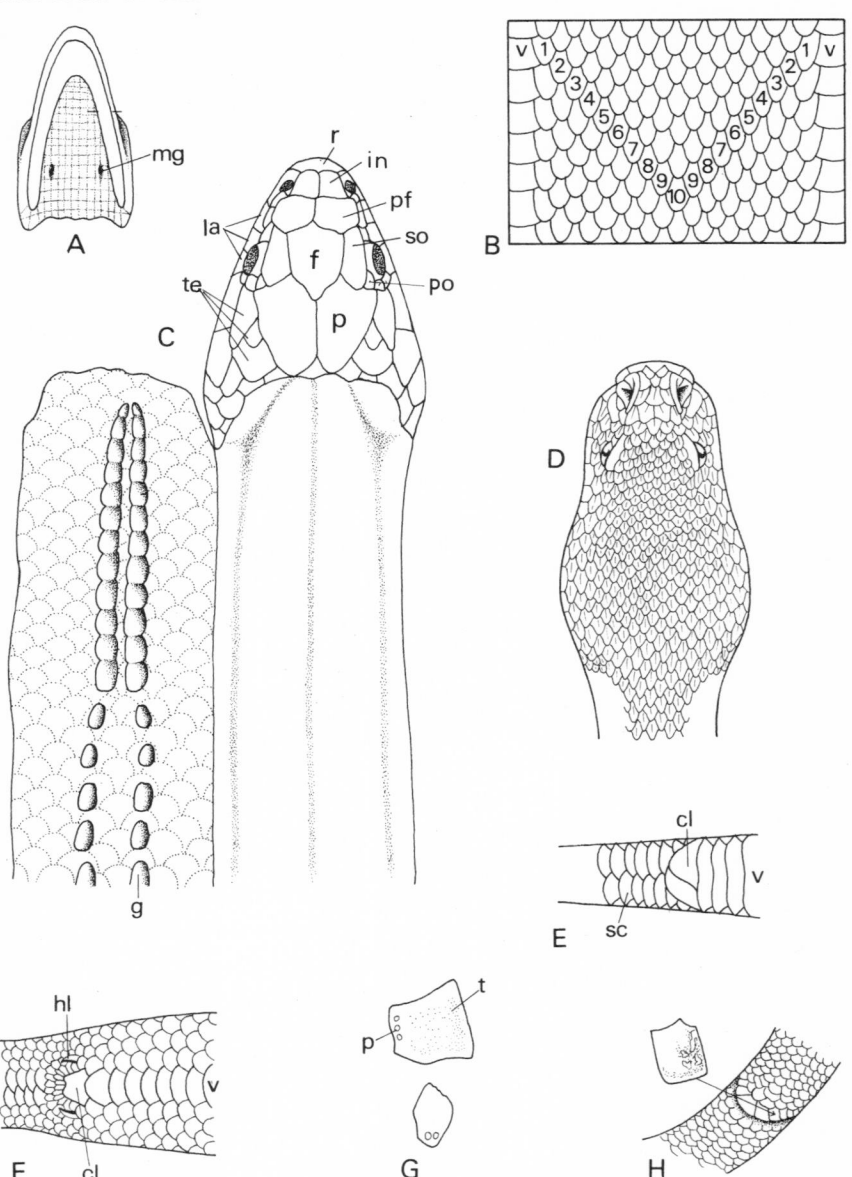

Figure 89   A. Under side of head of baby alligator showing openings of musk glands. After Reese, A. M. (1921) *J. Morph.* **35** 581 (figure 30, p. 609). B. Body scales of smooth snake (*Coronella austriaca*) showing method of counting dorsal scales in oblique transverse. series. After Smith [395]. C. *Natrix nuchalis* with dorsal skin of neck reflected showing the attached nucho-dorsal glands. The

nomenclature of some of the head shields is also given. After Smith, M. A. (1938) *Proc. Zool. Soc. Lond.* **107** 578. D. Head of *Vipera russelli*; covered by small scales instead of large shields. E. Under surface of cloacal region of colubrid snake *Natrix* [= *Amphiesma*] *stolata* showing broad ventrals, divided cloacal or anal shield, and paired subcaudals. F. Cloacal region of Indian *Python molurus* showing comparatively small ventral shields and rudimentary hind limb claws. D–F after Wall [443]. G. *Above*: upper labial shield of the colubrid *Alsophis leucomelas sanctorum* showing scale tubercles (tiny dots) and pits. They are most probably sense organs. *Below*: dorsal neck scale of same snake showing pair of pits. After Underwood [434]. H. Cloacal region of slow-worm (*Anguis fragilis*) showing small ventral scales. One of the shields bordering the cloaca is drawn separately to show the patchy distribution of melanin pigment; in the specimen the dots and enclosed areas showed up pale against the general dark background.

cl, cloacal or anal scale or shield. **f**, frontal. **g**, nuchodorsal glands. **hl**, hind limb claw. **in**, internasal. **la**, upper labial. **mg**, musk gland opening. **p**, pit, or parietal. **pf**, prefrontal. **po**, postocular. **r**, rostral. **sc**, subcaudals. **so**, supraocular. **t**, tubercle. **te**, temporal. **v**, ventrals.

inner surface which overlaps the scale adjacent to it. This is composed of the dead material keratin, a tough fibrous protein which is rich in sulphur-containing amino-acids such as cysteine; claws, hoofs, nails, horns, hair and feathers are also made up of it.

In lizards and snakes, and perhaps in other reptiles, the stratum corneum is composed of two separate layers. The outer or B-keratin layer is thick and hard, and in many species there is a series of fine ridges or sculpturings on its surface. These are clearly seen in material examined by electron microscopy, but are also discernible under the higher magnifications of the light microscope [76]. German workers have called this sculptured surface the *Oberhautchen* (outer skin). The details of the sculpturing may show differences which help one to distinguish between closely related species, and hence may be of interest to systematists. The deeper layer of A-keratin is more flexible and predominates in the regions of thinner skin between the scales where bending mostly takes place. It consists of flattened keratinised strands separated by bounding membranes which are quite distinct. These layers of keratin do not appear in the embryo until the time of hatching or birth approaches.

Beneath the A-keratin layer is an intermediate zone of cells which become flatter individually as they approach the horny layer, from within outwards. The deepest layer of all is the basal layer or stratum germinativum. Its cells give rise to all the more superficial layers; as they divide they are pushed off into the stratum intermedium and are progressively displaced towards the surface, where they become keratinised and form the new horny layer.

Beneath the basal layer of epidermis, and separated from it by a rather conspicious basement membrane, is the dermis. This consists of connective tissue, rich in collagen fibres, and contains a network of blood and lymphatic vessels, and nerves. Some of the latter pass into the epidermis where they may either end in little swellings or supply specialised sensory 'spots' or the bristle-like scale organs found in certain lizards [285]. The numerous pigment cells described later are also mainly found in the dermis. In many reptiles it also contains plates of bone known as osteoderms or osteoscutes (figure 90) which correspond, rather than the horny scales, with the scales of many bony fishes, and with the plates of mammals such as armadilloe.

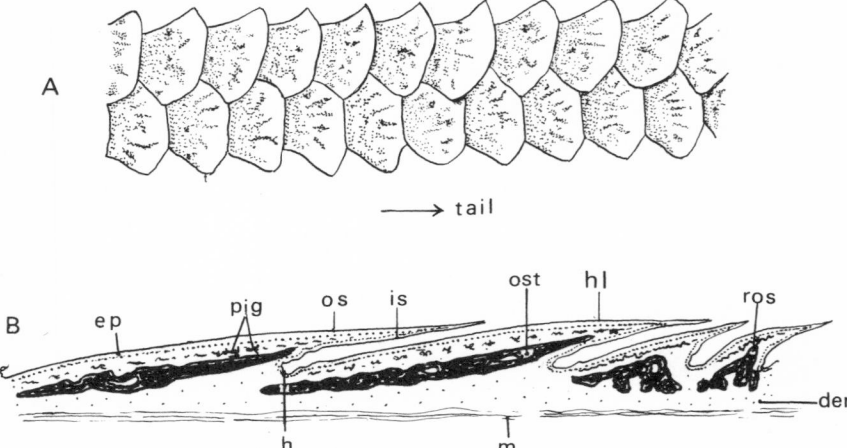

Figure 90   A. Two rows of osteoderms from dorsal skin of slow-worm (*Anguis fragilis*). Some of the fine pits are probably canals for blood vessels. B. Longitudinal microscopic section through scales of tail of slow-worm; the two smaller scales on the right belong to the regenerated tip.

der, dermis. **ep**, epidermis with superficial horny layer. **h**, hinge region. **hl**, horny layer (stratum corneum). **is**, inner scale surface. **m**, muscle. **os**, outer scale surface. **ost**, osteoderm. **pig**, pigment in dermis. **ros**, regenerated osteoderm.

The dermis forms a complete investment for the body and in certain regions such as the head or tail of lizards, is quite firmly attached to the underlying bone or muscle; in other places, however, there is a zone of loose tissue between the dermis and the deeper structures so that the whole thickness of the skin can be stripped off quite easily. The looseness of this tissue probably explains why a snake can be so readily skinned.

We know that many extinct amphibians and reptiles had a well developed armour of bony scutes or osteoderms. The horny scales, however, are not normally preserved as fossils and we can only speculate about their evolutionary history. Possibly they arose from warty thickenings of the epidermis like those seen in the more terrestrial amphibians of the present day, such as toads. In some cases, however, the horny scales have left impressions in the rocky matrix surrounding a fossil skeleton and there is direct evidence of their presence in a number of reptiles from the later Mesozoic, including mosasaurs and some dinosaurs.

Skin replacement

The skin of an animal must be able to make good by renewal the life-long ravages of wear and tear. In mammals such as man the dead horny layer of the skin is continually being rubbed off in tiny pieces and replaced by the growth and keratinisation of the deeper living cells. This continuous but piecemeal method of renewal seems to take place also in chelonians and crocodiles, where the outer horny parts of the scales and shell are probably shed individually and at different times in different places. We know comparatively little about skin replacement in these reptiles.

In lizards and snakes there are definite moulting periods when the outer part of the skin is shed all over the body. There is, of course, some parallel here with the moulting of many birds and furry mammals. In most lizards the skin is shed in quite large irregular flakes which come off everywhere at more or less the same time, although there may be slight regional variations; the head skin, for example, may be shed a few days before that of the tail. In the softer skinned species such as geckos, and also in some snake-like lizards such as the slow-worm (*Anguis*), the skin tends to be shed in very large pieces or even in a single continuous slough, as in most snakes. Geckos, and sometimes other lizards, may help themselves to moult by tearing away flakes of skin with their jaws; in some cases the shed skin is eaten by the reptile. Although a snake usually sheds its skin entire, or at least in very large fragments, piecemeal shedding may occasionally take place; this is often attributed to ill-health or unsuitable environmental conditions such as lack of moisture. In sea snakes both piecemeal and entire shedding have been described.

Two or three weeks before a snake is due to slough, its skin becomes dull and its eyes take on an opaque bluish tinge which is probably due to changes in the minute structure of the spectacle eye-covering (p. 351). The reptile may refuse to feed and become bad-tempered, perhaps because it cannot see very well. It often spends much of its time in water, and since there is evidence that the permeability of the skin is increased before moulting, it is possible that the snake soaks itself to avoid becoming uncomfortably dry. It may also be that the water helps to soften the keratin.

A few days before the moult actually takes place the spectacle clears again and the skin may regain something of its normal colour; one might suppose that it had already been shed were it not for the absence of the slough. The snake may then become restless, crawling about and rubbing its head against obstacles to break the skin around the mouth. Klauber [240] states that a healthy snake may be able to moult without such obstacles, but if available they are often utilised.

Both lizards and snakes are said to possess a physiological mechanism which facilitates the shedding process. The return of venous blood from the head to the heart can be obstructed by constriction of the jugular veins [390]. This causes the head to swell with blood, especially around the eyes where there are big venous sinuses, and helps to crack the dead horny layers. Inflation of the body with air may be of further assistance. Once the old skin has been torn away from the jaws escape from the rest of it is usually quite easy. If it can be caught against a stone or between the stems of vegetation it can readily be pulled off and often becomes turned inside out in the process. Frequently the whole slough is turned inside out except for the tip of the tail which slips off without becoming reversed.

It is clear that only the outer layers of the skin are shed since the slough is thin and fragile, quite different in texture from the full-thickness skin of a skinned snake, and has only faint, ghost-like traces of pigmentation. Shed snake-skins, complete even for the spectacle over the eye, can sometimes be picked up in the country-side, and enable the naturalist to identify the ophidian inhabitants of the neighbourhood.

The frequency of skin-shedding varies a great deal, in different species, in different individuals and even in the same individual. There is certainly little foundation for the popular belief that reptiles only slough once a year, in the spring. Some lizards may shed their skins as often as every month. Klauber [240], summarising the accounts of many observers, concludes that wild rattlesnakes usually slough between one and three times a year; shedding is more frequent in those species which live in warmer climates than in those which live further north and are only active for six to eight months out of the twelve. Rattlesnakes kept in artificially warmed cages may shed at least three times a year, and the frequency both in captivity and in the wild is greatest in young animals. The latter have been observed to slough up to seven times a year in captivity. Even greater frequencies have been observed in pythons. The first moult often takes place a few days after birth, and indeed it has been stated that in some viviparous reptiles the skin may be shed *in utero*.

The fresh colours of a snake which has recently shed its skin, and the creature's ability to renew its coat at intervals throughout its life have impressed poets and naturalists since the days of antiquity. Colonel Frank Wall [443], the herpetologist of Ceylon, has given a nice description of sloughing in the Russell's viper 'which may renovate it as completely as a mess uniform transforms an officer when exchanged for his khaki.'

Despite the fact that so much has been written about sloughing in snakes it is only quite recently that detailed studies have been made of the cellular changes in the skin which are responsible for it. These have been investigated by P. F. A. Maderson [267] who took daily samples of living skin from the colubrid snake *Elaphe taeniura* (the striped racer), which is found in Hong Kong. After a snake has sloughed its skin goes into a quiescent phase during which it shows the comparatively simple type of structure previously described (p. 287). There is the outer horny region with its *Oberhautchen* and keratin layers, an innermost layer of basal cells, and an intermediate zone consisting of a couple of rows of cells sandwiched between the two (figure 91 A: see also Plate 40 and ⊞; addenda).

After a variable period this resting condition changes rather suddenly as preparations for the fresh moult begin. Most of the cells of the basal layer start to divide at the same time and continue to do so until several rows of cells, becoming increasingly flattened from within outwards, are produced. It is now possible to recognise two successive generations of epidermal layers (figure 91 B). On the outside are the original horny and intermediate zone layers; these make up what is called the outer epidermal generation. The intermediate zone has changed in character and has become partly incorporated into the deeper part of the A-keratin layer. The several rows of new cells formed by the basal layer proliferation constitute the inner epidermal generation. The great thickening of the epidermis and

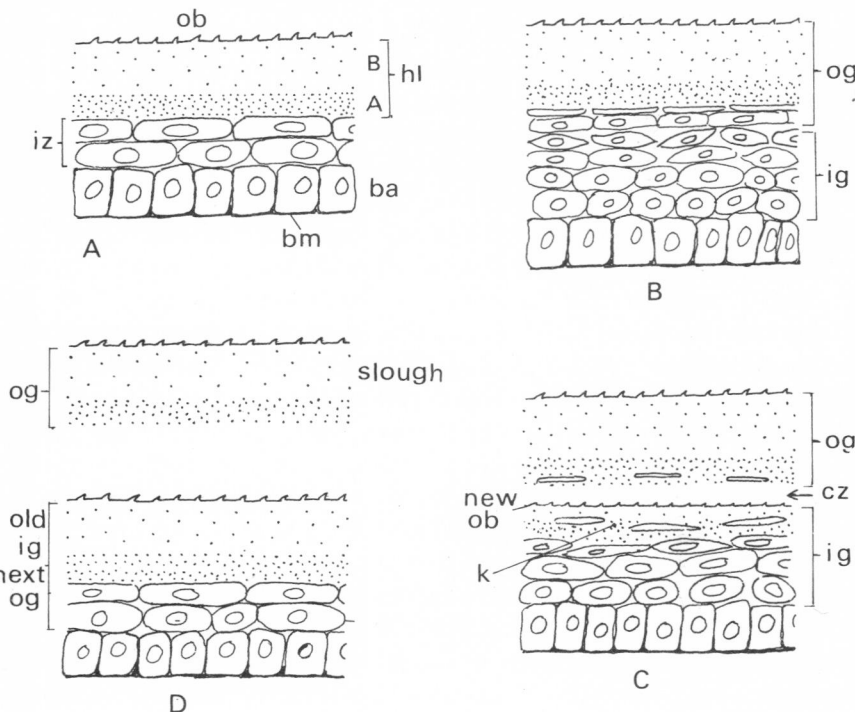

Figure 91. Simplified diagrams showing changes in the epidermis during the sloughing cycle of a snake. Based partly on Maderson [267]. A. Resting stage. B. Before sloughing. The basal cells have divided to form a new, inner epidermal generation (**ig**). The snake's colour is dulled. C. Shortly before sloughing. A cleavage zone appears between the two generations; the superficial part of the inner generation is becoming keratinised (**k**) and a new serrated *Oberhautchen* is being formed. This stage probably coincides with the clearing of the skin. D. Sloughing. The original outer generation is shed and the old inner generation becomes the next outer generation.

A, B, A- and B- keratin layers together comprising horny layer (stratum corneum). **ba,** basal cell layer (stratum germinativum). **bm,** basement (or basal) membrane between basal cells of epidermis and dermis. **cz,** cleavage zone. **hl,** horny layer. **iz,** intermediate zone cells (this layer does not altogether correspond with Maderson's stratum intermedium). **ob,** *Oberhautchen*. **ig, og,** outer and inner epidermal generations.

perhaps also the change in the character of the intermediate zone, are probably responsible for the fading of the snake's colours which has been previously noted.

In the next stage (figure 91 C) a cleavage zone appears between the outer and inner generations and the inner one matures so that it comes to resemble the original condition of the outer one. Its superficial cell rows become keratinised forming a new horny region with A- and B- layers and a sculptured *Oberhautchen*. The remaining deeper rows become the new intermediate zone. These changes seem to coincide with the clearing of the skin which is noticeable just before the actual sloughing takes place.

It now remains only for the outer generation to become detached as the slough (figure 91 D), after which the skin returns to the 'resting' condition and the cycle begins anew. The exact way in which the cleavage zone is established and the detachment of the old from the new 'skin' takes place is not fully understood. Part of the original intermediate zone of the outer generation seems to break down and it is possible that this dissolution is brought about by the liberation of proteolytic enzymes from eosinophil blood cells; these appear in the outer parts of the epidermis around this time. The dermis does not participate in these cyclical changes.

I have given a rather over-simplified version of Maderson's account which holds good in its essentials for other Squamata such as the tokay gecko [268] and probably also for *Sphenodon* [271].

The initiation of the sloughing cycle and the determination of its frequency is controlled, or at least strongly influenced by agents outside the skin itself. Endocrine glands, in particular the thyroid, are concerned in the process [99; see 371]. These in turn are probably influenced, directly or indirectly, by factors such as temperature, humidity and food-supply, and perhaps, as many vivarium-keepers believe, by the general health of the reptile.

The skin as a protective barrier

The tough, horny, and sometimes bony skin of reptiles gives good mechanical protection against wear and tear and is also said to form an effective barrier against penetration by certain wave-lengths of light, notably at the ultra-violet and infra-red ends of the spectrum. Its capacity for healing has been little studied but one has the impression that after extensive injury the scales take a long time to regenerate and may be irregular in arrangement. These remarks do not apply to the regeneration of tails by lizards, where new epidermis is formed very quickly and a regular, though sometimes atypical pattern of scalation is soon established (p. 481).

The reptilian skin is, as has been mentioned, much less effective as an insulator against changes in the temperature of the surroundings than the feathery or hairy coats of birds and mammals. It is partly for this reason that the reptiles have had to adopt a less precise method of temperature regulation than the 'warm-blooded' vertebrates and are so dependent for the maintenance of activity on external sources of heat.

The conservation of water is another important problem in which the skin is involved – particularly important to the numerous types of reptiles which live in arid surroundings. One might imagine that the dry and almost non-glandular skin would be extremely resistant to water loss. It appears, however, that there are great variations in the skin permeability of different species and that amphibious forms lose water more readily than terrestrial ones. The rate of water loss in *Caiman sclerops*, for example, is 19 times higher than that in the desert iguanid *Sauromalus* [38]. Burrowing reptiles may also lose water through the skin if they are placed in dry soil, and the amphisbaenid *Rhineura* becomes dehydrated more easily than the anguid *Anniella* which normally lives in drier places [52]. Some amphisbaenids are particularly prone to cutaneous water loss and the occurrence of certain species in semi-desert regions may be due to the habit of living along the beds of seasonal water-courses or at the roots of vegetation.

It is uncertain how much water reptiles can take up through the skin, and again, there are likely to be important differences between species. The fact that *Rhineura* soon regains weight after it has been transferred from dry to moist sand suggests that there is some absorptive mechanism. On the other hand, the old idea that the spiny little desert lizard *Moloch* of Australia (Plate 47 B) soaks up water through its skin like a sponge appears to be erroneous. What really happens is that the water creeps along by capillary action towards the mouth through minute channels in the horny epidermis, and is drunk by the lizard when it reaches the angle of the jaws [377].

Whatever conclusions about the permeability of the skin in reptiles are eventually reached, there can be little doubt that by comparison with the scaleless, glandular skin of most amphibians it is very waterproof. Even caimans (which for reptiles have very permeable skins) lose water by evaporation about half to a third as quickly as amphibians [38]. Iguanas and rattlesnakes lose water through the skin about 1/40th as quickly as do certain burrowing toads which also inhabit dry regions [257]. The comparative impermeability of the reptilian skin has probably played an important part in the evolutionary radiation of the class, enabling the reptiles to become the first really successful vertebrate colonists of the hot dry land. The significance of other methods of water conservation, such as the excretion of uric acid, has already been mentioned (p. 278).

As we have seen, the skin is also important in marine reptiles as a barrier against the loss of water by osmosis. Marine birds and mammals are probably protected in the same way and it may be supposed that the evolution of a comparatively waterproof skin was an essential prerequisite for vertebrates which have secondarily returned to life in the sea, as well as for desert-living forms. The salt water is an environment which the amphibians, with their permeable skins, have never been able to invade successfully, although one or two species have managed to adapt themselves to brackish water [257].

Colour and colour change

The colours of animals have interested many zoologists and have been studied from two points of view; the nature of colours and the physiological mechanisms which certain animals have evolved for changing them, and the part which colouration plays in the life of the creature as a whole. In this chapter the first of these topics will be considered; the adaptive significance of colour for such purposes as concealment and display is considered in Chapter 12.

The colour of skin and of other membranes such as the lining of the mouth and of the body cavity depends to a large extent on the presence of special pigment cells or chromatophores [71, *]. In reptiles these are mostly situated in the outer regions of the dermis. The commonest type of cell is one which contains the dark brown pigment melanin; it is known as a melanophore and possesses branching processes which extend outwards towards the basal cells of the epidermis. As a rule the melanophores form a dense and almost continuous sub-epidermal layer (figure 90, p. 288: Plate 41). There are also some smaller melanin-containing cells called melanocytes within the epidermis itself. These probably pass on granules of melanin to the cells which become keratinised, and are the source of the faint pigmentation seen in the sloughed skin.

The melanin-containing cells are primarily responsible for dark colouration and seem to be present in the great majority of reptiles. In one form at least, the burrowing skink *Voeltzkowia*, they are said to be the only pigmented cells found [310]. Presumably they predominate in all dark-skinned species, and in melanistic races or individuals which crop up from time to time among populations of normally lighter-coloured forms [250]. Deficiency of melanin is probably responsible for the white or very pale colours of a few reptiles, such as the burrowing lizard *Rhineura* and the race of earless lizards *(Holbrookia)* which lives in the White Sands area of New Mexico (p. 510). Cases of albinism among reptiles, such as the beautiful white python figured in C. H. Pope's book *The Giant Snakes* [333], are sometimes described, and here again, lack of melanin seems to be the immediate cause of the condition. Even a 'piebald' python with large white areas of skin has been recorded (Plate 48). One account [102] of a batch of albinoid American water snakes *(Natrix sipedon)* is of particular interest; although the eyes of these reptiles were pink and their bodies semi-transparent when held to the light, their skins contained at least three types of colouring agents, red, yellow and white; the dark melanin pigment, however, was apparently absent.

The cells containing yellow and red pigments are frequently called lipophores and allophores, although they have alternative names; the terminology of colour cells presents many problems and J. A. Peters' *Dictionary of Herpetology* [322] is a useful guide. They lie immediately beneath the epidermis and above (or outside) the bodies of the dermal melanophores and produce yellow or red colours which may be toned to various shades of brown when their effects are combined with those of the melanin-containing cells (figure 92).

It is noteworthy that blue and green pigments as such seem to be absent in reptiles. The fact that these colours are evident in many lizards and snakes is due to the presence of another type of colour cell, the iridocyte or guanophore, which also lies in the superficial part of the dermis (Plate 41). The iridocytes contain particles of semi-crystalline material which is generally regarded as guanine, a substance related to uric acid. Although this material is more or less colourless, it is a good reflector and has a strong modifying effect upon the light which falls on it. By themselves, iridocytes produce the effect of white, but in combination with the melanin-containing cells they scatter light of certain wave-lengths and produce the colour blue. If there is a layer of yellow lipophores superficial to them, it acts as a filter and a green colour results. By producing optical interference effects, the iridocytes are also responsible for the iridescence shown by the skin of many snakes, especially after slough-ing. The iridocytes therefore produce structural colours, like those of the wings of certain butterflies, which depend on the physical conditions rather than on the presence of actual colour pigment. The varied hues of some reptiles are therefore due to a combination of both structural and pigmentary colours, the latter being provided by the brown, yellow and red pigments of the other chromatophores.

Although some reptiles are more or less uniform in colour, many of them have striking spotted or banded patterns. These are probably produced by variations in the distribution, or at least in the activity, of the different types of pigment cell over different regions of the same individual. In a black scale, for example, both melanocytes and melanophores are conspicious and heavily charged with melanin, whereas the other types of pigment cell are inconspicuous or absent. In a neighbouring green scale, on the other hand, the iridocytes are well developed, but the melanin-containing cells have little or no pigment in their branches.

Whimster has drawn attention to the fact that in some species of lizards, at least, the colour pattern is built up like a mosaic from combinations of different coloured scales. Individual scales are often of uniform colour and scales of similar colour tend to be arranged in groups, so that well defined spots and bands are formed. Exceptions to this can, however, be observed (figure 89 H). It is interesting that if a particular spot on a lizard together with the skin immediately around it is excised, another spot with a roughly similar appearance will eventually be regenerated. On the basis of such results, together with those of transplantation experiments, Whimster believes that the skin pattern is influenced by some general factor, probably by the nervous system [455].

The pigment cells are not confined to the skin, but may be present in the membranes lining the mouth, the body cavity and in the mesenteries of the viscera. In some lizards the peritoneum is darkly pigmented owing to the presence of abundant melanin-containing cells. It has been suggested that this hidden pigmentation protects the viscera themselves from excessive radiations of heat and light, and attempts have been made to correlate its presence with the habits of the animal. Such a correlation has been found in certain *Anolis* lizards; some species in which the pigmentation is only slight or restricted to certain areas of the body cavity live in shady woodland, whereas others in which the pigmentation is more extensive live in more open country and are exposed to greater radiation intensities [111]. It has been shown, however, that the skin of some reptiles is impervious to ultra-violet radiation of the shorter wave-lengths. Furthermore, the slow-worm *(Anguis)* has a deeply pigmented, shiny black peritoneum, although it spends much of its time in hiding and seldom basks in the sun.

Colour variation and colour change Apart from 'freak' colouration such as is seen in albionos, the colours of reptiles often vary a good deal within a species; individuals of the African boomslang snake *(Dispholidus typus)*, for example, may be predominantly brown, black or green on the upper surface of the body [166]. The colour variant of the male slow-worm with flecks of blue on the back is familiar to European herpetologists. Sometimes these colour phases are sufficiently constant to justify the distinction of subspecies or races, especially when they are correlated with differences in geographical distribution. Many Mediterranean island races of the wall lizard *(Lacerta muralis)* have been recognised partly on the basis of colour. There may also be sexual differences in colour (p. 393), especially in lizards, and there are often age differences, a single individual changing from a juvenile colour phase to one characteristic of maturity. The golden-brown or silvery back colour of many young slow-worms and the yellowish bands on the flanks of young alligators are examples of juvenile colouration which tends to disappear in later life.

So far we have been considering colours which remain more or less static throughout the animal's life, or colour changes which come on slowly like the greying of human hair. Some reptiles also have powers of rapid colour change, and this may be brought about by two different methods. The first consists of the 'flashing' of concealed colours at the scale hinges by the sudden stretching of areas of skin; it can occur almost instantaneously and is used by some lizards and snakes in threat and other kinds of display (p. 397). The use of the throat-fan of *Anolis* is a good example (figure 92; Plate 7). Colour change as it is more usually understood, however, is due to changes in the pigmentary system; these can become apparent in a matter of hours, minutes, or even seconds.

Figure 92.   One type of flash colouration exhibited by reptiles. As the throat-fan of an *Anolis* lizard is flared out the coloured skin (shown in black here) in the hinge regions of the scales is stretched and suddenly displayed. In the green anole (*A. carolinensis*) the scales are whitish or buff and the skin between them is red.

So far as is known, this type of colour change in reptiles depends mainly or entirely on the movement of melanin pigment within the dermal melanophore cells. Generally speaking, the animal grows darker when the pigment is dispersed along the branching processes of the melanophores, and paler when it is concentrated in the bodies of these cells. The possibility that similar changes may take place in the other kinds of pigment cells has not been thoroughly investigated, but these cells are usually regarded as having only a passive role. If this is correct, the complex colour changes seen in certain lizards such as chamaeleons, *Anolis** and *Agama* are due to the partial or complete masking of these cells by the shifting brown pigment in the melanophores. The way in which the skin may change from orange to chocolate brown in a species like *A. agama* in which white pigment cells (iridocytes or guanophores), red and yellow cells, (lipophores, etc) and melanophores are all present is shown in figure 93, taken from Harris' book on the rainbow lizard [213]. Slight differences in the arrangement or distribution of these cells and of the state of the melanin pigment may account for the production of the partly structural blue and green colours.

Among reptiles, really striking powers of colour change are found only in certain more or less arboreal lizards of the infraorder Iguania (which contains the chamaeleons, agamids and iguanids),

---

* As previously mentioned, the dramatic colour change of the throat-fan in *Anolis* is due to the simpler 'flash' mechanism; pigmentary colour change is important over the rest of the animal.

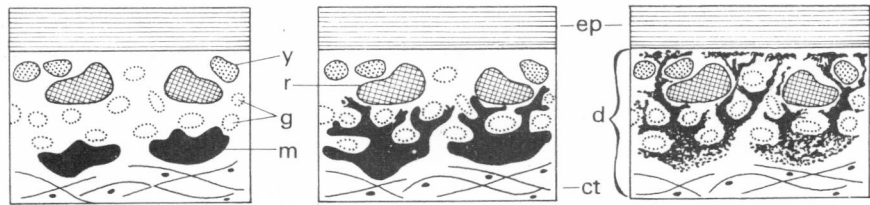

Figure 93.   Diagrams showing mechanism of pigmentary colour change in the rainbow lizard (*Agama agama*). The change from orange (left picture), through terracotta (middle) to chocolate brown (right) is primarily due to the dispersal of pigment through the branches of the dermal melanophores. After Harris [213].

ct, dermal connective tissue. **d**, dermis, **ep**, epidermis. **g**, guanophore (white). **m**, melanophore (black). **r**, red cell. **y**, yellow cell.

and perhaps also in some geckos. Of these the chamaeleons are probably the most accomplished, although even their colour range has its limitations. The best account of it which I have come across is that by Miss E. M. Stephenson [409] who was mainly familiar with the small species *Lophosaura pumila* found in South Africa. The general body colour of this reptile ranges from black, through various shades of green to primrose yellow, while the flanks are patterned with markings of orange, brown, blue or grey. Localised areas of skin, even individual tubercles, can change colour independently. In the 'common chamaeleon' (*Chamaeleo chamaeleon*) of southern Spain, a few Mediterranean islands and North Africa, the colour range is rather similar but the body often takes on an overall brownish hue; in other types, such as the little short-tailed chamaeleons (*Brookesia*) from Africa and Madagascar, the play of colours is more restricted and varies only from fawn to grey [376].

Although the chamaeleon's power of colour change is proverbial and has fascinated naturalists since the days of Aristotle, a great deal still remains to be learnt about it. The physiological mechanisms involved seem to be extraordinarily complicated, and what is true for chamaeleons does not necessarily hold good for other reptiles; this much is clear from the reviews by G. H. Parker [310] and by H. Waring [445]. Unfortunately, little original research has been done on the subject in recent years, and there are still many unresolved problems. Most of our information about chamaeleons is based on the 'common' *C. chamaeleon*, and on *Lophosaura pumila* which was much studied by Lancelot Hogben and his collaborators who were working in South Africa during the 1920s and 1930s[*].

300

Conditions of lighting seem to be the most important of the several factors influencing colour change, and *Lophosaura* apparently shows two different, and sometimes contradictory, types of response. In complete darkness the animal becomes very pale, and it tends to darken when exposed to light; either side of the creature may be darker than the other if it is more brightly illuminated. Even dim light may elicit some darkening so that the chamaeleon changes from its nocturnal shade of pale fawn to one of greyish green at dawn; during the day it assumes darker shades of green and brown. These changes occur in nature as a kind of circadian rhythm, which has been observed in other colour-changing lizards.

At the same time, laboratory experiments have shown that under some circumstances at least, chamaeleons react to the shade of the background against which they are placed. Generally speaking they become pale on a white, light-scattering background, and dark on a black background which absorbs light. Since the effect of a white background would be to raise the general intensity of illumination and that of a dark background to decrease it, it would seem that this reaction is to some extent antagonistic to the simple response to light previously described. The experimental results here are difficult to interpret, but it appears that under certain conditions the background response predominates. Thus, *Lophosaura* becomes pale on a white background despite the fact that it is brightly lit.

The eyes are important in both types of response, but are especially so in the animal's adaptation to its background. There seems to be no evidence that they can register colour as well as shade, but it is quite possible that they can. *Anolis* lizards are believed to respond specifically to green light (p. 304), and diurnal lizards in general are thought to have powers of colour vision.

The skin is also sensitive to light, although not to the same extent as the eyes, and is probably more important in the response to general illumination than in that to background. The skin reaction can be demonstrated in blinded animals, and also, by a simple and striking experiment, in intact ones. If an object of distinctive shape is held against the flank of a chamaeleon for a couple of minutes its outline will appear as a pale print on the darker skin. It is likely that the skin owes its sensitivity to the presence of special light-receptive cells, but these have not yet been identified under the microscope.

Changes in temperature are also important in provoking colour change, although the physiological mechanism involved has not been worked out. In *Lophosaura*, and indeed in lizards generally, the effect of high temperature is to induce pallor, and this reaction may play some part in temperature control (p. 225). It is uncertain, however, if temperature responses are important in wild chamaeleons, since these lizards avoid extreme heat by retreating into the depths of the foliage. 'Emotional' factors also come into the picture, and when a chamaeleon is angry or frightened it often changes colour in quite a dramatic fashion. Some lizards respond to noxious stimuli by turning pale, but chamaeleons usually end up a good deal darker than they were originally.

It can be appreciated, therefore, that the colours of a chamaeleon at any time are likely to result from several different environmental factors which may be pulling different ways to effect a kind of 'compromise decision'. The vexed question as to how far this result helps the chamaeleon to conceal itself is discussed on pages 512–4.

Students of colour change have devoted much attention to the problem of how the melanophores are controlled (figure 94). One of two principal alternative methods (or a combination of both) seem most probable – nervous control or glandular control. In the first instance, the retina, stimulated by light, would initiate a train of nerve impulses passing through the optic nerve to the brain, down the spinal cord, and ultimately through the peripheral nerves to the melanophores. Similarly, the light-sensitive cells in the skin would initiate impulses which passed along nerves to the spinal cord, and then out again by other nerves to the melanophores, completing a spinal reflex.

On the other hand, the melanophores could be controlled by the circulation in the blood of hormones produced by ductless glands such as the pituitary or the adrenals; the production of adrenalin may be responsible for the 'excitement pallor' exhibited by certain lizards after unpleasant stimulation. The nervous system would still be involved to some extent in so far as it would provide a pathway for messages between the eyes or skin receptors and the gland, but the melanophores themselves would not be under nervous control directly and would not need to have any nerve fibres distributed to them.

So far as chamaelons are concerned, the evidence suggests that the reactions of the melanophores to light (and probably to certain other types of stimulus as well) are directly controlled partly or entirely by the nervous system. It has been shown that if the spinal

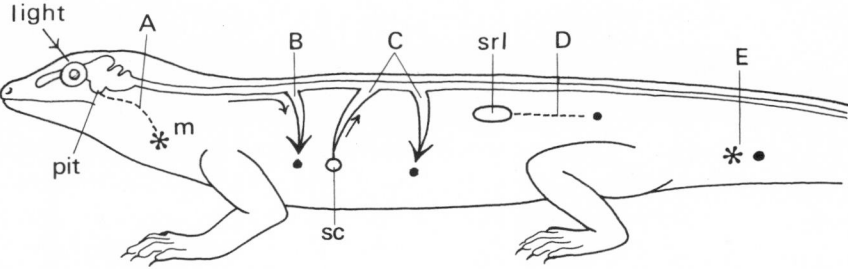

Figure 94. Diagram showing possible methods for control of melanophores, which are shown by star when pigment is dispersed, and by black spot when pigment is concentrated. These methods may occur singly or in combination in a given species. Only responses to light (and not to temperature) are shown.
A. Action of pituitary (intermediate lobe). Light transmitted via eye and brain to pituitary gland (**pit**) stimulates production of hormones which act on melanophores (**m**), probably causing pigment dispersal and darkening of skin.
B. Nervous control. Effect of light transmitted via eye and brain initiates passage of nerve impulse down spinal cord and out to melanophores through peripheral spinal nerves, probably relaying in sympathetic ganglia which are not shown. Probable effect is to concentrate pigment so that skin pales. C. Nervous control (spinal reflex). Hypothetical light-sensitive cells (**sc**) in skin initiate impulses passing to cord in afferent nerve fibres as shown by small arrow. Impulses relay in cord and pass out through efferent nerves (large arrowhead) to melanophores. Probably same effect as B. D. Possible action of suprarenal (adrenal) gland (**srl**). Adrenalin liberated, perhaps in response to nervous stimulation or hormones produced by other glands, and carried to melanophores causing concentration of pigment. E. Melanophores respond directly to light, the pigment becoming concentrated in dark or dispersed in light. Either this response, or C, are presumably involved when a part of a chamaeleon's skin is made to go pale by covering it over.

cord is severed the skin behind the level of the injury darkens and fails to respond to changes in the environment by any further alteration in colour. This reaction is also evident in animals with transected cords which are stimulated electrically in the mouth, a procedure which normally causes generalised blanching. Moreover, a chamaeleon with its head cut off and its viscera removed will continue to give skin responses to light and darkness if the spinal cord and peripheral nerve trunks are left intact. It is supposed that here a spinal reflex initiated by skin receptors is involved since under these conditions the eyes and the endocrine glands are eliminated.

The nerve-supply to the melanophores is probably derived from branches of the sympathetic system which originate within the spinal cord and relay in the ganglia of the sympathetic chain. Experiments involving electrical stimulation suggest that the effect of nervous activity is to concentrate the pigment in the melanophores, so that the chamaeleon turns pale. The dark condition of the skin, with the melanin granules dispersed, probably represents the relaxed condition when the nervous system is not working. Further work is necessary, however, before this explanation, which has the merit of simplicity, is completely acceptable.

Similar studies have been made on *Anolis carolinensis,* which belongs to a group of arboreal iguanids nearly as good at colour change as the chamaeleons of the Old World; indeed, anolis lizards are sometimes miscalled chamaeleons in the USA. *A. carolinensis* ranges in colour from brown to bright emerald green. The throat-fan of the male turns red when dilated, but this is primarily due to a 'flash' effect, and not to pigmentary colour change (see p. 299).

As in chamaeleons, lighting and temperature are both important in provoking colour change. At low temperatures, for example at 10°C, *Anolis carolinensis* is always brown, and at very high temperatures (over about 40°C) it becomes pale green; the green colour phase of *Anolis* corresponds with the pale whitish or yellowish phases of other colour-changing lizards. At intermediate temperatures the colour is mainly influenced by the lighting conditions [see 310, 390, 444].

The skin seems to respond to light in a fairly clear-cut fashion, so that blinded animals turn brown in strong light and green when taken into darkness. The visual response, however, appears to be extremely complicated, and until further work is done it is very difficult to generalise about it. Experiments show that *Anolis* can adapt to light and dark backgrounds in a rather similar fashion to *Lophosaura*. It is also probable that the lizard gives a specific visual response to green light which overrides the skin response to light of any colour. Wilson found that if his anoles were placed in jars covered with green cellophane, or if they were fitted with green hoods over one or both eyes they always turned green when they were illuminated; the response to green therefore brings about concentration of the melanin pigment. If the animals were fitted with black hoods the skin response became operative and the lizards turned brown owing to the dispersal of the pigment [see 444].

These experiments help to explain why anoles in the wild are usually green when they are among foliage and are consequently exposed to light which is mainly green in colour. If, however, they climb into an exposed position where the amount of green in the light is negligible, they become brown regardless of the background. Varying proportions of green in the light are responsible for intermediate shades of yellowish green and brown. Unfortunately, these interesting observations are hardly discussed in the more recent reviews on colour change.

Anolis differs from chamaeleons in that its ability to change colour is not impaired by cutting the spinal cord or peripheral nerves. It is thought that its melanophores are controlled, not by the nervous system, but by the hormone intermedin or melanin-dispersing hormone (M.D.H.), which is secreted by the intermediate lobe of the pituitary gland, and possibly also by adrenalin. There is the further possibility that the melanophores themselves respond directly to light, as well as to hormones liberated by glands when the eyes and light-sensitive cells in the skin are stimulated. There is no firm evidence for this type of direct response in *Anolis* or chamaeleons; it has been demonstrated more clearly, however, in another iguanid, *Phrynosoma,* in which the melanophores are also influenced by hormones, and possibly by the nervous system as well. Enough has now been said to indicate the extraordinary complexity of colour change control in reptiles and the need for further work on its problems.

A number of agamid lizards such as the African *Agama agama* and the oriental *Calotes* are also renowned for their chromatic abilities, their heads and bodies changing colour in a brilliant and striking fashion. The head of the male *A. agama* is normally orange and the body indigo during the breeding season. If the lizard is angry or frightened, the head turns chocolate brown, while patches of cream, fawn and mauve appear upon the body [213]. These displays are also evoked during courtship and rivalry (p. 398) and are unlikely to serve any purpose in concealment.

Quite striking colour changes have also been observed in some geckos such as the diurnal jewel gecko *Phelsuma andamense.* In bright light this is a most beautiful creature, vivid green with streaks of red on the back; in the dark, however, it becomes almost black [394]. This seems to be a reversal of the typical response to light and dark shown by the chamaeleon and *Anolis,* and it is possible that temperature changes rather than illumination are the operative factors here; as we have seen, responses to light and temperature may pull in different directions, and under certain conditions the reaction to temperature may predominate. Comparable, but more subdued

305

types of colour change are seen in certain desert lizards such as *Phrynosoma*. These reptiles are pale at night and in the middle of the day, but darken in the early morning and evening, a rhythm which is probably conditioned by both temperature and light and may be concerned with temperature control. There are probably many other species with similar chromatic ability.

Laboratory experiments have shown that slight powers of colour change are present in other reptiles besides lizards. Paling and darkening of the belly skin occurs in young alligators after injection of adrenal or pituitary hormones, or after they have been kept for a time on white or black backgrounds. A similar response to background has been described in the skin of the 'carapace' of soft-shelled turtles (*Trionyx*) and takes two to four days to complete [21]; the digital webs of the Australian turtle *Chelodina* also respond, but more slowly, over a period of nearly thirty days. Colour change can be provoked in some snakes and even in the tuatara under laboratory conditions [310, 445]. In the prairie rattlesnake (*Crotalus viridis*), for example, removal of the pituitary gland is followed by paling of the skin, and darkening can be induced again by injections of intermedin. There is no evidence that colour change in these non-saurian reptiles is under nervous control.

It is interesting that the snakes, which are so closely related to lizards and which often live in the same habitats (such as trees), should include no species which can change colour to any great extent. Walls regards this as a piece of evidence for his interesting theory that the ancestors of snakes lived underground (p. 31), a mode of life in which the power of colour change is unlikely to be of much value.

Special structures of the skin

In many reptiles certain regions of the skin have become modified to form tiny organs such as glands, appendages such as spines and crests, and in some cases, impressive systems of armour-plate. It is impossible to deal with all the products of the versatile integument in this chapter, and a few cutaneous structures such as the 'wings' of 'flying' lizards and the friction pads which enable geckos to climb have been more conveniently described in Chapter 3 on locomotion.

Glands, etc In many vertebrates such as amphibians and mammals the epidermis contains numerous glands which secrete their products on to the surface of the body in the form of slime, grease or scent. In reptiles, as in birds, such glands are far less common and when they occur they are usually restricted to localised regions of the body. In some chelonians, for example, such as the musk or stinkpot terrapin (*Sternotherus*) there are glands at the front of the hind limb pockets which produce a powerfully smelling secretion. Two pairs of musk glands have been described in the alligator, a large pair opening into the cloaca, and another pair with slit-like apertures on either side of the under surface of the lower jaw (figure 89, p. 286). These glands are present in both male and female and may play some part in sexual attraction. Crocodilians also have a whole series of minute glands under the skin of the back. These are arranged in two rows, each lying beneath the second row of scales from the midline; they open on to the surface by tiny pores between the scales. Their secretion is oily but odourless and their function is unknown.

In certain colubrid snakes of the genus *Natrix* and related genera there is a paired chain of glands beneath the dorsal scales (figure 89) which may extend for the whole length of the body [394]. Certain allied species possess two quite large areas of modified skin, one on either side of the dorsal midline of the neck, which are thought to be glandular in function. The secretion of these vertebral or nucho-dorsal glands is irritant to mucous membranes and perhaps has a defensive function, causing a predator to let go of a snake which it has seized in its mouth. It is possible that they may also produce some odour which is important in courtship. The chin-rubbing procedure followed by many snakes before mating would certainly bring the nose into close proximity with any glands on the neck and back of the female. Among other species, curious gland-like structures (figure 40, p. 114) have been described on the head of the blind snakes (*Typhlops*), and the occurrence of glandular cells or scales in various regions of the integument of Squamata appears to be widespread [175, 176, 270].

Epidermal organs of a rather different type are the well-known femoral pores and glands (figure 95) found in many lizards, for example in lacertids, and in many iguanids and geckos [110]. The pores are situated along the back of the under surface of each thigh, usually in a row, but sometimes in small clusters; some geckos and amphisbaenids have similar pre-anal pores in front of the cloacal opening. Such pores may be present in both sexes, as in lacertids, but are usually better developed in the males. In female geckos the pores are usually absent or rudimentary, when they are represented by a series of small pits in the scales. Although the number of femoral pores may vary considerably within a single species, as in the common lizard *Lacerta vivipara* which has 7–13 on each side, they are sometimes useful as taxonomic characters.

Each pore opens on to the surface of a slightly enlarged scale. It leads into a small blind sac or tube, the femoral gland, lined with epidermal cells which periodically die and are shed into it. This cellular debris accumulates until it projects from the opening of the pore as a little waxy cone or crust. It is interesting that these organs, like most of the skin glands which have been described in reptiles, are glands of the holocrine type. They resemble the grease-producing sebaceous glands of mammals in that their secretions are derived from the actual breakdown of their own cells instead of being filtered off from the bloodstream.

There has been much discussion about the function of the femoral pores and their glands. One idea is that by virtue of the roughness which they give to the skin they help to prevent the thighs and cloacal regions of the male and female from slipping apart during the sexual act, but this is by no means certain. They seem to have some

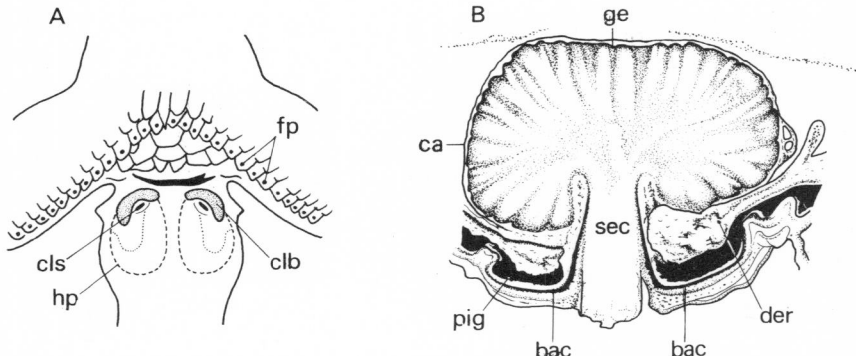

Figure 95. A. Femoral pores, cloacal bones and sacs of gecko, *Gymnodactylus pulchellus*. After Smith [394]. B. Microscopic section through middle of femoral pore and gland of a male iguanid lizard, *Crotaphytus collaris*. After Cole, C. J. (1966) *J. Morph.* **118** 119 (Figure 5, p. 129).

bac, basal cell layer of surrounding epidermis. **ca**, capsule of gland. **clb**, cloacal bone. **cls**, opening of cloacal sac; outline of sac dotted. **der**, dermis. **fp**, femoral pore. **hp**, hemipenis (outline). **ge**, germinative epithelium of gland. **pig**, pigment in dermis. **sec**, plug of secretion in duct of pore.

association with sexual activity, however, for the femoral pores of male lacertid lizards regress after castration.

Some geckos have a pair of small blind sacs of unknown function on the under surface of the tail behind the cloaca, and in the male there is a small curved bone on either side related to the sac (figure 95). In the males of many species of geckos there are also one or more horny tubercles or spurs on either side of the tail base. The use of these has been described in the American banded gecko *Coleonyx* where they are used to pull back the posterior lip of the female's cloaca just before copulation [331].

Various kinds of small pits and tubercles formed from thickenings of the epidermis have been described on the scales of reptiles (figure 89 G, p. 286) and are generally credited with a sensory function. Larger tubercles, well supplied with nerves, are present around the throat and chin of crocodilians, and on the chin and cloacal region of some natricine snakes. These latter organs are said to be involved in certain phases of courtship (p. 406). The fine bristles found on the tips of scales in lizards such as *Agama* (figure 96) and *Pygopus* are also believed to be touch-sensitive, but no very specific function has been ascribed to them. Some workers have regarded them as the forerunners of mammalian hairs.

The presence of luminous organs in the skin has actually been claimed in one species of rare teiid lizard, *Proctoporus shrevei*, found in Trinidad. This creature possesses a series of black spots along the flanks, each containing a small white area in the centre. These white beads were described as lighting up in the dark like the portholes of a ship, especially when the lizard was agitated. Study of these spots in

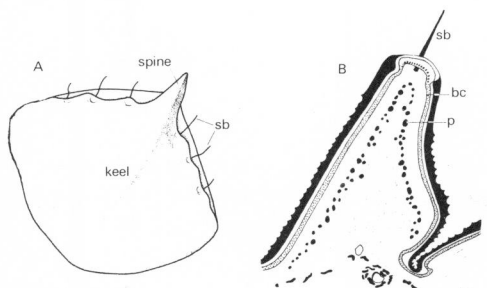

Figure 96. A. Body scale of rainbow lizard (*Agama agama*) showing spine and sensory bristles. After Harris [212]. B. Section through scale with sensory bristle of agamid lizard (*Calotes*). Modified from Elias, H. and Bortner, S. (1957) *Amer. Mus. Novitates* No. 1820, 1, and Schmidt, W. J.

bc, basal cell layer of epidermis. **p**, dermal pigment. **sb**, sensory bristle.

309

related species, however, shows no evidence that they are really luminous organs; the white central bead differs mainly from the rest of the skin in containing no melanin pigment; there are no special concentrations of the reflecting pigment guanine [362]. Further observations are obviously needed to clear the matter up.

Crests, etc Many lizards possess spines or crests formed from modified scales, while others have more elaborate appendages such as dewlaps and throat-fans in which the muscles and skeleton participate. Such excrescences are mostly found in members of the iguanid, agamid and chamaeleon families, which, as we have seen, may be further distinguished by their powers of colour change. The spines of lizards usually consist of single enlarged scales with sharp points, or arise from the tips of scales; crests are made up of rows of spines down the neck, back or tail, or else from flaps or ridges of skin covered with small scales. In some forms such as the male rainbow lizard (*Agama agama*) the crest on the back of the male can be erected by the dilatation of blood-vessels in the underlying skin [212].

Perhaps the most prickly of all lizards are the little short-tailed iguanids known as horned lizards or horned toads (*Phrynosoma*) and the very similar-looking agamids called thorny devils (*Moloch*) from Australia. The squat bodies of these reptiles are well furnished with spines and spiny tubercles, and there are longer spines on the head which suggest miniature replicas of horned dinosaurs. The heavily built agamid *Uromastyx* is another spiny form, but here the spines are restricted to the thick powerful tail. The African zonurès or girdle-tailed lizards also have tails ringed with spiky scales and some species have a formidable protection of spines on the head and body as well (figure 146, p. 506; Plate 47); these lizards are neither agamids nor iguanids, but belong to the family Cordylidae. All these animals are inhabitants of sandy or rocky arid places and resemble many other creatures of the desert in their tendency to spinescence.

A few kinds of lizards have quite spectacular crests. In male basilisks (*Basiliscus*), for example, there are prominent crests (figure 20, p. 74) on the head, back and tail which give these tree-living iguanids a most heraldic appearance; the dorsal crest is said to have a stiffening of bony rays. The sailed dragon (*Lophura amboinensis*), a big agamid from the East Indies, has a spiny crest along its back and a much higher one without spines on the tail. It is interesting that the caudal crest of this species and the rather similar crest along the back and base of the tail in the West African *Chamaeleon cristatus* are supported by the very long spinous processes of the vertebrae. The crests of these lizards, which are present in both sexes, are therefore analogous in a way to the huge dorsal crests of some of the extinct pelycosaurs such as *Dimetrodon* (figure 2; 14).

Certain lizards such as the helmeted iguanids *(Corythophanes)* of tropical America (figure 145, p. 505), the chamaeleon-like agamid *Lyriocephalus* of Ceylon, and many chamaeleons have crests or casques of a rather different type on their heads. Such casques are composed primarily of bony elevations from the parietals and the skin merely provides a covering for them. In certain chamaeleons such as the African flap-necked species *(C. dilepis)* there are movable scaly flaps at the back of the head.

Some chamaeleons are further embellished with horns, or horn-like structures; in some species such as *C. fischeri* (figure 45, p. 132) and *C. gallus* there is a single scaly projection arising from the snout, while in *C. furcifer* there is a forked appendage of the same type. In others, structures with a greater resemblance to mammalian horns are present, with bony cores (figure 54, p. 152), a keratinised integument [183, 376]. Such horns are present in the three-horned species *C. oweni* and *C. jacksoni* (Plate 27), one arising from the nose and another from each side of the forehead, above the eye.

Conspicuous nasal appendages also occur in some agamid and iguanid lizards (figure 97). The highly adorned *Lyriocephalus*, for instance, has a scale-covered knob of spongy tissue on its snout as well as a crest along its neck and back and a dewlap beneath its throat. One species of *Ceratophora*, another Ceylonese form, has a large spine on the end of the nose, while in another species the snout bears a thick club-like projection with prominent scales. Among the iguanids the rare *Anolis phyllorhinus* from Amazonia has a remarkable leaf-like appendage on its snout (figure 97 D), while the big rhinoceros iguana *(Metopoceros cornutus)* of Haiti and some other species have a pointed tubercle on the nose formed from enlarged scales.

Many iguanid and agamid lizards have a kind of dewlap (Plate 45) consisting of a fold of loose skin and connective tissue beneath the throat. It is sometimes called a gular pouch or sac, but since it has no cavity and does not communicate with the mouth, this does not seem a very good name for it. A moderate-sized dewlap is present in many species, at least in the male sex, and can usually be expanded

311

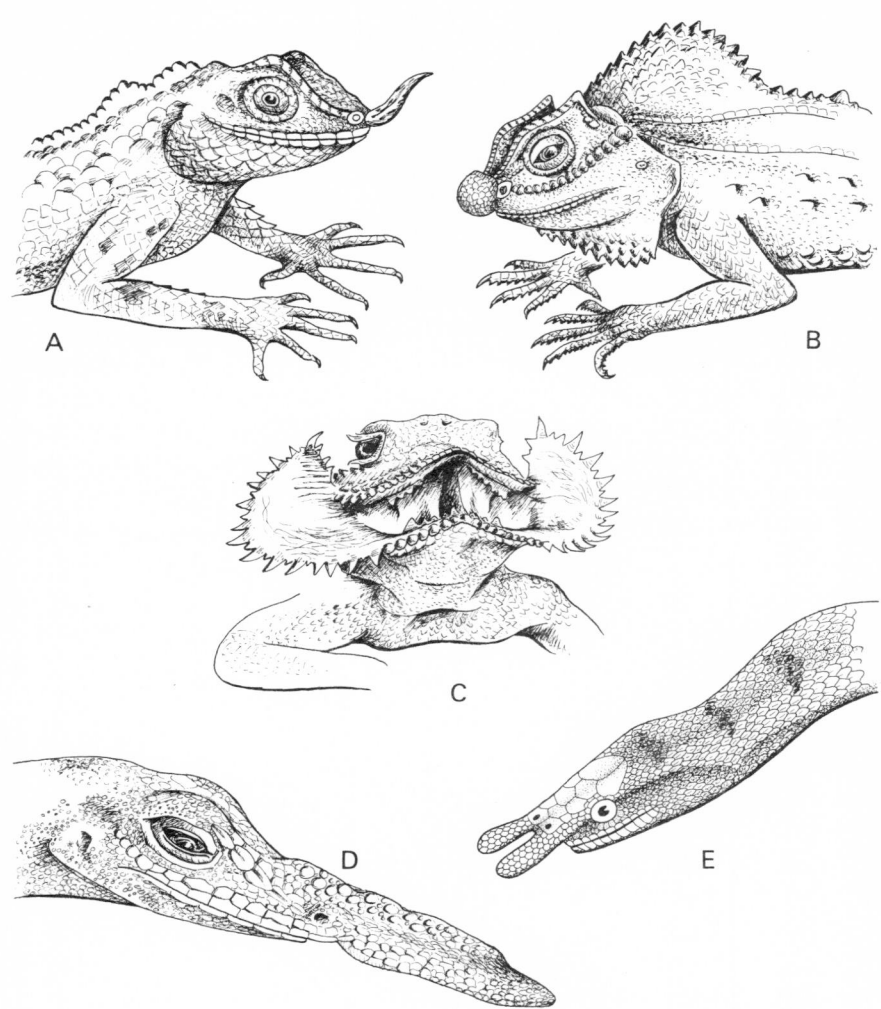

Figure 97. Some reptiles with cutaneous appendages. A, B. Agamid lizards from Ceylon. A, *Ceratophora stoddarti*; B, *Lyriocephalus scutatus*. After Deraniyagala [135]. C. Sand agama *Phrynocephalus mystaceus* spreading its check flaps in a defensive posture. Based on photo by Senckenberg Museum in Mertens [280]. D. Leaf-nosed *Anolis phyllorhinus* from Amazonia. After Myers, G.S. and de Carvalho, A.L. (1945) *Bol. Mus. Nac. Rio de Jan.* No. 43. E. Colubrid water snake *Erpeton tentaculatum*. After Jan, G. and Sordelli, F. (1881–6) *Iconographie générale des Ophidiens*. Paris, J.B. Bailière et fils. This atlas-type work contains many fine illustrations of snakes.

to some extent when the creature is excited, giving the throat a dilated appearance. In some forms such as the *Anolis* lizards (Plate 7), and the oriental genera *Draco* and *Sitana,* the structure is very large and can be rapidly dilated in a manner which suggests the opening of a fan. The dramatic effect of the throat-fan, as this kind of expansile dewlap is often called, may be enhanced by the flashing of colours normally concealed in the hinges of the scales (figure 92, p. 299). A few iguanas such as the common or green species *(Iguana iguana)* of tropical America have pendulous skinny dewlaps which possess a limited power of independent movement.

The throat-fan of *Anolis* and other lizards is expanded by the movement of the hyoid apparatus, which has already been described (p. 128). Contraction of the paired ceratohyoid muscles, which arise from the relatively immovable 1st ceratobranchials and are inserted on the ceratohyals, makes the whole apparatus pivot like a see-saw. The 2nd ceratobranchials which are very long and close together in the midline are consequently rotated downwards and forwards,

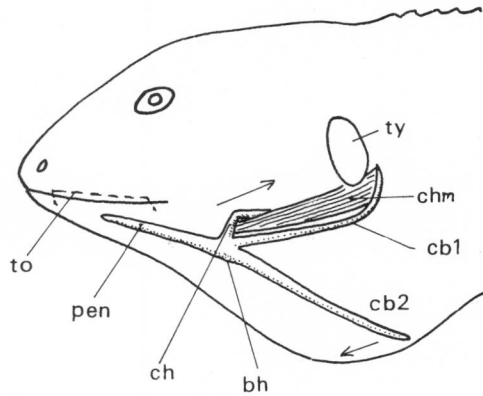

Figure 98.   Diagram showing method of operating throat-fan in agamid or iguanid lizard. The 1st ceratobranchials of the hyoid are more or less fixed by muscular and other attachments. Contraction of the ceratohyoid muscle (origin from the 1st ceratobranchials, and insertion on the ceratohyals) and retraction of the tongue rotates the front part of the hyoid apparatus upwards and backwards. The apparatus pivots on the basihyal region, and the 2nd ceratobranchials sweep forwards and downwards, raising up the loose skin of the throat-fan. Arrows show direction of movement.

cb 1 and **2,** 1st and 2nd ceratobranchials. **bh,** basihyal. **ch,** ceratohyal. **chm,** ceratohyoid muscle. *pen,* processus entoglossus. **to,** tongue (outline in broken lines). **ty,** tympanic membrane.

313

raising up a flap or ridge, the throat-fan, in the loose skin of the throat (figure 98). In the flying lizards *(Draco)* the throat-fan is particularly large and when fully extended it projects in front of the head. There is also a pair of smaller erectile appendages, one on either side of the throat.

Another type of neck appendage is the large frill of the well-known frilled lizards *(Chlamydosaurus)* (Plate 46) and the spiny 'beard' of the bearded lizard *Amphibolurus barbatus,* another big Australian agamid. These structures are normally folded back around the neck, but can be raised and lowered rapidly; here again the muscles and skeleton of the hyoid apparatus are responsible for movement. It is interesting that the frill and 'beard' are only slightly developed at hatching, but increase rapidly in size later on. *Phrynocephalus,* a smaller kind of agamid found in the stony deserts of western Asia, has a large flap of skin fringed with spines at the angle of the jaws; when the lizard is annoyed these stick out like ears on either side of the gaping mouth (figure 97 C).

Works on systematic herpetology, such as Boulenger's great museum catalogues [60], contain many descriptions of these and other skin appendages found among the diversity of lizards. Unfortunately such accounts are usually concerned only with external appearances. Far less is known about their internal anatomy or about the part which they play in the life of the animal.

Some appendages such as crests and dewlaps are undoubtedly used in display and kindred social activities (p. 397). It is possible that their presence may help an animal to distinguish other members of the same species or to recognise the sex of other individuals; the adornments may be present, or only well developed, in one sex, the male being generally better endowed than the female. This is true for the crests of *Agama* and the basilisks, for example, and for the throat-fan of *Anolis* and other lizards which possess this structure. The 'horns' of certain chamaeleons, at any rate those of the true horny rather than the scaly type, afford further instances of sexual difference. In *Chamaeleo oweni,* for example, the three horns of the male are said to be completely absent in the female, while in *C. montium* the female has only a pair of small tubercles in the place of the two long horns on the snout of the male [60].

Other appendages, however, such as the scaly nasal processes of *Chamaeleo fischeri,* the big pendulous dewlap of *Iguana* and the frill of *Chlamydosaurus* seem to be of equal or nearly equal size in both sexes.

A thorough survey of such sexual differences in reptiles would be of great interest.

It appears that among lizards elaborate skin appendages of the kind which have been described are almost restricted to members of the families of the Iguania group. They are also rare among reptiles of other orders. Nevertheless, a few interesting examples are to be met with among the snakes. A number of vipers such as the horned adder *Bitis cornuta* (figure 99 A) and the desert-living asps *(Cerastes)* of the Old World, and the sidewinder rattlesnakes *(Crotalus cerastes)* of North America have pointed tubercles formed from enlarged scales over each eye, giving them a horned appearance. In the big Gaboon viper *(Bitis gabonica)* and the rhinoceros viper *(B. nasicornis)* there is usually a pair of horn-like tubercles on the snout, though these are sometimes poorly developed; in the European *Vipera ammodytes* (figure 99 B) there is a single blunt tubercle. Some tree snakes have the snout drawn out into a long pointed tip, and in the Madagascar genus *Langaha* this ends in a remarkable nasal appendage which differs in the two sexes (figure 99 C, D). In the male of the species *alluaudi* the appendage has the form of a simple elongated cone, projecting in front of the nostrils and the ends of the jaws, but in the female there is a more elaborate leaf-shaped structure with

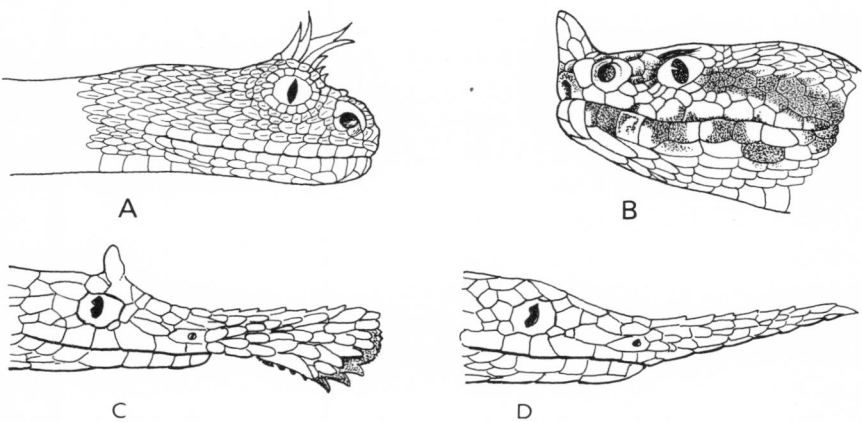

A   B

C   D

Figure 99.   A. Head of *Bitis cornuta*, a horned adder from South-West Africa. After Fitzsimons [166]. B. Adder, *Vipera ammodytes* from Central Europe, with tubercle on snout. After Boulenger [1913]. C, D. Colubrid snake, *Langaha alluaudi*, from Madagascar. C, Female; D, male. Other forms of this genus may show similar types of sexual dimorphism, but have previously been regarded as distinct species. After Guibé, J. (1949) *Mem. Inst. Sci. Madagascar* **3** 148.

serrated edges. A final unique example of a different type may be mentioned. The snout of the curious water-snake *Erpeton tentaculatum* is furnished with two scaly tentacles (figure 97 E) which do not appear to be particularly sensitive although they are freely movable. They are pointed forwards when the snake is entirely submerged, but are laid back on either side of the snout when the head is protruded above the surface [394]. The use of all these appendages in snakes is problematical, though it is possible that in *Langaha* they help to camouflage the head among leaves.

Such specialised skin structures are even more unusual among chelonians and do not appear to be present at all in crocodilians. Horny spurs are present, however, on the thighs of certain tortoises such as *Testudo graeca* (distinguishing this species from related European forms), while the head and throat of the matamata *(Chelus)* is embellished with curious tags of skin (figure 42, p. 122). In the giant extinct tortoise *Meiolania* the head had horns with bony cores (figure 2, 13).

One of the most interesting of all reptilian skin structures is the rattlesnake's rattle, which has been thoroughly described by Klauber [240]. It consists of a number of interlocking horny segments which take the place of the conical scale found over the tail tip of other snakes. Each segment of the rattle normally consists of three lobes, and the segments are so disposed that the two hinder lobes of each fit inside the two front lobes of the one behind it. Each segment therefore has a strong but freely movable articulation with its neighbours. The only part of each segment which can be seen in the intact rattle is the front lobe (ie the lobe towards the head of the snake) – except in the case of the last segment which has nothing to fit over it so that all its lobes are visible (figure 100 A).

The rattle is higher from above downwards than it is wide from side to side, and there is a furrow along both sides of each segment which is thus partly divided into upper and lower portions. Owing to differences in the respective sizes of these portions and the way in which the lobes of the different segments interlock (figure 100 B) the rattle as a whole has an upward slant which tends to keep it off the ground and reduces wear and tear. This slant, which can be increased by tilting of the end of the tail so that the rattle is held nearly vertically, also seems to be the most favourable position for sound production.

Hidden inside the front or basal segment of the rattle is the true

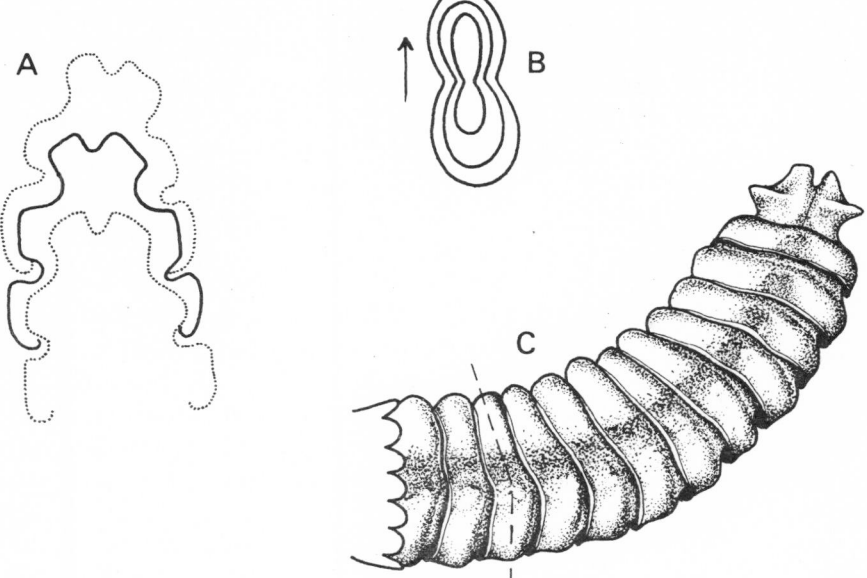

Figure 100. The rattlesnake's rattle. A. Vertical longitudinal section through rattle showing three interlocking segments. B. Transverse section showing three interlocking lobes. The fit between the lobes is tighter dorsally than ventrally, an arrangement which allows the rattle to bend further in an upward (shown by arrow) than a downward direction. A and B after Klauber [240]. C. Side view of rattle showing upward tilting. This is caused by the arrangement shown in B, and by the fact that the part of each lobe dorsal to the furrow (stippled) slants slightly forwards (i.e. towards rattle base), as shown by broken line.

tip of the tail, which is called the end-body or matrix (figure 101). This contains a bony core, the style or shaker, which is developed, either in late embryonic or early post-natal life, from the fusion of a number of tail vertebrae. Its front end articulates with the last normal vertebra and the muscles which vibrate the tail are attached to it. The spinal cord enters the style and gives off spinal nerves which issue from small holes in the bone and supply the rest of the end-body.

The soft tissue of the end-body is shaped like a mould of a rattle segment and has a similar lobed outline. Its epidermal covering resembles that of the skin elsewhere and possesses an inner basal or germinatival layer of cells and an outer horny layer. This epidermis is of vital importance since it actually produces each of the horny segments in rather the same way as the normal body skin produces a slough. In fact the formation of each new segment coincides with

317

each moult and is the result of a localised modification of the general sloughing process.

If the end-body simply produced a succession of new segments of much the same shape, one might imagine that these would just accumulate inside each other, so that the rattle would increase in thickness but not in length. We know, however, that the rattle does get longer by the length of one visible lobe, the front one of each new segment, every time the snake sheds its skin. The rather complicated way in which this is brought about has been described by Zimmermann and Pope [476].

The first stage in the process, which more or less coincides with the blue-eyed stage which precedes the skin-shedding, is the development of an extra, fourth, lobe on the front of the end-body (ie the end toward the head of the snake). This has the effect of forcing the soft tissues of the rest of the end-body backwards in relation to the style and is directly responsible for the rattle increasing in length. The style itself undergoes little change during the process. The horny layer of the last three lobes of the end-body is then shed and forms the new rattle segment, and at the same time the hinder lobe of the end-body is rapidly absorbed, restoring it to its original three-lobed condition. In this way the rattle gets longer without any alteration in the relationship between its different segments (figure 101). The whole process depends on the occurrence of periodic bursts of cell division in the basal epidermal layer of the end-body, coupled with the formation of new tissue at the front of the end-body and the absorption of old tissue at its rear.

At birth the baby rattlesnake has no rattle, only a horny knob called the pre-button at the tip of its tail. Within a few days, however, it usually sheds its skin for the first time and acquires its first rattle segment, the button, which differs from the later segments in only having two lobes. It will go on adding one new segment (and hence one new visible lobe) with every skin-shedding, and since it may slough as often as six times a year, the rattle will get longer quite quickly. It often happens, however, that the rattle breaks after about six or eight segments have been formed, and rattle strings containing more than about a dozen segments are rare in the wild. Strings much longer than this are sometimes seen in captive specimens which tend to lead more peaceful lives and a record figure of twenty-nine rattle segments has been reported. Complete rattles can be quite easily distinguished from broken ones by the presence of the two-lobed

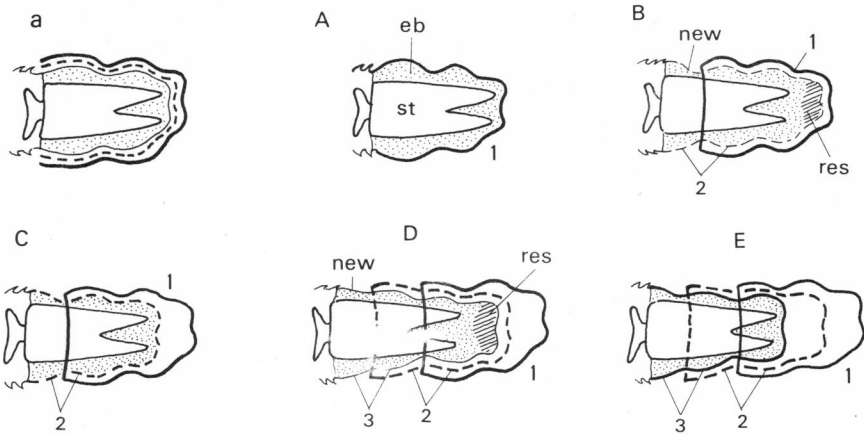

Figure 101. Schematic diagrams illustrating growth of rattlesnake's rattle, as seen in longitudinal section. a. Hypothetical condition in which the successive keratinised generations are formed without rearrangement of their relationships, so that each nests inside the last and the rattle does not lengthen. This does *not* occur. A. Rattle consists of a single 3-lobed, keratinised segment (**1**) with underlying matrix or end-body (**eb**) surrounding bony style (**st**) with last free caudal vertebra attached. B. New lobe added at proximal (anterior) aspect of end-body, shifting previously formed tissue backwards relative to style and establishing 4-lobed end-body with covering (**2**) shown in broken lines. Horny layer of original segment (**1**) shed but remaining in articulation. C. Distal lobe of 4-lobed end-body resorbed (**res** in B) restoring 3-lobed condition as in A. Covering of end-body keratinised (**2**, in thick broken lines). Two interlocking segments now established. D. Another new segment added proximally, producing 4-lobed end-body (covering designated **3**) again. Horny layer of second segment (**2**) shed and distal lobe of end-body resorbed (**res**). E. Epidermis of third segment (**3**) keratinised, as shown by thick lines. Rattle consists of three interlocking segments with end-body filling proximal or third segment. The button of a baby rattlesnake after its first moult has two lobes only. The subsequent production of the three-lobed condition is probably due to failure to resorb the distal lobe of the end-body after the second moult.

button at the tip. It can be appreciated that it is impossible to determine the age of a rattlesnake from a broken rattle string. The number of segments in a complete string, however, will indicate the number of moults which the snake has undergone, and from this basis a very rough estimate of age may be obtained. The use of the rattle and the part which it plays in the life of the snake is discussed on p. 508.

Skin armour As has been mentioned, many reptiles have an armour of bony scutes or osteoderms in the dermal layers of the skin, beneath the horny scales. These tend to develop late in embryonic life or after birth, long after the appearance of the rest of the skeleton, and have a characteristically pitted and ridged appearance, due to the penetration of the bone by minute blood vessels (figure 90, p. 288).

Generally speaking, osteoderms are well developed in reptiles of the archosaurian lineage (p. 33) and are beautifully preserved in some dinosaur skeletons, although all traces of the horny scales usually disappear in the process of fossilisation. The great bony plates along the back and tail of the stegosaurs, for example, are ossifications of this kind. All present-day crocodilians possess bony scutes beneath the enlarged horny scales of the upper surface of the neck, of the back and the base of the tail, as well as a few scattered nodules of bone on the outer sides of the limbs. In the Chinese, though not in the American, alligator, and in the caimans, there are also osteoderms on the belly. These are exceptionally well developed in the smooth-fronted and dwarf caimans *(Paleosuchus)*, and like the scutes on the back, interlock with each other. The very complete dermal armour of these caimans is said to protect them from being injured by rocks in the fast-running streams which they inhabit. A specialised osteoderm often called the palpebral or supraorbital bone, is found supporting the upper eyelid of crocodiles and some lizards. Protected by their shells, chelonians have little need of additional armour, but some species have scattered bony nodules in the skin of the legs, while in the snappers *(Chelydra)* there is a well-developed sheath of osteoderms over the long and barely retractible tail.

Osteoderms are present in many groups of lizards. Those over the head often become fused with the underlying bones of the skull roof and may cover over the top of the orbits and the temporal vacuitkes. In some families such as the Lacertidae the osteoderms are confined to the head, but in others they are present over the body and tail. They may be small separate ossicles, as in the few species of geckos which possess them, or big plates which touch at their edges like the tiles of a mosaic or overlap each other, as in the African plated lizards *(Gerrhosaurus)* and the slow-worm *(Anguis)* (figure 90, p. 288). In some lizards the outlines of the osteoderms coincide exactly with those of the horny scales, in others the correspondence is less exact, while in a few others there is little correlation at all [88].

Although the presence and arrangement of osteoderms in the different lizard groups is sometimes a useful guide to classification, there may be much variation within a family, or even within a genus. In the monitors *(Varanus)* for example, they are absent altogether or very small, except in the Komodo dragon where they are quite substantial structures. Osteoderms are reduced or absent in many (though not all) burrowing lizards, and their complete absence in snakes could be regarded as a further piece of evidence that this group originated from subterranean ancestors.

Crocodilians and the tuatara have a curious system of bony rods known as gastralia or 'abdominal ribs' in the dermal layer of the skin of the belly (figure 6, p. 52). They occur in the region between the pectoral and pelvic girdles and lie outside the true ribs, to which they have no connection. Gastralia were also present in many extinct reptiles and are probably a remnant of the more complete ventral armour of the primitive fossil amphibians. Possibly they served to protect the long, low-slung body wall of these animals. Their distinctness from the parasternum or inscriptional ribs of lizards has already been noted (p. 54).

The chelonian shell The chelonian shell is such a remarkable piece of biological engineering that it deserves a section of its own. It may make up some 30 per cent of the total body weight of a tortoise, though it tends to be relatively lighter in the larger species [37]. The shell is one of the best examples of defensive armour found among verte- brates. However, it is paralleled by (though differently constructed from) the carapaces of bony plates found in certain extinct reptiles – for example in the placodont *Henodus* (figure 2:10), a relative of the plesiosaurs – and among mammals, in the armadillos and their giant extinct relatives, the glyptodons.

The chelonian shell consists of two main pieces, the carapace above, and the plastron below, which are usually firmly joined between the legs by a bridge on either side, formed mainly by an upgrowth of the plastron. In typical forms the shell is composed of a thin outer layer of horny plates or laminae and a thicker, inner one of bony plates (figure 104). The laminae correspond with the horny parts of the scales on the back and belly of other reptiles and are laid down by an underlying basal layer of living epidermal cells which lie between them and the bony plates. The outlines of the laminae seldom coin- cide with those of the plates, and the fact that they overlap increases the strength of the shell. The general arrangement of the laminae and bones shows a certain similarity, however, especially on the

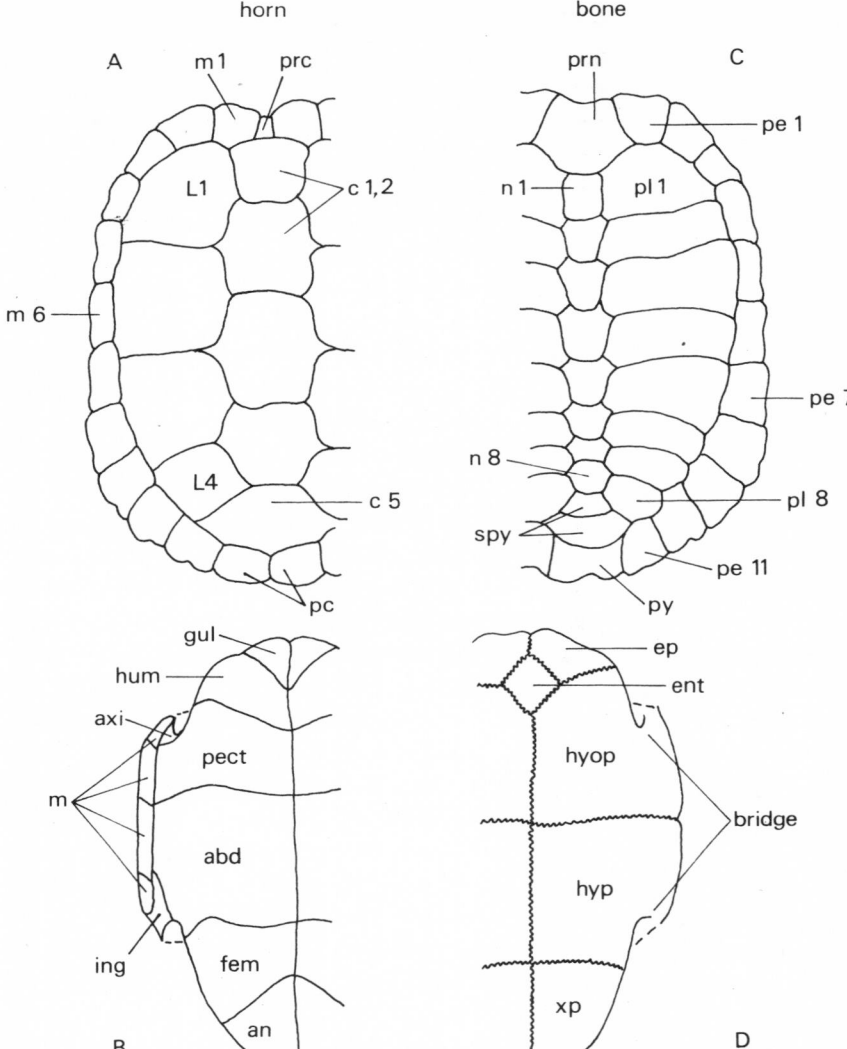

Figure 102.   Horny shell (A, carapace, and B, plastron) and bony shell (C and D) of emydid terrapin (*Pseudemys scripta*), after Carr [89].

Horny plates or laminae : **abd**, abdominal **an**, anal. **axi**, axillary. **c**, central. **fem**, femoral. **gul**, gular. **hum**, humeral. **ing**, inguinal. **L**, lateral. **m**, marginal. **pc**, postcentral. **pect**, pectoral. **prc**, precentral.

Bony plates : **ent**, entoplastron. **ep**, epiplastron. **hyop**, hyoplastron. **hyp**, hypoplastron. **n**, neural. **pe**, peripheral. **pl**, pleural. **prn**, proneural (nuchal). **py**, pygal. **spy**, suprapygal. **xp**, xiphiplastron.

322

carapace. Here there is a row of each down the middle, another row of larger ones on either side of this, and a series of small ones round the margins of the shell. Additional small laminae are present in some forms; in the cheloniid sea turtles, for instance, there is a row of elements (inframarginals) between the carapace and plastron in the region of the bridge. Separate systems of nomenclature are now used to designate the laminae and bones respectively although some older workers used the same terms (eg marginals) for horny and bony structures alike. The arrangement of the various elements of the chelonian shell is illustrated in figure 102. Abnormalities of the shell are not uncommon in the wild, and have been produced experimentally, sometimes in combination with other malformations, by partial drying of the eggs during incubation [263].

As described in chapter 3 the evolution of the shell has involved drastic changes in other parts of the skeleton, the trunk vertebrae and most of the ribs being typically fused with the bony plates.

The sternum of chelonians has entirely disappeared and parts of the shoulder-girdle have been incorporated into the plastron. The remaining bones of the shoulder (scapula and coracoid) and the pelvic girdle lie within the ribs instead of outside them as in almost all other vertebrates. This is one of the most remarkable features of chelonian anatomy and arises during embryonic life as the result of complicated growth changes in the proportions of the body, and in the carapace and skeleton. In early embryonic stages the body is fairly long and rounded in cross-section, as it is in other reptiles. Soon, however, the trunk begins to grow more rapidly in the lateral or horizontal plane than it does in the dorsi-ventral or vertical plane, so that the embryo becomes relatively broader and flatter. At the same time the carapace is foreshadowed as a thick layer of connective tissue covered by epidermis which grows outwards until its rim projects from each side of the trunk (figure 103). The ribs first appear as short rods of cartilage. Since there is no sternum their outer ends are quite free, and they soon become attached to (or very closely associated with) the thick connective tissue dermis of the carapace. As this grows outwards it raises the ribs and carries them with it until they have become shifted into a position above and outside the limb girdles [363].

During late embryonic and early post-natal life the bony plates develop in the deepest part of the dermis, each plate arising from a separate centre of ossification. Ossification of the pleural series of

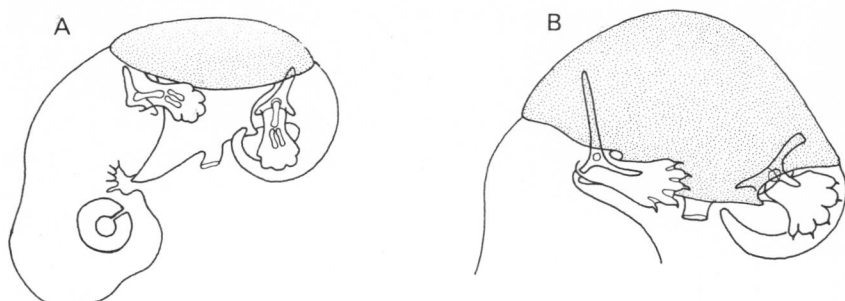

Figure 103. Relationship of carapace (stippled) to limb girdles in embryos of snapping turtle (*Chelydra serpentina*). A, 10 mm. embryo, carapace just beginning to enclose girdles. B, 20–25 mm. embryo with girdles nearly overgrown. After Ruckes [363].

plates begins around the ribs and spreads outwards from them; in *Pseudemys* the rib cartilages are not ossified at all but degenerate and are replaced by blood-forming marrow tissue [413]. At about the same time the epidermis keratinises to form the horny laminae of the shell surface. The plastron seems to develop in a rather different fashion from the carapace, as a series of bony bars which later become fused. No true ribs, of course, are associated with it but there are indications that it may have been partly derived from the abdominal rib system found in other reptiles, as well as including elements of the limb girdles. Thus the developing epiplastra are similar in shape to the clavicles of primitive reptiles, while the entoplastron bears a strong resemblance to the interclavicle [see 473].

The fact that the development of the shell is still incomplete at hatching underlines the importance of an adequate dietary intake for the baby tortoise or turtle. Unless it obtains adequate supplies of calcium and probably of vitamin D at this stage in its life the ossification of the shell, and indeed, of the skeleton in general, will be impaired and the creature will succumb to a condition of bone softening analogous to the human disease of rickets.

Interesting variations in shell structure are found in different kinds of chelonians. In its general shape the carapace may be high and dome-like, as it is in most land tortoises, or very flat, as in the highly aquatic matamata *(Chelus)* and the soft-shelled turtles (Trionychidae). Presumably the domed type of shell gives good protection against the jaws of predators since it is hard to grasp, while the flat shells of most freshwater species are easily concealed when their owners are resting on the bottom. In some races of the Galapagos giant tortoise such as *Testudo elephantopus ephippium* the carapace is raised up in front and the neck is very long. These 'saddle-back' races, as they are called, inhabit the most arid islands. The shape of their shells gives them a long reach and enables them to browse on high-growing cactus pads [337].

As a rule the laminae of the chelonian shell are fairly smooth, but in the matamata, in some individuals of the snapper and alligator turtles *(Chelydra* and *Macroclemys)*, and in the leathery turtle the carapace bears longitudinal ridges or keels. In some land tortoises the centres of the carapacial laminae are raised up into blunt bosses.

A number of tortoises and terrapins have developed hinges (figure 104) across the plastron, dividing it into lobes which can be raised to some extent, and which give more complete protection to the head, limbs and tail when these are retracted. These hinges pass between adjacent pairs of plastral elements and are formed of connective tissue, or possibly of cartilage. Presumably the sutures between the laminae and bony plates coincide along the line of bending. Such mechanisms have been evolved independently in different groups. In the box turtles *(Terrapene)*, for example, there is a single hinge across the plastron between the pectoral and abdominal laminae (figure 104 C; Plate 16), and the hypoplastral and hyoplastral bony plates; these animals are able to box themselves in so tightly that a knife-blade can scarcely enter. A similar but less well-developed hinge is found in the European pond terrapin *(Emys orbicularis)*, while in the American mud turtles *(Kinosternon)* there is also a second hinge further back so that the plastron is trilobed, the middle lobe being immovable (figure 104 D). A few chelonians, such as the African tortoises of the genus *Kinixys* possess a hinged carapace (figure 104 B). One species *K. erosa* is further distinguished by the fact that the front of the plastron projects forwards beyond the carapace as a forked ram-like structure. In captivity it is said to attack tortoises of other species by thrusting the ram 'beneath the side of an opponent in an attempt to turn the latter on its back' [301].

Perhaps the most specialised of all mechanisms for shell closure are found in some of the soft-shelled terrapins such as the Indian pond terrapin *Lissemys* of the family Trionychidae. In these flat, bottom-living creatures there is a hinge across the front of the carapace to close the head opening, and another across the plastron. Additional protection is given by flaps or valves of soft tissue (sometimes

325

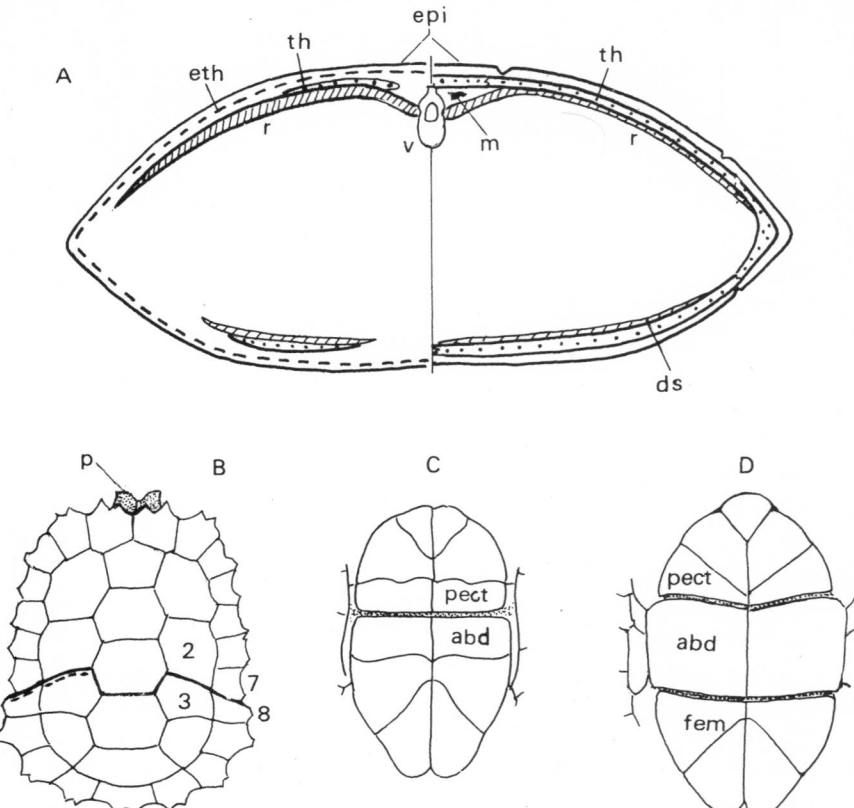

Figure 104.   A. Diagrammatic cross-section showing possible components of chelonian shell. The condition on the right side represents that found in the great majority of chelonians. The outermost layer is made up of horny epidermal plates (**epi**) or laminae; deep to this are the bony thecal plates (**th**; dotted), fused with the ribs (**r**) and neural spines of the vertebrae (**v**). The reduced epaxial muscles (**m**) lie between the rib heads and the thecal plates. Ventrally, parts of the dermal shoulder-girdle (**ds**) such as the clavicle have been incorporated into the plastron.

On the left side there is an outer layer of epidermis (**epi**) which may not be differentiated to form hard plates. Beneath this is a layer of epithecal ossifications (**eth**; broken lines). Beneath this again are reduced elements of the thecal armour (**th**; dotted), ribs and (in the plastron) parts of the dermal skeleton. This condition is more or less realised in the leathery turtle (*Dermochelys*), and to a lesser extent in the soft-shelled turtles (Trionychidae) where many of the bony plates of the carapace have been interpreted as epithecals. Modified from Zangerl [473].

B–D, hinged or kinetic shells (surface views of horny plates). Mainly after Wermuth and Mertens [448]. B, carapace of the African tortoise *Kinyxis erosa* with plastron (**p**) projecting in front. The hinge passes between the 7th and 8th marginals and the 2nd and 3rd laterals (horny plates), and the 7th and 8th peripherals and 4th and 5th pleurals (bony plates; adjacent margins of these shown in broken lines on left only). The hinge is less evident towards the midline but there is some flexibility in the region of the 4th central horny plate. In *Kinyxis* the hinge only develops in maturity, spreading inwards from the margins of the shell. This contradicts the common biological principle that the body becomes stiffer with age! C. Plastron of box tortoise *Terrapene carolina*. Single transverse hinge between pectoral and abdominal horny plates, and bony hypo- and hyo-plastra. D. Plastron of mud turtle *Kinosternon subrubrum*. Two hinges. (1) between pectoral (**pect**) and abdominal (**abd**) horny plates and epi- and hyo-plastra; (2) between abdominal and femoral (**fem**) horny plates and hypo- and xiphiplastra.

supported by plates of cartilage) which are moved by special muscles and occlude the openings in the shell for the limbs and tail.

It may seem strange that chelonians, having gone to so much trouble, as it were, to evolve their elaborate armour should then lose some of it, but this has apparently happened in several different groups. The shell bones are said to be quite thin in some of the giant tortoises; this may confer some advantage by reducing the weight and would be no handicap to tortoises which live on isolated islands devoid of non-human predators.

A more interesting example of shell reduction is shown by the curious *Malacochersus tornieri* which unlike other land tortoises has a very flat carapace. Joan Procter [338] has given a graphic description of it under its synonym of Loveridge's tortoise.

In general appearance it looks as if it had been crushed in youth and had only survived by a miracle. When taken in the hand alive it has a boneless feeling which is uncanny; both carapace and plastron react to pressure on the abdominal region with a springy motion, and the animal is able to inflate itself to a slight degree.

This flexibility has been achieved by reducing the bones of the carapace to a framework surrounding large vacuities; there is also a large opening in the centre of the plastron. It is interesting that the general condition resembles that of the young of related species before the shell has fully ossified, and has therefore been evolved by the process of neoteny (see p. 474). Even within the species various degrees of shell reduction are seen in different individuals. The shell of *Malacochersus* is an adaptation to its habitat among arid, rocky kopjes in Tanzania. It climbs well and squeezes itself into crevices and under stones from which it resists attempts to dislodge it by inflating its body with air. Here we find a parallel with the habits of certain lizards such as the spiny-tailed agamids of the genus *Uromastyx*.

Reduction of the bony shell has also occurred in many aquatic chelonians and is often regarded as advantageous, on the grounds that it renders the animal lighter and more buoyant. There may, for example, be a large gap in the middle of the bony (though not of the horny) plastron as in the sea turtles (figure 105). In the latter also the

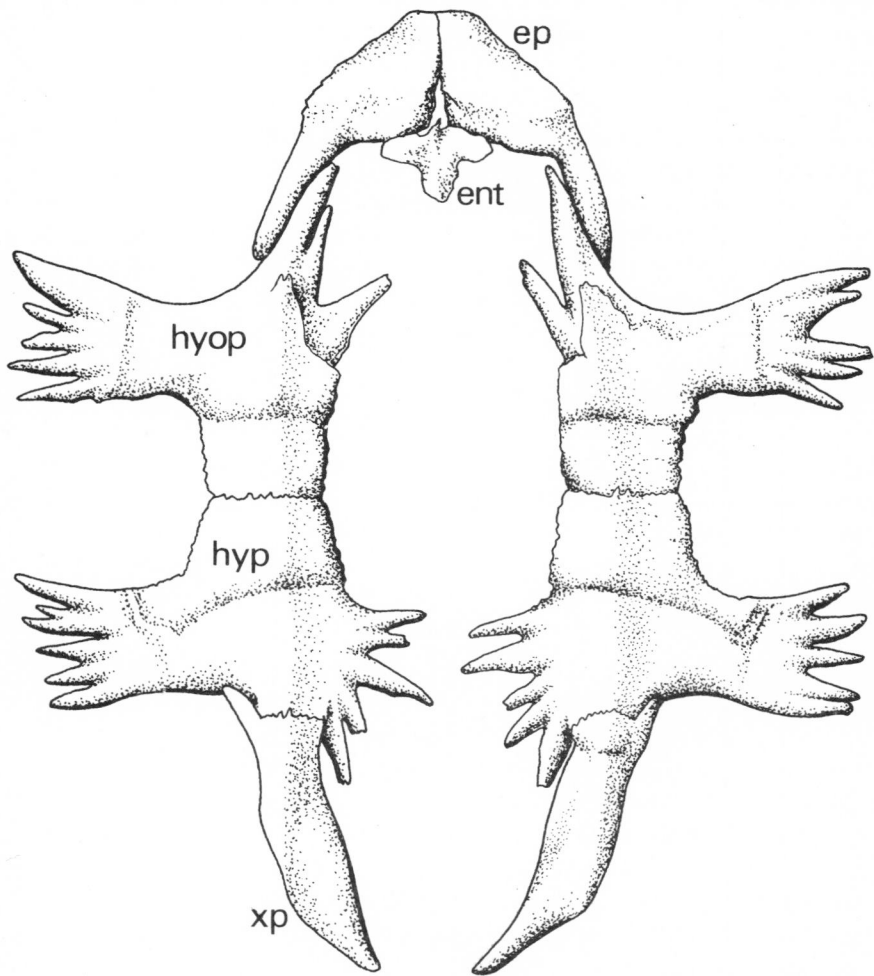

Figure 105.   Bony plastron of hawksbill turtle (*Eretmochelys imbricata*). The entoplastron (**ent**) is probably broken off short.

ep, epiplastron. **hyop**, hyoplastron. **hyp**, hypoplastron. **xp**, xiphiplastron.

328

pleural bony plates of the carapace are short so that there are gaps or fontanelles between them and the peripheral bones, and between the ends of the ribs (figure 16, p. 66). In the loggerhead *(Caretta)* these gaps tend to become filled in by ossification during maturity or old age [394]. The bony shell was cut down even further in some of the extinct turtles such as the giant Cretaceous *Archelon*.

The types of shell reduction which have been considered so far involve only the bony plates of the shell, but in a few chelonians the epidermal laminae have also degenerated. In *Carettochelys* (figure 29, p. 89) and the soft-shelled turtles (Trionychidae) (Plate 37) the carapace and plastron are covered only with leathery skin; in the Trionychidae the bony plastron is poorly ossified and the bony plates round the margins of the carapace (the peripherals) have generally been lost so that the ends of the ribs project. These turtles are prone to a curious humpbacked abnormality which is possibly due to some disharmony of growth between the bones of the carapace and the vertebral column and ribs, occurring in early life.

The only other existing chelonian without a horny shell is the leathery turtle *(Dermochelys coriacea)* (Plate 57) the largest and most remarkable existing member of the whole order. Young leatherbacks possess small horny scales over the body and limbs but these disappear in the adult which is covered entirely by smooth, dark skin. Beneath this is an extraordinary carapace or corselet consisting of many hundreds of small, roughly polygonal platelets of bone sutured at their edges like the tesserae of a mosaic (figure 106). Seven ridges run down the length of the back, produced by rows of platelets bigger than the others; each of these has its right and left halves set at an angle to each other. The large bony plates present in the carapace of other turtles are absent, except for a single nuchal bone, shaped like a butterfly, at the back of the neck, which articulates with the spine of the eighth neck vertebra. Apart from this, the carapace is quite free from the vertebrae and ribs, which hence have a more 'normal' appearance than they do in other chelonians. There is no comparable mosaic on the belly, only several widely separated longitudinal rows of platelets. There is also a ring of slender bones which correspond with the outer edges of the plastral plates of other Chelonia (figure 104); the entoplastral element is absent.

The curious shell of the leatherback has been the starting point of much discussion, not only about the zoological position of the animal itself, but also about the nature of the chelonian shell in general.

329

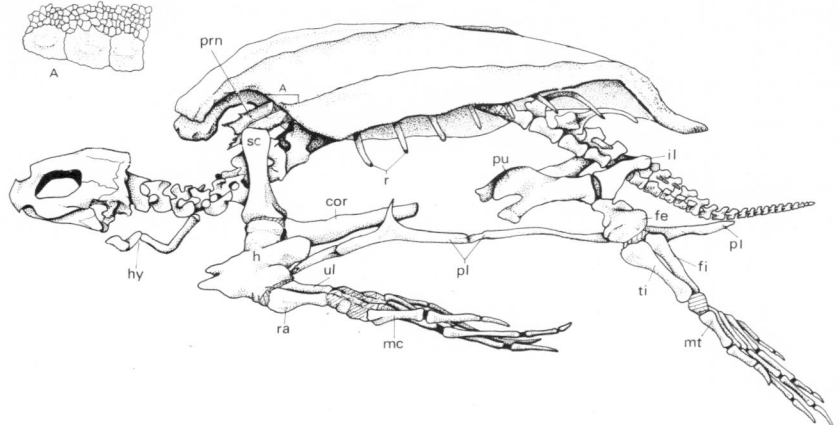

Figure 106. Shell and skeleton of leathery turtle (*Dermochelys coriacea*). The carapace of this specimen, mounted in the British Museum (Natural History) is made of plaster. It actually consists (apart from the proneural bone) of thousands of bony platelets sutured together, and would probably be extremely difficult to prepare for museum purposes. It is not attached to the ribs or vertebrae. The inset figure (A) shows a small portion of this epithecal dermal armour (after Deraniyagala [134]) which corresponds roughly with the area marked A in the main figure. The longitudinal ridges are formed by rows of the larger platelets. The sparse plastral and the flank platelets are not preserved. The carpal and tarsal regions of the specimen are also partly restored in plaster which probably represents cartilage or connective tissue in which the small bones are imbedded. These regions, like the joint surfaces of the large limb bones which are restored in the same way, are shown by slanting lines. The humerus is broad and flattened and has strong processes for muscle attachment. Paired structures are mostly shown on the near side only.

cor, coracoid. **fe**, femur. **fi**, fibula. **h**, humerus. **hy**, hyoid skeleton. **il**, ilium. **mc**, 1st metacarpal. **mt**, 1st metatarsal. **pl**, plastral bones. **prn**, proneural (nuchal) bone. **pu**, pubis. **r**, rib (distal end). **ra**, radius. **sc**, scapula. **ti**, tibia. **ul**, ulna.

Although there is no clear-cut evidence from fossils, modern opinion inclines to the view that conditions in *Dermochelys* are specialised rather than primitive, and that it has evolved from forms which had an armour like that of other turtles [356, 359]. Subsequently this degenerated, as the armour of marine reptiles tends to do, leaving as its remnants the nuchal bone and the reduced plastral elements. At the same time, the mosaic of platelets arose as a secondary development, perhaps to compensate for the loss of the original shell. These platelets are sometimes referred to as 'epithecals' to distinguish them from the broad 'thecal' plates of the typical chelonian carapace. The epithecals appear later in embryonic life than the thecals and ossify in a more superficial stratum of the dermis; probably they correspond with the osteoderms of other reptiles, whereas the thecal plates seem to have no counterparts outside the Chelonia [see 473].

It should be added that some workers have identified epithecal ossifications in other types of turtles, and it has even been suggested that they were present, together with and outside the thecals, in the carapace of the ancestral Chelonia; this theory is an alternative to the view that they arose secondarily after the ordinary shell had begun to degenerate. The relative positions of the thecal and epithecal elements are shown in figure 104. Probably we should be well advised to forego further speculation until good fossil evidence is available, and until more detailed studies of the embryonic development of the shell of living chelonians have been made.

Chapter 8

Nervous System, Psychology and Sense Organs

The nervous system

THE NERVOUS system receives information from the sense organs about the outside world, integrates and stores this knowledge and initiates activity appropriate to the occasion. One might therefore imagine that studies of this system in different animals would tell us much about their ways of life, but in fact the subject of comparative neurology contains disappointingly little of interest to the naturalist, at any rate where the Reptilia are concerned. This is perhaps because many students of the reptilian nervous system have concerned themselves with it mainly in so far as it throws light on the evolution of the mammalian condition; they have been less interested in such diversities in pattern which may exist within the reptiles themselves.

The brains of reptiles are small by mammalian standards, usually not much bigger and sometimes smaller than the brains of fish or amphibians of similar bulk. When considering brain sizes, however, it must be remembered that large animals of any kind tend to have relatively smaller brains (in proportion to body size) than small animals. One must make allowance for this tendency when one is comparing brain sizes in members of different vertebrate classes. The human brain, which is one of the largest mammalian brains in absolute size, amounts to about $\frac{1}{48}$ or 2·1 per cent of the total body weight. The tiny brain of a shrew, on the other hand, is equivalent to approximately $\frac{1}{23}$ or 4·3 per cent of the weight of the intact animal; its *relative* brain weight is therefore about twice as great as that of man.

It is not surprising that the dinosaurs should have had brains which were relatively minute in proportion to their vast bulk, even though these may have been absolutely larger than the brains of modern reptiles. It has been estimated that in a giant sauropod such as *Brontosaurus* the brain may have weighed only 1/100,000 or 0·001 per cent, of a total body weight of perhaps 30,450 kilograms (30 tons). At the other extreme, the brain of a small gecko may have a relative weight of nearly 1 per cent.

Figures for some weights of brain and body in some reptiles and other vertebrates are shown in the following table [436].

Species	Brain wt. as % body wt.	Absolute wt. brain	(gm.) body
Esox lucius (pike)	0·04	4·9	12,700
Cyprinus carpio (carp)	0·07	1·3	1,817
Perca fluviatilis (perch)	0·2	0·16	67
Gasterosteus aculeatus (stickleback)	1·5	0·02	1·4
Rana catesbiana (bull frog)	0·08	0·2	244
R. temporaria (frog)	0·2	0·1	53
Bufo bufo (toad)	0·2	0·1	44
Salamandra maculosa (salamander)	0·2	0·05	25
Triturus cristatus (newt)	0·28	0·02	7
Varanus niloticus (monitor)	0·03	2·4	7,500
Testudo hermanni (tortoise)	0·04	0·4	994
Naja melanoleuca (cobra)	0·04	0·65	1,770
Vipera berus (adder)	0·16	0·1	64
Anguis fragilis (slow-worm)	0·2	0·04	19
Lacerta viridis (green lizard) (i)	0·6	0·1 (0·093)	17
Lacerta viridis (green lizard) (ii)	0·5	0·1 (0·125)	24
Lacerta viridis (green lizard) (iii)	0·4	0·1 (0·130)	32
Lacerta agilis (sand lizard)	0·6	0·08	12
Hemidactylus brooki (gecko)	0·9	0·043	5
Gallus gallus (fowl)	0·2	3·8	1,665
Troglodytes troglodytes (wren)	5·3	0·48	9
Balaenoptera sibbaldi (whale)	0·01	12,000	100,000,000
Homo sapiens (man, European male)	2·1	1,360	65,000
Felis catus (cat)	0·9	29	3,284
Sorex araneus (shrew)	4·3	0·125	2·9

These figures refer to more or less adult animals and have mostly been altered from the original data to the nearest decimal point. The fact taht the brain weight differs so little in three different-sized specimens of the green lizard suggests that the brain stops growing before the rest of the body, much as in man. There is very little critical information, however, about the relative growth rates of the brain and body in reptiles.

Actual measurements of brain size (as opposed to weight) in reptiles are seldom recorded; the brain of a green lizard about a foot long would measure approximately half an inch from olfactory bulb to the back of the cerebellum. In a crocodile of between three and

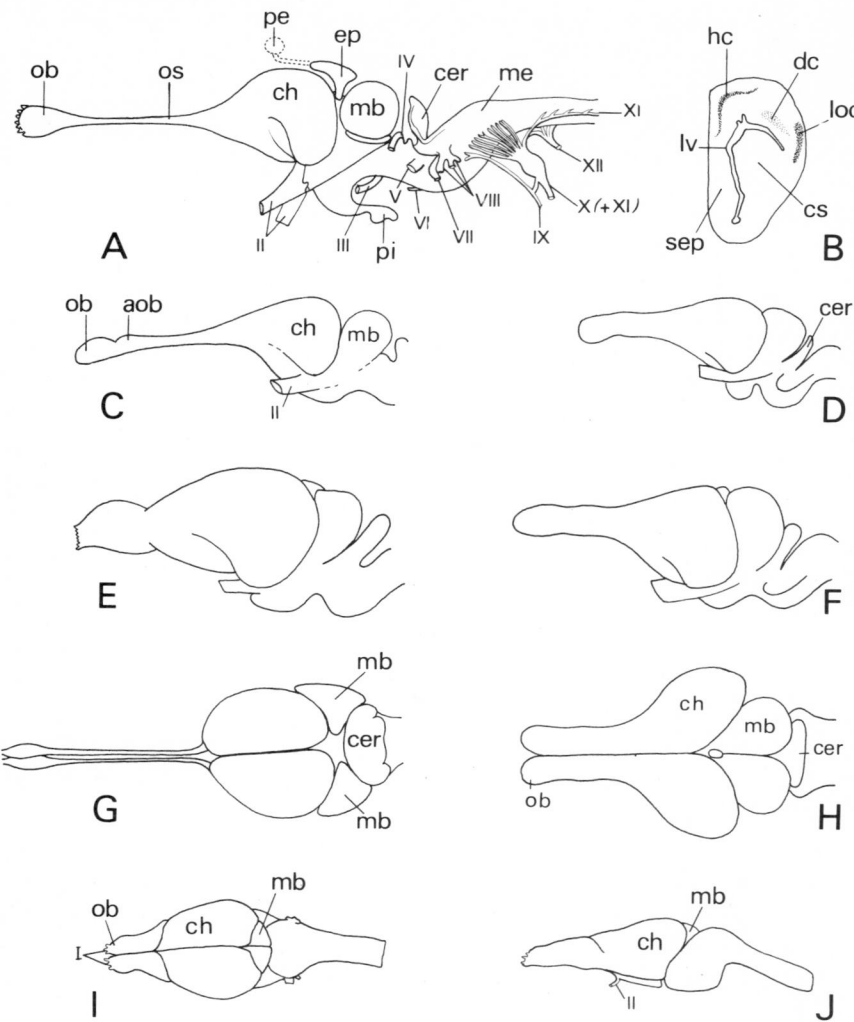

Figure 107. Brains of reptiles. A. Tuatara (*Sphenodon punctatus*) from left side with parts of pineal apparatus, pituitary and cranial nerves. B. Transverse section through fore-brain of green lizard (*Lacerta viridis*). C.–J. Diagrammatic outline drawings to show external features of brain of C, green lizard; D, slow-worm (*Anguis fragilis*); E, tortoise (*Testudo graeca*); F, grass snake (*Natrix natrix*); all from left side: G, *Anolis garmani*; H, grass snake; I, blind snake (*Leptotyphlops humilis*); all from above: J, *Leptotyphlops* from left side. See Plate 50 for *Crocodylus*. A, after Wiedersheim (see figure 54 H). B, after Goldby, F. *J. Anat.* 1934, **68** 157; C–G after Goldby and Gamble [197]. I, J, after Senn [381].

aob, accessory olfactory bulb. **cer**, cerebellum. **ch**, cerebral hemisphere. **cs**, corpus striatum. **dc**, dorsal cerebral cortex. **ep**, epiphysis. **hc**, hippocampal cortex. **loc**, lateral olfactory (pyriform) cortex. **lv**, lateral ventricle. **mb**, mid-brain (optic lobes). **me**, medulla. **ob**, olfactory bulb. **os**, olfactory stalk (peduncle). **pe**, parietal ('pineal') eye. **pi**, pituitary gland. **sep**, septal region. Cranial nerves: **II**, optic. **III**, oculomotor. **IV**, trochlear. **V**, trigeminal. **VI**, abducent. **VII**, facial. **VIII**, auditory and vestibular. **IX**, glossopharyngeal. **X**, vagus. **XI**, accessory. **XII**, hypoglossal.

four feet, the brain is about 5 cm. (2 in.) long, and about 2 cm. in its greatest width, across the cerebral hemispheres (Plate 50).

The brains of most reptiles do not completely fill the cranial cavity and are separated from its walls in places by loose strands of dura mater, the outer membrane surrounding the brain. This fact introduces obvious difficulties in the task of restoring the brain from the skulls of fossil forms. Thus, in the dinosaur *Tyrannosaurus*, an endocranial cast of the skull cavity was about 20 cm. (8 in.) long and no more than 5 cm. across. The brain may well have been considerably smaller than this, but at least we have some indication of its maximum possible size [106].

The reptilian brain (figure 107), like that of vertebrates in general, is divided into three main parts, the fore-, mid- and hind-brains. Each of these has one or more of the twelve (or sometimes only eleven) pairs of cranial nerves attached to it. A large part of the fore-brain is made up by two pear-shaped swellings, the cerebral hemispheres; these are hollow, their cavities being called the lateral ventricles. The surface of the hemispheres is smooth, although it may have one or two faint grooves. This contrasts with the richly folded or convoluted appearance of the hemispheres which is so characteristic of the brains of man and many other mammals.

The front of each hemisphere is drawn out into a stalk which ends in a swelling, the olfactory bulb. These bulbs lie just behind the nose and the fibres of the olfactory nerves pass back into them. In most reptiles there is another smaller swelling, the accessory olfactory bulb, behind each main bulb, and this receives the fibres of the vomeronasal nerve from the organ of Jacobson (p. 365). The appearance of the front region of the brain differs considerably among reptiles. In lizards such as *Agama* and *Lacerta*, in the tuatara and in crocodiles, the olfactory stalks are long and thin. In tree lizards such as *Anolis* and chamaeleons, where the sense of smell is poorly developed, the bulbs are minute and their stalks exceedingly slender – so much so that they have been mistaken for the olfactory nerves. In the slow-worm and in snakes and turtles generally, which have a good sense of smell, the olfactory bulbs are large and their stalks are thick and fairly short, especially so in the Chelonia. These differences in the proportions of the brain probably depend to some extent on the relative sizes of the nose and eyes which are in turn related to the differences in the proportions of the skull.

In mammals the greater part of the cerebral hemispheres is made up of a layer of grey matter known as the cortex which is particularly well developed in man and other higher Primates. Many sensory fibres enter this region from other parts of the brain, and many motor fibres originate from it and are distributed directly to the muscles of the body and limbs. It is also a co-ordinating centre of great importance and is deeply involved in what may be called the 'higher faculties' such as learning and memory. In reptiles, however, the cerebral hemispheres are concerned mainly with the sense of smell, as they are in the majority of vertebrates. A small area on the upper surface of each hemisphere has often been regarded as the evolutionary forerunner of the mammalian cortex, but there is no firm evidence for this. Experimental removal of this area in lizards has very little effect on the animal's behaviour, and does not even appear to destroy the effects of previous training to associate particular colours or geometrical patterns with the offer of food. Experiments in which this part of the brain is stimulated electrically have also failed to show conclusively that motor fibres to the limbs and body originate from it; it is possible that the crocodilian brain differs from the others in this respect [see 197].

If both cerebral hemispheres are entirely removed or very seriously damaged, however, lizards become sluggish and seldom make spontaneous movements, although they are still able to move in a more or less normal way if forced to do so, as by handling. They are also unable to perform the coordinated sequence of movements which is necessary for capturing and eating prey. These effects are probably due to damage to the large mass of grey matter known as the corpus striatum, which is very well developed in reptiles and forms most of the outer and lower wall of each hemisphere, bulging into the lateral ventricle (figure 107 B). The corpus striatum could well be of great importance in the coordination of complicated instinctive behaviour, such as reptiles show in attack and defence, and in territorial display, though there appears to be little experimental evidence on this point.

Lying deeply between the hinder parts of the cerebral hemispheres is another part of the fore-brain known as the diencephalon, which surrounds the cavity of the third ventricle. The 'pineal' or parietal eye and the epiphysis arise from the roof of this region (figure 113, p. 356) while the pituitary gland is attached to its floor; only a part of this gland is developed from the brain in the embryo, however; the anterior lobe, concerned with regulating growth and reproduction, arises from a little pouch which grows up from the pharynx. In some gigantic extinct reptiles the depression or fossa in the skull which lodges the pituitary is very large, and it has been suggested that the gland was of corresponding size. The fact that part of the fossa in certain modern forms such as monitor lizards is occupied by eye muscles shows again the dangers of deducing the size of soft tissues from that of the bony cavities which contained them.

Above the stalk of the pituitary is a region of the brain called the hypothalamus which seems to play some part in sexual activity and temperature control, and above this again is another region, the thalamus. In mammals the thalamus is large and constitutes an important relay station for sensory nerve impulses travelling from various parts of the body to the cerebral cortex. The much smaller thalamus of reptiles seems also to act as a relay station but the fibres which originate in it pass mainly to the mid-brain, and by way of large tracts known as the fore-brain bundles, to the corpus striatum.

Behind the cerebral hemispheres another pair of swellings are conspicuous on the upper surface of the brain. These are the optic lobes of the mid-brain, which receive most of the fibres from the optic nerves. The optic lobes are extremely well developed in reptiles such as chamaeleons where the visual system is highly efficient, and are small in burrowing forms such as *Leptotyphlops* (figure 107, I, J) [381].

In fish and amphibians the mid-brain, besides being associated with the visual system, is also a general coordinating centre of great importance and performs functions analogous with those of the cerebral cortex of mammals. This is probably also true in reptiles, though here the dominant role of the mid-brain seems to have been partly taken over by the corpus striatum; this tendency has been carried much further in birds.

The hind-brain of reptiles consists of the cerebellum and the medulla oblongata which is continuous with the spinal cord. The cerebellum is small and its lateral lobes, which are so prominent in

337

birds and were also apparently large in the extinct flying reptiles, are poorly developed. Presumably the small size of the cerebellum in modern reptiles is correlated with the fact that their locomotion does not usually involve sustained muscular control or critical powers of balance. It must be admitted, however, that the brains of exceptionally agile reptiles such as the fast-swimming leather turtle, of tree snakes and of flying lizards, do not seem to have been investigated.

The medulla is of great importance in the regulation and control of internal bodily activities which it achieves mainly through the agency of the vagus nerve attached to it; this far-ranging nerve supplies the heart and lungs, as well as much of the alimentary tract and contains both motor (parasympathetic) and sensory fibres. The medulla is also concerned with hearing and balance, since it receives fibres from the auditory and vestibular (balancing) organs of the inner ear.

Generally speaking the brain of modern reptiles resembles that of birds in many important respects; this is especially true in the case of the brains of crocodiles, and of lizards such as *Anolis*, where the sense of smell is poorly developed. The fact that the reptilian brain is so much more like the avian brain than the mammalian one is only to be expected in view of the fact that modern reptiles (other than chelonians) are more closely related to birds than to mammals. The main differences between the avian and reptilian brain lie in the much greater development of the corpus striatum and of the lateral lobes of the cerebellum in the former. The brain of chelonians seems to be more primitive (ie more like the amphibian brain) than is that of other reptiles.

The spinal cord of reptiles passes down to or almost to the tip of the tail. This condition contrasts with that in mammals where the cord ends in the lumbar region and the spinal canal in the vertebrae behind this level is occupied by a leash of elongated nerve-roots known as the chorda equina. In typical reptiles the cord shows the usual cervico-dorsal and lumbo-sacral enlargements in the regions opposite the fore- and hind limbs, from which the limb nerve plexuses arise (Plate 51). In many dinosaurs the lumbo-sacral region of the spinal canal was greatly dilated, sometimes having a volume of perhaps twenty times that of the cranial cavity. It is uncertain whether this cavity was entirely filled by nervous tissue; however, it has often been suggested that the lumbo-sacral enlargement was particularly well developed in dinosaurs and acted as a centre for controlling the tail and hind limbs which could act independently of the distant brain.

Certainly the lumbar spinal centres seem to have considerable powers of autonomy, and it has been shown that in tortoises and lizards these centres can by themselves maintain coordinated walking movements of the hind limbs. A lizard in which the spinal cord has been cut just in front of the lumbar region can move itself along with its hind legs if the front part of its body is supported on a trolley [417].

In limbless lizards and snakes the enlargements of the cord are absent, as one might expect in view of the absence or extreme reduction of the limb plexuses (Plate 51). In chelonians the dorsal region of the cord between the limb plexus enlargements is narrow; this again seems to be correlated with a reduction of the trunk muscles, and perhaps also with some reduction of the sensory nerve fibres when the skin was replaced by the shell – though this is by no means insensitive.

Intelligence

Although many reptiles have quite elaborate patterns of instinctive behaviour, no one could claim that they are good at adapting to unfamiliar situations, or have much ability to learn from experience. For example, lizards *(Lacerta* species*)* do not seem able to learn to climb deliberately over the rim of a shallow glass dish in which mealworms are visible. They are only successful in obtaining the food by chance after vigorous clawing and biting at the dish has accidentally resulted in raising their heads over the rim. This simple experiment has been repeated three times a week for three months, but the creatures never managed to learn [114].

On the other hand, some species can certainly be tamed in the sense that they grow accustomed to being handled and may even take food from the hand. Large and potentially harmful reptiles such as alligators, pythons and Komodo dragons may become quite amenable in captivity and can usually be trusted not to bite. While many snake-charmers are frauds who rely on snakes whose fangs have been put out of action, there are authentic accounts of genuine devotees of the art who tame even the deadly king cobra in full possession of its venomous faculties [290].

Although there are many anecdotes about the intelligence (and, alternatively, the stupidity) of reptiles, only a few workers have tried to study their mental powers in a scientific fashion. Most comparative psychologists with an interest in reptiles have used chelonians as experimental subjects. It has been known for many years that these animals can learn their way about a simple maze if they are offered rewards for taking the right turning and punished for taking the wrong one. If circumstances are altered they can change their habits eventually, and will learn to go, for instance, to the right instead of the left at a T junction. Similar studies on snakes have produced inconclusive results [464].

Both lizards and chelonians can be trained to distinguish between various colours such as orange, blue and green, and between various shapes and patterns, such as circles and squares. Some chelonians are even able to distinguish between vertical and horizontal lines and between lines of varying widths [see 89]. In some more recent experiments, the ability of terrapins (Pseudemys scripta elegans) to correlate certain smells with unpleasant stimuli was tested. The animals were offered meat by itself, which they were allowed to eat; alternatively, the meat was offered when a strongly smelling substance such as amyl acetate was liberated into the tank water and an electric shock followed. Most of the terrapins soon became able to distinguish between the meat by itself, and the 'dangerous' meat offered with amyl acetate, vanillin or eucalyptus, and did not attempt to snap at it. Cutting of the olfactory nerves prevented the turtles from making the distinction and showed that smell was the sense involved. These animals could be trained more readily to avoid 'dangerous' meat by a visual stimulus – the display of a strip of black perspex [65].

Further experiments [293] on a related species (Pseudemys ornata callirostris) made use of the fact that if placed on a stand beside their tank, the terrapins would rapidly scuttle down into the water. The tank was divided into two compartments, one side being black and the other white, both being equally accessible (figure 108). After a number of trials it became clear that nearly all the animals had a definite preference for white. They could often be induced to overcome their colour prejudice by the appropriate electric shock treatment and would enter the black compartment. Sometimes, however, they refused to cooperate and just remained on their platform. Some individuals retained memories of their training for several weeks after the experiment had ended. It should be added that a preference for white is not a characteristic of all species of terrapins and that with Pseudemys scripta elegans some individuals choose a white compartment and others a black one [294].

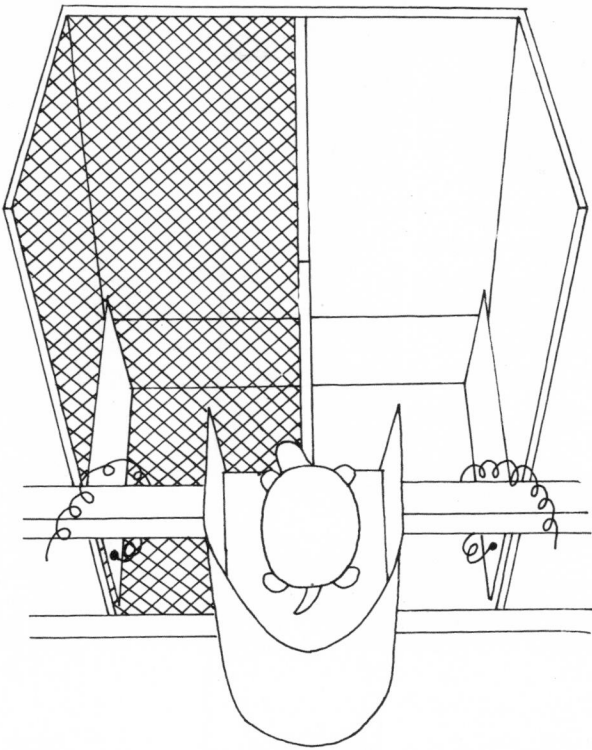

Figure 108.   Terrapin training-tank with black and white compartments. After Mrosovsky [293].

Reptiles are not the easiest of animals to use in such studies. Many species are prone to go off their food and become difficult to tempt with rewards, while chelonians may respond to shock treatment by retiring into their shells. Furthermore, they show individual idio-syncrasies; as an early experimental psychologist has written 'The mind of the turtle is very erratic.' [see 294] One may perhaps wonder whether these experiments really tell us much about the life of the animal in its natural surroundings. They may help us to understand, however, which particular qualities of its environment it can appre-ciate and respond to; whether, for example, its choice of food or a mate can possibly be influenced by such qualities as smell or colour. The preference of certain terrapins for a tank with white walls is interesting, for it has been suggested that hatchlings are guided by the brightness of an open horizon or of moonlit water when they

341

make their first perilous journey from the nest down to the river or sea[*].

One may mention here the curious observation that some reptiles can apparently be 'hypnotised' by suitable manual techniques [440]. A sudden grip or pressure on the throat of a crocodilian is said to reduce it to a state of immobility; if turned on its back it will remain immobile for as long as an hour. The same result can be obtained by suddenly snapping together the open jaws. I have myself seen a small crocodile rendered motionless by holding it round the neck and turning it over on its back, but the effect only lasted for a few minutes. It has been suggested that the animals possess certain 'hypnogenic zones' which are stimulated by such techniques, sending the creatures into a kind of cataleptic trance. Further and perhaps more critical studies of these interesting phenomena are clearly desirable.

Sense organs

The principal sense organs, the nose, eyes, and the ears with their primitive function of detecting changes in the animal's position in space, have remained remarkably stable throughout some 450 million years of vertebrate evolution. Perhaps the most important change was the loss of the lateral line organs which give the fish or tadpole its powers of perceiving disturbances in its watery surroundings. This must finally have occurred among the ancestors of reptiles when they began to lay their eggs on land and to dispense with aquatic larval stages.

Sometimes we find the regression of certain sense organs when they are no longer needed; in burrowing animals, for example, the eyes tend to degenerate. There are also a few instances of existing sense organs being elaborated in such a way that they acquire new functions. The evolution, in the early amphibians, of an instrument for perceiving airborne sounds out of the balancing organs of the inner ear, and the addition to it of a sound-conducting apparatus derived from the gill arch skeleton, is perhaps the most striking example. The elaboration of the organ of Jacobson in Squamata to supplement and perhaps even supplant the nose as an organ of smell is an interesting but less radical innovation. Only exceptionally does one encounter among vertebrates what appears to be an important sense organ of completely new type; the remarkable heat-sensitive pits on the snout of certain snakes may genuinely fall into this category.

342

The eyes The eyes are perhaps the most fascinating of all the sense organs. This is partly because they are such overwhelmingly important members of our own sensory equipment, and partly because they show such diverse and complex adaptations to the habits of their owners. The book by G. L. Walls on the vertebrate eye [444], first published in 1942 and embodying years of research, is still almost the only general source of information – at least in English – about the eyes of reptiles (and of many other animals). It is a massive and most scholarly work, yet written in a highly individual style, and seems to me one of the masterpieces of modern biological literature.

Most diurnal reptiles which lead active lives above the ground probably rely more on their eyes than on any other sense organs, even than that of Jacobson (p. 365), and this is certainly true for species like chamaeleons which live in trees. They respond, like many other keen-sighted animals, much more readily to moving objects than to stationary ones, though it is possible that here the brain rather than the eye is involved.

Many lizards such as agamids and lacertids can certainly distinguish between different colours, as one might expect from the importance of colouration as a secondary sexual character. If lizards (*Lacerta agilis*) are offered as alternatives tasty mealworms and unpleasant salty ones on discs of different coloured paper they can learn to distinguish red, orange, yellow, yellowish-green, blue and violet from each other and from various shades of grey [see 444]. *Anolis* lizards can recognise insects with bright patterns of warning type such as red on black and usually reject them as food, even though, if they do eat them, they do not find them all distasteful [382]. Giant tortoises can be trained to distinguish between orange, blue and green [see 89], and certain terrapins appear to be particularly sensitive to colours of long wave-length towards the red end of the spectrum; they may even be able to perceive infra-red radiations. Crocodiles and snakes, on the other hand, are probably colour-blind.

Binocular vision, in which the fields of the two eyes overlap considerably, gives a good perception of depth and a nice judgement of distance. It is characteristic of man and other Primates, and of creatures which pounce or swoop upon their prey such as cats and raptorial birds. Among the reptiles, land tortoises, crocodiles and many diurnal lizards such as lacertids have only narrow binocular fields which overlap by 25° or less. Though sharp-sighted enough, these creatures depend on monocular vision. One may often notice an alert lizard cock its head to bring an object under the critical scrutiny of one eye alone. Binocularity is better developed, however, in many freshwater chelonians and in snakes, which may have 30° or more of visual overlap. It is particularly good in the snapping turtle (*Chelydra serpentina*) which captures its prey with a sudden strike, in monitors and *Anolis* lizards, and in certain agile, arboreal snakes. In the tree snake *Ahaetulla* and some of its relatives there are grooves along the sides of the elongated snout along which the two eyes can sight on the same object, their fields overlapping by some 45° (figure 111).

The chamaeleons are remarkable in that they enjoy the advantages of both wide-angle monocular, and binocular vision. Their very large eyes project from the head, and unlike the eyes of most reptiles, have a wide range of movement; indeed they can swivel independently like guns in twin movable turrets, each traversing a field of about 180° in the horizontal and 90° in the vertical plane. A hungry chamaeleon will use his eyes in this independent fashion, looking forwards with one and backwards with the other while he scans his surroundings for the movement of an insect. If one is sighted nearby, his two eyes converge upon it and hold it in binocular view, while he slowly stalks it until it is within range of his projectile tongue. A similar power of moving the eyes independently has been observed in the Cuban iguanid *Chamaeleolis*, a relative of the anoles which shows an extraordinary parallel with the Old World chamaeleons in habits and appearance [461].

Although all vertebrate eyes are basically much alike, those of reptiles differ in certain interesting ways from the more familiar mammalian condition. For example, the tough fibrous coat or sclera of the eyeball is usually reinforced with cartilage, and towards the front of the eye where the sclera becomes continuous with the transparent cornea, there is a ring of about fourteen little bones, the scleral ossicles (figures 8, p. 55 and 109 A). These bones are also present in birds and are often preserved in fossil reptiles, being very conspicuous in ichthyosaurs. They are absent in modern crocodiles though some of the extinct, Mesozoic types possessed them. Both scleral cartilage and ossicles are lacking in all snakes.

The task of accommodating the eye for near vision is performed by the little ciliary muscles which are situated near the corneo-scleral junction. In man and most other mammals they act in such a way that they relax the tension of the elastic envelope which surrounds the crystalline lens. The lens, which is slightly supple, can then be moulded by the pressure of its envelope so that it becomes more spherical and hence more sharply curved in front.

In typical reptiles and birds the method of accommodation is rather different. The effect of their ciliary muscles is to squeeze the front of the eyeball until the thick bulge of tissue, known as the ciliary body which lies on the inside of the corneoscleral junction, presses against the sides of the lens itself (figure 109 A). As the result of this pressure, the lens becomes longer from front to back, like a

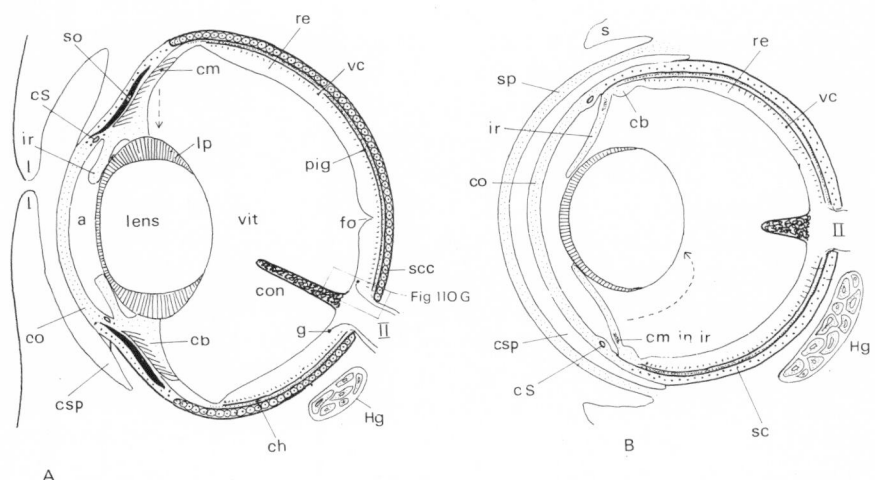

Figure 109. Diagrams showing essential features of the eyes in A, typical lizard and B, typical snake, as seen in transverse section through the middle of the lens. In A two optic nerve fibres are shown arising from ganglion cells in the retina; the area in the rectangle corresponds with figure 110 G. The arrows show the direction of force applied to increase the curvature of the lens in the process of accommodation for near vision. In the lizard contraction of the ciliary muscles forces the ciliary bodies against the lens pad and squeezes the lens. In the snake the ciliary muscles have shifted into the iris and those near its root press the iris against the vitreous; this raises the intra-vitreous pressure and pushes the whole lens forwards. The iris muscles which contract and dilate the pupil are not shown in A or B. Modified from Walls [444].

a, anterior (part of aqueous) chamber of eye. **cb**, ciliary body. **ch**, choroid. **cm**, ciliary muscle. **co**, cornea. **con**, conus papillaris. **cS**, canal of Schlemm (drains aqueous chamber). **csp**, conjunctival space. **fo**, fovea. **g**, ganglion cell giving rise to optic nerve fibres. **Hg**, Harderian gland. **ir**, iris. **l**, eyelid. **lp**, lens pad. **pig**, pigment layer of retina. **re**, retina. **s**, projecting supraocular scale. **sc**, sclera. **scc**, scleral cartilage. **so**, scleral ossicle. **sp**, spectacle. **vc**, visual cell (rod and cone) layer. **vit**, vitreous. **II**, optic nerve.

rubber ball squeezed round its middle, while again its front surface becomes more sharply curved to bring close objects into focus. The scleral ossicles are important in this process, since they help to maintain the bulge of the ciliary body and to keep it in contact with the periphery of the lens, which is modified to form a special pad-like structure. The loss of the scleral ossicles in crocodilians is perhaps correlated with the fact that these creatures are mainly active at night and may not need critical powers of accommodation.

In snakes the mechanism of accommodation is different again, and recalls that of the squid, and of sharks and amphibians. The eye is more or less spherical, without a groove around the corneo-scleral junction, the scleral ossicles are absent, and the small ciliary body is too far away from the lens to exert any pressure on it (figure 109 B). The ciliary muscles have migrated into the root of the iris, the structure which acts like a camera diaphragm and controls the amount of light entering the eye. When the muscles contract they pull the corneo-scleral junction inwards and increase the pressure of the gelatinous, vitreous material which fills up the interior of the eyeball behind the lens. Owing to this rise in pressure the lens is forced forwards without changing its shape, like the lens of a camera focused for a close-up.

The retina, the light-sensitive part of the eye, consists of an outer, heavily pigmented layer, a layer of visual cells and several other layers of nerve cells and fibres. The optic nerve originates from the inner-most layer before it passes back through the sclera to the brain. It can be seen that the visual cells are situated round the outside of the retina; in order to reach them the light must pass through the various nervous elements which lie nearer the cavity of the eye. This arrange-ment is an inevitable result of the way in which the retina develops in the vertebrate embryo, from a sac-like outgrowth of the brain which is later pushed in or invaginated to form a cup (figure 113).

Outside the retina is another pigmented layer, the choroid, which contains blood vessels from which the retinal cells derive their nourishment. Lizards possess another device for augmenting retinal nutrition in the form of an elongated cone of tissue which projects into the semi-fluid vitreous from the back of the eye, and is thought to secrete food substances into it. This cone is analogous with the bigger and richly pleated structure known as the pecten in birds. Snakes also have a retinal cone, but it is smaller and of a different type.

346

Some animals, such as cats, possess a special layer called the tapetum, between the retina and the choroid, which reflects light back through the visual cells and so allows a greater proportion of light to be utilised under conditions of poor illumination, as at night. Such a tapetum, containing guanine crystals like those in the guanophores of the skin, is well developed in crocodiles and is responsible for the reddish eye-shine which betrays them to the torch of the nocturnal hunter *.

The visual cells of the retina with which an animal actually 'sees' are of two principal kinds, known from their respective shapes as rods and cones (figure 110). The rods are concerned with vision at night or in dim light, and contain rhodopsin, the 'visual purple' pigment which becomes deficient if there is not enough vitamin A in the diet, and which used to be so important to the pilots of night-flying aircraft. The cones are responsible for vision in bright light, and probably also for colour vision in those animals which possess it. They appear to be the more primitive type of visual cell, and rods are believed to have originated from them in the evolutionary sense, as an adaptation to nocturnality. In many animals the retina has a thin spot or depression, usually near its middle, known as the fovea. This characteristically contains very large numbers of slender, closely packed cones and is particularly important in permitting optical resolution of fine detail.

Many reptiles, including chelonians, crocodilians and the tuatara apparently have 'duplex' retinas, containing both rods and cones of various kinds. In diurnal lizards, however, cones are the only visual cells present, so that the creatures may be virtually blind at night. Some of these cones are of the 'double' type, looking as if they have been formed by the fusion of two separate cells. The cones contain yellow oil droplets which filter off light at the violet end of the spectrum and reduce chromatic aberration and glare. The fovea is nearly always present, and in some chamaeleons is larger than that of man. *Anolis* lizards possess two foveas on each eye, one in the usual central position, and one further back in what is called the temporal position [428]. The latter is probably correlated with binocularity as in tree snakes, since light rays from the overlapping parts of the visual fields will tend to fall on the retina near its hinder edge, rather than on its central part.

The majority of geckos are most active at night or in the dusk, and in these lizards the visual cells resemble rods which appear to have arisen from the transmutation of cones; this is a change which seems to have occurred on various occasions in reptilian evolution. Only a few species of geckos such as *Sphaerodactylus parkeri* possess a fovea, which is in the temporal position [428].

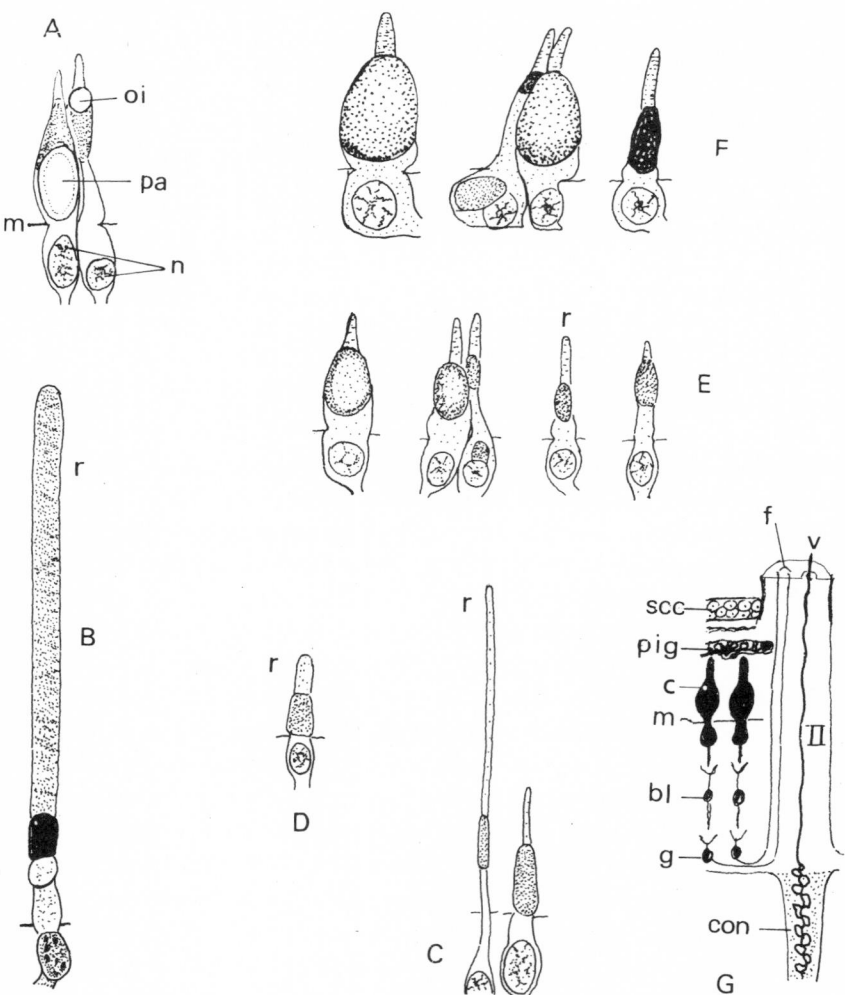

Figure 110. Visual cells of Squamata. Rods are labelled **r**; other elements are cones of various types. B and F after Walls [444]; A, C, D, E after Underwood [434]. A. Double cone from pure cone retina of diurnal lizard *Anolis lineatopus*. B. Single rod of nocturnal gecko, *Coleonyx variegatus*; doubles are also present. C. Rod and cone of boa, *Epicrates subflavus*. D. Rod of blind snake, *Leptotyphlops humilis*. No other types of visual cell are present. E. Visual cells of *Vipera berus*.

348

These consist of three types of cone, including one double form, and a single type of rod. F. Visual cells of diurnal colubrid, *Natrix natrix*. Three types of cone including one double form are present. There are no rods. G. Diagram of retina (see rectangle in figure 109 A). Two cones only are shown. The upper ends of the rods and cones, as drawn in the other pictures, point away from the light and are in contact with the outermost, pigmented layer of the retina. The bases of these cells project through a limiting membrane beneath which lies their nuclei. From each nucleus fine processes pass inwards to make contact with the bipolar nervous elements of the next layer of the retina. Actually, each cone makes multiple synaptic contacts with a number of bipolar cells, not single ones as is shown for clarity. The bipolar cells are in turn connected with the ganglion cells from which the fibres of the optic nerve arise. These fibres course along the inner (i.e. vitreous) aspect of the retina and then leave the eyes as a compact bundle, the optic nerve.

bl, bipolar layer of nerve cells. **c**, cone. **con**, conus papillaris. **f**, fibres of optic nerve. **g**, ganglion cells layer. **m**, external limiting membrane. **n**, nucleus. **oi**, oil-droplet. **pa**, paraboloid, an intracellular body which is lacking in snakes. **pig**, pigmented layer of retina. **r**, rod. **scc**, scleral cartilage. **v**, blood vessel supplying conus. **II**, optic nerve.

The evolution of the retina of snakes (figure 110) has been extraordinarily complex. As Walls has written, these animals 'have rung as many changes upon their visual-cell pattern as have all the other vertebrates put together'. Garth Underwood, one of the few contemporary students of the reptilian eye, has discussed the problem in his book on ophidian classification. Primitive snakes of the python-boa group possess rods and cones of fairly simple type, while in the 'blind' scolecophidians (eg *Typhlops*) the cones have been lost and only tiny rods are present. Snakes such as the adder of the subfamily Viperinae possess rods and cones somewhat like those of boas, but they have in addition two larger types of cone, one of which is a curious double form which is characteristic of the 'higher' snakes (figure 110). Underwood [434, 435] suggests that the various visual cell patterns found among the families of advanced snakes have been derived from the same general type as that found in the adder. In many diurnal colubrids the rods have disappeared and the retina contains only cones of single and double type. All snakes have lost the retinal oil-droplets which are found in most lizards; as a substitute, diurnal serpents have acquired a new intra-ocular colour filter in the form of a yellow lens which cuts down the blue light.

Much can be learnt about an animal's habits from the shape of its pupils. In most diurnal reptiles and a few nocturnal ones such as coral snakes the pupil is circular; this is the case in chelonians. The majority of nocturnal or crepuscular forms, such as crocodilians, *Sphenodon,* and most pythons, vipers and geckos, have pupils which generally assume the form of a vertical slit. Walls has suggested that this type of pupil is not so much the sign of an exclusively nocturnal animal, as of one which is active at night but also appears in bright light, perhaps to bask in the sun. The function of the pupil is to regulate the amount of light which reaches the lens and ultimately the retina through the iris diaphragm. A pupil which contracts to a slit can be closed more completely in bright light than one which remains circular, and hence gives better protection to the type of rod-rich retina which night-prowling animals possess. The domestic cat provides an excellent example of the utility of this adaptation.

The vertical slit pupil has been further refined in many geckos (figure 111; Plate 49), such as *Tarentola,* found along both shores of the Mediterranean, which is quite fond of basking. The edges of the golden-coloured iris are serrated, so that when they are brought together a vertical series of tiny holes remains. It has been suggested that the separate images formed by each of these pinholes can be superimposed on the retina to form a single very sharp image, sharper than it would be if formed by a single opening of equal area to the sum of the pinholes. In this way the gecko can retain its visual acuity even when the very minimum of light is allowed to enter the eye. Walls believes that such geckos have the best all-purpose vision of any vertebrates, apart from certain mammals.

A few tree snakes such as *Ahaetulla* (figure 111) possess curious pupils, elongated horizontally and shaped something like a keyhole with the slot in front. This seems to be a device for increasing the binocular fields of vision, for the front of the keyhole slot is aligned with a groove down the snout in front, and behind with the temporal fovea on the hinder rim of the retina.

Accessory organs of the eye Around the eye are a number of accessory structures: eyelids to protect it from injury and to exclude light when the animal is asleep, muscles which move the lids, and others which turn the eyeball as a whole, and tear glands to lubricate the cornea and the conjunctival space between the cornea and the lids.

In most reptiles the upper eyelid is the smaller and less freely movable of the two (the reverse of the mammalian condition) and in

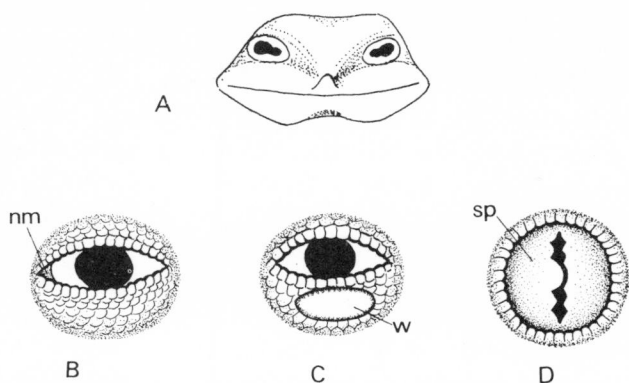

Figure 111 A. Head on view of oriental tree-snake *Ahaetulla* [= *Dryophis*] *mycterizans* showing keyhole pupils and grooves along snout which allow good binocular fields. After Walls [444]. B. Left eye of typical lizard with upper and (larger) lower eyelid, and nictitating membrane (**nm**) at front of eye. C. Lizard with window (**w**) in lower eyelid. This condition is seen in certain skinks (e.g. some species of *Mabuya*) and other forms. D. Condition seen in many geckos (e.g. *Tarentola*) with spectacle (**sp**) instead of movable eyelids, as in snakes. The vertical slit pupil has serrated edges (see also Plate 49). B, C and D after Bellairs and Carrington [32].

crocodiles and some lizards it is stiffened by a small supraciliary or supra-orbital bone. There is usually also a well-developed third eyelid or nictitating membrane as in birds (figures 111 B, 112). This is a more or less transparent fold of tissue strengthened by cartilage which is seen at rest in the front angle of the eye. It can be swept quickly backwards across the cornea, cleaning and lubricating its surface, by a tendon and special muscle of its own. The nictitans muscle has apparently split off from another, the retractor bulbi, which is present in amphibians and many mammals, and serves to draw the eye deep into its socket for protection. In chamaeleons, the upper and lower lids have more or less joined together at the front and back so that the eye opening is reduced to a small oval; the nictitating membrane in these aberrant lizards has been lost.

Snakes cannot blink for these ingenious creatures have solved the problem of keeping dust out of their eyes by joining their eyelids together to form a fixed transparent watchglass or spectacle (figure 112); the German name *brille* is sometimes given to it. The fusion of the two initially separate lids can be followed in embryos, and it can be seen that the lower lid forms the greater part of the spectacle. The cells of the skin and subcutaneous tissue which becomes incorporated

351

into the spectacle have in some mysterious way become transparent, like those of the underlying cornea. Its outer surface is formed from the horny layer and is hard enough to resist abrasion; even if it does become scratched it is periodically shed with the skin over the rest of the body. The well known bluish colour of the spectacle seen in a snake before shedding is probably due to the accumulation of new cells between the two epidermal generations (p. 291) of its outer surface. So far as one can tell, all traces of the nictitating membrane have disappeared so that the spectacle is separated from the cornea only by the narrow chink of conjunctival space.

Many lizards have also replaced their movable eyelids by a spectacle. This is present in the majority of geckos (figures 111, 112), for instance, and these lizards sometimes clean their spectacles by wiping them with their tongue [84]. Only a few genera such as *Eublepharis* and *Coleonyx* (Plate 73A), sometimes placed in a separate subfamily, have normal eyelids and nictitating membrane. Spectacles are also found in the limbless pygopods of Australia, in the night lizards *(Xantusia)*, in the burrowing amphisbaenids, in some skinks, and in one lacertid genus *(Ophisops)*. Other lizards such as the skink *Mabuya vittata,* the lacertid *Cabrita* and the earless monitor *Lanthanotus* possess movable lids but have a transparent window in the lower one; possibly this represents a stage in spectacle evolution. Obviously the spectacle has been 'a good idea' and has been evolved independently among various groups of Squamata including the snakes, but one cannot really correlate its presence with any particular habitat or set of habits. It is found in some burrowers and desert-dwellers, but also in climbing geckos.

Generally speaking, reptiles have two large glands (figure 112) associated with each eye which produce the 'tears'. The lachrymal gland lies near the back of the eye and discharges its secretions into the conjunctival space beneath the lids; it is sometimes reduced, or absent as in most snakes. The enormous size of this gland in marine turtles was a mystery for many years, until Schmidt-Nielsen and Fange [380] showed that it was important in ridding the body of excessive salt (p. 281). The other gland is known as the Harderian after its discoverer Johann Jacob Harder (1656-1711) who was successively Professor of Rhetoric, Physics, Anatomy and Botany, and Medicine at the University of Basle, and was clearly a man of wide interests. This gland lies mainly on the inner side of the eye, though its body may stretch back behind the eye, as in snakes

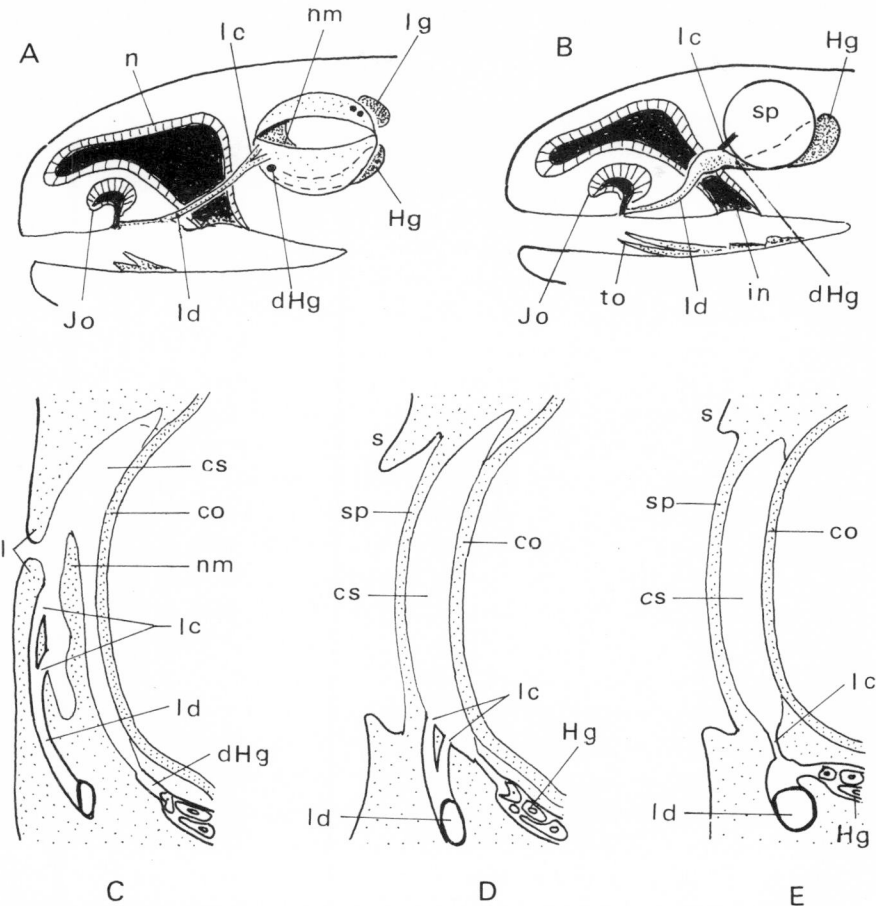

Figure 112 A, B. Diagrams showing Jacobson's organ, nose, lachrymal duct, etc. from left side, partly in section, in A, typical lizard; B, snake. In the lizard there are two lachrymal canaliculi and the lachrymal duct opens in front into the duct of the organ of Jacobson, and often into a groove in the palate close by. In the snake the lachrymal duct opens into the duct of Jacobson's organ, the Harderian glands leads directly into the lachrymal duct and there is generally a single canaliculus. C–E. Diagrammatic transverse sections through front of eye of C, typical lizard (eyelids, nictitating membrane, two lachrymal canaliculi); D, typical gecko (spectacle instead of movable lids, no nictitating membrane, two canaliculi); E, snake (spectacle, no *nictitans*, one canaliculus).

co, cornea. **cs**, conjunctival space. **dHg**, duct of Harderian gland. **Hg**, Harderian gland. **in**, internal nostril. **Jo**, Jacobson's organ. **l**, eyelids. **lc**, lachrymal canaliculus. **ld**, lachrymal duct. **lg**, lachrymal gland. **n**, nasal sac. **nm**, nictitating membrane. **s**, projecting scale. **sp**, spectacle. **to**, tongue.

(figure 112). In chelonians, crocodilians and lizards the Harderian gland discharges by several ducts into the front angle of the conjunctival space on the inner or deep surface of the nictitating membrane. In most snakes, however, its single duct by-passes the conjunctival space altogether and joins the lachrymal or tear duct instead.

The tears are carried away by minute canals which lead off from the front of the conjunctival space at the base of the lower eyelid, and at the outer side of the nictitating membrane when this is present. In *Sphenodon* and lizards (apart from amphisbaenids) there are two of these canals which soon join to form a single lachrymal or tear duct; this escapes from the orbit through a hole in the lachrymal bone (or where this is absent, the pre-frontal). In most crocodilians there are three canals or more, while in snakes there is only a single one which joins the much wider lachrymal duct.

In crocodilians the lachrymal duct opens in front into the nose on either side (figure 116, p. 364) much as it does in man, and in the tuatara it discharges in the region of the internal nostril, where the mouth and nose communicate. In lizards and snakes it opens into, or very close to the duct of Jacobson's organ; in many lizards it also communicates with a groove or gutter which runs along the palate on each side. The rather complicated anatomical relationships which I have described are shown diagrammatically in figure 112.

It is clear that in Squamata the eye glands, tear ducts and organ of Jacobson form a rather interesting functional system [31]. In lizards with movable eyelids the tears wash the conjunctival space and then run down through the tear canals and duct; some of the fluid will reach the mouth, but there is reason to believe that some of it will also enter the organ of Jacobson and act as a solvent and a carrier for scent particles which are picked up by the tongue. Once a spectacle has been evolved the conjunctival space becomes closed off and no longer needs such copious washing; the Harderian secretions, therefore, tend to side-track the eye and pass by a more direct route to the organ of Jacobson, as in snakes.

Chelonians are remarkable in having no lachrymal duct at all to carry away their tears, and this must be a reason for the copious weeping which has often been described in sea turtles as they laboriously dig their nests and lay their eggs.

It should have emerged from this description that the eyes of snakes show many unique features, and it was these which led Walls to work out his attractive theory that the snakes as a group had originated from burrowing ancestors in which the eye had virtually 'touched bottom' in degeneracy. The scleral skeleton had disappeared, the standard reptilian method of accommodation had been lost, the visual cells had degenerated, and various other less dramatic retrogressions had taken place. When the snakes came back above ground they were compelled to re-furbish their eyes with what they had left, retaining the spectacle which had in this case arisen as an adaptation to burrowing. This idea explains many ophidian ocular peculiarities; the camera-like method of accommodation using the iris as the motive force, the yellow lens, and the unique type of double cone which is present in diurnal snakes with highly efficient eyes. It also provides a *rationale* for the importance of smell and Jacobson's organ sense in even the most keen-eyed snakes, and for the great size of the Harderian gland, when the lachrymal gland, which is never so closely associated with Jacobson's organ, has disappeared.

It is interesting that the parts of the brain concerned with vision, particularly the optic lobes of the mid-brain, show signs of this evolutionary history. They are reduced, as one would expect, in primitive burrowers such as *Leptotyphlops* (figure 107, p. 334), *Typhlops,* and to a lesser extent in the secretive Aniliidae [381]. By comparison with 'higher' snakes such as colubrids and vipers, the optic parts of the brain are also reduced in the semi-arboreal boa constrictor and rainbow boa *(Epicrates),* both of which must be regarded as primitive snakes on other grounds, such as the possession of vestigial hind limbs. It can be argued, therefore, that the reduction of the 'optic' nervous system is a feature of primitive snakes in general, irrespective of their habits, and this is further evidence that the whole group passed through a subterranean phase in its ancestry.

The eyes of burrowing lizards and snakes are very interesting, though it must be admitted that none of them show an ocular condition which quite bridges the gap between the two groups. The eye of *Lanthanotus* has not yet been described. In some of the less extreme fossorial types such as the limbless lizard *Anniella* [28], a Californian relative of the slow-worm, the eyes are certainly very small, but 'have all their works', as Walls puts it; eyelids, scleral cartilage and ossicles, muscles, lens and visual cells. The same may be said for the eyes of burrowing skinks such as *Typhlacontias* and some of the less specialised amphisbaenids such as *Trogonophis* (Plate 53), except that these forms possess a spectacle [353]. Certain other amphisbaenids (Plates 52, 53), such as *Rhineura* and *Loveridgea,* are perhaps the

355

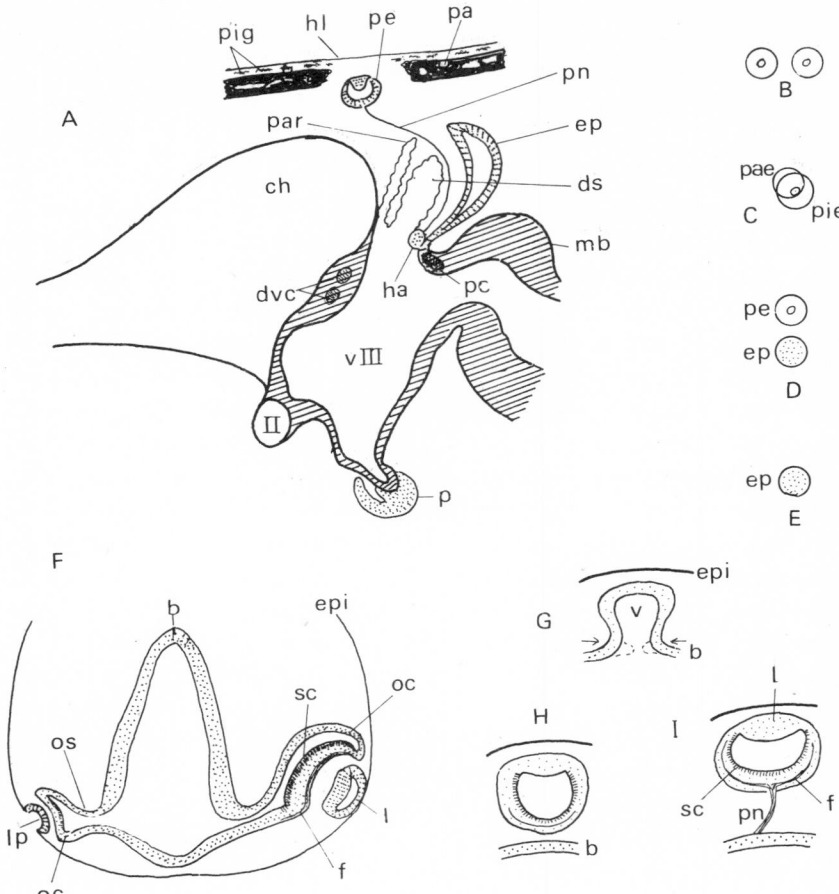

Figure 113   A. Diagram of median longitudinal section through part of brain of lizard showing pineal apparatus. After Romer [358] and other authors. B–E. Diagram of parts of pineal apparatus in vertebrates. B, hypothetical condition with two dorsal eyes side by side. C, dorsal eyes of lamprey; the pineal eye is the larger and the functional one. D, lizard with parietal eye and epiphysis. E, chelonian, bird or mammal with epiphysis only. F–G. Diagrams illustrating differences in mode of development between lateral eye (F) and parietal eye (G, H, I). In F the left side represents an earlier developmental stage than the right; G, H, and I show three successive stages. Arrows and broken lines in G show way in which vesicle separates from brain. Modified from Dendy [133].

b, brain (roof of dienceophalon). **ch**, right cerebral hemisphere. **ds**, dorsal sac. **dvc**, dorsal and ventral commissures connecting the two sides of the fore-brain. **ep**, epiphysis cerebri. **epi**, epidermis. **f**, fibres of developing optic or parietal eye nerve. **ha**, habenula. **hl**, horny layer of epidermis of parietal scale. **l**, lens of parietal or lateral eye. **lp**, lens placode. **mb**, mid-brain. **oc**, optic cup. **os**, optic stalk. **p**, pituitary. **pa**, parietal bone. **pae**, parapineal eye. **par**, paraphysis. **pc**, posterior commissure. **pe**, parietal eye. **pie**, pineal eye. **pig**, pigment (in dermis). **pn**, parietal eye nerve. **sc**, sensory cells of developing retina of lateral or parietal eye. **v**, vesicle, primordium of parietal eye. **vIII**, third ventricle of brain. **II**, optic nerve.

most highly modified of all reptiles for burrowing life. Their eyes are much more degenerate, though they can apparently respond to light [58]. The scleral ossicles (and in some species the scleral cartilage) have disappeared, the lens and eye muscles are highly degenerate or absent and the optic nerve is very difficult to identify. The retina is heavily pigmented so that the minute eye appears as a tiny spot beneath the spectacle, which is itself barely distinguishable from the surrounding scales. Curiously enough, the visual cells resemble cones, rather than rods which are normally responsible for dim-light vision. The little burrowing snakes *Typhlops* and *Lepto-typhlops* are typically ophidian in lacking the scleral skeleton and possess well differentiated visual cells which are interpreted as rods. Underwood [428] believes that the condition in these reptiles, rather than that in amphisbaenids, could be envisaged as capable of re-elaboration in the fashion required by Walls' hypothesis. In all these burrowing squamates, the Harderian gland is relatively enormous and the minute eye is practically buried in it [Plate 52]; most, if not all of its secretion passes into the lachrymal duct, *en route* for the mouth and the organ of Jacobson.

The parietal eye and pineal apparatus It is well known that the tuatara and many lizards have an eye-like structure on the top of their heads beneath a hole in the parietal bone. The slow-worm has a good one, and it is also well developed in monitors, lacertids, some iguanids and skinks, and lizards of several other families. Although this parietal, pineal or third eye, as it has been variously called, has all the appearances of a sense organ for perceiving light, its precise functions have been an enigma to biologists for many years. In fact there is hardly another organ in the body which has so stubbornly resisted researches to elucidate its significance.

Beneath and behind the parietal eye is a conspicuous structure which looks like a gland, known as the epiphysis, pineal gland or pineal body. It is pear-shaped in longitudinal section (figure 113) and has thick, folded walls, enclosing a central cavity. It is connected by a solid stalk with the roof of the diencephalon, the part of the fore-brain which lies between the cerebral hemispheres and the optic lobes of the mid-brain. In front of the epiphysis are two sac-like structures, found in many other vertebrates and called the para-physis and dorsal sac; they communicate with the third ventricle, the cavity of the diencephalon. Their walls contain many blood vessels and they appear to be parts of the choroid plexus system which secretes the cerebro-spinal fluid – the liquid which circulates through the cavities of the brain and spinal cord. It is not known whether they have any other functions.

There are grounds for believing that the epiphysis was once an eye also, so that at one stage in evolution there was a pair of eyes on the top of the head rather than only one. Something approaching this condition is actually seen in those primitive vertebrates, the lampreys, where there are two eye-like structures, the larger and more dorsal one being called the pineal and the smaller, the parapineal (figure 113 C). Although they lie one above the other, the parapineal is placed slightly to the left of the midline and is connected with the left side of the brain, while the pineal has a corresponding position and attachment on the right. This suggests that in the most ancient vertebrates the two organs lay side by side, like the 'ordinary' or lateral eyes, but on the top of the head (figure 113 B).

In most vertebrates one of these organs has disappeared altogether, while the other has ceased to be an eye and has perhaps acquired a glandular function, becoming the epiphysis. The pineal region of most fish is hard to interpret, but in some larval and adult frogs there is a rudimentary sac which appears to represent the pineal eye of lampreys, and an epiphysis which probably corresponds with the parapineal. In crocodiles both eye and epiphysis are absent, while in chelonians, snakes, birds and mammals only the epiphysis is retained. The human organ, usually called the pineal body, is about the size of a pea and hidden beneath the enormous cerebral hemispheres; the philosopher Descartes thought that it was the residence of the soul.

A parietal foramen in the skull was present in many fossil amphibians and reptiles, presupposing the presence of an eye beneath it. Among existing land vertebrates, however, a well-developed parietal eye is a unique possession of the lepidosaurs, and even in this group there is a tendency for it to disappear. It is absent in geckos and certain other lizards, including the burrowing amphisbaenids, and, as previously mentioned, in snakes, although these creatures all possess the epiphysis. It is interesting that the parietal foramen of the Californian footless lizard *Anniella*, which burrows in sandhills, is vestigial, and the parietal eye is considerably smaller than it is in its European relative *Anguis* [28]. The slow-worm is much less specialised for burrowing life and not infrequently exposes its head to the light of day. The absence of both parietal foramen and eye in snakes can be taken as another piece of evidence for their subterranean ancestry, since such structures could be of little use to reptiles which spend all their time underground. The foramen is absent in *Lanthanotus*, the 'putative' snake ancestor (p. 31); nothing is known of its parietal eye.

The homologies of the parietal eye and epiphysis of higher vertebrates with the two eye structures in lampreys are uncertain. Arthur Dendy [133], who wrote the classical description of the pineal apparatus of the tuatara in 1910, believed that in this reptile the eye was connected with the left or 'parapineal' side of the brain and the epiphysis with the right or 'pineal' side, whereas in lizards the opposite conditions prevailed. He suggested that two eyes may have lain side by side beneath the large parietal foramen of some extinct reptiles. This does not seem proven, however, and it is best to avoid the terms parapineal and pineal eye in reptilian context, and to use the non-committal 'parietal' or 'median eye' instead. The term pineal may be retained for the whole apparatus collectively: paraphysis, dorsal sac, eye and epiphysis.

It is perhaps a relief to turn from these rather theoretical problems and to consider what the parietal eye of reptiles actually looks like and what functions it is likely to perform. Apart from the question of its attachment to one or other side of the brain, its structure is essentially similar in the tuatara and in lizards such as *Anguis*, *Varanus* and *Sceloporus*. It consists of a cup-shaped retina surrounded by a fibrous capsule and closed in above by a lens-like structure which joins the retina on either side. The space between retina and lens is filled by a gelatinous material resembling the vitreous of the lateral eyes (figure 114). The interval between the lens and the foramen in the skull is occupied by connective tissue which in *Sphenodon* is modified to form a massive plug; this plug is much less evident in lizards. The foramen is covered over by the interparietal scale which is usually thinned out and devoid of pigment in its central region overlying the lens, so that it forms a kind of transparent cornea.

The retina has an inner layer of cells which show many resembl-

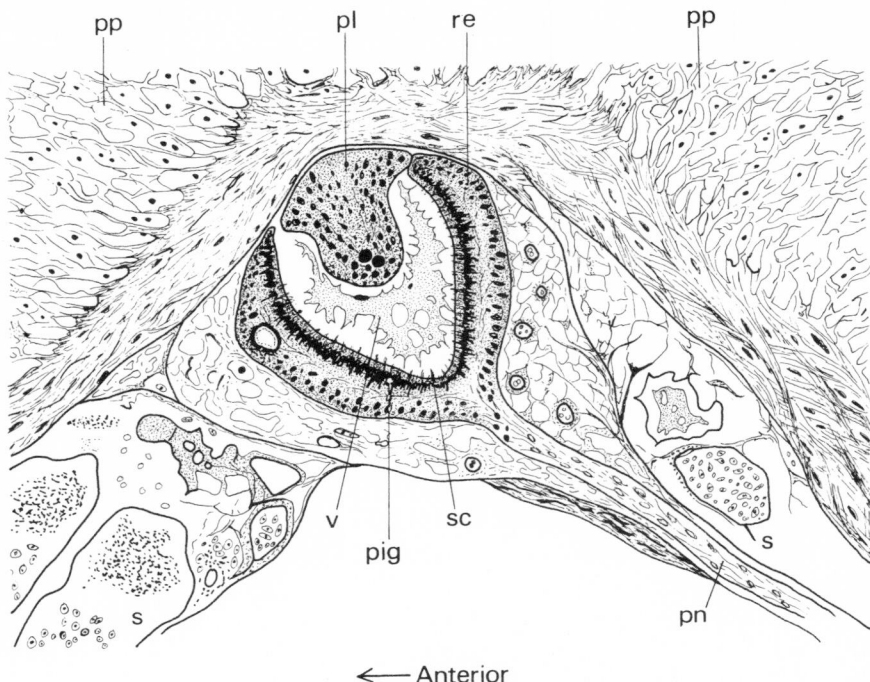

← Anterior

Figure 114   Longitudinal section through parietal or median eye of tuatara (*Sphenodon*). After Dendy [133].

pig, pigment layer of retina. **pl**, pineal eye lens. **pn**, pineal nerve. **pp**, pineal plug. **re**, retina. **s**. venous sinus. **sc**, sensory cells. **v**, vitreous body.

ances, both under the light microscope and the electron microscope, with the rods and cones of the lateral eyes. Many pigment cells are also present, and more peripherally are structures regarded as ganglion cells and nerve fibres (figure 115). In *Sphenodon*, *Anolis* and *Sceloporus* and no doubt certain other forms, a fine nerve can be identified, though sometimes with difficulty [151]. This originates from the retina and passes down between the dorsal sac and epiphysis to enter a part of the diencephalon called the habenula (figure 113 A). Its ultimate nervous connections are obscure. The parietal eye nerve of *Sceloporus* contains about 250 fibres, all of the type which lack myelin sheaths. It will degenerate if the eye is destroyed. Some workers, however, have failed to find the nerve in other adult lizards which they have studied, and it is possible that it is absent in some species, at least in the adult.

360

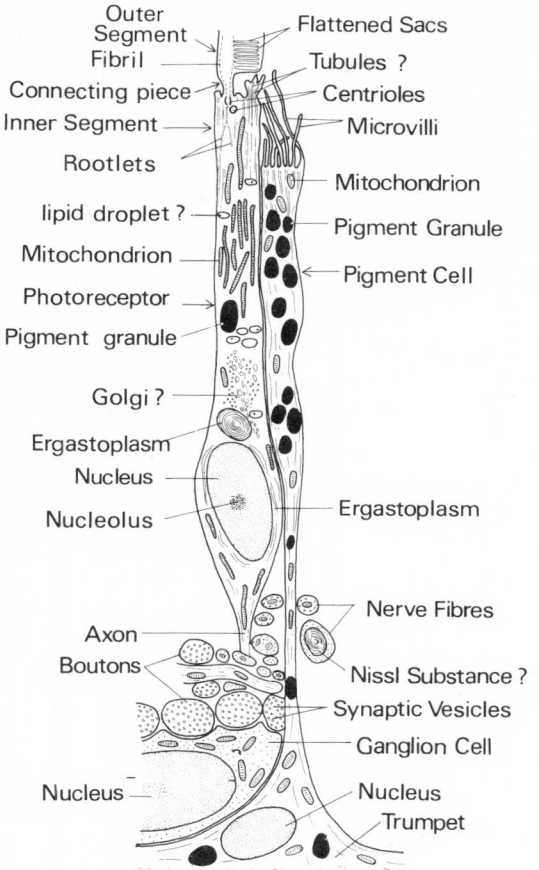

Outer Segment — Flattened Sacs
Fibril — Tubules ?
Connecting piece — Centrioles
Inner Segment — Microvilli
Rootlets — Mitochondrion
lipid droplet ? — Pigment Granule
Mitochondrion — Pigment Cell
Photoreceptor —
Pigment granule —
Golgi ? —
Ergastoplasm
Nucleus —
Nucleolus — Ergastoplasm
Nerve Fibres
Axon
Boutons — Nissl Substance ?
Synaptic Vesicles
Ganglion Cell
Nucleus — Nucleus
Trumpet

Figure 115 Diagram showing three principal elements in the retina of the parietal eye of the lizard *Sceloporus occidentalis*, based on electron microscope studies. The elements are (1) light (photo-) receptor (base only of outer segment shown); (2) pigment cell (minus its fibrillar apparatus); (3) ganglion cell. After Eakin and Westfall [151].

From the previous description it will be apparent to the reader acquainted with embryology that the development of the parietal eye differs in several important ways from that of the lateral eyes in vertebrates. The sac-like outgrowth from the brain from which the parietal eye arises is not cupped by invagination; consequently the layer of cone-like and presumably sensory cells lie nearest the cavity of the organ (and the entering light) instead of being at its outer surface like the rods and cones of the lateral eyes (p. 347). Moreover, the parietal lens is developed from the same outgrowth of the brain as its retina, instead of arising from the skin like the lens of the lateral eye (figure 113).

Although the parietal eye of reptiles and the pineal and parapineal eyes of lampreys are in many ways like the lateral eyes, they lack certain of the latters' refinements such as lids and muscles, the iris, and powers of accommodation. They are better developed in these animals than in any other vertebrates, but we do not really know whether they are vestiges of once more perfect eyes, or whether they have always existed in their present state. The pineal and parapineal eyes of lampreys are sensitive to light and are involved in the daily rhythm of colour change, which is abolished if they are removed. The parietal eyes of lizards react in subtle ways to continued bright illumination by shifts in the distribution of retinal pigment and other intracellular changes [149]. Despite numerous experiments, however, no reptile has been seen to make a simple or direct response to any stimulus (such as light or warmth) applied to the organ under circumstances approaching those in nature.

Various workers have suspected that the parietal eye is involved in sexual activity or in temperature control. It might, for instance, be concerned in registering environmental changes, such as a seasonal increase in daylight, which evoke breeding behaviour. The few experiments which have been made to investigate this possibility suggest that the sex glands mature more rapidly if the parietal eye is put out of action.

Recent work has been more concerned with the possible role of the organ in the regulation of body temperature, or at least of activites which influence this. In 1958 Stebbins and Eakin [408] published the results of an important and ambitious experiment which they had carried out in California. They removed the parietal eye from a large number of young and adult fence lizards *(Sceloporus occidentalis)* and performed a 'sham' operation (incising the interparietal scale) on a similar number of controls. The operation was easy to perform and caused no deaths. The lizards were then marked by clipping one or more toes, and liberated in the same area of countryside where they were originally captured. This has circumscribed natural boundaries which discouraged emigration. Visits were repeatedly made to the area over a period of months, and the behaviour of the animals was carefully observed. It was found that the lizards which had had their parietal eyes removed spent more time basking and exposing themselves in the open than the sham-operated controls, although there was no difference between the body temperature of the two groups. The genuine experimental animals also moved about restlessly in an aimless fashion; they were less inclined to retreat at the approach of the observer than the controls. Similar

362

results were obtained from other groups of this and related iguanid species in which the parietal eye was covered with aluminium foil instead of being excised, or which were kept in cages instead of being liberated.

It therefore seemed that the parietal eye was acting as a kind of register of solar radiations, informing the lizard in some way when it was time to come in out of the sun. The organ may also have the more generalised and pervasive function of conserving energy, since lizards only become active and run about when they have warmed themselves up by basking or exposing their bodies to the warm surface of the ground.

Unfortunately, subsequent laboratory experiments on another species of *Sceloporus* and on the only two tuataras which Stebbins could obtain have given less clear-cut results which emphasise the complexity of the problem [403, 406]. One might guess that the eye responds to light by inhibiting rather than by stimulating the activity of other organs, and it is possible that its actions are linked with those of other influential endocrine glands, particularly with the pituitary and thyroid. The parietal eye could, theoretically, pass on the information it receives from the environment either through nervous pathways, or by secreting some hormone into the blood-stream, or by a combination of both. Such secretion may, perhaps, be produced by the cells of the lens or retina, though no obviously glandular elements have been discovered within the organ. If, as some workers have claimed, the parietal nerve is absent in certain lizards, it would have to act like a gland if it was to have any function at all.

The epiphysis or pineal sac of reptiles contains cells which bear some resemblance to those of the parietal eye retina. Like the eye, it has, at least in some species, a nerve which passes down through its stalk into the roof of the diencephalon. These similarities, together with the fact that the parietal eye and epiphysis arise from little brain outgrowths of the same kind (possible from a single outgrowth which later divides), supports the idea that they are basically organs of the same kind.

Experiments on the epiphysis or pineal body of lizards have been less conclusive than those on the parietal eye, especially since it is difficult to interefere with it without damaging the parietal eye nerve also; there is some indication that *Sceloporus* shows increased loco-motor activity after removal of the organ [404]. In terrapins *(Clemmys leprosa)* this operation has been followed by degeneration of the testes [420]. There seems to be no evidence that interference with any part of the pineal complex in reptiles affects either the skin-shedding cycle or the pigmentary system. Perhaps I have said enough to indicate the interest and possible importance of the pineal structures, to which so much painstaking research has been devoted, and about which so little is certainly known.

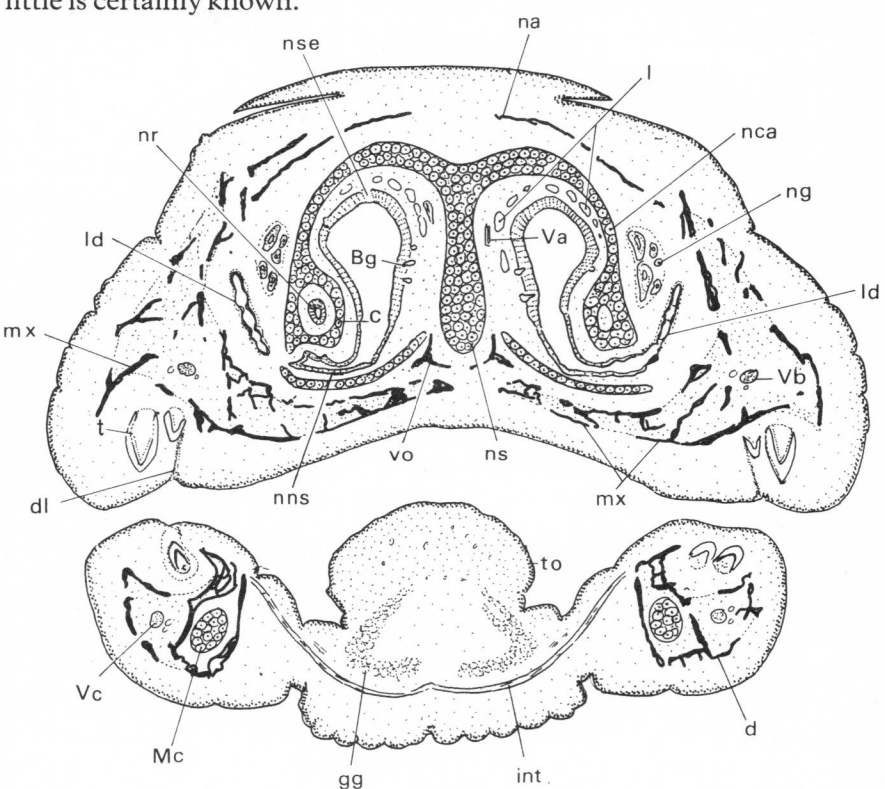

Figure 116   Transverse section through middle of snout and lower jaw of late (26 mm head-length) embryo of American alligator, showing anterior nasal concha and lachrymal duct opening into the nose beneath it. (X 14).

Bg, Bowman's gland. **c**, part of anterior nasal concha (preconcha). **dl**, dental lamina. **fr**, frontal. **gg**, genioglossus muscle. **ilg**, inferior labial gland. **int**, inter-mandibularis muscle. **ld**, lachrymal duct. **Mc**, Meckel's cartilage. **mx**, maxilla. **n**, nasal cavity. **na**, nasal. **nca**, cartilaginous nasal capsule. **ng**, nasal gland. **nns**, non-sensory epithelium of nose. **nr**, recess of nasal sac within concha. **ns**, nasal septum. **nse**, sensory epithelium of olfactory chamber of nasal sac. **t**, tooth germ, with successional tooth on its inner side. **to**, tongue. **vo**, vomer. **I**, olfactory nerve. **Va, b, c**, ophthalmic, maxillary and mandibular divisions of fifth (trigeminal) cranial nerve. **d**, dentary.

The nose and organ of Jacobson The nose is not only the organ of smell, but also the front part of the respiratory system, and some of its attributes have already been dealt with in Chapter 6 (p. 234). The part of the nose concerned with smell is the olfactory chamber; usually one or more processes of cartilage called conchae project into its cavity from its outer wall. In Squamata there is generally a single concha (figure 117); the tuatara has two and there are three in crocodiles (figure 75, p. 237; figure 116). In Chelonia there is no true concha at all, though there may be a bulge in the outer nasal wall which somewhat resembles one [320].

The sensory cells which register smell lie in the membrane or epithelium of the nasal sac; they are situated in the roof, inner wall and often part of the floor of the olfactory chamber and along the upper surface of the conchae. In some reptiles such as the arboreal *Anolis* lizards and chamaeleons, and also in marine snakes and turtles, these sensory areas are reduced in extent. The rest of the nasal sac has no sensory function.

Each of the sensory cells possesses a rod-like process ending in a tuft of olfactory 'hairs' which project into the nasal cavity; a fine nerve-fibre also arises from the cell body. The fibres come together in groups to form a number of olfactory nerve bundles on each side and escape through a large opening at the back of the nasal capsule to enter the olfactory bulb of the brain (figure 117). A number of small glands called Bowman's glands are also found in the sensory epithelium of the nose (figure 116); their secretions adhere to the hair of the olfactory rods and perhaps play some essential part in their function.

In the embryo each nasal sac begins as a tiny plate or placode of thickened skin on either side of the front of the head (figure 117 B). This plate sinks into the underlying tissues and becomes a sac; its original opening remains as the nostril and it acquires a new opening, the internal nostril, into the roof of the mouth. In lepidosaurian reptiles a pocket appears on the inner side of each nasal sac near its front (figure 117 C); this is the vomeronasal organ of Jacobson, first described (in mammals) in 1809 by the Danish anatomist Ludwig Levin Jacobson. Sensory cells similar to those of the nose develop in its walls and their nerve fibres, known as the vomeronasal nerves, pass back into the accessory olfactory bulb of the brain, which is situated behind and on the inner side of the main bulb. Jacobson's organ must therefore be regarded as a specialised and more or less isolated region of the nasal sac.

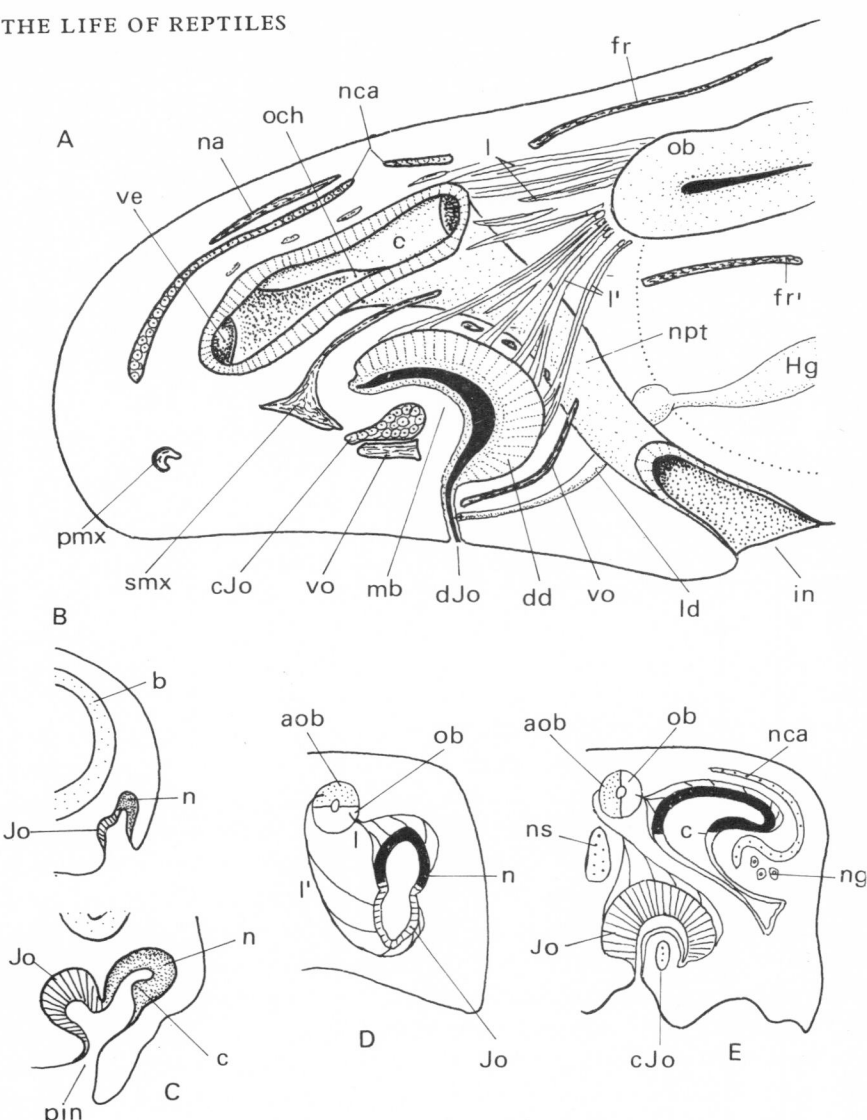

Figure 117   A. Partly reconstructed longitudinal section through snout of late embryo of grass snake (*Natrix natrix*). The section passes a little to the right of the midline so that the organ of Jacobson and other structures cut through belong to the right-hand side. The lateral or outer wall of the right nasal sac with its concha is seen, and the outline of the front of the right eye is shown in dotted lines. The very large size of Jacobson's organ is striking. The posterior ends of the vomeronasal nerves are cut, since they enter the accessory olfactory bulb nearer to the midline than the plane of section. B, C. Transverse sections through side of snout of snake embryos. In B, which represents the earlier developmental stage,

366

the nasal placode has already sunk in to form a pit; the walls of this are differentiating to form the organ of Jacobson medially, and the nose proper (**n**) laterally.
In C, Jacobson's organ and the nose have become more distinct but they still
communicate with the mouth by a common opening, the primitive internal
nostril (**pin**). D, E. Diagrammatic transverse sections through one side of the
snout of turtle (D) and snake (E), showing the nerve-supply of the nose proper
(**I**- fibres enter olfactory bulb) and of Jacobson's organ (**I'**- fibres enter accessory
olfactory bulb). As can be seen from A, the front of the brain actually lies behind
the level of Jacobson's organ and would not be seen in a real section through the
organ. Sensory parts of the nose proper are shown in black, and of the organ of
Jacobson in lines; non-sensory parts of both organs are unshaded. It is possible
that the region marked Jacobson's organ in the turtle is not homologous with
Jacobson's organ in snakes and lizards. B–E mainly after Parsons [320].

aob, accessory olfactory bulb. **b**, brain. **c**, nasal concha. **cJo**, cartilage of **Jo**
(Jacobson's organ). **dd**, dorsal dome of **Jo**. **dJo**, duct of **Jo**. **en**, external nostril.
fr, frontal. **fr'**, downgrowth from frontal. **Hg**, Harderian gland. **ilg**, inferior
labial gland. **in**, internal nostril. **Jo**, Jacobson's organ. **ld**, lachrymal duct.
mb, mushroom body of **Jo**. **mx**, maxilla. **n**, nose, nasal sac. **na**, nasal. **nca**,
cartilaginous nasal capsule. **ng**, nasal gland. **npt**, nasopharyngeal tube. **ns**, nasal
septum. **ob**, olfactory bulb. **och**, olfactory chamber of nasal sac. **pin**, primitive
internal nostril. **pmx**, premaxilla. **slg**, superior labial gland. **smx**, septomaxilla.
t, tooth in lower jaw. **to**, tongue. **ve**, vestibule of nose. **vo**, vomer. **I**, olfactory
nerve (of nose). **I'**, vomeronasal nerve (of Jacobson's organ).

In the tuatara the organ is a relatively simple tubular structure
which retains its primitive connection with the nose, opening into the
nasal cavity at the front of the internal nostril. In many ways it is much
more like the mammalian organ of Jacobson than that of Squamata,
and one may suppose that its function is to smell food as it is being
eaten or held by the jaws.

The organs of Jacobson in Squamata have become much more
elaborate affairs and have virtually taken on the role of a pair of new
sense organs. They become completely cut off from the nose during
embryonic life and acquire ducts of their own which open on to the
front of the palate on either side of the midline, and are separate from
and anterior to the internal nostrils [31]. The two organs lie one on
either side of the lower part of the front of the nasal septum, and each
is enclosed in a capsule formed by a cartilage called the paraseptal and
by the vomer and septomaxillary bones (figure 117; Plate 32).

In most lizards and in snakes each organ of Jacobson is shaped
rather like a ball the lower surface of which has been pushed up into
the cavity, so that the latter is now crescentic when seen in section.
The upper part of the organ may be called the dorsal dome and the

367

lower pushed-in part the mushroom body; this is usually supported by a concha-like projection from the paraseptal cartilage and sometimes by one from the vomer as well. The epithelium of the dorsal dome has no Bowman's glands, but in most other respects resembles that of the olfactory part of the nose, containing sensory cells. These are furnished with tiny processes called microvilli which can be recognised under the electron microscope [14]. Their nerve fibres stream up from the dome on either side of the nasal septum and come to lie beneath the roof of the nasal capsule and quite close to the olfactory nerves before they enter the brain. If the olfactory and accessory bulbs are destroyed experimentally in lizards the sensory cells of both the nose and the organ of Jacobson will degenerate [10]. The epithelium covering the mushroom body is of a different type to that of the dome. It is not sensory, but it is provided with tiny movable hairs or cilia. The duct of the organ leads down between the dome and the mushroom body to reach the palate.

In snakes, including the marine species, and in the majority of lizards, the organ of Jacobson is quite a substantial structure; the dorsal dome measures about 1 mm. from front to back in the adult slow-worm with a head length of some 14 mm. Possibly its sensory area is comparable with that of the nose proper in extent, but no one seems to have made a critical comparison. The organ is fairly small, however, in certain agamids and iguanids such as *Anolis* where it lacks a concha [10]. In chamaeleons it is absent or rudimentary. As in our own arboreal ancestors, the whole olfactory apparatus of these tree-dwellers has degenerated. So far as I know, the nose of specialised tree snakes has not been studied.

It can be seen that the ducts of the two Jacobson's organs are strategically placed in relation to the tip of the tongue, especially in snakes and those lizards where this is forked (figure 112, p. 353). The protrusion and intermittent flickering of the tongue of a snake or monitor lizard exploring its surroundings and using it to test both air and ground, is very characteristic. In a film which I have seen of wild Komodo dragons these huge lizards played their tongues in and out almost with an air of relish as they were tempted from their lairs by the smell of rotten meat. Even species with much shorter and less deeply forked tongues such as *Anguis* and *Lacerta* will often use them to investigate objects of interest.

This use of the tongue has fascinated naturalists for many years, long before its true significance was understood. During the 1930s,

G. K. Noble and his collaborators at the American Museum of Natural History and other workers in Germany showed that the tongue of snakes and lizards picked up scent particles and carried them to the organs of Jacobson where they could be 'smelt' by the sensory cells [298]. This important discovery does not necessarily invalidate the older ideas that the tongue is an organ of fine touch, as well as perhaps playing some part in taste; taste buds have been described on the tongues of snakes as well as lizards, but the importance of this sense in the former is problematical.

How do the scent particles actually reach the cavities of Jacobson's organs? It is possible that in snakes and monitor lizards the very fine tongue tips may actually be passed up the Jacobson's ducts. Some workers have suggested, however, that these are too narrow for this to happen, and it has been shown that in the garter snake the organs of Jacobson are still effective after the tips of the tongue have been cut off [see 47]. Even if one believes that insertion of the tongue tip is the normal procedure in these reptiles and that the organs only reach their fullest efficiency in forms where this is finely forked, it is necessary to envisage an alternative method of transport, at least in some species. It is true that in some lizards such as anoles which do not have forked tongues the organ of Jacobson is probably unimportant. Nevertheless there are others such as geckos and certain skinks which have blunt tongues and well developed organs of Jacobson at the same time. It is hardly conceivable that such a tongue could be thrust into the duct of Jacobson even if this was capable of undergoing dilatation like the throat of a snake.

We have seen that in Squamata the secretions of the Harderian gland enter the lachrymal duct and are then conveyed to the neighbourhood of the opening of Jacobson's duct on each side. In the absence of Bowman's glands, this fluid probably acts as a solvent and a medium of transport for scent particles wiped off the tongue. The movement of the cilia on the mushroom body and in some species of lizards on the palatal groove (figure 118) with which the lachrymal duct communicates are thought to set up a circulating current which wafts the particles through the organ. There is experimental evidence for this idea, though certain details are hard to understand. C. W. M. Pratt has shown that particles of carbon placed at the opening of Jacobson's duct, or further back on the palatal groove of a freshly killed *Lacerta vivipara* can be demonstrated among the cilia of the mushroom body after thirty seconds [335].

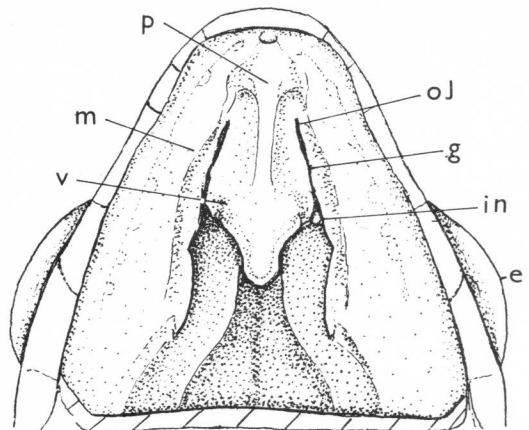

Figure 118   Palate of late embryo of *Lacerta vivipara* with lower jaw cut away;

e, eye. g, palatal (choanal) groove (communicating in front with oJ). in, internal nostril. oJ, opening of Jacobson's organ. m, p and v, maxillary, premaxillary and vomerine parts of palate.

Noble and others have carried out many experiments on the sense organs of lizards and snakes in which the animals were blindfolded with pieces of adhesive tape or had their nostrils plugged with grease, or substantial parts of their tongues removed; they are said to recover quickly from this last operation without losing their general health. It is clear that the combined olfactory sense of the nose proper and Jacobson's organs plays an immensely important part in the lives of many species, especially of snakes. The role of this sense in recognition and courtship is described elsewhere (p. 406). It is probably also important in enabling lizards such as monitors and the Gila monster to locate concealed food [53]; certain skinks employ it to recognise their own eggs when they return to their nests to brood (p. 429). By means of this vomeronasal sense snakes can follow trails left by prey such as a frog hopping through grass and leaving minute traces of slime behind. Species such as deKay's snake, which like to hibernate in company, probably rely on it to track their fellows to their winter retreats.

C. M. Bogert [47] has shown by some clever experiments that rattlesnakes employ their organs of Jacobson in recognising their king snake enemies. Rattlesnakes adopt a peculiar and characteristic defence posture when confronted by a king snake, raising a loop of the body and preparing to administer with it a vigorous slapping blow (p. 496). Even a blindfolded rattler will react in this way if a king snake is placed near it, or if it is put into a container in which a king snake has recently been housed. The same response can be elicited if a stick which has been rubbed along a king snake's back is held in front of a rattler, whether blindfolded or not, so long as it can test it with its tongue. It is interesting that the rattlesnake does not respond to smears of the king snake's cloacal glands; as in the case of sex recognition among other species, the stimulating agent seems to be the scent of the dorsal skin. These reactions on the part of the rattlesnake are completely abolished if the tongue is amputated, even when the eyes and nostrils are left unobstructed.

The relative importance of the nose and organ of Jacobson in the combined olfactory sense is not yet clear. Under normal circumstances one would imagine that they worked in conjunction, but it may be possible for either to act alone. Inactivation of Jacobson's organ, either by cautery, by amputation of the tongue, or by the more difficult technique of cutting the vomeronasal nerves has been shown to prevent snakes of various kinds from trailing prey or striking at food, even when their other senses were unimpaired. These findings, like those of Bogert on enemy recognition, suggests that Jacobson's organ is more important than the nose proper. Noble [298] found, however, that obstruction of either of these organs generally was sufficient to inhibit courtship; blocking of both was always effective. It is possible that there is some division of labour between the two sets of organs. The nose may respond to very minute concentrations of scent in the air so that the animal becomes aware of food or some other relevant stimulus at a fair distance; then the tongue and Jacobson's organs are applied to the problem of locating it more precisely [123]. The compelling nature of these experiments should not blind us to the importance of vision in most lizards and snakes; one can perhaps look on the combined olfactory sense as a vital supplement to vision rather than as a substitute for it. It is curious that no experiments of this kind seem to have been carried out on mammals, in which the organs of Jacobson are surgically accessible, and though less elaborate than in Squamata, are often quite appreciable structures.

In adult crocodilians, as in birds, the organ of Jacobson is absent, though a rudiment of it can be identified in the embryo. In Chelonia the structure of the nose differs radically from that of other existing reptiles, and in some ways recalls the condition in Amphibia, especially the urodeles (newts etc). No little vomeronasal pocket appears in the embryo and there is no distinct organ of Jacobson in the adult, in the sense that there is in lepidosaurs and mammals. The olfactory chamber of each nasal sac is partly divided by ridges into an upper and lower compartment (figure 117). The upper one possesses both Bowman's glands and sensory cells, the nerve fibres of the latter passing back to the olfactory bulb in the usual fashion. The lower compartment also contains sensory areas, but no Bowman's glands, and its sensory nerves enter the accessory, and not the main olfactory bulb. Whether one regards this lower compartment as an organ of Jacobson or merely as a subdivision of the nose is just a matter of terminology. Chelonians are often stated to have a keen sense of smell, and they can be conditioned to associate certain strong odours with an unpleasant stimulus (p. 340). Aquatic forms such as the loggerhead *(Caretta)* and the diamond-back terrapin *(Malaclemys)* probably smell under water; they have been observed in tanks to open their nostrils and pump the floor of the mouth up and down, presumably drawing water through the nose [442]. We know little about the importance of this sense in their everyday lives, however, and practically nothing at all about the matter in crocodilians, where the structure of the nose is more complicated than in any other reptiles.

The ear The ear is more difficult to describe than the eye since there has been no otological counterpart of the late Dr Walls to write about it in so masterly a fashion. We tend to think of the ear principally as an organ of hearing, and I shall describe it first in this capacity; yet its primitive functions in connection with sense of position and balance are probably more important in reptiles.

When the first fish-like amphibians began to spend a part of their time on land they evolved a complicated apparatus for perceiving airborne sounds, and this has been retained (though often modified) by higher vertebrates. It consists of an ear drum or tympanic membrane upon which sound waves impinge, a rod for transmitting the resulting vibrations to a tube filled with fluid, and an area of sensory cells (with appropriate nervous connections) inside the tube which respond to fluid disturbance. All these three basic components of the auditory apparatus are present in the majority of existing reptiles; the snakes have perhaps departed furthest from the 'typical' condition.

The ear drum is a thin membrane, covered on its outer surface by modified skin, usually pigmented and devoid of scales; it is generally attached to the hinder surface of the quadrate and adjacent parts of the skull which are often shaped so as to form a kind of 'otic notch' across which it is suspended (fig. 49). In modern forms this does not necessarily correspond in position with the otic notch of primitive reptiles. In many reptiles the ear drum is more or less on level with the surrounding skin instead of lying at the bottom of a deep 'ear-hole' as in mammals. In some lizards, however, such as the big tokay (*Gekko gecko*) the drum is sunk a millimetre or more beneath the surface and the hole over it can be closed by a constrictor muscle. In sand-living lizards the ear opening may be guarded by a fringe of projecting scales, but the crocodilians are the only reptiles which have anything resembling the movable ear-flap or pinna of mammals.

Beneath the ear drum is a space called the middle ear cavity or tympanic cavity, which may be partly recessed into the skull. It leads inwards to the pharynx through the Eustachian tube on each side, and this connection helps to equalise the air pressure inside the cavity with that in the throat and therefore in the outside world. The Eustachian tube and middle ear cavity, including the inside of the ear drum, are lined by mucous membrane which becomes continuous with that of the pharynx.

In reptiles, as in the more generalised amphibians and in birds, there is a single bone called the stapes for conducting vibrations from the drum to the inner ear. It passes across the middle ear cavity and is surrounded by a thin sleeve of mucous membrane (figure 119 A). The name 'stapes' means a stirrup, and in mammals the bone looks like one. In most reptiles, however, it is shaped like a rod or column (hence its alternative name of columella auris) with an expanded boss or footplate at its inner end. Its outer end is applied to the ear drum and is usually furnished with one or more projections or processes which may be attached by ligaments to the surrounding bones. This outer part of the stapes is cartilaginous and is known as the extrastapes or extra-columella. In some reptiles such as crocodilians and geckos a tiny muscle is attached to it which corresponds with the stapedius of mammals. The stapedius is said to have a protective damping effect upon sound vibrations reaching the inner ear.

The mammals differ from reptiles and birds in having two more little bones, the malleus (hammer) and incus (anvil) inside their middle ears, as well as the stapes. Many studies on the ear region of the extinct mammal-like reptiles, supported by work on the embryology of modern mammals, have shown that the incus and malleus correspond respectively with the quadrate and articular – the upper and lower bones which form the jaw joint in the reptilian skull. It is

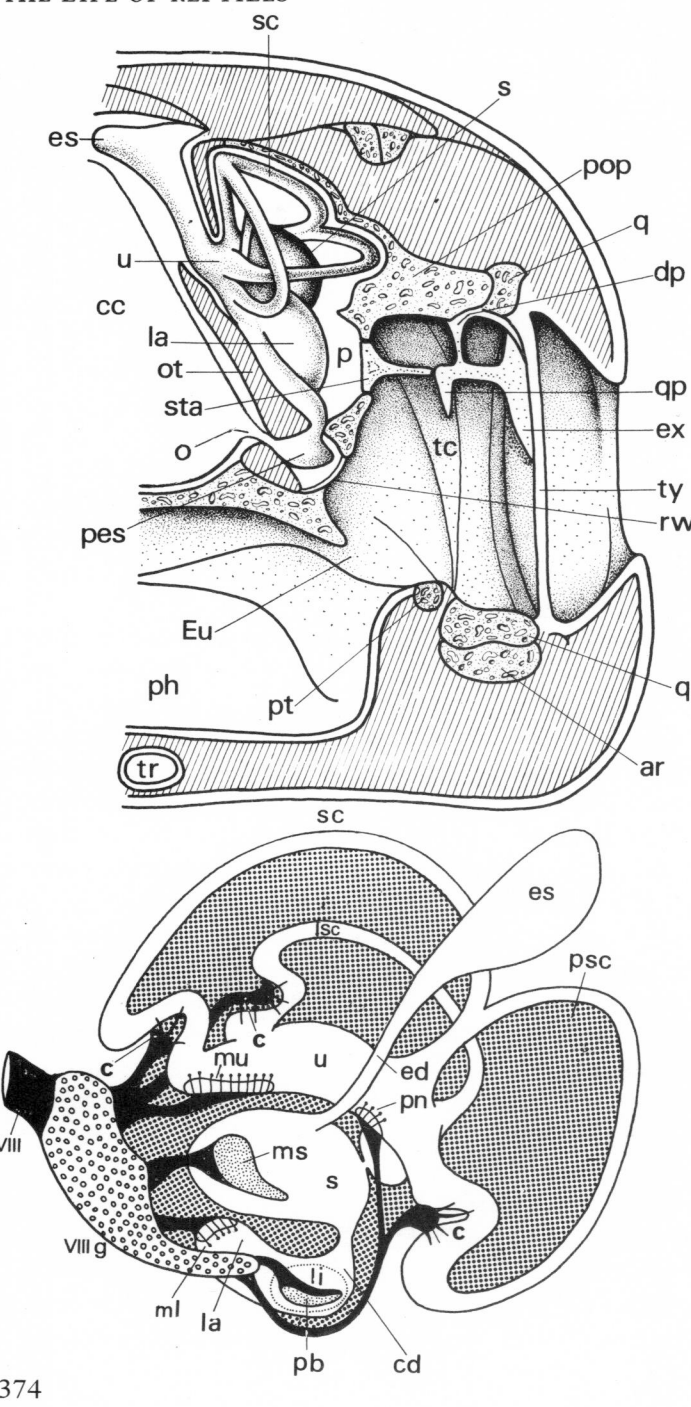

Figure 119   *Top*. Diagrammatic cross-section through ear region of lizard, seen from behind. The membrane lining the middle ear and covering the stapes and extra-stapes is not shown. After Goodrich, E. S. (see figure 75), and Versluys, J. *Bottom*. Diagram of various parts of the right inner ear of a lizard seen from the medial aspect; after Shute, C. C. D. and Bellairs, A. d'A. (1953) *Proc. Zool. Soc. Lond.* 123 695. The machine-stippled areas represent the space between the various regions of the inner ear. The position of the limbus is shown in dotted outline. The cristae are the special sensory areas of the semicircular canals, the maculae and papillae are the sensory areas of other regions of the inner ear. The functions of the macula lagenae and papilla neglecta are obscure. The papilla basilaris corresponds with the mammalian organ of Corti.

ar, articular. **c**, crista. **cc**, cranial cavity. **cd**, cochlear duct. **dp**, dorsal process of extra-stapes (intercalary). **ed**, **es**, endolymphatic duct and sac. **Eu**, Eustachian tube. **ex**, extra-stapes. **la**, lagena*. **li**, limbus. **lsc**, lateral semicircular canal. **ml**, macula lagenae. **ms**, macula of saccule. **mu**, macula of utricle. **o**, opening of perilymphatic duct into **cc**. **ot**, otic capsule (inner wall). **p**, perilymphatic space. **pb**, papilla basilaris. **pes**, perilymphatic sac. **ph**, pharynx. **pn**, papilla neglecta. **pop**, paroccipital process. **psc**, posterior semicircular canal. **pt**, pterygoid. **q**, quadrate. **qp**, quadrate (internal) process of extra-stapes. **rw**, round window. **s**, saccule. **sc**, superior semicircular canal. **sta**, stapes (columella auris): pointer in 119 top indicates footplate in oval window. **tc**, tympanic (middle ear) cavity. **tr**, trachea. **ty**, tympanic membrane (ear drum). **u**, utricle. **VIII**, auditory nerve with its ganglion, **VIIIg**. **IX**, **X**, glossopharyngeal and vagus nerves (course of). * or cochlear duct.

possible to reconstruct many of the steps by which the back end of the reptilian jaw became incorporated into the ear of mammals, and by which the latter evolved a new jaw joint out of the neighbouring squamosal and dentary bones. This remarkable transformation was associated with changes in the biting muscles and jaw mechanics [see 317]. One might suppose that the evolution of a triple lever system for conducting sound waves has helped to increase auditory efficiency; the majority of mammals have better powers of hearing than modern reptiles. On the other hand, some birds such as owls have exceptionally keen hearing despite the fact that like reptiles they have only a single ossicle system.

The inner ear consists of an intricate series of membranous tubes and sacs which probably originated from a part of the cranial lateral line system in the ancestors of vertebrates. In the embryo it develops from a vesicle called the otocyst which itself arises from a plate of thickened epidermis on each side of the head, in a rather similar fashion to the nasal sac. The uppermost part of the otocyst differentiates into the three semicircular canals, two vertical ones and a horizontal one, all at right angles with each other and communicating with a rounded chamber, the utricle (figure 119). This leads in turn into another chamber, the saccule, and this communicates with yet another, called in reptiles the cochlear duct, which contains the organs of hearing. Arising from the saccule is a tube known as the ductus endolymphaticus which ends blindly in the endolymphatic or otic sac. In many reptiles this sac extends into the cranial cavity and lies within the meningeal membranes which surround the brain. In geckos and certain other lizards, however, the duct and sac are enlarged and issue from the skull to end among the neck muscles behind the ear on each side of the head. This sac contains calcified particles and is sometimes called the endolymphatic gland. It has been suggested that its function is to provide a reserve of calcium for the formation of the hard-shelled eggs, and the amount of material it contains fluctuates with the egg-laying cycle. Similar calcified deposits are found in the embryos of other reptiles but disappear in the adult [386].

The various regions of the inner ear are filled with fluid, the endolymph, and contain patches or maculae of sensory cells furnished with fine hairs which are embedded in a gelatinous membrane; the membrane is loaded with small calcareous particles called otoliths or statoconia which are particularly conspicuous in the saccule.

Little experimental work has been done on the functions of the non-auditory parts of the inner ear in reptiles. It is probable, however, that as in other vertebrates, the semi-circular canals are concerned mainly with dynamic position sense as the animal turns and twists in space. The inertia of the endolymph when the head is turned in any direction causes the sensory hairs in at least one of the canals to stream out in the fluid, setting up impulses in the nerve fibres which supply their parent cells. The utricle, and possible the saccule also, give information about static posture, registering the tilt of the head, and about acceleration, as for instance when a slowly creeping lizard makes a sudden dart to escape an enemy. The otoliths act like the lead weight on a plumbline, pulling on the sensory hairs in response to gravity, or to centrifugal force when the animal accelerates. The nervous inflow from these organs of equilibration enters the hindbrain via the vestibular division of the VIIIth cranial nerve and is relayed to the cerebellum; it initiates righting reflexes such as enable an animal to return to its normal position after falling on its back, and other responses necessary to maintain equilibrium. It is interesting that these organs, in contrast with the parts of the ear responsible for hearing, seem to have remained almost unaltered throughout the course of evolution, keeping vertebrates the right way up as effectively on land or in the air as in their ancient watery home.

The cochlear duct of reptiles is shaped like a pear or a sausage; in mammals it has become longer and is coiled on itself like a snail. It has originated from a shorter, more simple type of structure known in fishes and amphibians as the lagena; indeed, this term rather than cochlear duct is used by some writers for a whole or a part (the tip) of the reptilian organ (figure 119). Its principal sensory area is the papilla basilaris which resembles the more elaborate organ of Corti in the mammalian cochlea, though in some of its features it cannot be compared directly with the latter [see 210, 284]. The papilla basilaris is supplied by the cochlear division of the VIIIth nerve. There is also another small sensory area, the macula lagenae, at the tip of the cochlear duct; this probably corresponds with the original macula of this part of the inner ear of fishes, but its function is not known.

The papilla basilaris is supported by a ring or plate of thickened connective tissue which looks rather like cartilage, called the limbus. Although more specialised, its sensory cells are basically similar to those of the maculae of other parts of the ear, and are furnished with fine hairs covered by a roofing (tectorial) membrane. It has been estimated that there are between 100 and 1000 of these hair cells in the papilla of lizards, as compared with 9000 to 18,000 in the mammalian organ of Corti [323]. They are stimulated not by movement or posture but by sound waves transmitted from the ear drum through the stapes. To understand this mechanism we must consider the relationship of the inner ear to the structures which surround it.

The various regions of the inner ear are invested by the otic capsule, developed as cartilage in the embryo but later ossifying to form the prootic and opisthotic bones. Between inner ear and skeleton is a perilymphatic or periotic space which is partly occupied by strands of connective tissue and contains fluid known as perilymph. This connective tissue is so arranged as to enclose a large perilymphatic cistern beneath and around the cochlear duct; the latter is suspended in it like a balloon filled with fluid and held in a bath (figure 119).

The footplate of the stapes fits into a hole called the oval window in the outer wall of the otic capsule where it covers the perilymphatic cistern. Movements of the stapes will therefore be transmitted through the perilymph in the cistern to the cochlear duct and the

377

endolymph inside it; they will ultimately stimulate the sensory hairs of the papilla basilaris, setting off impulses in the cochlear nerve. In mammals the different regions of the papilla, or the organ of Corti, as it should be called, respond selectively to vibrations of different frequency, set up by sounds of different wave-length or pitch. Their response depends upon their position along the wall of the coiled and progressively narrowing cochlear duct; high notes are registered most effectively near the base of the cochlea and low ones near its tip. The cochlear duct of birds, though shorter and uncoiled, can also discriminate pitch in this way, and the same is probably true in some reptiles such as geckos, though to a more limited extent [453].

In order to allow for the fluid waves in the perilymph set up by the plunging movements of the stapes a special recoil mechanism has been developed. This consists of another opening known as the round window, covered by membrane and situated below the oval window; in reptiles it is situated in the floor of the otic capsule above the Eustachian tube. In some species the perilymphatic cistern bulges out into the middle ear cavity through the round window, or inwards, into the cranial cavity through a fissure in the skull. Here it ends as the perilymphatic sac (not to be confused with the endolymphatic sac described previously) within the dura mater around the brain.

These conditions appear to represent the basic pattern of the reptilian ear as seen in many lizards. We may now say something of the more striking specialisations of the auditory apparatus found in various groups, and discuss its functional capacity.

Crocodilians are the only reptiles which have large flap-like outer ears. These are quite conspicuous structures though they are normally held in the closed position, flush with the surface of the head. They stretch from just behind the eyes to the back of the head on each side and completely cover the ear drums. Presumably the flaps are a useful protection for these sensitive membranes against injury from underwater snags and possibly from increased pressure when the animal dives. At the front of each flap is a small slit aperture which is generally open when the crocodile's head is out of water (figure 120, Plate 12) and closed when it submerges. This opening seems to be the normal route by which airborne sound waves reach the drum. The whole ear-flap is also movable, however, being hinged to the skull along its upper edge. It can easily be lifted up in a docile animal, and dissection shows that there are two little muscles at its hinder end which raise and lower it. Yet the only occasion on which I have

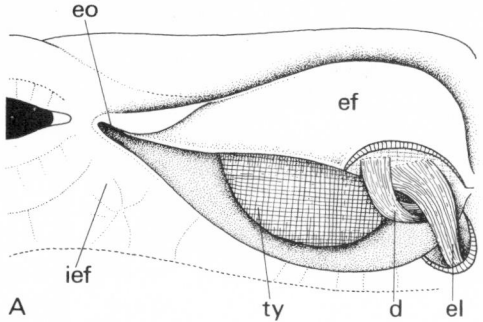
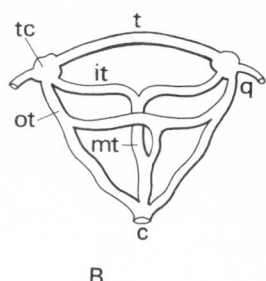

Figure 120   A. Left side of head of alligator with the ear-flap drawn upwards to show tympanic membrane, and its muscles partly dissected out. After Shute and Bellairs [385]. B. Diagram of Eustachian tubes of a crocodilian, as if removed from the head and seen from in front (see Wettstein [452]).

c, common median opening of Eustachian tube into pharynx. **d,** depressor muscle of ear-flap, **ef. el,** elevator muscle of ear-flap (obtains leverage in indirect fashion, being inserted into flap from behind). **eo,** external opening of ear normally visible when the ear-flap is closed. **ief,** inferior ear-fold (pulled upwards to close **eo**). **it,** inner branch of Eustachian tube. **mt,** median tube. **ot,** outer tube. **q,** extension from tympanic cavity into quadrate, eventually leading through siphonium into lower jaw. **t,** transverse connection between tympanic (middle ear) cavities, **tc. ty,** tympanic membrane (ear drum).

seen a crocodilian raise one of these flaps is when I have inserted a pipette beneath it and squirted a little water on to the surface of the ear drum. Then the flap rapidly flicks open and shut several times, as if to shake out the water, and finally remains closed as before [385]. I have seen it stated that when a crocodile is angry or frightened its ear-flaps flutter up and down like humming-birds' wings, and although I have never seen this the description has an authentic ring. It remains a mystery, however, why a crocodile should possess large movable ear-flaps when the opening and closing of the small apertures in front (by means of a movable fold) seem adequate for normal purposes of hearing on land and underwater protection.

The middle ear cavities and Eustachian tubes of crocodilians are extraordinarily complicated [105, 387]. They are almost completely enclosed by bone so that the back part of the skull is permeated by a system of communicating, air-filled passages. Each middle ear cavity is connected with the pharynx by two Eustachian tubes, an outer and an inner one. The inner one soon joins its opposite fellow to form a single median tube which issues from the skull base through

379

a foramen in the basisphenoid, behind the internal nostrils (figures 53, p. 149; 120). The outer tubes, one from each cavity, emerge from the skull by small holes on each side of the bigger, median foramen. They then join each other and the median tube to form a single short, common duct which opens into the pharynx in the midline. Two further branches from the outer pair of tubes join and lead into the front of the median tube inside the skull.

In addition to these connections, the two middle ear cavities communicate with each other across the head beneath the roof of the skull. Another extension from each cavity excavates the quadrate, and emerges from the back of this bone to join a membranous tube called the siphonium. This enters the lower jaw through a small hole on the inner side of the joint surface, and finally leads into a cavity within the articular bone.

The remarkably intricate arrangement of these tubes and spaces is difficult to visualise, even from the descriptions of Richard Owen [308] and T. H. Huxley [227], the master-anatomists of the nineteenth century, a time when biologists were really interested in such matters.

The middle ear cavities and Eustachian tubes of birds are in some ways rather similar, particularly in the manner in which they enter and pneumatise the bones of the skull. It is uncertain whether their complexity in crocodilians is a part of a common archosaurian heritage, or whether it is related to the mode of life of these animals. Various suggestions that the tube system helps a crocodile to equalise the pressure in its two ears very quickly when it dives have been made, but the problem is still quite obscure.

The cochlear duct of crocodilians, though uncoiled, is relatively longer than that of other reptiles, and it is generally agreed that they possess good powers of hearing. This is certainly suggested by their use of challenge and mating calls during the breeding season (p. 396), such sounds being produced by the aid of folds in the mucous membrane of the larynx which may resemble the vocal cords of mammals. In captivity, bull alligators will respond by roaring to low notes of 57 cycles per second (c.p.s), corresponding to B flat two octaves below middle C, and played on an instrument such as a French horn. Such sounds are thought to resemble the bellowing of rivals [23].

The ears of geckos are also of special interest. In the first place, the middle ear of these lizards is particularly easy to examine, even during life. The ear drum is more or less transparent and if one holds a gecko up to the light it is possible to see through both ears beneath the skull, right across the head. When handled these animals often gape their jaws, exposing the back of the pharynx and the short, wide Eustachian tubes. The stapes and inner surface of the ear drum are clearly visible within the cavity of the inner ear, and it is surprising that these delicate structures are not injured when the creature swallows struggling prey.

Geckos have a better auditory apparatus than most other lizards, the cochlear duct and papilla basilaris with its supporting limbus being extremely well developed. This again is what one might expect from the extremely vocal behaviour of these reptiles (p. 402). Rather striking resemblances have been found, however, between the cochlear duct and limbus of geckos and pygopods, a group of Australian snake-like lizards whose habits are little known. This is one of several features which suggest an affinity between these two outwardly very dissimilar families of Sauria [see 210].

During recent years, E. G. Wever and his colleagues at Princeton University have investigated the auditory sensitivity of various reptiles by means of electrophysiological techniques [see 453]. Essentially these involve the subjection of anaesthetised animals to pure sounds of known frequency (pitch) and loudness. The resulting electric current or potential set up in the inner ear can be measured and gives an indication of response – circumstantial evidence that the animal can hear the sound which is reaching it.

The ears of the dozen or so species of lizards studied were found to respond to sounds of between 100 and 10,000 cycles per second, a greater range than was reported in crocodilians. The sensitivity of lizards to high notes falls off greatly, however, at around 4000 c.p.s. The performance of the geckonids *Coleonyx variegatus* and *Gekko gecko* is comparable with that of other species in range, but their ears respond to fainter sounds. The ear of *Coleonyx* is as sensitive as the ear of the guinea-pig over its optimum frequency range of 300 to 1000 c.p.s., although at higher frequencies its sensitivity is much inferior to that of mammals. The guinea-pig ear, for example, has an upper limit of about 100,000 c.p.s, and a range of maximum sensitivity extending from 300 to 35,000 c.p.s. [323].

In many lepidosaurs there is a tendency for the ear drum, middle ear cavity and Eustachian tube to disappear and for the extra-stapes to become attached to the quadrate bone. These trends are not always related in any obvious way to the creature's mode of life. They are evident, to a greater or lesser extent, in *Sphenodon,* in certain iguanids such as the earless lizards *(Holbrookia)* and in agamids such as *Lyriocephalus* and *Ceratophora* from Ceylon, as well as in the chamaeleons. Presumably these animals are dependent on the conducting properties of bone for the reception of sounds, like a person whose auditory ossicles have become immobile. This is perhaps surprising since they are mostly terrestrial or arboreal creatures which might be expected to benefit from good powers of hearing.

Similar but more explicable modifications have occurred in many burrowers, both with and without legs; in skinks such as the 'sand-fish' *(Scincus)* and the snake-like *Acontias* and *Typhlosaurus,* in the pygopod *Aprasia* (perhaps the only lizard which lacks a stapes) and in amphisbaenids. The slow-worm *(Anguis)* shows an early stage in this process, since its ear-opening, though almost overgrown by scaly skin, is just visible, at least in some individuals. The tissue beneath it represents a small thickened ear drum, encroached on from in front and behind by the jaw muscles. The middle ear cavity is small, with narrow but functional Eustachian tubes. The semi-fossorial earless monitor *Lanthanotus* has no ear drums, but possesses a large extra-stapes said to be in contact with the quadrate [264]. In the amphisbaenids the extra-stapes, instead of being attached to the

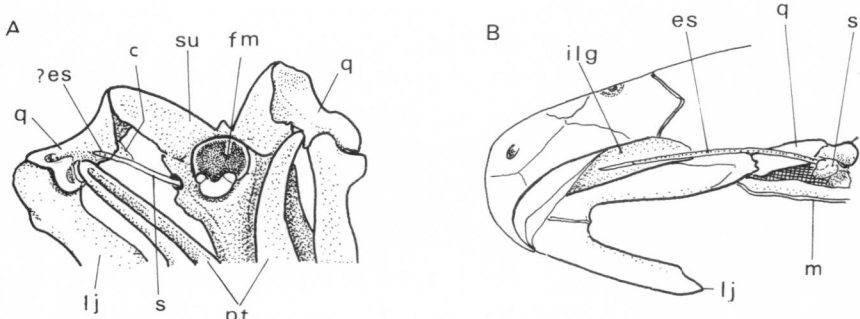

Figure 121   A. Oblique view of back of skull of *Python* showing relationship of stapes to quadrate. B. Partly dissected head of *Amphisbaena* sp. showing extra-stapes running forwards along side of jaw. A and B after Versluys [see 56].

c, nodule of cartilage attached to quadrate (possibly intercalary or extra-stapes). **es,** extra-stapes (extra-columella). **fm,** foramen magnum. **ilg,** inferior labial gland. **lj,** lower jaw bones. **m,** sheet of membrane (cut). **pt,** pterygoid. **q,** quadrate. **s,** stapes (columella). **su,** supratemporal.

quadrate as in other burrowers, runs along the outside of the lower jaw bones beneath the skin for some distance. In these and other specialised burrowing lizards the footplate of the stapes is enlarged and the shaft of the bone is surrounded by large fluid-filled cavities which may be lymph spaces, or more probably, extensions of the perilymphatic system [425]. In the inner ear the papilla basilaris and limbus tend to be reduced [284].

In snakes the ear drum, middle ear cavity and Eustachian tube are also absent, and the extra-stapes is absent or perhaps represented by a small nodule of bone or cartilage between the end of the stapes and the inner side of the quadrate (figure 121). The fact that these conditions are present in burrowing and non-burrowing forms alike has been interpreted as another link connecting the snakes as a group with burrowing saurian ancestors which were nearly deaf as well as nearly blind. It had been suggested, however, that the presence of a large middle ear cavity would be incompatible with the great mobility of the quadrate which is so characteristic of the majority of snakes; the loss of the middle ear might therefore be correlated with strep-tostyly (p. 154) rather than with ancestral burrowing habits.

It must also be admitted that the inner ear of snakes shows features which do not obviously support the attractive 'burrowing theory'. One might expect that the papilla basilaris, the organ of hearing in the cochlear duct, would be reduced in burrowing snakes as it is in burrowing lizards, but this is not the case; in forms such as *Anilius* and *Xenopeltis* the papilla basilaris and limbus are actually better developed than they are in the majority of surface-dwelling species. They are reduced, however, in sea snakes. The evolutionary significance of the inner ear structures of snakes is not yet well understood, but there are indications that these reptiles originated from lizards with a more primitive type of cochlear duct structure than any now living [284].

The question as to how well snakes can 'hear' in the generally accepted sense of the word is extremely difficult to answer. The absence of the ear drum and the anatomy of the middle ear of these animals does not suggest great sensitivity to airborne sounds, even though the papilla basilaris of the inner ear may be quite well developed. Experiments have failed to show that snakes respond to such sounds in any obvious way, and stories of their being charmed or lured out of their retreats by music have generally been discounted by zoologists. Nevertheless, Wever and Vernon [454] have demonstrated that the inner ear of the colubrids *Pituophis, Thamnophis* and *Natrix* gives electrical responses when the head is exposed to airborne sounds of low pitch at frequencies of around 100 to 500 cycles per second; indeed over part of this range the ears of the snakes gave a better performance than the ear of a cat. At higher frequencies the responses of the snakes' ears fell off very markedly and it was concluded that the inferiority of their hearing lies in its limited range, and not in its absolute sensitivity. The quadrate was shown to act as a receiving surface for the sounds, and thus to have a similar function to the ear drum of mammals. Removal of this bone was followed by a marked reduction in sound transmission and had a greater effect on the responses than breaking the stapes.

While the ability of a snake to perceive airborne sounds has been established, it seems to be limited, and is perhaps not very relevant to their normal way of life. It is possible, however, that the auditory conducting apparatus, both of snakes and of burrowing lizards, is specially adapted for receiving vibrations set up by touch-contact. In snakes electrical responses can readily be elicited from the ear if such vibrations are communicated directly to the head, especially to the region of the quadrate. This bone, as we have seen, is in contact with both the stapes and the lower jaw in snakes; in amphisbaenids the stapes itself is connected with the lower jaw through the medium of the extra-stapes. When its head is resting on the substratum or enclosed within a tunnel, the animal would be in an excellent position to pick up vibrations and in this way would obtain warning of the approach of enemies or of the movements of prey on or beneath the surface. Vibration sense could thus be very useful to a burrowing or secretive reptile which must, literally, keep its ears to the ground.

The importance of this sense to a surface-living or arboreal snake is less obvious. Snakes generally raise their heads when they are crawling about, and when stationary will often rest the head on a coil. It is possible that ground vibrations are effective when transmitted through the body, but Wever and Vernon found that responses from the inner ear fell off substantially when the vibrator was moved on to soft tissues away from the head. Nevertheless, most naturalists believe that a snake is quickly alerted by any ground disturbance, such as an approaching footstep.

Some Chelonia such as the Greek tortoise have distinct ear drums not unlike those of typical lizards, but in many others such as the marine turtles the drums are covered or replaced by scaly skin, or by a large tympanic scale. The bony parts of the middle ear are always remarkably specialised. The cavity is more or less divided into two compartments by a ridge which projects back from the quadrate (figure 122). The outer compartment, seen as one looks at a turtle's skull from the side, is shaped like a crater with a hole or notch near its bottom through which the outer end of the bony stapes projects (figure 50, p. 145). The cartilaginous extra-stapes occupies most of the outer compartment and its tip is expanded into an oval plate which is applied to the ear drum or to the tissue which corresponds with it. The shaft of the stapes lies in the inner compartment and is surrounded by a fluid-containing space which may represent an extension from the perilymphatic cistern. Here we have a condition rather similar to that in snakes and burrowing lizards, though it must have evolved quite independently. The functional significance of these peculiarities is not yet understood.

The auditory sensitivity of chelonians seems on the whole inferior to that of crocodilians and lizards, particularly to notes of over one or

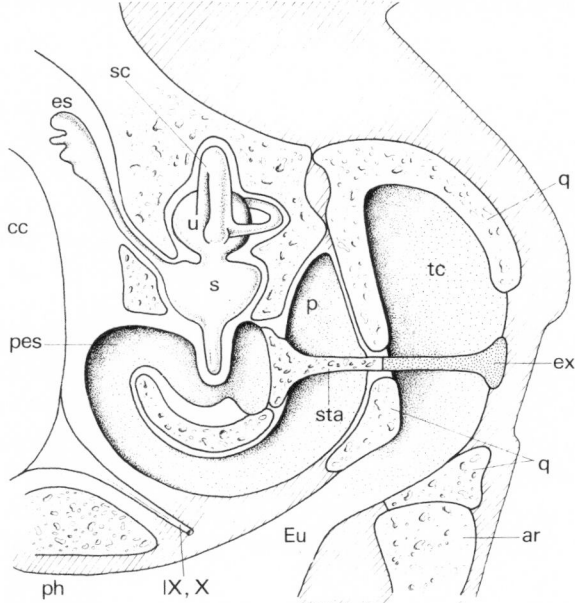

Figure 122   Diagrammatic transverse section through ear region of a chelonian. After Romer [356]. The portion of the perilymphatic space (**p**) above the bony stapes is called the pericapsular sinus. Only two semicircular canals (**sc**) are shown.

Abbreviations as for figure 119, p. 375.

two thousand cycles per second, which have to be loud in order to evoke an electrical response in the inner ear or cochlear nerve. E. D. Adrian [2] found that the ear of the 'common land tortoise' and of the box turtle (*Terrapene*) was particularly responsive to sounds of about 110 c.p.s., even when they were only just audible to the human ear; he suggested that there might be some special mechanism behind this selectivity, and that the stapes itself might vibrate at the same frequency. The animals did not react in any obvious behavioural fashion to these sounds. More recent work has shown that the north American wood turtle (*Clemmys insculpta*) shows rather good sensitivity for tones of up to 500 c.p.s., and then a very rapid decline above 1000 c.p.s. [323]. Rather similar results have been obtained for other species. Sounds seem to play little part in chelonian life, except before and during mating, when cries and grunts are sometimes heard.

One has the impression that the sense of hearing is more variably developed, and generally speaking, less acute in reptiles than in birds or mammals. Experimental studies in which reptiles were conditioned to associate noises with rewards and punishments might tell us a good deal about the importance of hearing in their behaviour.

The sensory pits Rattlesnakes and other crotalines such as the copperhead and bushmaster possess a conspicuous pit on each side of the snout, between the eye and the nostril (figure 123). It is partly enclosed by a hollow in the maxillary bone, an osteological feature which enables one to distinguish between the skull of a pit-viper of the subfamily Crotalinae and that of a pit-less one such as an adder belonging to the subfamily Viperinae.

Each pit is subdivided into an outer chamber and a smaller inner one by a membrane of about 0·025 mm. in thickness. This is composed of two sheets of epidermis with a layer of connective tissue sandwiched between them. Small blood vessels and many fibres of the ophthalmic and maxillary divisions of the trigeminal nerve enter the membrane from its periphery, and some of these fibres terminate among the cells of the outer epidermal sheet. The inner chamber communicates with the exterior by a minute pore opening beneath one of the scales at the front of the eye.

Similar though less elaborate pits are present along the upper and lower labial scales which border the mouth in pythons and a few boas. They vary in size in any individual, some being quite deep and

386

occupying most of a scale, while others look like little dots. They are also well supplied with blood vessels and fibres from the maxillary and mandibular nerves, but are not subdivided. It has been suggested that this kind of pit represents the primitive condition. The two-chambered crotaline pit may have evolved through the approximation of two simple pits of the python type, the tissue between them becoming thinned out to form the membrane. The idea is supported by the way in which the pit develops from two separate ingrowths in the rattlesnake embryo.

Although the German herpetologist Franz Leydig suggested 100 years ago that these pits were sense organs of some kind, their precise function remained mysterious until the 1930s, when it was dis-covered that they were sensitive to temperature changes. Noble and

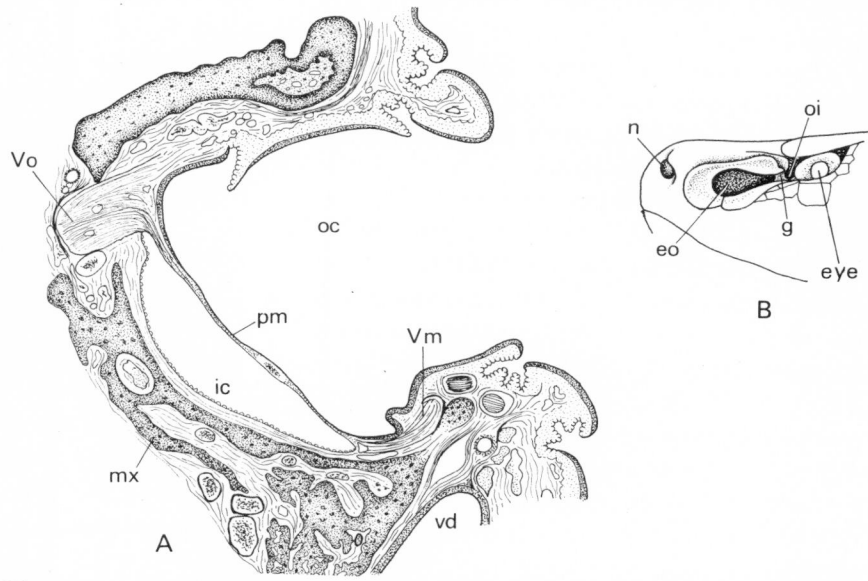

Figure 123   A. Microscopic section through sensory pit of rattlesnake (*Crotalus terrificus*). B. Left side of snout of bushmaster (*Lachesis muta*). The flap of tissue partly covering the external opening of the pit is lifted up, showing the groove between the pit and eye, and the external opening of the inner pit chamber. A and B after West, G. S. (1900) *Quart. J. microsc. Sci.* **43** 49.

ic, inner chamber of pit. **eo**, external opening of pit. **g**, groove between pit and eye. **mx**, maxilla. **n**, nostril. **oc**, outer chamber of pit. **oi**, opening of inner pit chamber to exterior. **pm**, pit membrane. **vd**, venom gland duct. **Vm**, branch of maxillary division of trigeminal (Vth) nerve. **Vo**, branch of ophthalmic division of Vth nerve.

Schmidt [300] found that garden boas and green tree boas *(Boa hortulana* and *B. canina)* could distinguish between warm and cold electric light bulbs when these were covered with a cloth and moved in front of them. When blindfolded the snakes continued to strike at the warm bulbs only, at distances of up to 30 cm. Accurate responses continued after the other principal sense organs – nose, tongue and organ of Jacobson – had been put out of action. They immediately ceased after the labial pits had been filled with collodion, indicating that these were the organs responsible for temperature discrimination. The experiments showed that the boas were able to distinguish temperature differences of 0·2°C or even less which were produced in the air around the pit when the warm and cold bulbs were alternately waved in front of them about 20 cm. away.

Very similar results were obtained with rattlesnakes and copperheads, except that these reptiles, when blindfolded and deprived of their combined olfactory sense and tongues would sometimes strike at moving cold bulbs when warm ones were not available. This suggested that the facial pits of crotalines with their sensitive membranes might respond to air vibrations as well as heat.

More recent studies on crotaline pits in which the electrical activity of their nerves was recorded have confirmed these observations to a large extent [79]. The pits were found to respond primarily to the heating effect of infra-red radiations and were even more sensitive than was originally believed, registering a radiation gradient comparable with that produced by a human hand held 30 cm. (nearly a foot) away. Cold objects also elicited a nervous response so that the organs probably help the snake to recognise bodies which are slightly colder, as well as warmer, than their surroundings. Like other paired sense organs the pits may have a kind of 'stereoscopic' function, helping the snake to direct its strike. The fields of the two organs in rattlesnakes overlap slightly like those of the eyes in animals with weak binocular vision. The actual sensory radius of each pit was found to extend horizontally from 10° across the midline to a point at right angles to the long axis of the head, and from 45° upwards to 35° downwards in the vertical direction.

The way in which the organs register infra-red radiations is not yet understood. It is possible that the nerves in the pit membrane (probably the only sensory component of the crotaline pit) react directly to very minute temperature changes caused by infra-red absorption. Alternatively, there may be some more subtle mechanism

388

akin to the photochemical reactions of rhodopsin in the retina. One theory supposed that the membrane was stimulated by a rise in pressure in the inner pit chamber due to gaseous expansion; this seems to be invalidated by the fact that nerve responses are unimpaired if the membrane is punctured. Observations recorded when the undamaged membrane was lightly touched or if puffs of air were directed upon it suggest, contrary to earlier views, that the pits are not very important as organs of vibration sense.

How effective are these organs under natural conditions? Noble and Schmidt found that their snakes could choose between freshly killed warm and chilled rats in the same way as between warm and cold electric light bulbs. The presence of a live rat was shown to raise the temperature of the atmosphere by $0.1°C$ at a distance of 18 cm. (7 in.), a temperature gradient which is now believed to be within the organs' capacity. Furthermore, had they taken flickering of the tongue as the first indication that a snake was interested in a warm object, instead of the more unequivocal strike response, they might have credited the organ with a greater range of sensitivity. One may conclude that the pits enable their possessors to locate warm (and possibly cold) blooded animals which pass close to them as they lie in ambush; this could be especially useful at night when these reptiles often hunt their prey. The possible sensory function of certain small cavities present above the nostrils in vipers such as *Bitis* which lack typical pits deserves investigation.

Chapter 9

Sex and Reproduction

Sex

THE SEXUAL urge has a whimsical and sometimes tragic character; it was evolved for the benefit of the species, but may be disastrous for the individual. When it is at its peak it overrides almost all other forms of behaviour. This is dramatically illustrated by the life of the green turtle, which migrates for vast distances away from rich feeding grounds to mate and breed on a far-off shore, devoid of nourishment and fraught with imponderable danger.

Differences between the sexes The first essential step in sexual reproduction is to find and recognise a suitable mate. Belonging as we do to a species in which the recognition of sex is seldom a serious problem, we may wonder how animals which do not possess distinctive sexual features manage to obtain this vital information. Instinctive reactions to subtle differences in appearance, smell and behaviour no doubt suffice in many species, but there is a tendency to make life easier by providing obvious clues in the form of secondary sexual characters.

Such characters are evident in many reptiles, at least to the trained observer. Only some of them, however, such as the bright colours and other adornments of certain male lizards, appear to play a genuine part in sexual advertisement. Others, such as the shape of the plastron in male tortoises, seem to be direct adaptations to the act of coitus, while others again, such as differences in body and tail proportions, may be the incidental by-products of growth patterns controlled by the sex hormones. So far as I can discover, no critical review of sex differences in reptiles has been made since Darwin's account in *The Descent of Man* [128]; no doubt many interesting examples which I have missed could be added to the following particulars.

The growth rates of the young and the size and age when sexual maturity is reached may differ in males and females (p. 465), while size is often a guide to the sex of an adult reptile. Among the Chelonia the females of many, though not all species tend to grow bigger than the males. The greatest discrepancy is found in the map and diamond-back terrapins *(Graptemys* and *Malaclemys)* in which the females have shells twice as long as those of the mature males. In the red-eared terrapin *(Pseudemys scripta elegans)* (figure 124) the females are also much the larger [89].

The biggest Nile crocodiles, on the other hand, are usually males, though females are heavier than males of comparable length. One of the longest of these crocodiles ever recorded, however, measuring 5·58 metres (18 ft., 4 in.), is alleged to have been a female [119]. Female American alligators seldom exceed 2·28 metres (7½ ft.), whereas the males grow to 3·66 metres (12 ft.), or even more. Males of the gharial *(Gavialis gangeticus)* are also said to grow bigger than the females [394], and this is probably the rule with crocodilians generally.

In most, though by no means all lizards the male is also the larger sex, and this is probably the general rule among species such as the rainbow lizard *(Agama agama)* where marked territorial behaviour and rivalry occurs during the breeding season. It is also true for the tuatara which is not known to be territorial. A big male *Sphenodon* may measure slightly over 61 cm. (2 ft.) with a snout-vent length of 29 cm., and a weight of more than 1,000 gm. The females seldom exceed 51 cm. (20 in.) overall, a snout-vent length of 24 cm., and a weight of 500 gm. [130]. Female snakes, however, usually grow larger than their mates; big female pythons, for instance, may be nearly 2 metres longer than the biggest males, and male reti-culated pythons of over 4·6 metres (15 ft.) are seldom found [333]. In the slow-worm *(Anguis)* the female is said to grow longer than the male [395] and it would be interesting to know whether this was usual in other snake-like lizards.

The proportions and shape of certain parts of the body may also vary according to sex. In tortoises such as the common Greek species the posterior part of the plastron is somewhat concave in the male and fits over the domed carapace of the female during the sexual act, helping him to preserve his balance. Male chelonians also have longer tails than the females, and the base of the tail is relatively thicker since it contains the penis. In some species such as the green turtle the front claws are enlarged for clasping the female, or as in the red-eared terrapin, for preliminary nuptial stimulation. Sex dimorphism (apart from size differences) is not evident in crocodilians, but mature male gharials can be distinguished by a protruberance on the tip of the snout. The resemblance of this to a 'ghara' or earthenware pot may have been responsible for the animal's name [394].

In many lizards, including the slow-worm, the male has a larger, broader head than the female; big males of the eyed lizard *(Lacerta lepida)* and the tegu *(Tupinambis)* acquire a definitely 'jowly' appearance which seems to be due to hypertrophy of the jaw muscles. Secondary sexual characters of a rather specific kind are often found in lizards, especially in members of the Iguania group. These include dorsal and caudal crests, throat-fans, horns (in certain chamaeleons and agamids) and femoral pores, which are usually better developed in, or the exclusive property of the male sex. These structures are described in Chapter 7 (p. 311), which deals with the skin.

Male and female snakes seldom differ strikingly in appearance; the curious excrescences on the snout in tree-snakes of the genus *Langaha* (figure 99, p. 315) are exceptions to the general rule. Male snakes tend to have relatively longer tails and shorter bodies than the females, however, and this difference is reflected in the numbers of ventral and subcaudal scales. As in lizards the tail base is swollen in the region of the hemipenes, which lie side by side beneath the superficial tissues, behind the cloacal opening (figure 128, p. 416) In dead specimens eversion of these organs can sometimes be induced by pressing on them from behind, and both hemipenes may be protruded in a snake's death agony, occasioned, for example by a heath fire. This finding has given rise to a belief among countrymen that snakes such as the adder possess rudimentary hind limbs, and even a biologist can be misled in the same way about a snake embryo; the hemipenes are everted during embryonic life, though they are normally withdrawn before hatching.

Certain minor differences in scalation are found in a number of colubrid snakes, the males possessing keels or tubercles on the scales of the cloacal region, beneath the chin or elsewhere on the body; in some cases these structures have an erotic significance. The vestigial hind limbs of many boid snakes, which are also used in courtship, are likewise better developed in the male sex and may be two to three times larger than in the female.

Sexual differences in colour are seldom evident in crocodilians or chelonians, although in certain terrapins of the *Pseudemys* group such as Troost's terrapin, mature males often become much darker than the females, so that they have been described as members of a different subspecies or even species. Colour differences are common among lizards, especially those of the agamid and iguanid families, and, generally speaking, the male is far more striking and conspicuous than his mate, as in many birds. The mature male of the rainbow lizard, for example, assumes the most vivid hues during the breeding season, his head being bright orange-red and his body blue; the females and young on the other hand, are dull brownish yellow, with olive green on the head. The bright green flank colour of the male sand lizard in England is another example of sexual colouration. Even in the sombre slow-worm the sexes often show some difference in hue, the females tending to retain the dark stripe along the back, and the black belly, which are so characteristic of the young. In some snakes such as the adder colour differences may also be apparent. Thus, male adders in southern England usually have a jet-black dorsal zigzag marking on a background of white or cream; in the female the colours are less contrasting, the zigzag being dark brown on a reddish-brown ground colour. The colour of the eyes (often golden or yellowish green in reptiles) shows a sexual difference in a few species. In females of the adder and of the box turtle (*Terrapene carolina*) the iris is brown, whereas in the male it is red; the eyes of the male adder, seen close up, have quite a sinister glow.

Sex ratio

In most vertebrates the numbers of females and males in any natural population are roughly equal. There is evidence, however, that both in alligators and in certain chelonians the females outnumber the males by two to one or even more; a ratio of one male to 5·9 females was found in a study of 1,433 specimens of the terrapin *Malaclemys* [167]. Further work is needed before the significance of this interesting discrepancy can be understood. A sex ratio which is heavily biased in favour of the females may suggest that some of the population are reproducing parthenogenetically, like the Caucasian rock lizards described later (p. 456).

Hybridisation

Hybridisation between related species or subspecies of reptiles such as the tortoises *Testudo marginata* and *T. graeca* and the adders *Vipera berus* and *V. ammodytes* has been recorded in captivity and there is much evidence that it occurs from time to time in the wild [279].

Courtship, breeding and territorial behaviour

Mating in reptiles is generally preceded by some form of courtship, and in some species there is much rivalry between the males who occupy and defend areas or territory like many other animals such as birds and some mammals. In the wild these activities are, as a rule, confined to the breeding season, which may be defined as the period during which courtship, mating, egg-laying and embryonic development occur, and which ends with the hatching or birth of the young.

Gilbert White [456] gave a nice description of the courtship of his tortoises in his garden at Selborne, the male walking on tiptoe; his fancy intent on sexual attachments, 'which transport him beyond his usual gravity, and induce him to forget for a time his ordinary solemn deportment'. More recent accounts suggest that the male conducts his affair in a somewhat aggressive fashion, chasing the female about, butting the hinder part of her shell with the front of his carapace, and biting at her legs. Such behaviour is often difficult to distinguish from fighting between two males, or between individuals of different species, which has often been observed in captivity. Immediately before copulation the male mounts the carapace of the female (Plate 56), sometimes gripping the front of it with his claws and biting her neck. Finally, he pushes his tail region down towards that of the female, behind the back of her shell, so that intromission of the penis can take place. In the box tortoises *(Terrapene)* the tail is very short, and in order to achieve coitus the male has to assume an almost vertical position, perched on the rear of the female's shell with his large hind claws hooked between the carapace and the movable posterior lobe of the female's plastron (figure 124). The female helps to maintain his precarious balance by pressing her hind legs inwards, against the ankles of the male.

In some species, such as the giant *Testudo elephantopus* of the Galapagos, the male heralds his approach to the female by nodding movements of his head rather like those of lizards, and the sexual act is preceded or accompanied by the emission of sounds by the male. These vary from the low-pitched roar of the Galapagos giant to the thin high shriek which D. H. Lawrence has described in his poems on the mating of one of the European species [247].

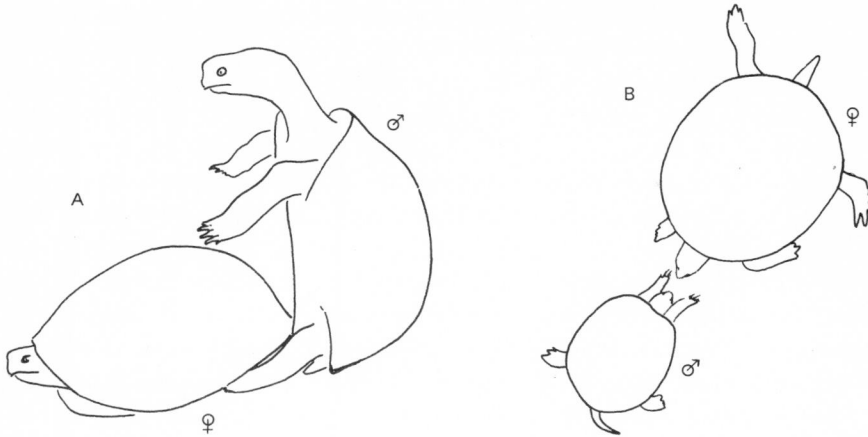

Figure 124   A. Mating posture of box turtle, *Terrapene carolina carolina*.
B. Courtship of red-eared terrapin, *Pseudemys scripta elegans*. The male swims
backwards in front of the much larger female, 'titillating' her face with his long
front claws. After Oliver, J. A. (Copyright 1955) *The Natural History of North
American Amphibians and Reptiles*. Princeton, New Jersey, D. Van Nostrand
Company, Inc. A, modified from L. T. Evans; B, modified from F. R. Cagle.

Freshwater and marine chelonians mate in the water, and in some
species there are quite elaborate patterns of courtship. Courting
couples of the red-eared and western painted terrapins *(Pseudemys
scripta elegans* and *Chrysemys picta bellii)*, for example, perform a
curious aquatic parade, the male swimming backwards in front of the
female with his nose about an inch apart from hers (figure 124). At the
same time the male extends his front legs and tickles the chin of the
female with his elongated front claws, back-paddling with his hind
legs to maintain his progress [89]. Eventually the female sinks to the
bottom and the male swims on to her back and assumes the conventional coital position of chelonians, with his claws gripping the rim
of her carapace. Copulation may continue for an hour or more.

There is evidence that some tortoises show territorial behaviour
and in captivity a kind of peck-order has been observed among
individuals of certain species. It is still uncertain, however, how far
these activities are related to sexual behaviour, and indeed, there is
certainly much to be learnt about the social customs of chelonians.

Our knowledge of the mating habits of crocodilians is almost
confined to the American alligator and the Nile crocodile. During
the breeding season the males become very pugnacious and inflict

395

severe injuries on each other which sometimes result in death. Some vicious and unprovoked attacks by Nile crocodiles on small motor boats have been recorded; it has been suggested that the reptiles, perhaps incensed by the noise of the outboard motor, were acting in defence of territory. Crocodiles are known to defend their basking sites and other areas both during and outside the breeding season. In some of these attacks the crocodiles were surprised on the bank and then plunged into the water and made straight for the boat in a flurry of spray with their jaws opening and shutting. In other cases the attack began when the crocodile was already in the water. An account by two American zoologists of their encounter with a huge crocodile when they were crossing a lake in Northern Rhodesia in a small dinghy is one of the most thrilling pieces of writing in the annals of herpetology. The authors eventually had to swim for the shore, while the crocodile fortunately concentrated its attention on savaging their damaged boat [349].

Vocalisation, especially at night, is another feature of crocodilian breeding behaviour. The roar of the bull alligator is (or formerly was) well known in the swamplands of the southern USA and the noise of one individual seems to act as a stimulus to other males nearby who start up in turn until the whole wilderness is echoing. Roaring can be evoked on captive males by various sounds which may resemble those made by a rival bull. An alligator will sometimes advance in a menacing fashion towards the source of the noise with the back arched and the body held high off the ground, as if he suspected a rival and was looking for trouble [23].

Cott [119] describes two types of sound made by bull crocodiles during the breeding season. One is an abrupt bark or cough often emitted when the reptile is basking. The other is a deep rumbling roar, 'like distant thunder' made with the head raised and the jaws wide open. Cott believes that the roar is made to attract females rather than as a challenge to rivals. Female crocodiles seem to be much less vocal than their mates but are said also to have a mating call – a growling roar quite distinct from that of the bull.

Copulation takes place in the water and has seldom been witnessed, although Cott describes a kind of pre-nuptial display in which the female Nile crocodile rears up out of the water with gaping jaws pointed to the sky. Burrage [81] has recently given a short but careful account of mating in a pair of captive alligators. The bull caressed the back of the female's head with his own head for several minutes and then mounted her body which she had, cooperatively, submerged. He then depressed his tail and protruded his penis externally so that it could enter the cloaca of the female. Coitus lasted for fifteen minutes.

Perhaps the most highly developed forms of courtship and territorial behaviour in reptiles are found among certain agamid and iguanid lizards. V. A. Harris has recently described the natural history of the rainbow lizard *(Agama agama)* in Nigeria; his fascinating book [213] contains one of the most thorough accounts of reptilian social life in the literature, and is based on several years' observation of these colourful reptiles in their acquired habitat among the campus buildings of Ibadan University. One of his first problems was to find methods of identifying individuals; paint marks on the thighs which could be recognised through binoculars usually lasted long enough to be useful. For more permanent recognition he photographed the colour pattern beneath the throat, which is almost as characteristic as a human finger-print. It was, of course, necessary to catch the lizards before this pattern could be examined.

In this locality, the rainbow lizards breed throughout a good deal of the year, and the males occupy territories during the breeding period. Each territory consists of a fairly circumscribed area, such as a wood-pile, which must possess certain amenities. One or two display posts, tree-stumps for example, are needed on which the male can pose in his conspicuous breeding colouration. There should also be suitable shelters against attacks of birds of prey and other enemies, and a tree nearby for roosting at night; territorial competition ceases during the hours of darkness and rivals from adjacent territories can sleep in peace on the same roost.

Each adult male or 'cock' lizard shares his territory with one or more of the duller coloured females, and sometimes with several young. The females tend to stay around the same territory with the same mate for considerable periods, sometimes throughout a whole breeding season, but stray from it at various times, as for instance when they lay their eggs. If another male approaches the resident cock immediately challenges him and tries to drive him away.

Harris has described a range of gestures which are used in the appropriate situations by these gregarious agamas (figure 125). When a cock is confronted by a rival he distends his gular fold (which is of modest size as compared with that of certain other lizards such as *Anolis)*, and raises his head and fore-quarters up and down on his front legs several times in a manner suggestive of the human gymnastic exercise of 'press-ups'. If the intruder holds his ground he is treated to a more threatening type of gesture in which the resident lizard raises his whole body up and down on all four legs, instead of the front pair only, with his gular fold fully extended. This threat is accompanied by fairly rapid pigmentary colour change; *Agama* has no means of producing 'flash' colour effects, like those of the throat-fan of *Anolis*. The head of the threatening cock changes from orange to dark brown, while his body becomes a paler bluish-grey. The same colour change may occur when the lizard is frightened by an enemy.

This performance is sometimes adequate to daunt the intruder who turns tail and allows himself to be chased off the territory. If he stands his ground, however, a real fight begins. The method of fighting between cock lizards is quite characteristic. They stand side by side, but with their heads facing in opposite directions and their jaws open, and lash out at each other with their tails until one is knocked over and runs away. The victor either retains or usurps the territory and the females which go with it. Portions of tail may get broken off in these combats, despite the fact that the tail of *Agama* is not fragile and has no fracture planes (p. 500). The jaws may also be broken or dislocated by the lashing strokes. Such injuries are seldom fatal, however, and the rivals do not try to bite each other with their sharp teeth. The female agamas, in contrast, are much more vicious and have no compunction about snapping at each other when they fight together. They are also status-conscious and have a hierarchy or peck-order of their own.

Challenge and threat display are only used by males towards other males, and, as in polite human society, males only fight males and females only fight females. The young are generally ignored by adults of both sexes. The male uses a different type of greeting when he is courting a female; this is called the head 'bob', and it resembles challenge display except that the 'press-ups' are slowly and deliberately carried out and the gular fold is not extended. It frequently terminates in the act of mating, which is similar to that in lizards generally. The male mounts the back of the female, and usually seizes her by the neck with his jaws. He then twists his tail beneath hers and inserts one or other of his hemipenes; probably the organ on the side nearest to the female is used.

Yet another kind of gesture involving nodding of the head only is made by rainbow lizards to each other, irrespective of sex or age.

Figure 125   Social behaviour in lizards. A. Ritual combat of male Galapagos sea
iguana (*Amblyrhynchus cristatus*). After photos in Eibl-Eibesfeldt [154]. B–E.
Rainbow lizard (*Agama agama*), after Harris [213]. B: the male is in an alert
posture about to give a courtship bob; the female is in the mating posture with tail
raised. C: male in threat posture and about to attack a rival. D: head bobbing, as
performed by male at beginning of courtship. The male makes a similar type of
gesture when challenging another, except that in challenge the throat-fan is
lowered as in threat posture. Females also show challenge and threat postures
towards other members of their own sex. E, the head nod, a group response of
uncertain significance. F. Pre-coital posture of sand lizard (*Lacerta agilis*). From
Smith [395] after Kitzler.

This head 'nod' (figure 125 E) seems to be unrelated to reproductive activity but may have some significance in group orientation, rendering each individual conspicuous to its fellows like a raised hand at a meeting.

It has been suggested that the role of the female is purely a passive one in lizard courtship. This may be true in some species, but it is not so in *Agama agama*. Female rainbow lizards posture actively in front of the male, turning from side to side with jerky steps, arched back and tail raised in the air. To the human observer such behaviour looks as if it is meant to arouse the male's interest, and often elicits the appropriate mating response from him. Sometimes, however, the male turns away to guard his territory, and on other occasions the female will not allow the male to catch her, despite her provocative behaviour.

There is some evidence that the female rainbow lizard actually seeks out her mate in the first instance, and moves in on him and his territory. Harris suggests that one of the main functions of territorial behaviour is to provide a stable background for reproductive activity and to strengthen the sexual bond between male and female. Other workers, however, have seen the significance of territory in a different light. Wynne-Edwards [469] has discussed the problem very fully in a book of far-ranging scholarship – though he deals with reptiles only to a limited extent. He believes that many species have built-in homeostatic mechanisms for adjusting the numbers of their populations to the natural resources available. Territorial behaviour and its accompanying manifestations of competitive display are among the most important methods of achieving this object; they tend to maintain the populations inhabiting a particular area at the optimal density, and also promote the dispersal of excess individuals to wider pastures.

Experiments with models have shown that sex recognition in the rainbow lizard is primarily visual and depends upon the ability to discriminate certain combinations of colour and movement in its fellows. These qualities act as stimulants or 'releasers', to use a current term in animal behaviour studies, which trigger off the appropriate reaction of one individual to another. Colour seems to be the most important factor, while gesture, rather surprisingly, plays a subsidiary part. Thus, models painted to resemble males were challenged and threatened by other males even when they did not move. The same response was made to living females painted up in male colours. Furthermore, movable models which could be made to bob up and down in characteristic male fashion were only challenged if they were given the appropriate male colouring. The females also seem to recognise their mates by colour.

Recognition of the females by the males, however, depends to a greater extent on movement, the female assuming her mating posture in the presence of the male only. This enables him to distinguish between females and the similarly coloured immature lizards which are too young to display mating or challenge gestures. In certain other species movement may be the principal factor in sex-recognition; in *Agama sankoranica*, for instance, the adult males and females are always much the same colour, but the female postures in the same way as in *A. agama*.

Similar patterns of breeding behaviour have been described in other agamid and iguanid species by many herpetologists. In the north American *Anolis* lizards, rapid extension of the huge throat-fan which flashes bright pink as its skin is stretched (see figure 92), p. 298) is a prominent feature of both challenge and threat display. The males of the flying lizards (*Draco*) use their brightly coloured wings as well as their throat-fans in the same fashion as they run among the branches or glide through the air. Territorial behaviour is well developed in some of the big iguanas such as the marine *Amblyrhynchus* of the Galapagos [154]. The males fight to defend small areas of beach and their combats have a curiously ceremonial character, like the jousts of medieval knights (figure 125). Each individual tries to overthrow the other by doughty butts of his head, and as in fights between male rainbow lizards, the formidable teeth are seldom if ever used. In some forms, such as the Mexican iguana *Ctenosaura*, territorial behaviour is complicated by a kind of peck-order, one male in a colony being dominant over all the others. Although the males defend their territories against each other, they allow the tyrant male to patrol them all.

Elaborate social behaviour might be expected in chamaeleons since they belong to the same group, the Iguania, as the agamids and iguanids. Bustard's studies on captive specimens show that this is indeed so, at least in certain species [83], and his account of a colony of *Chamaeleo hohnelii*, a small viviparous species from Kenya, is reminiscent of Harris' observations on the rainbow lizard. Male chamaeleons in their bright blue and yellow colour phase soon acquire territories in the vivarium and attack any rivals which encroach on them. The resident chamaeleon is nearly always the winner in these contests which consist largely of bluff and threat display and futile attempts to nip each others' flanks. After several minutes the invading male gives up despite the fact that he is normally quite unharmed, and signals his defeat by changing to a drab greyish-brown. Males begin to court the females with a series of rapid backward jerks of the head, corresponding with the head bobs of *Agama,* but the reactions of the females are much more aggressive. It is interesting that there are certain 'bully females' in a colony, which resemble males in colour and appearance (ie in the shape and the casque) and are particularly combative in their behaviour. Chamaeleons have their own form of nuptial embrace in which the male climbs on to the back of the female and grips her round the body with all his four prehensile limbs, his front pair behind her neck and his back pair in front of her hind legs.

Territorial behaviour is known or suspected to occur among other groups of lizards, but much less is known about it. The customs of geckos, in particular, would repay study for many species are gregarious and live in places such as crevices in walls or buildings which might lend themselves to territorial activity. Moreover, many kinds of geckos seem to have some form of verbal communication; the cheeping and clicking sounds which they make are familiar to anyone who has been used to taking an evening drink on his verandah in the tropics. The little ground-living geckos of the Kalahari in South-West Africa aptly named *Ptenopus garrulus* emerge from their holes in the sand just before sunset and being a chirping chorus which ceases abruptly when darkness falls. The significance of these gecko noises is not understood, but it is probable that they represent some form of group display or act as releasers in territorial and courtship behaviour, like the gestures of the rainbow lizard and its relatives. Arching of the back is used as a form of display by male geckos of some species [84].

Male monitor lizards *(Varanus)* sometimes indulge in spectacular contests, the rivals rearing up and grappling with each other with their front legs until one is pushed over and allows himself to be chased away (figure 126). After such a combat the backs of the pair are bleeding from each other's claws but the teeth are not used in earnest [137]. Such contests between a couple of seven foot-perenties *(Varanus giganteus),* the largest and most powerful of Australian monitors, must indeed be worth watching.

Figure 126   A. Male monitor lizards (*Varanus bengalensis*) in ritualistic combat.
Drawn from a photo by R. Y. Deraniyagala [137]. B. Combat posture of male
rattlesnakes (eg *Crotalus atrox*). C. Lyre-shaped combat posture supposedly
assumed by male Aesculapian snakes (*Elaphe longissima*) – possibly the prototype
of the medical caduceus emblem. This posture seems unusual among colubrid
snakes; other species seldom elevate their heads in combat. D. Characteristic
combat posture of many male colubrids. B, C and D after Bogert and Roth [54]
and other authors. E. Courtship phase of king cobra, *Ophiophagus hannah*, as
observed in the New York Zoological Park. Drawn from a photo in Oliver [305].

403

Male lacertids such as the sand lizard *(Lacerta agilis)* also threaten and fight with each other at the beginning of the breeding season. Lacertid lizards can sometimes be seen to raise the fore-feet and vibrate them rapidly; this has been interpreted as a submissive gesture by females in the presence of the male [258]. Male rivalry has also been described in slow-worms, which bite and scar one another with their teeth. In the act of mating the male seizes the female by the head or neck and the pair, sometimes with jaws interlocked and bodies entwined, may remain together for several hours. It is sometime stated that the mating behaviour of legless lizards is essentially lizard-like rather than snake-like, but it is unwise to generalise until more is known about other species.

Snakes are not known with certainty to defend territories, although individuals of some species may patrol particular localities or 'home ranges' in which they reside for long periods. Male snakes of many kinds, however, such as rattlesnakes, copperheads, vipers, mambas and various colubrids indulge in ritualistic combats in which no serious damage seems to be inflicted [54]. They entwine their bodies in a characteristic fashion and in some cases rear up and push against each other until one of the pair becomes exhausted and glides away. Males of the handsome Aesculapian snake *(Elaphe longissima)* of southern Europe assume a lyre-shaped posture (figure 126) which perhaps formed the model of some versions of the caduceus; this was the snaky emblem of Aesculapius, the ancient Greek god of healing, and has become the badge of medical institutions in many civilised countries.

People who have been lucky enough to witness one of these performances in the wild have generally regarded them as courtship dances performed by male and female, and it is possible that certain phases of courtship and combat look rather similar, at least in some species. Nevertheless, whenever it has been possible to determine the sexes of the pair they have always, or almost always turned out to be males, usually of the same species but occasionally of related species or genera. Although it is possible that some of these displays may have been prompted by competition for food, or even be manifestations of homosexual behaviour, they can be more reasonably interpreted as exhibitions of rivalry which take place in association with mating. In some instances a female has been seen resting nearby and has been courted by the victorious male after he has put his rival to flight.

These contests seem to be comparable with the jousts between male lizards, and the posture of rival rattlesnakes and other snakes which rear up when fighting is reminiscent of the stand-up pseudo-combats between male monitor lizards. One wonders if this could be another of those rather numerous resemblances in form and habit which have led to the idea that there was a special relationship between the snakes and the Varanidae.

Although snakes do not appear to have the same range of social gestures as certain lizards, a curious type of behaviour which is sometimes called 'head-bobbing' may occur in some species such as the cottonmouth moccasin. It does not resemble the head-bobbing of lizards but consists of jerky contractions of the front part of the body. It may be elicited when the snake is excited, especially by the movements of another individual, and perhaps also occurs during courtship.

Snakes such as garter snakes and the more northerly species of vipers and rattlesnakes which live in temperate countries sometimes hibernate in communal dens, and when they emerge in the spring they do not have to travel far to find their mates. They sometimes cluster together and begin mating, thus giving rise to stories of 'snake-balls' occasionally recounted by countrymen. Such gregarious mating seldom occurs in tropical species which do not hibernate.

The courtship of snakes has been described in a classical paper by G. K. Noble [298], a pioneer in experimental herpetology. Before mating the male snake often follows the female around, flicking out his tongue and running his head and neck over her body. Such behaviour has been described in the king cobra, the male nudging the extended hood of the female with his snout at the same time [305]. Intertwining of the tails is another feature of courtship, and the male may use his own tail to lift up that of the female, so that the cloacal regions of the pair can be held against each other. In many colubrids such as *Thamnophis* (the garter snake) and *Storeria,* the body of the male is thrown into a series of waves passing from tail to head which may continue for ten minutes or more; this activity appears to precede copulation rather than actually coinciding with the orgasm. In other species such as rattlesnakes the male thrusts or jerks his body instead of undulating it. Male boas and pythons use their rudimentary hind limbs for scratching against the flanks of the female, making a rasping noise which may be audible several feet away. This stimulation apparently persuades the female to move herself into a position where the male can easily twist his tail under hers and insert his hemipenis.

405

Only in a few snakes, such as the smooth snake *(Coronella)* does the male try to bite the female or grip her with his jaws, as many male lizards do. Copulation may be maintained for as long as an hour, or even longer; in captivity, attempts at homosexual mating have some-times been observed.

Some of G. K. Noble's ingenious experiments to test the import-ance of the various sense organs in courtship and mating have already been mentioned (p. 370). He found that male snakes *(Thamnophis* and *Storeria)* were attracted from a distance by the movement of other individuals, and that courting males were not put off even if the backs of the females were dyed a bright purple red, quite a different colour from their normal olive green hues. If a male was blindfolded with caps of adhesive tape it was of course at a disadvantage in locating a female some distance away, but once it had come close to her it had as good a chance of mating with her as a snake with its vision un-impaired.

Interference with the sense of smell had a more drastic effect. For example, either plugging the nostrils with greased tape or collodion or cutting off the tips of the tongue to inactivate the organ of Jacobson (p. 365) usually stopped all courtship behaviour, and control experi-ments seemed to show that this was due to the specific loss of the olfactory sense rather than to any general discomfort caused by the operation. Noble also found that normal males took no interest in females which had been smeared all over with vaseline but were not put off by apparently more unpleasant substances such as picric acid or quinine.

Male snakes can track females by means of smell, using both the nose proper and the organ of Jacobson. It has been suggested that in vipers the scent trail is produced by the pungent secretions of the female's anal glands but Noble found no evidence for this in the colubrid species which he studied. He did discover, however, that a male would readily follow a trail left across a glass plate by rubbing it with a piece of skin from a female's back, and was forced to the rather unexpected conclusion that the skin was leaving some subtle odour despite the fact that it contains no glands in the species which he studied, and seems almost odourless to man.

The sense of touch also proved to be important especially in immediate pre-coital activity. *Thamnophis, Storeria* and their allies are provided with touch-sensitive corpuscles on the labial and mental scales beneath the chin, and in the male *Storeria* there are also tactile organs in the skin around the region of the cloaca. The chin-scale organs of the male are presumably stimulated by the male when he rubs his head along the female's back; if they are artificially covered over the male refused to court. The cloacal tubercle touch organs seem to help the male adjust his posture to the lie of the female's body and copulation cannot take place if they are put out of action.

It would appear from these experiments that the chemical and tactile sense play the paramount part in the sex life of snakes, whereas in lizards the role of vision is more important. Such a difference might be expected if the snakes were in fact derived from burrowing ancestors rather than from typical surface-dwelling lizards like the rainbow lizard which are attracted to their partners primarily by behaviour, shape and colour. Our knowledge of sexual activities in lizards, however, is still largely based on conspicuous, diurnal agamid and iguanid types; the habits of burrowing or secretive species are much more difficult to observe. There is evidence that these animals rely on touch, smell and the Jacobson's organ sense to a much greater degree as guides to social behaviour and sex discrimination; Study of a wider range of species is necessary before one can safely generalise about behaviour in such large and diverse groups of animals.

Breeding cycles and their control

Reptiles, like most other wild animals, usually breed only at certain fixed times in the year. The species which live in temperate regions such as northern America and Europe generally have a single annual breeding season only. In southern England, for example, lizards and snakes mate in April or early May and the young hatch from their eggs or are born in July, August and early September. An interval between the end of hibernation and mating may be necessary to allow the eggs to develop sufficiently in the ovaries before fertilisation.

Some species which normally reproduce every year do so at longer intervals in the colder parts of their geographical range, as determined either by latitude or by altitude. Certain rattlesnakes, for example, probably breed only every other year in the northern areas of their distribution, and the adder *(Vipera berus)* is thought to have a similar, biannual reproductive cycle in Finland and northern Sweden. The North African amphisbaenids of the genera *Trogonophis* and *Blanus,* outlying members of a more or less tropical group, normally appear not to breed every year. These observations refer to the breeding of individual females only and not to the population as a whole, which will naturally contain members at different stages of their reproductive cycles. Such limitations on breeding appear to involve the female sex only; in the males the testes have an annual cycle, producing fertile sperm each year [59, 240, 370, 441].

As one might expect, there is a general tendency for sub-tropical and tropical species to reproduce at more frequent intervals. There may be a second breeding season in the autumn, as in the case of certain reptiles which inhabit the countries round the Mediterranean; indeed autumn matings are reported from time to time in northern Europe [395]. The laying of multiple clutches of eggs per season may occur among chelonians such as the box turtle (*Terrapene*), at least in parts of its geographical range [249]. In the vicinity of New Orleans the green anolis lizard lays a single egg at fortnightly intervals throughout the summer; the eggs are apparently liberated from the right and left ovaries alternately [211]. In southern parts of the United States females of the skink *Lygosoma laterale* produce three or more clutches of one to seven eggs at intervals of about five weeks throughout a breeding season which may last for four months [164].

Of the reptiles which inhabit truly tropical regions, some, such as the Nile crocodile in most parts of East Africa, seem to have fairly definite, circumscribed breeding seasons. In others, however, especially those which inhabit rain forests and other types of environment where the climate is relatively uniform, reproduction continues throughout all or most of the year, though there may be fluctuations in its intensity. The classical example of such a breeding pattern was described in 1947 by J. R. Baker, who studied two species of skinks of the genus *Emoia* living in the New Hebrides (Pacific) where the climate is remarkably stable. Populations of these lizards breed the whole year round but there is a peak period in November and December when the daylight lasts longest, and a minimal period in May and June [13]※.

In some animals the reproductive cycle is controlled mainly by an internal rhythm, a built-in biological time-clock, as it were, such as that responsible for the monthly changes in the reproductive tract of the human female. Little is known about the importance, or even the existence, of such rhythms in reptiles. As we have seen, however, there is much evidence [229, 462] that the breeding of reptiles is largely influenced by the environment, especially by the climate.

Temperature, light and humidity may all be involved, though their relative importance may vary in different species. It is presumably because of low temperature, and perhaps also restriction of daylight, that the eggs of the female adder in the near-Arctic parts of its range require two summers to mature in the ovaries before they are ready to be fertilised. Slight seasonal reductions in the duration of daylight may be responsible for the breeding fluctuations in the skinks which Baker studied in the New Hebrides. In some other tropical reptiles, rainfall seems to be the decisive factor. Cott has shown that in many localities in East Africa the Nile crocodile lays its eggs during the dry season and that the young hatch after the onset of rains when the lakes and rivers are becoming flooded. Another, and indirect way in which climate may affect the breeding of reptiles is by its influence on food-supply. This is apparently the case with some populations of the African lizard *Agama agama* living near Nanyuki in East Africa, almost on the equator, where both temperature and duration of daylight remain stable throughout the year [275]. This reptile is virtually omnivorous and its stomach often contains as much vegetable as animal food remains. The month of April, however, is a period of very heavy rainfall which is followed by an upsurge of insect reproduction. Breeding is timed to coincide with this rich harvest of animal protein and occurs almost exclusively during the four months of the year (June to September) when caterpillars, beetles and other arthropods are most abundant. In view of the great sensitivity of reptiles to their surroundings, it is easy to see how their reproductive patterns may vary from one place to another. This is true not only for different species, but even for races or populations of the same species, such as the adder, which live under different climatic conditions.

It might theoretically be possible to make reptiles breed in the laboratory at any time by providing the appropriate environment. Common lizards (*Lacerta vivipara*), for example, have been induced to mate and produce fertile eggs in mid-winter by keeping them warm, well-lit and plentifully supplied with food [309]. As a rule, however, the embryos failed to develop properly and very few normal young were born. This might indicate that reproduction in these reptiles is to some extent controlled by an inherent rhythm which could not be entirely repressed by controlling the environment. Reptiles are, however, remarkably difficult to keep in the laboratory in a normal state of health and activity, and it is possible that the lizards' failure to reproduce successfully was due to the absence of some unknown but essential factor from their artificial surroundings.

The mechanism by which changes in the environment can somehow be transmitted to the reproductive organs and initiate the breeding cycle is still incompletely understood. Very probably, as in birds and mammals, a part of the fore-brain, the hypothalamus, is involved. This may respond directly to changes in temperature; in an ectothermic animal the temperature of the bloodstream tends to vary with that of the surroundings. Alternatively, the hypothalamus may receive information originally perceived by the sense organs; the eyes, for example, and possibly also the parietal or 'pineal eye' may register the duration and intensity of daylight at different times in the year.

It is then supposed that the hypothalamus releases some kind of stimulus, nervous or chemical, or a combination of both, which acts on the anterior lobe of the pituitary gland lying beneath it. This gland then in turn produces its gonadotrophic hormones, chemical substances which are carried in the blood to the gonads or sex glands, the ovaries or testes, and brings them to a state of activity.

The activity of the gonads must, of course, be timed to occur at the same time of year in the males or females of any population, but it is interesting that this synchronisation is not always complete. As we have seen, the males of some species may be able to breed every year, while the females have a biannual or even triannual cycle. In some tropical and sub-tropical reptiles, the testis has a much longer period of activity than the ovary; the males in fact would be able to breed almost continuously throughout the year, but the females have a more circumscribed period of reproductive activity which naturally limits the actual breeding season of the species.

Removal of the pituitary by means of experimental surgery has been performed on the females of several species of lizards and snakes, but the results of the operation are not always easy to interpret. Ovulation, the liberation of eggs from the ovaries, is apparently prevented, but other effects of the operation, especially during pregnancy, are not easy to interpret. The embryos of *Lacerta vivipara* continue to develop normally after the mother has been subjected to the procedure, but are sometimes retained beyond the usual term, dying *in utero*, or being born dead [309]. Other glands such as the adrenal and thyroid may also be involved in the reproductive cycle although the part which they play is still obscure. In some reptiles

410

they are known to undergo periodic changes which can be correlated with those in the pituitary and gonads, but it is possible that these changes are associated rather with the annual cycle of hibernation and activity than with the specific function of reproduction.

The sex organs

The gonads of both sexes lie in the posterior part of the abdominal cavity, near the kidneys, and are suspended by mesenteries or folds of peritoneum. In snakes and some snake-like lizards they are markedly asymmetrical in position, the right being further forwards than the left (figure 82, p. 256). In certain burrowing snakes, the Typhlopidae, only the right ovary is well developed, the left one together with its oviduct having practically disappeared [175].

The sex glands possess two rather distinct functions. In the first place they act as glands of internal secretion, like the pituitary and thyroid. Their hormones, produced in response to those of the pituitary, provoke the appropriate type of sexual behaviour which leads to courtship and mating, and also induces changes in some of the other reproductive organs, such as the oviduct of the female. The secondary sexual characters may also be affected; the brilliant colouration which some male lizards assume in the breeding season and the activity of the femoral pores (p. 307) are subdued if the animal is castrated. In the male of some species of lizards and snakes parts of the kidneys also respond to sex hormones. Each kidney tubule has a thicker portion known as the sexual segment which is absent in the female and undergoes changes at the beginning of the breeding season. During this period its cells show marked secretory activity and it is possible that their products may help to nourish the sperm, or perhaps alter the viscosity of the seminal fluid so that it flows more readily down the groove in the hemipenis [43].

The other more obvious function of the gonads is, of course, the production of germ cells. The spermatozoa develop from cells in the walls of the seminiferous tubules of the testis and are then carried to the epididymis, an organ consisting of a long coiled tube lying against the testis. The epididymis probably acts as a reservoir of spermatozoa and contains large numbers of them during the mating season. Its cells probably also contribute some special secretion to the seminal fluid, and like those of the gonads they undergo seasonal changes in activity. The epididymis leads in turn into another tube, the vas deferens which carries the sperm back to the cloaca, a complicated chamber through which both germ cells and excretory products must pass before they reach the outside.

It has been shown experimentally in night lizards *(Xantusia)* that the ability of the testes to produce potent sperm is prevented by quite moderate degrees of heat (38°C). Keeping the adult males at this temperature did not appear to affect their general health, but it did render them completely sterile during the period when they were living under these conditions. This has been confirmed by experiments on other species in which parts of the excised testes were kept in tissue culture [252]. Further work on *Uta* lizards has shown that exposure to X-rays also inhibits the production of sperm, much as it does in mammals. Mass irradiation of colonies of these lizards captured and then returned to the wild resulted in a drastic reduction in birth rate, and a striking decrease in the population density a year later. No increase in the number of young born with congenital malformations was observed, however [424].

The eggs are formed from primary germ cells within the ovaries; each consists of a single cell laden with an enormous mass of yolk and is surrounded by a sac known as the follicle which is formed from the surrounding ovarian tissue. The follicles rupture when the eggs have reached a certain size and state of maturity, and the latter are then shed or ovulated into the body cavity. They then normally enter the front ends of the oviducts, which in some species are widened out into funnel-shaped openings called infundibula. Dissection of a reptile at the beginning of the breeding season will generally reveal two types of eggs; comparatively small, immature eggs in the ovaries which will not ripen until the next season, and large mature eggs lying along the inside of each oviduct like a chain of sausages, awaiting their opportunity for fertilisation.

The oviducts, which open behind into each side of the cloaca (figure 87, p. 276), are quite complicated structures and can be differentiated into several regions. Their walls are thinner than those of the mammalian uterus, but contain muscle fibres which force the eggs backwards towards the cloaca, and thread-like cilia whose lashing movements help to carry the sperm in the opposite direction. They also possess many mucous-secreting cells, and more specialised glands which produce the egg-shell and the albumen or white of the egg. In viviparous reptiles a large part of each oviduct is thicker and more muscular than the rest and is modified for the retention and maintenance of the eggs. There is a tendency among those who study the reproduction of these reptiles to call this part of the oviduct the uterus, though it differs from the human uterus in being one of a pair instead of a single structure.

Each ovary normally discharges its eggs into the oviduct of the same side, but in certain turtles and snakes some of the eggs may wander across the body cavity by chance and enter the opposite oviduct; this is also known to occur in mammals. The occasional discovery of eggs in the body cavity which are in the process of absorption or calcification, or which may even contain living embryos, is proof that ovulation does not always proceed according to plan. Possibly such eggs never reached the haven of an oviduct; it is also possible that they entered it and were extruded again, either before or after fertilisation, owing to the contraction waves passing the wrong way along the oviduct muscle. Ectopic pregnancies of a comparable type are well known in human gynaecological practice.

After ovulation, the follicle in the ovary from which each egg was discharged becomes converted into another kind of ductless gland known as the corpus luteum (yellow body) owing to the fact that in mammals yellow pigment is deposited in it. In mammals the secretions of these bodies are necessary for the establishment of pregnancy, and for its maintenance, at least for a while. The function of the corpora lutea in reptiles, however, is by no means understood. Their removal by cutting out the ovaries seems to have little effect on the development of the embryos even in viviparous forms. In *Lacerta vivipara*, however, the operation apparently has much the same result as removing the pituitary gland during pregnancy; the birth of the embryos is either premature or delayed, and they are frequently born dead owing to disturbances of parturition [309].

Fertilisation always takes place internally, the sperms travelling up the oviducts to reach the eggs. The tuatara, the most generalised of modern reptiles, is unique in possessing no male organ of intromission; presumably the sperm is transferred by direct cloacal contact as in many birds, but there is in both sexes a prominent transverse fold within the cloaca which may be protrusible and possibly helps to guide the sperm.

In male chelonians a portion of the floor of the cloaca is modified to form the penis (figure 127). This consists of a flattened shaft of fibrous tissue along the upper surface of which runs two ridges composed of spongy erectile tissue. Between these ridges is the seminal

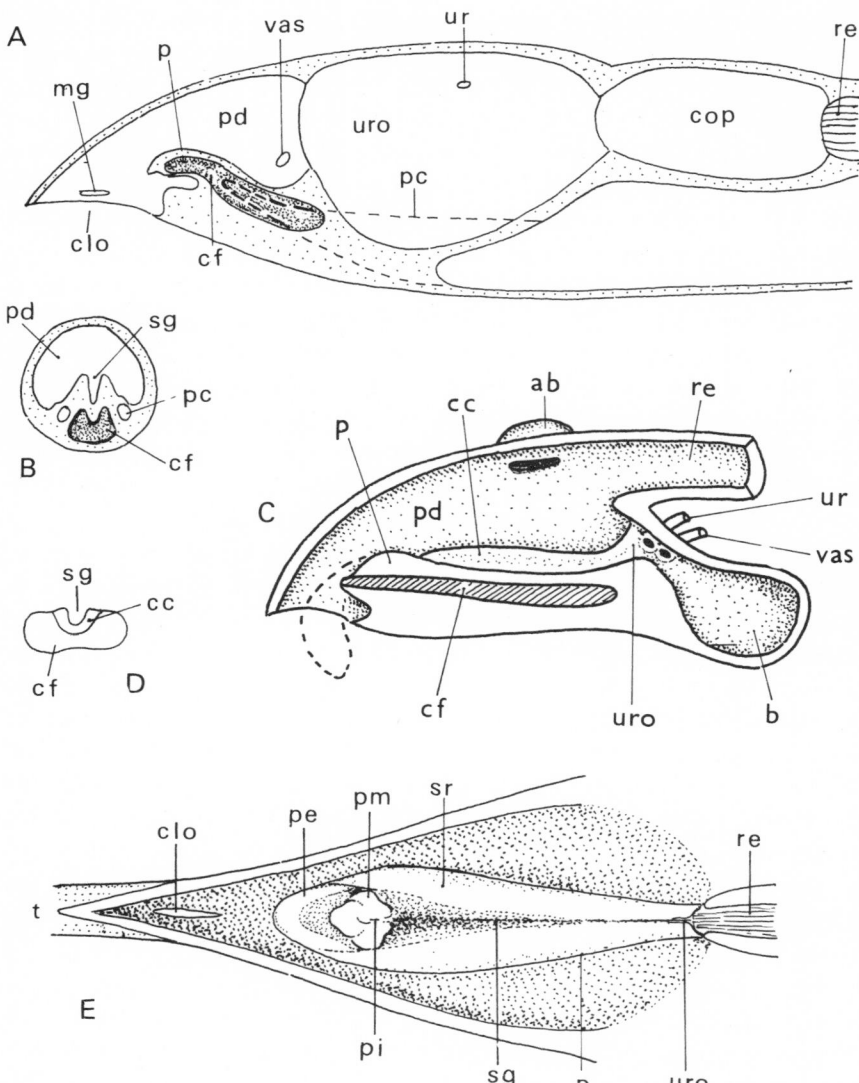

Figure 127   A. Diagram of longitudinal section through cloacal region of
crocodilian, showing penis and position of peritoneal canals. B. Transverse
section through proctodaeal part of cloaca and middle of penis of crocodilian. A
and B after Moens, N. L. (1912) *Morph. Jb.* **44** 1. C. Longitudinal section through
cloacal region of chelonian, showing penis. Outline of erected organ in broken
lines. After Romer [358] and Moens. D. Transverse section through middle part
of penis of chelonian. After Zug [478]. E. Cloaca of *Clemmys leprosa* opened from
above to show penis in dorsal view. After Wood Jones, F. (1915) *J. Anat.* **49** 393.

ab, accessory cloacal bladder. **b**, bladder. **cc**, corpus cavernosum of penis. **cf**, corpus fibrosum. **clo**, cloacal opening (anus). **cop**, coprodaeum. **mg**, opening of musk gland. **p**, penis. **pc**, peritoneal canal. **pd**, proctodaeum. **pe**, **pi**, **pm**, plica externa. interna and media (folds seen on dorsum of terminal part of penis). **re**, rectum. **sg**, seminal groove. **sr**, seminal ridge. **t**, tail. **ur**, ureter. **uro**, urodaeum. **vas**, deferens.

groove which conducts the sperm from the region of the cloaca where it is delivered by the vasa deferentia to the genital tract of the female. The free end of the penis is called the glans and is expanded and complicated by the presence of grooves and folds which vary in pattern among the different families; in fact it has been shown that the form of the penis serves as a valuable guide in chelonian classification [478]. In the female there is a small clitoris which resembles the penis in its basic structure.

The penis is erected by the engorgement of blood vessels within the spongy tissues; this also has the effect of closing the margins of the seminal groove so that it is converted into a canal. When erected, the organ projects obliquely downwards and forwards from the cloacal opening so that in this position the seminal groove faces downwards. It is pulled back into the cloaca by special retractor muscles which originate from the sacral ribs or from the pelvis. A copulatory organ of much the same kind is found in crocodiles (figure 127 A), and it is thought that the penis of certain birds such as the ostrich, and also the mammalian penis, could have been evolved from such a condition.

The Squamata have developed paired copulatory organs of a different type known as hemipenes (figure 128). This rather misleading name is based on the old idea that the two organs had to be pressed together in order to conduct the sperm, or on mistaken observation of species in which each of the hemipenes is very deeply forked. It is now generally agreed that only one hemipenis is used at a time, the choice of right or left being determined by the side which is nearest the female. It has been suggested that these paired organs have been evolved as an adaptation to a type of copulatory posture in which the male twists his tail beneath that of the female from one side. The position of the everted hemipenis, which projects laterally from the cloaca, would be more favourable than that of a single median penis of the type found in other reptiles and in mammals. It may be argued against this idea, however, that alligators are said to

415

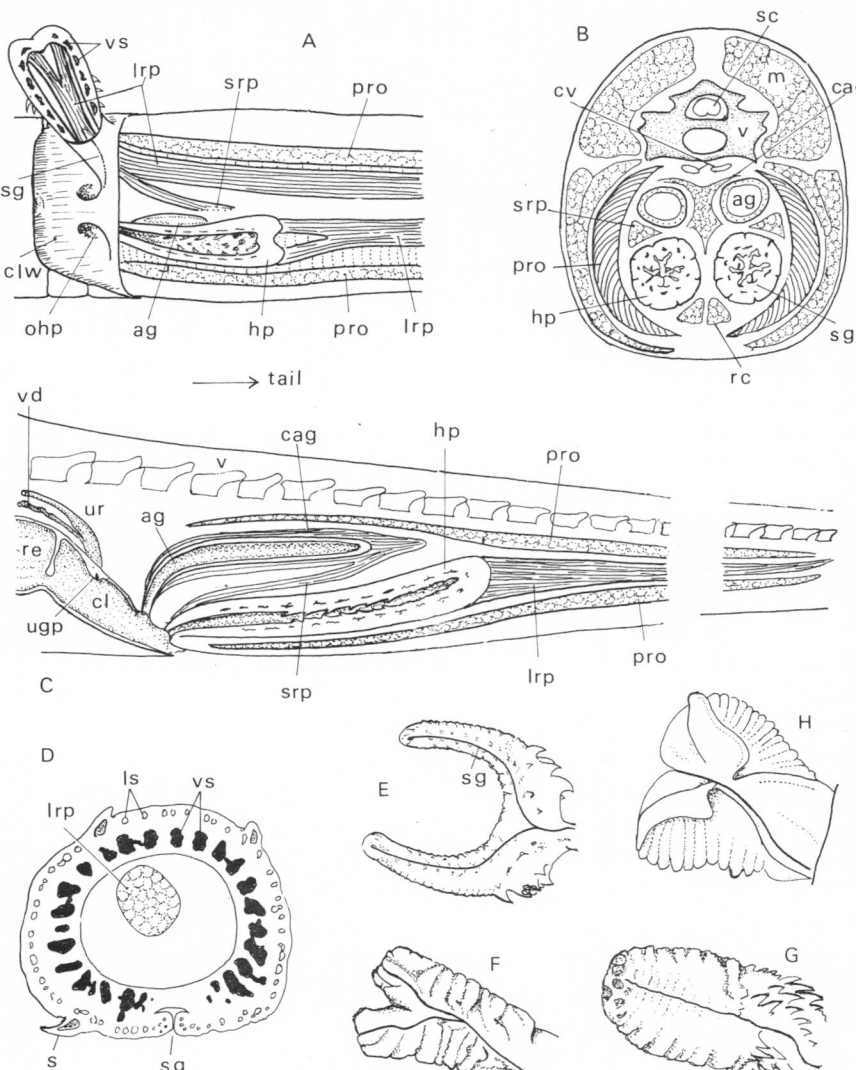

Figure 128   A. Diagrammatic ventral view of hemipenes and their muscles in a snake. The structures are seen in horizontal section with the upper and posterior parts of the cloacal wall left intact. The right (lower in figure) hemipenis is retracted within the tail, with its spines, seminal groove etc on the inside, while the left organ with its venous sinuses engorged and its spines on the outside, is extruded. The hemipenes are shown as being of the bilobed type, with the large retractor muscle forking near its tip.   B. Transverse section through tail of king snake (*Lampropeltis*) showing retracted hemipenis, anal gland, etc.   C. Longitudin-al section slightly to left of midline and passing through left hemipenis and anal

gland of king snake. A section of tail is omitted. D. Transverse section through everted hemipenis of natricine snake. E–H. Ventral views of everted right hemipenes of E, copperhead (*Agkistrodon contortrix*) (bifurcated seminal groove on divided organ furnished with basal spines); F, boa (*Epicrates angulifer*) (flounced, with bifurcated groove); G, colubrid (*Spalerosophis diadema*) (single groove on single organ, with basal spines and calyces or cups at tip); H, sand lizard (*Lacerta agilis*). The form and ornamentation of the hemipenis is highly variable and is valuable as a taxonomic character, especially in snakes. B–G based on Dowling and Savage [144]; H after Smith [395].

ag, anal gland or sac. **cag**, constrictor muscle of anal gland. **cl**, cloaca. **clw**, cloacal wall. **cv**, caudal blood vessels. **hp**, hemipenis. **lrp**, large retractor muscle of hemipenis. **ls**, lymphatic sinus. **m**, dorsal muscles. **ohp**, opening of hemipenial sac. **pro**, propulsor muscle. **rc**, rectus caudae muscle. **re**, rectum. **s**, spine of hemipenis. **sc**, spinal cord. **sg**, seminal groove. **srp**, small retractor muscle of hemipenis. **ugp**, urogenital papilla. **ur**, ureter. **v**, caudal vertebra. **vd**, vas deferens. **vs**, venous sinus.

copulate in much the same fashion as lizards. There are accounts of belly-to-belly union in other species of crocodilians but their reliability is uncertain.

The anatomy and mechanism of the hemipenes has been most thoroughly studied in snakes [144, 441]. When in the retracted state they lie side by side in the front part of the tail behind the cloaca. Each organ is hollow, its cavity opening in front into the side of the cloaca, and ending blindly behind, near the tip of the hemipenis (figure 128). Its wall contains large sinuses for blood and lymph, and is traversed along its inner surface by the seminal groove. In most snakes the large, sausage-shaped anal glands lie above the hemipenes. One or more retractor muscles which originate from the tail vertebrae are attached to the tip and sides of each hemipenis. Both hemipenes with their retractor muscles, as well as the paired anal glands, are surrounded by the large propulsor muscle, which is attached above in the midline to the chevron bones of the caudal vertebrae. Its fibres sweep round in a circular fashion, investing all these organs in a single muscular sheath which extends backwards for some distance, beyond the hemipenes.

Erection and eversion of the hemipenis is brought about by a combination of muscular and vascular action; each organ is supplied by a large vein which can be blocked by a sphincter muscle so that the blood sinuses in the hemipenis become engorged with blood. At the same time the propulsor muscle contracts, squeezing the hemipenis inside out like the finger of a glove, so that the seminal groove is now on its outer surface. Retraction and inversion of the organ is brought about by the retractor muscles, together with relaxation of the venous sphincter. The mechanism is therefore quite different from that of the penis of other reptiles, which can be erected and protruded, but is not turned inside out. The hemipenes of certain Australian blind snakes (Typhlopidae) are exceptional in being solid structures which are presumably erected like the penis of chelonians [see 295]*.

The shape of the hemipenes is extremely variable, especially in snakes (figure 128), and as E. D. Cope showed at the end of the nineteenth century, may be of great value to the systematist as a guide to the relationships of different species and of larger groups [116]. In lizards the organ may be forked, as in *Lacerta agilis* (figure 128 H) or end in a knob-like expansion; its surface is often elaborated by folds or 'flounces', or by the presence of small papillae near the tip. In snakes the hemipenis may be cylindrical, conical, bulbous or corrugated; it may be divided into two lobes, each with its own cavity, or, as in the copperhead and rattlesnakes, very deeply forked. Its surface may also be ornamented with papillae and flounces and in many species it is armed with spines. In one genus of burrowing African colubrids (*Prosymna*) the hemipenes are worm-like and extraordinarily long, almost as long as the tail [8].

Clifford Pope has written an interesting account of the way in which the hemipenis fits inside the cloaca of the female, as observed in a pair of colubrid snakes *(Liophis poecilogyrus)* killed while copulating and preserved without dislodging the male organ [330]. The bilobed shape of the cloaca is well adapted to that of the hemipenis, and each branch of the seminal groove (which is forked in this species) ends in a kind of crater which fits over the orifice of each oviduct. The spines with which the base of the hemipenis is studded anchor it very firmly when it is tumescent; indeed this bond is so strong that male snakes are sometimes dragged about by the larger females during their protracted copulations. The fact that the hemipenis has to be inverted when it is withdrawn prevents injury to the female, since the spiny outer surface of the extended organ becomes the inner surface when it is retracted inside the tail. It has been found, however, that as a general rule, the walls of the female cloaca are thick in species where the hemipenis of the male is spiny, and are thin in species where the hemipenis is devoid of spines. Such differences may occur even in two species of the same genus and perhaps help to prevent hybridisation.

418

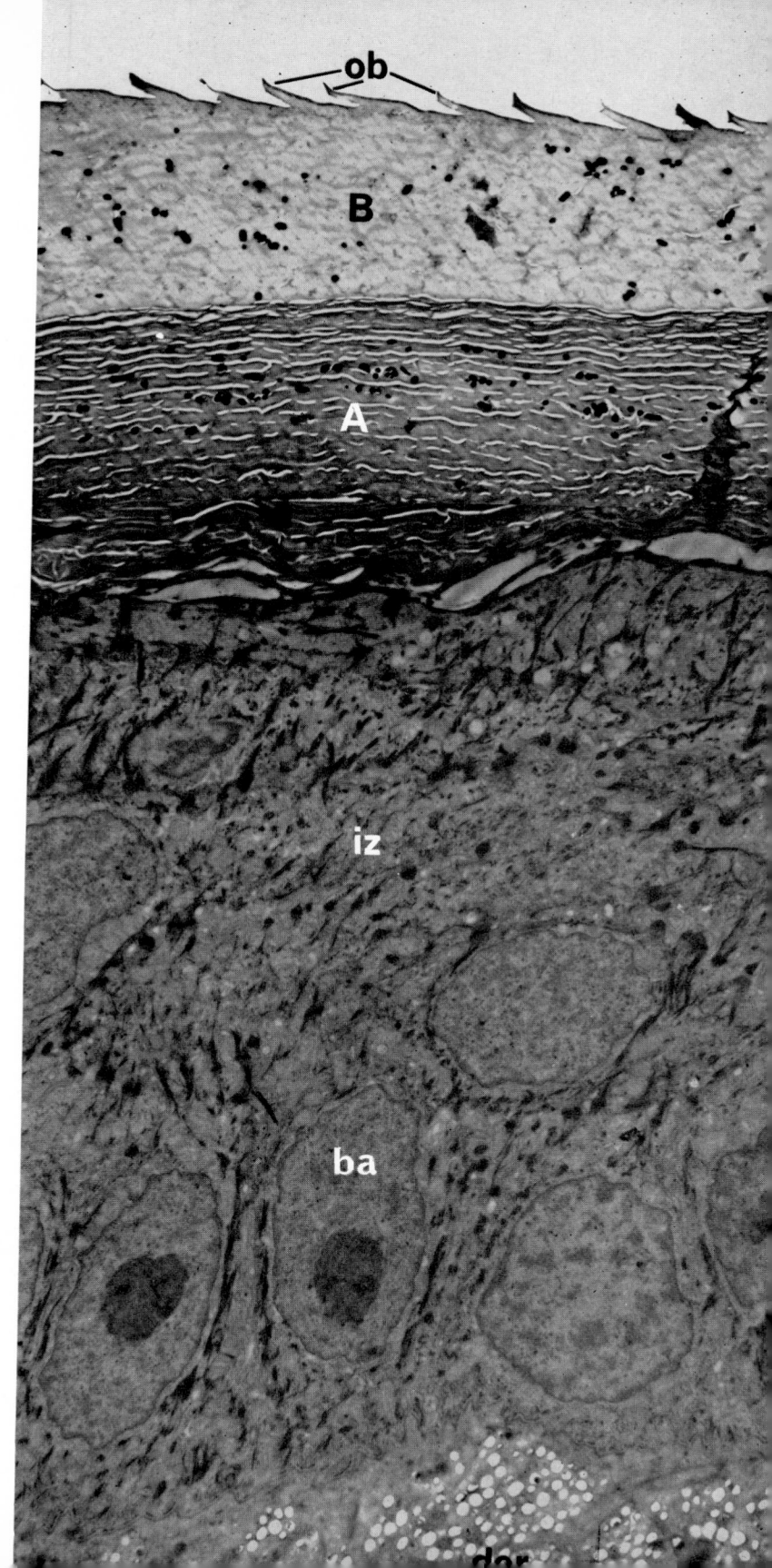

40 Electron
micrograph of
epidermis of tail skin of
the lizard *Lacerta
vivipara* one day after
sloughing. A similar
stage is shown
diagrammatically in Fig.
91A, p. 292. x5,800.
After Bryant *et al.* [76].
A, **B**, A- and B- keratin
layers of horny layer.
ba, basal layer cell.
der, dermis. **iz**,
intermediate zone. **ob**,
serrations of
Oberhautchen.

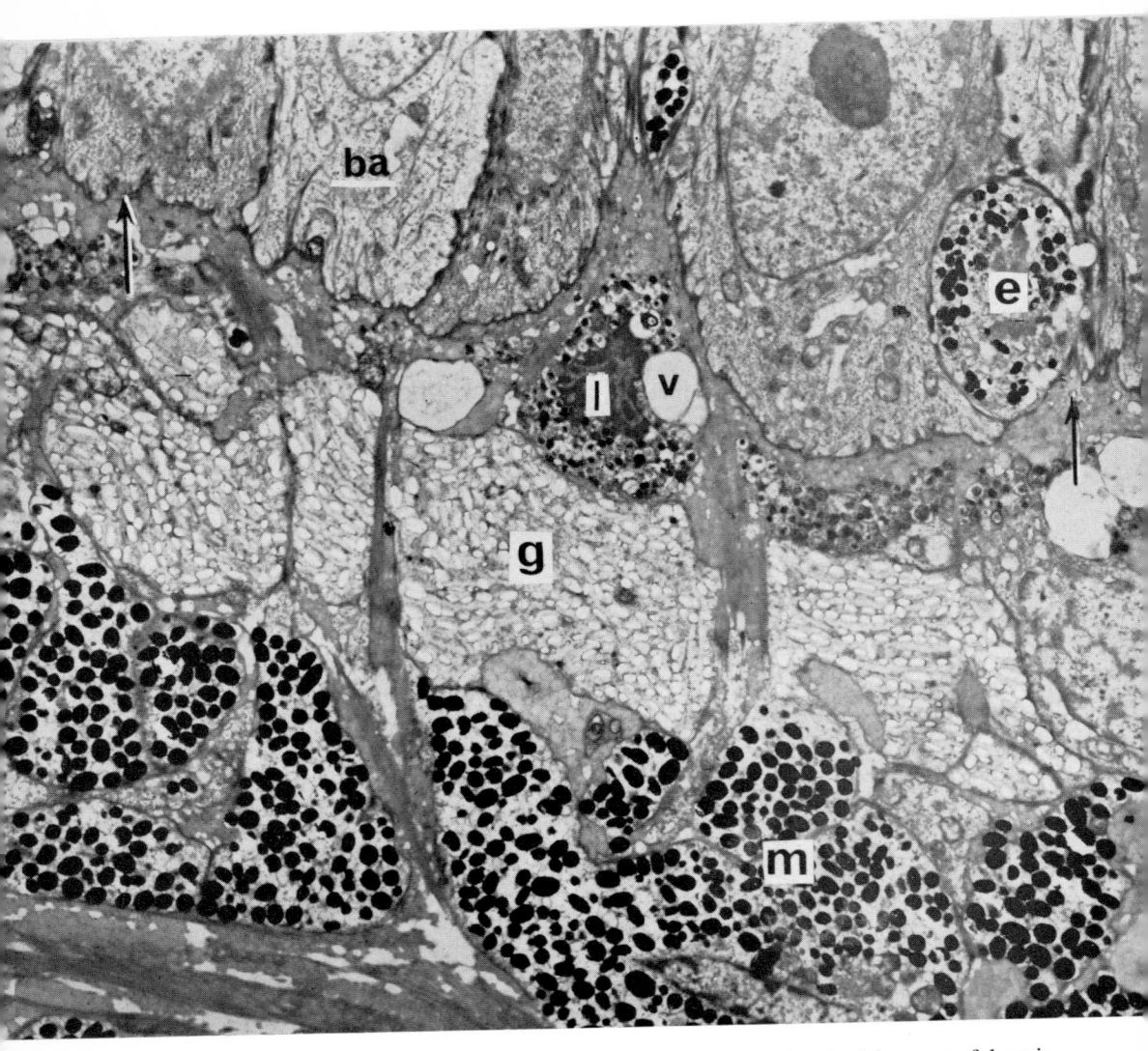

41 Electron micrograph of basal layer of epidermis and underlying part of dermis of tail skin of *Lacerta vivipara*, showing pigment cells. The lipophores (**l**) contain numerous cytoplasmic granules and occasional large vesicles (**v**). The guanophores (**g**) show a honeycomb appearance due to the loss of guanine crystals from the cytoplasm during processing. The dermal melanophores (**m**) are packed with melanin granules; basal layer cells (**ba**) and an epidermal melanocyte (**e**) can also be seen; arrows point to the basal lamina ('basement membrane') of the epidermis. × 5,500. From Breathnach and Poyntz [71].

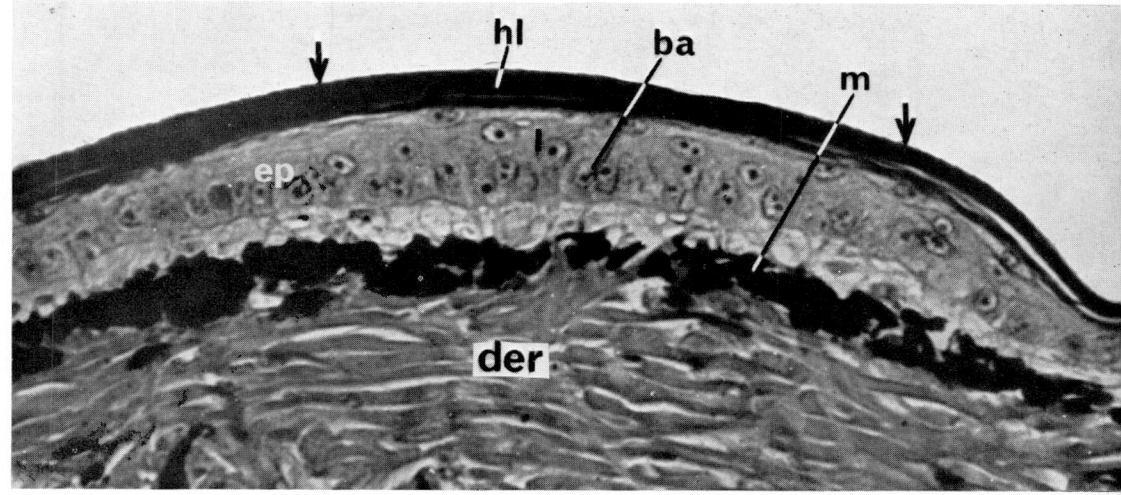

42 Light micrograph of skin of *L. vivipara* showing epidermis (**ep**), dermis (**der**) and horny epidermal layer (**hl**); the latter can be seen on the right to consist of inner and outer keratin layers; × 500. Other abbreviations as in 41.

43 (*Below right*) Scanning electron micrograph showing surface of epidermis of *L. vivipara* with its sculpturings formed by the serrations of the *Oberhautchen*, which here resemble overlapping tiles; × 5,050. 42 and 43 after Bryant *et al.* [76].

44 (*Below left*) Electron micrograph showing blister-like cytoplasmic protrusions (**b**) of basal cells (**ba**) of apical cap, taken from tail regenerate of *L. vivipara* one week after autotomy. The basement membrane (**bm**) is interrupted at the site of these protrusions into the underlying blastema; × 39,000.

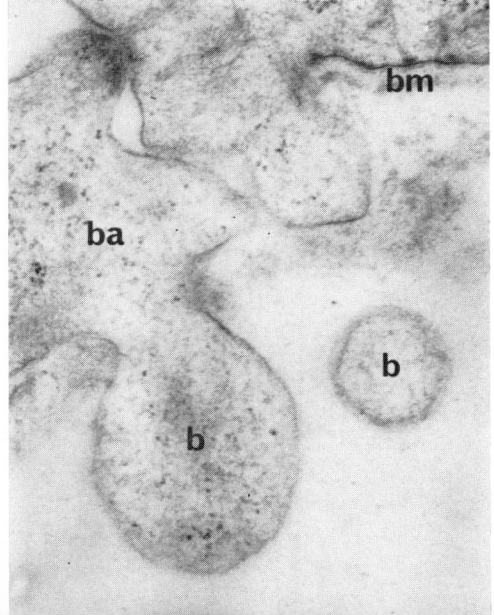

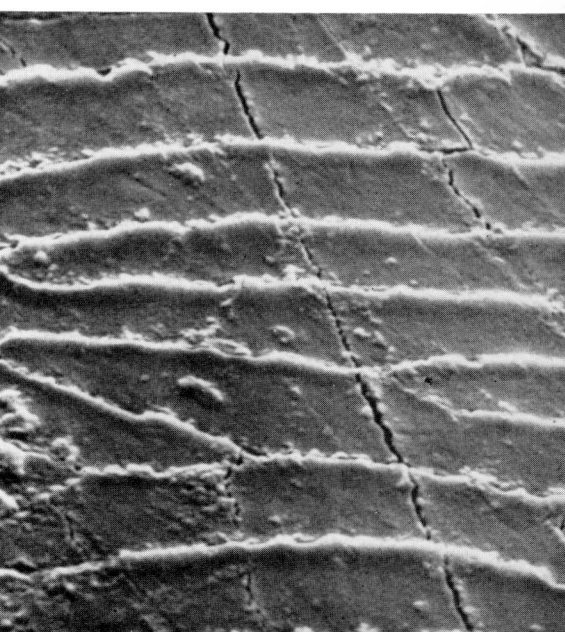

45 Adult male *Iguana iguana rhinolopha* from Mexico in posture assumed when intimidating intruders. The very large dewlap cannot be folded back like the throat-fan of *Anolis* and certain other lizards. This species grows to 1·5 metres (5 ft.).

46 The Australian frilled lizard (*Chlamydosaurus kingi*) gives one of the best-known examples of reptilian threat display. The frill is supported and erected by the hyoid skeleton and its muscles. The acrodont tooth row in the lower jaw is conspicuous. This agamid lizard grows to about 91 cm. (3 ft.) long, the frill being 15 to 25 cm. (6 to 10 in.) across.

47 Two lizards with spiny armour. Both are under 30·5 cm. (1 ft.) in length.
A The armadillo lizard, *Cordylus cataphractus*, from southern Africa.

B The thorny devil, *Moloch horridus*, from desert regions of Australia.

48 This 'piebald' royal python (*Python regius*) measuring 118 cm. (about 46½ in.) in total length (snout-vent, 107: tail, 11: sex, male) shows a very unusual colour abnormality. Pigment appears to be absent over extensive areas, leaving sharply defined regions of normal colouration which are confined to the dorsal surface; the belly is completely white. The snake was killed (1966) in a forest about 100 miles inland from Accra, West Africa, by villagers who wanted it for 'fetish' purposes, but its body was saved by Fr Henry Noordermeer and Mr Jim Landewe. Photo and information from Mr Barry Hughes, Zoology Department, University of Ghana.

49 Eye of the gecko *Ptyodactylus hasselquistii* showing scaly fringe around spectacle and serrated pupil almost closed but leaving pinhole apertures.

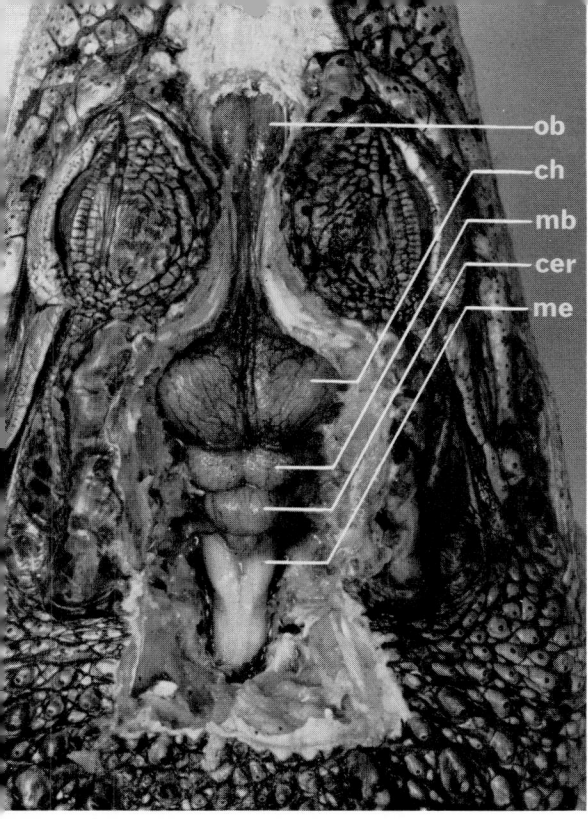
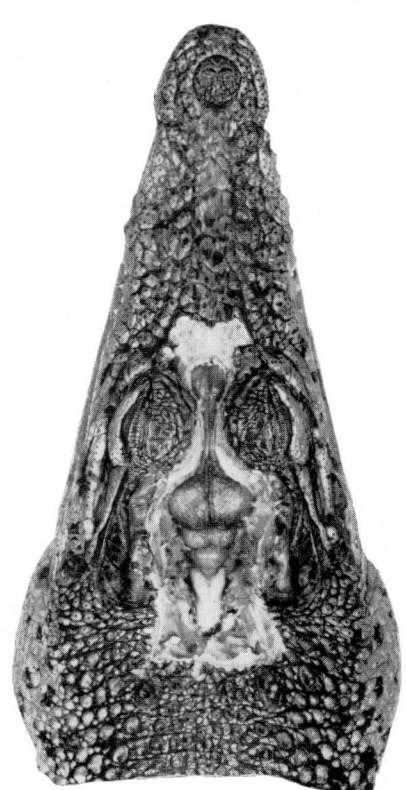

50 Brain of *Crocodylus porosus* exposed from above after removal of skull roof. From its head length (14·5 cm.) this crocodile would have been about 109 cm. (43 in.) long. **cer**, cerebellum. **ch**, cerebral hemisphere. **mb**, mid-brain. **me**, medulla. **ob**, olfactory bulb. ×1·2 and 0·55.

51 Dorsal view of dissected-out brains and spinal cords of (top) tortoise (*Testudo graeca*) and (bottom) slow-worm (*Anguis fragilis*). The brachial and lumbo-sacral enlargements of the cord associated with the nerve plexuses which supply the fore- and hind limbs are present in the tortoise (shown by arrows), but absent in the slow-worm.

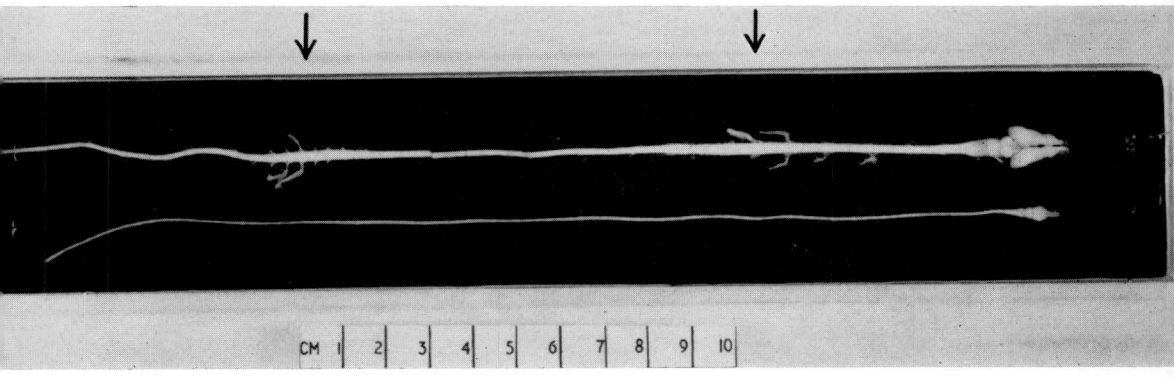

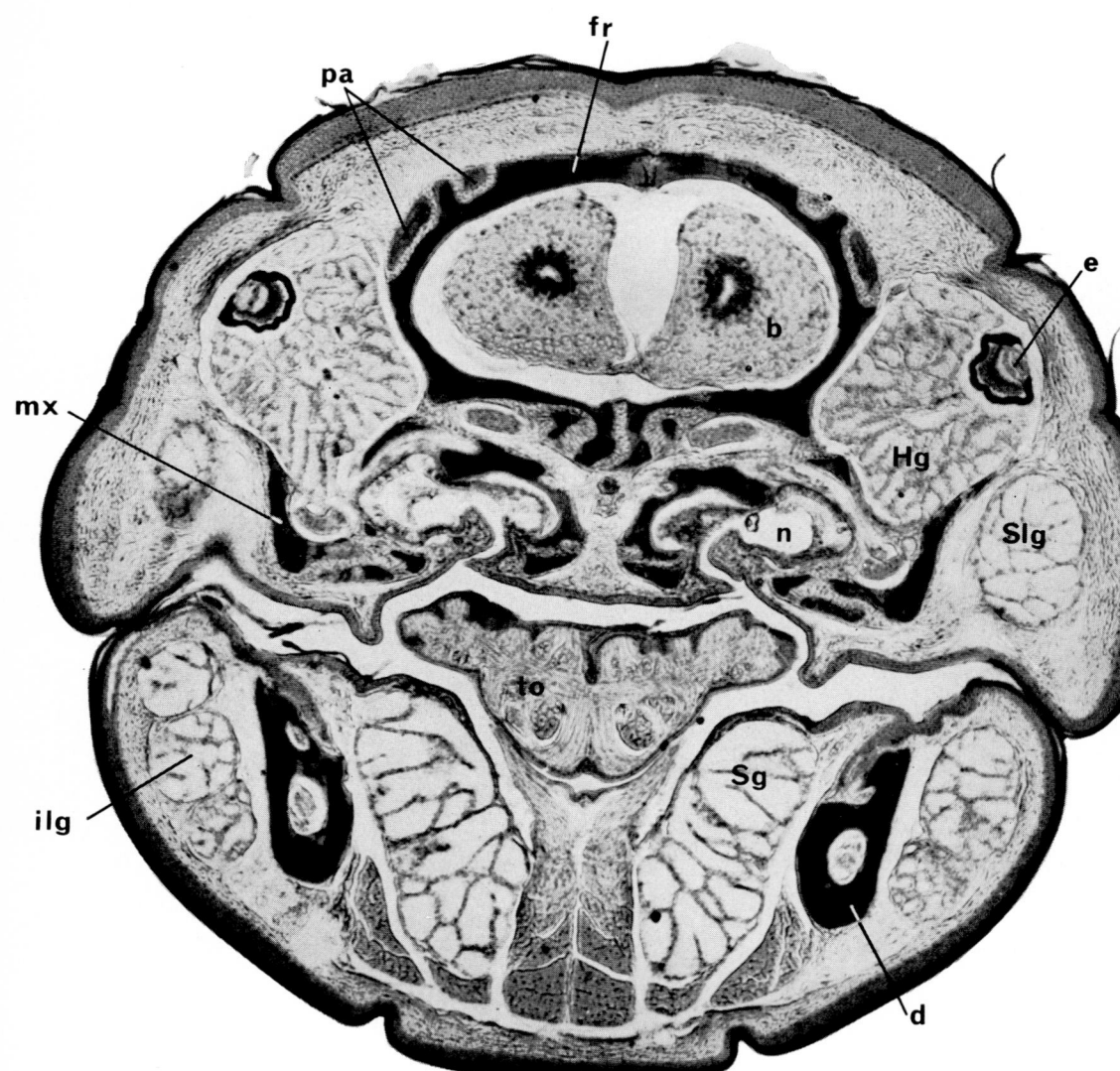

52 Transverse section through head of the African amphisbaenid *Loveridgea
ionidesi* at level of eyes, × 58. Pl. 53 shows eye at higher magnification. The
eyes, imbedded in the huge Harderian gland, are much reduced and covered by a
scale of normal thickness, but have a retina, probably a lens, and a heavily
pigmented outer coat (pigmented layer of retina and/or choroid). The scleral
cartilage and ossicles are absent, at least in this specimen. The amount of
glandular tissue present in this part of the head is very striking. Abbreviations
as for Pl. 53.

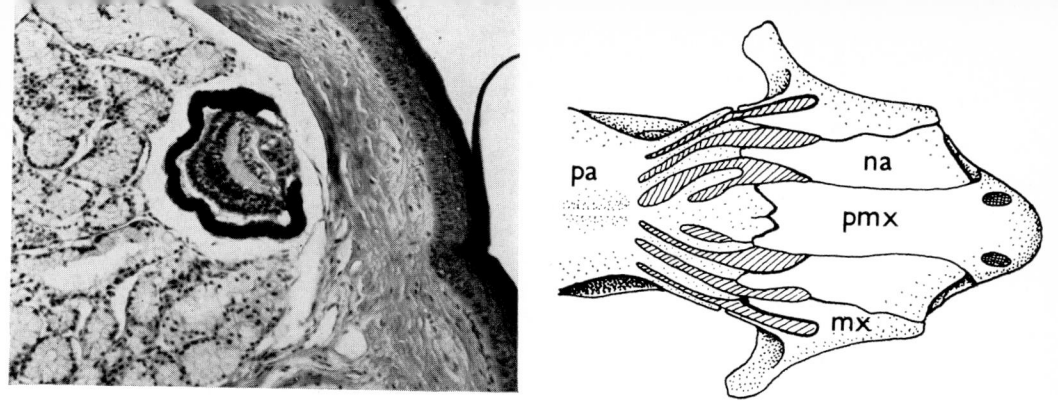

53 *Left:* Eye of *Loveridgea ionidesi*, × 128.

Right: Front part of skull roof of the North African amphisbaenid *Trogonophis wiegmanni*, after Gans [180]. The interlocking sutures are particularly complex in this species and are formed from splinter-like projections of the maxilla, nasal, frontal (in slanting lines), parietal and premaxillary bones. The prefrontal is small and hidden, and the contact between the fused parietals and premaxillae is exceptional among reptiles. × 10·5.

Below: Transverse section through part of head of *Trogonophis* showing the eye, which though very small is better developed than that of *Loveridgea ionidesi*. The lens, retina and scleral cartilage can easily be recognised. The optic nerve and scleral ossicles can also be identified in the section, but unfortunately the material, like that of *Loveridgea*, is not well preserved for microscopic examination. × 72.

b, brain (posterior part of olfactory stalk). **d**, dentary. **e**, eye. **fr**, frontal. **Hg**, Harderian gland. **ilg**, inferior labial gland. **l**, lens. **mx**, maxilla. **n**, nasal cavity (posterior part running into internal nostril). **na**, nasal.

p, eye pigment. **pa**, parietal. **pal**, palatine. **pmx**, premaxilla. **r**, retina. **s**, ossified 'sphenoid' bone. **sc**, scleral cartilage. **sg**, sublingual gland. **slg**, superior labial gland. **t**, fused trabeculae. **to**, tongue.

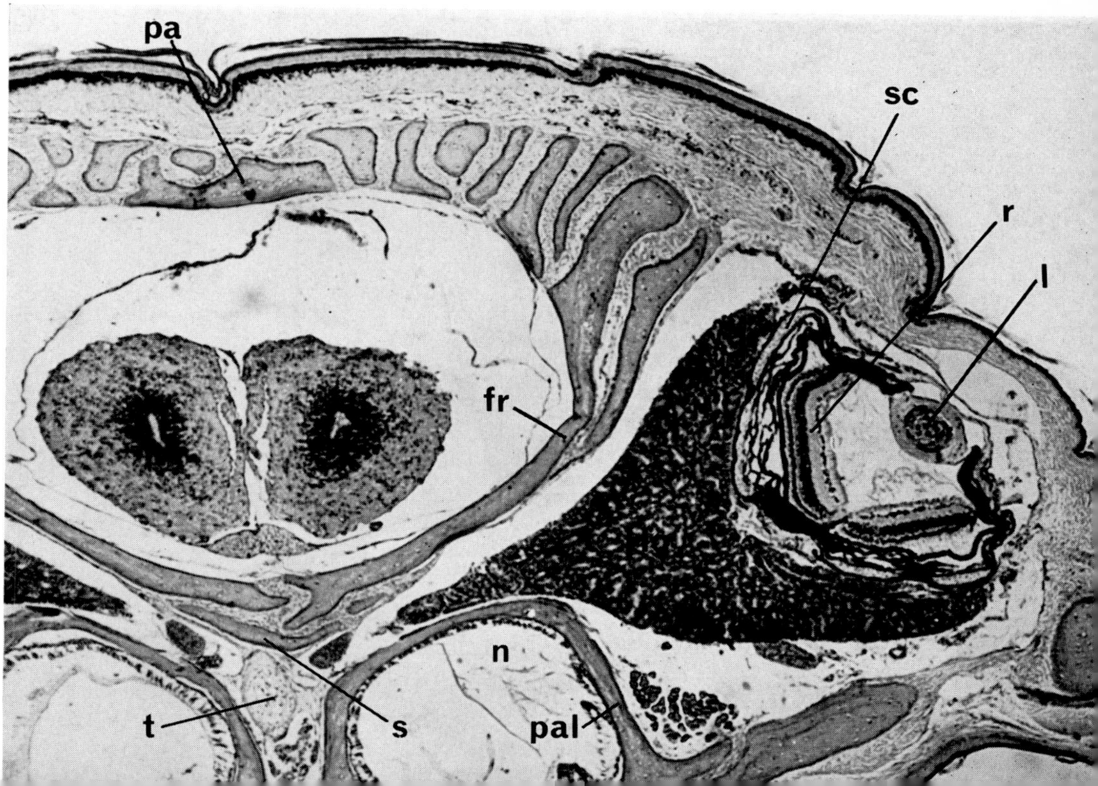

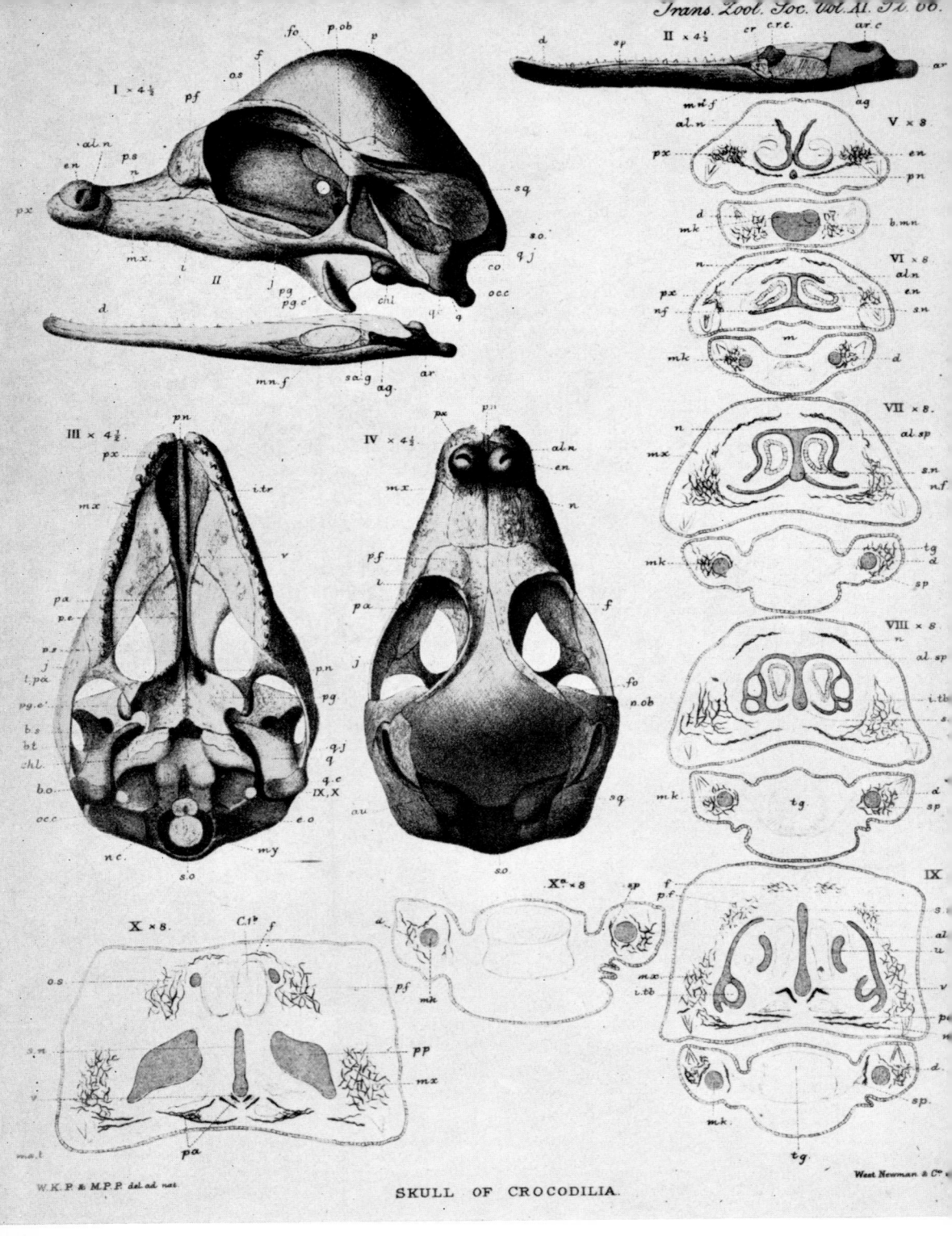

54 Illustration from W. K. Parker's monograph 'On the structure and development of the skull in the Crocodilia' (*Trans. Zool. Soc. Lond.*, 1883, **11**, 263), showing the skull and cross-sections through the snout of late embryos of the alligator. The relative shortness of the snout in the embryo is evident.

55 Transverse section through snout of young sand boa (*Eryx conicus*) from India showing nose (**n**; very front part of olfactory chamber) and Jacobson's organ (**dd**, dorsal dome of; the sensory epithelium contains many blood-vessels). × 43. Abbreviations as for Fig. 117, p. 366.

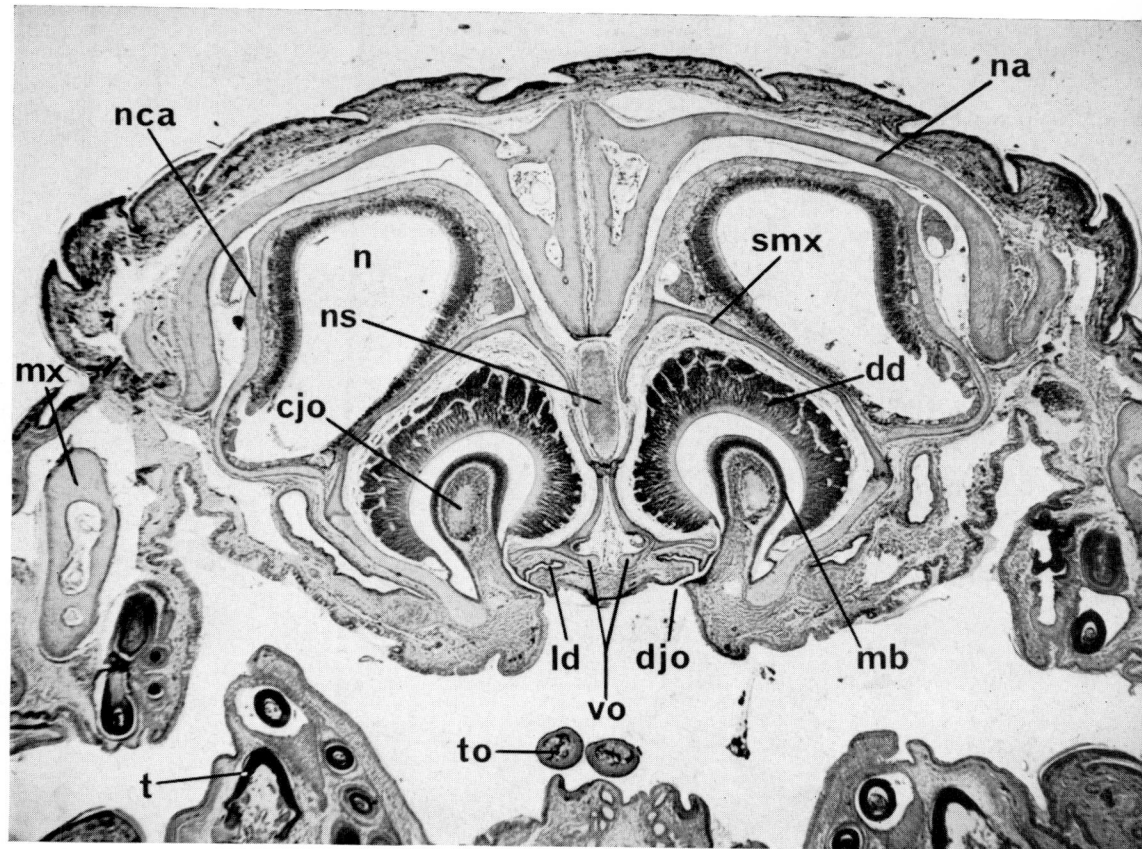

56 Captive giant Galapagos tortoise (*Testudo elephantopus*) about to mate.

57 Leathery turtle (*Dermochelys coriacea*) digging nest.

58 Green turtle (*Chelonia mydas*) digging body pit, and depositing eggs; the egg chamber is nearly full, containing 110 eggs at the moment when the photo was taken.

59 Hatchling green turtles making for the sea after emerging from nest; all face in the same direction.

61 The North American limbless glass lizard *Ophisaurus ventralis* brooding her eggs. After Vinegar [438].

60 Ghost crab (*Ocypode ceratophthalma*) preying on hatchling green turtle. Plates 58–60 taken in northern Australia.

62 Female Nile crocodile in East Africa covering her nest.

63 Dr Hugh Cott with Nile crocodile eggs in nest near Entebbe, Uganda.

64 Hatching of the New Guinea fresh-water crocodile, *Crocodylus novae-guineae*, a little known species.

65 Dissected-out oviduct of common lizard (*Lacerta vivipara*) containing eggs with living embryos; ×4.

66 Gravid slow-worm (*Anguis fragilis*) opened to show eggs in oviducts.

67 Embryo of *Lacerta vivipara* dissected out of its membranes, with chorioallantois and yolk; × 12. The embryo is at Dufaure-Hubert stage 37–38.

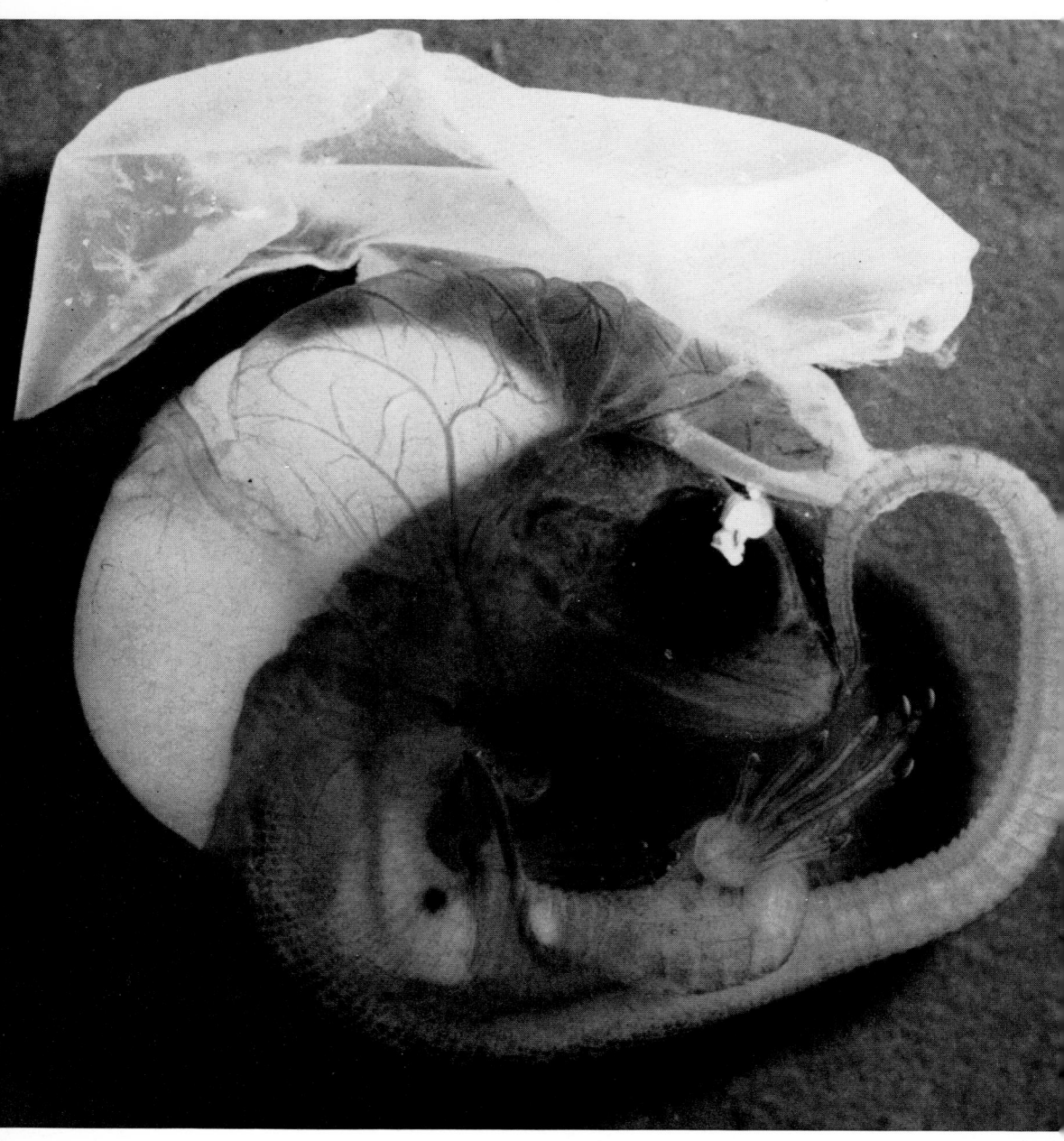

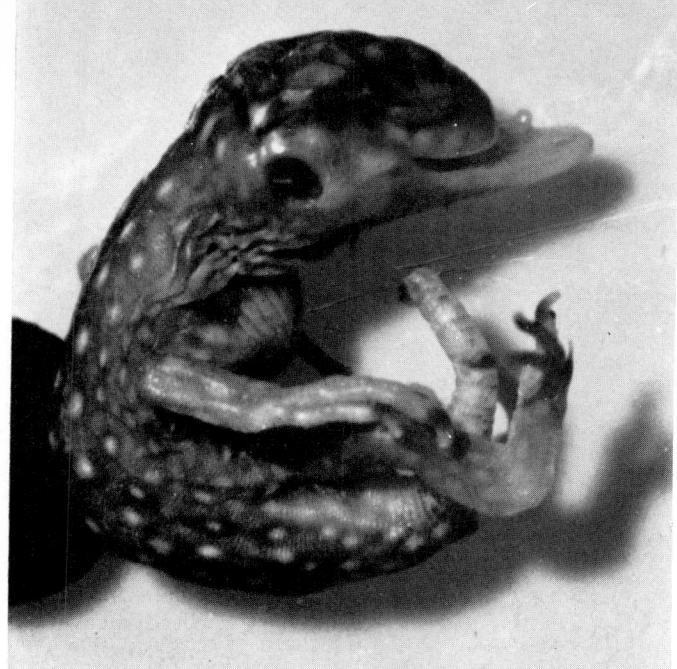

68 Abnormal embryo of eyed lizard (*Lacerta lepida*) with short upper jaw and reduced eyes, × 4. This type of abnormality is not exceptional among reptiles.

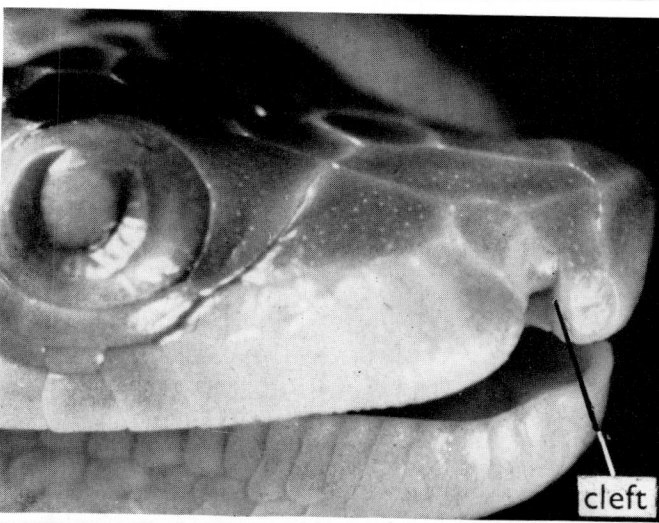

cleft

69 Late embryo of anaconda (*Eunected murinus*) showing abnormality of cleft lip and palate; × 9.

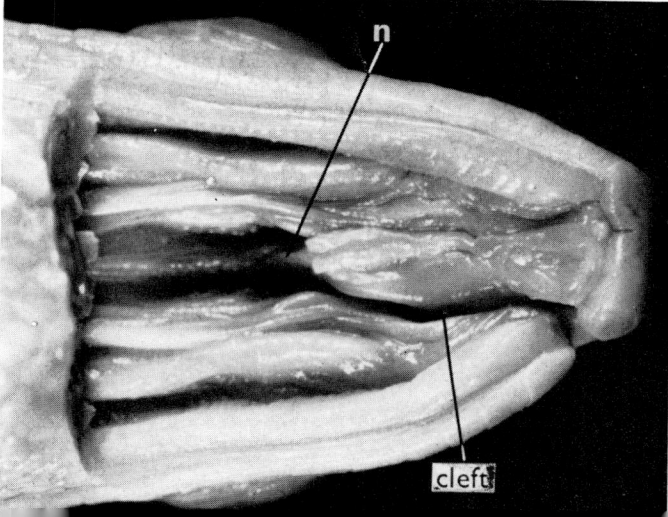

n

cleft

70 Palate of another sibling anaconda embryo (× 6·5) showing the unilateral cleft in the palate, on the other side from that in C. Apart from the cleft the palate is not malformed, and the position of the internal nostrils (**n**) is normal. Plates 69 and 70 after Bellairs, A.d'A. and Boyd, J.D. *Proc. Zool. Soc. Lond.*, (1957) **129**, 525.

71 Birth of slow-worm (*Anguis fragilis*).

72 *Lacerta vivipara* hatching from egg removed from mother and maintained in Panigel culture; × 1·8. The dressing was applied some days earlier to close an incision in the embryonic membranes when an operation was performed on the embryo.

73 (*Opposite above*) American banded gecko, *Coleonyx variegatus*, with immature tail regenerate. This species has true eyelids and lacks digital pads; the dorsal skin has a characteristic disruptive pattern.

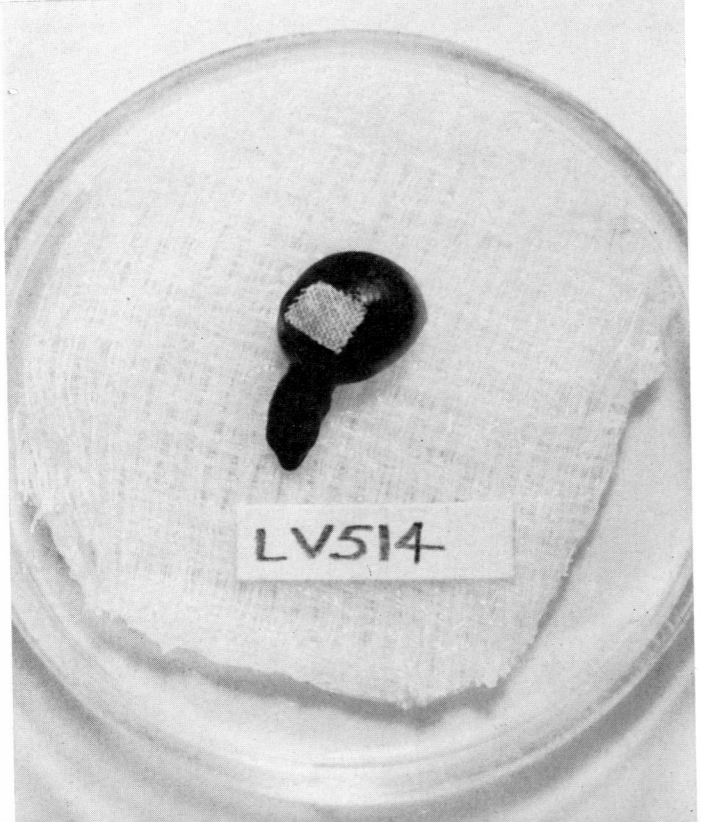

LV514

74 (*Opposite below*) Epidermal plate or lamina (4th central) of giant Aldabra tortoise (*Testudo gigantea*) showing growth rings, which indicate an age of about 25 years. The central boss is worn and the original horny surface present in the hatchling has disappeared. The specimen measures 25·5 x 19·5 cm., and the anterior edge of the plate is at the top. Information and photo from Dr. R. Gaymer.

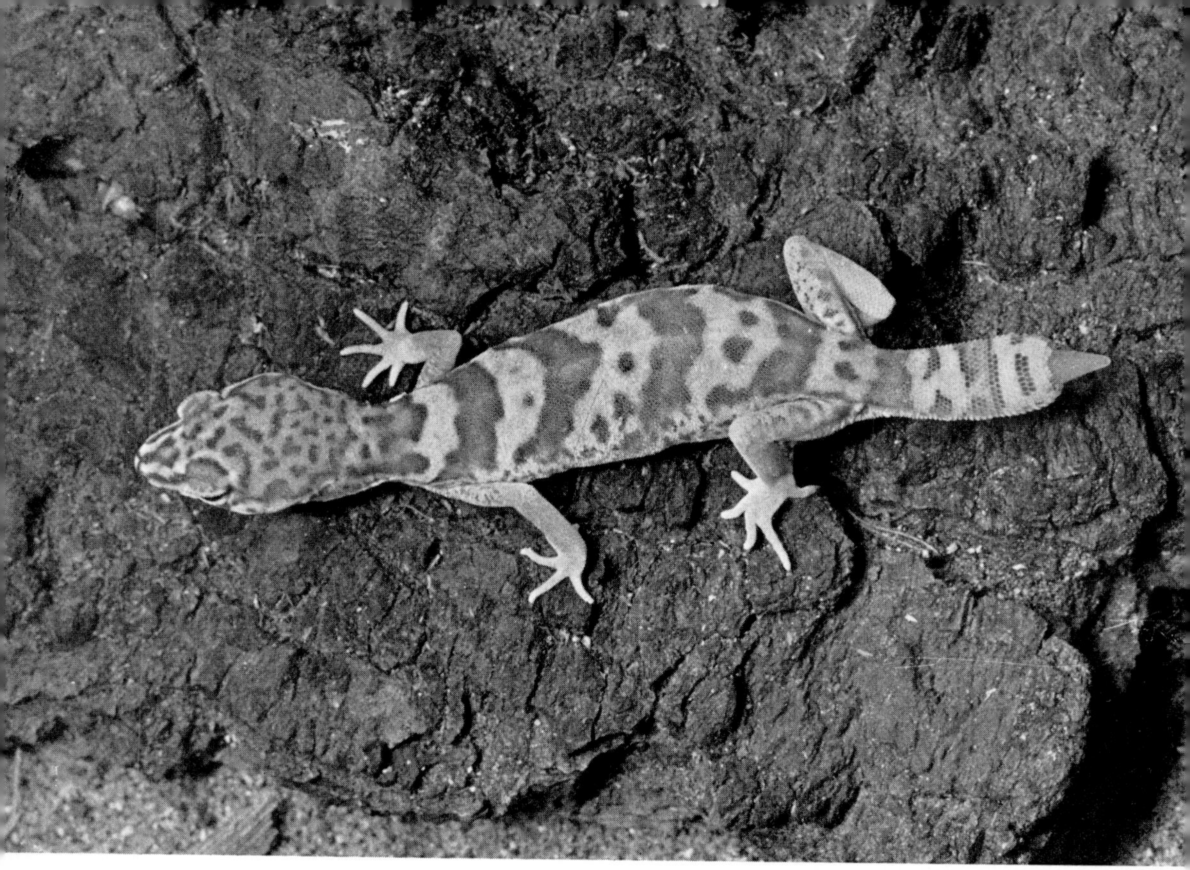

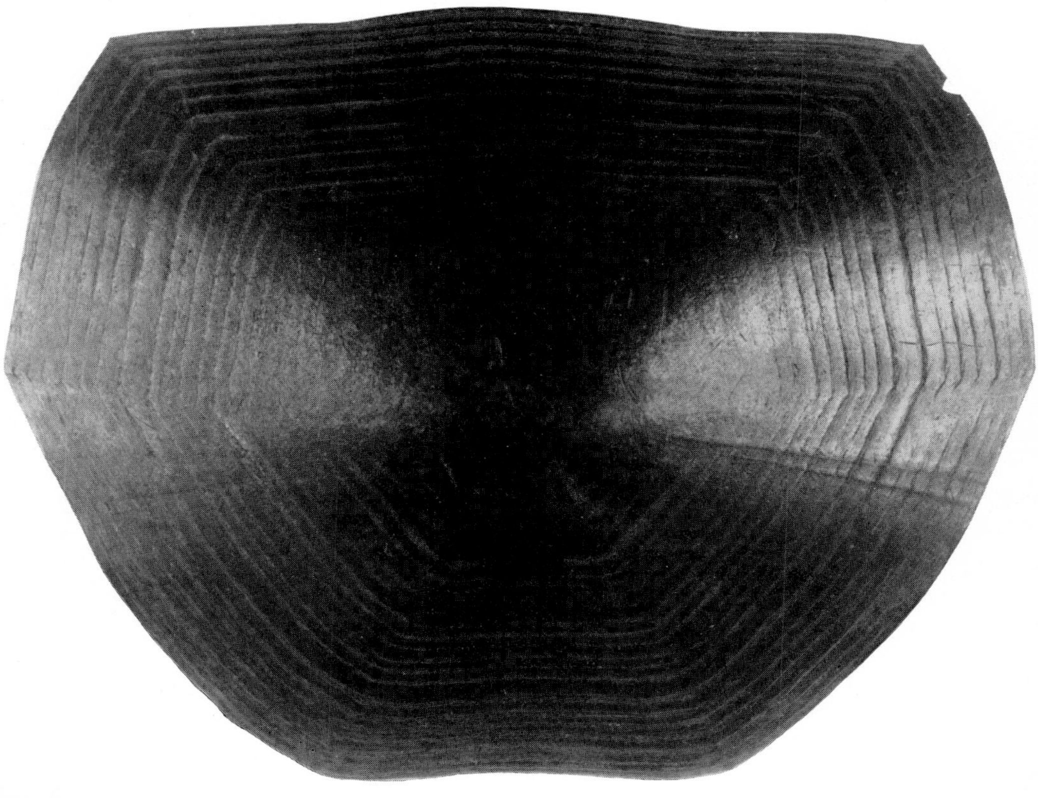

76 (*Opposite*) Part of skeleton of cobra (*Naja* sp.) with neck ribs. These are elevated to spread the hood.

75 African black-necked cobra (*Naja nigricollis*) in defensive posture. The gaping glottis is clearly visible. This species can spit venom.

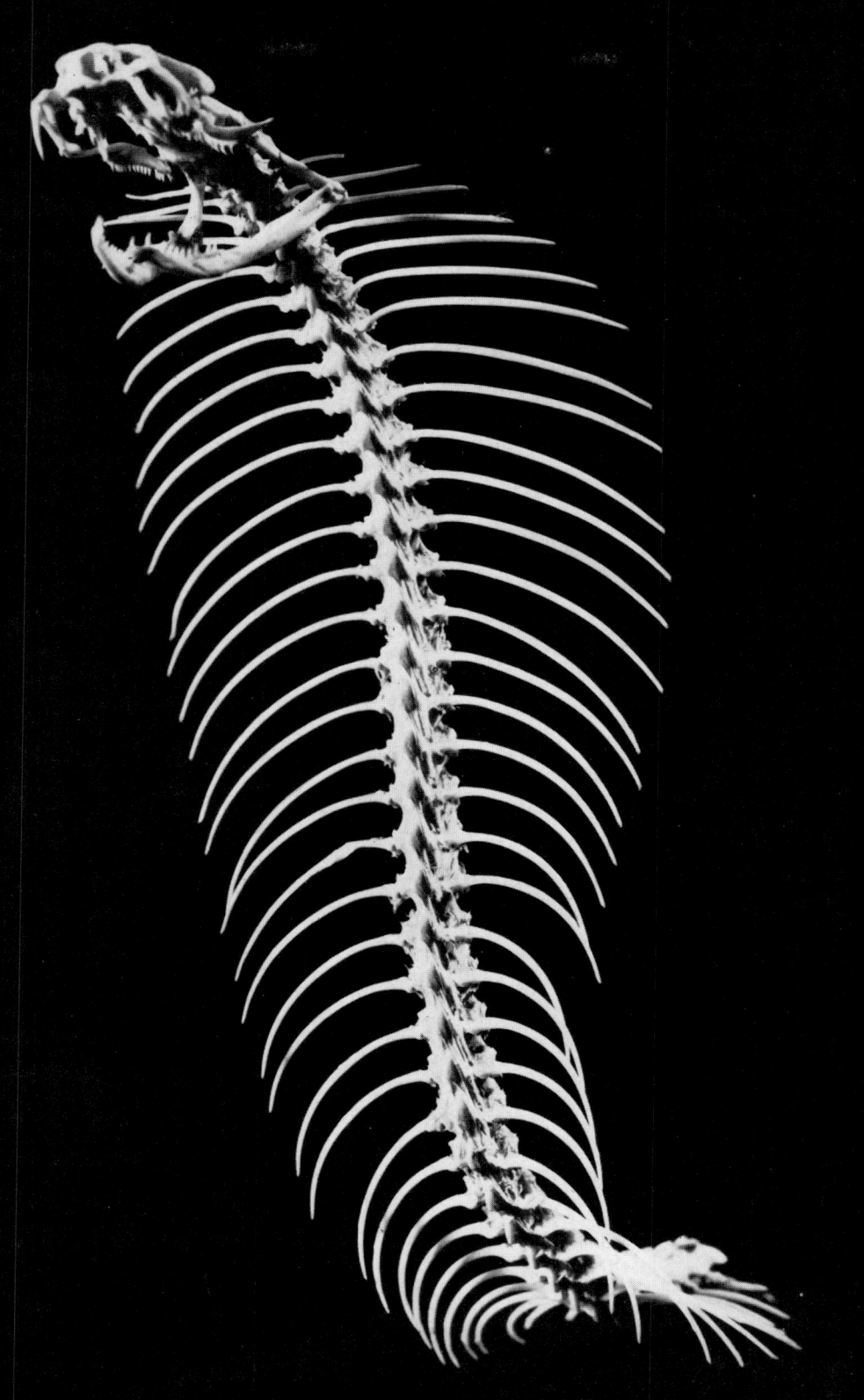

77 The arboreal vine snake (*Oxybelis aeneus*), a back-fanged colubrid found in Mexico, in threat posture.

78 North American hog-nosed snake (*Heterodon contortrix*), a harmless colubrid, feigns death when alarmed and unable to escape.

Sperm storage

It has been known for some years that in certain species of turtles, snakes and lizards the sperm can live in the genital tract of the female for long periods [see 124]. It is therefore possible for a reptile to produce successive clutches of fertile eggs, usually diminishing progressively in number, after a single insemination. Sperm from an autumn mating can therefore be used for fertilising the eggs in the following spring. Sperm survival for several months is probably quite a common occurrence. There are instances, however, where living spermatozoa have been recovered from the oviducts, or fertile eggs have been laid by isolated female captives after much longer periods: 4 years in the case of a diamondback terrapin (*Malaclemys centrata*) and a box tortoise (*Terrapene carolina*), 4½ years in an indigo snake (*Drymarchon corais*) and 6 years in another colubrid, *Leptodeira*. These last instances, however, are probably exceptional and the possibility of parthenogenesis (p. 456) must also be considered.

The sites where the sperm is stored have been studied in certain lizards and snakes [168, 175]. In the garter snake (*Thamnophis sirtalis*), a viviparous species, the sperm introduced at an autumn mating spend most of the winter in the female's oviduct. As spring approaches they migrate further forwards towards the base of the infundibulum. They then enter special seminal receptacles in the form of modified oviducal glands and are in a favourable position to fertilise the eggs when these are ovulated and enter the oviducts. As a rule the unused sperm die off after the young are born in the summer, though it is possible that they may occasionally survive for as long as a year.

Numbers of offspring

The great sea turtles are probably the most prolific of all reptiles. They are capable of laying immense clutches of over 100 eggs; 100 is an average figure for the green turtle (*Chelonia mydas*), and a maximum of about 200 has been recorded. As in reptiles generally, the biggest and oldest females tend to produce the largest clutches. Moreover, some of these turtles breed several times a year, at least in certain parts of their geographical range. The green turtle, for example, lays repeatedly (up to at least six times) at intervals of about a fortnight during three months of the year in parts of the Caribbean. It is probable that this immense reproductive effort is only made once in two or three years, so that with a bi- or triannual cycle the mothers have time to recuperate [94, 216].

The snapping turtle (*Chelydra serpentina*) is one of the most prolific freshwater chelonians and occasionally lays a clutch of 80 eggs. Many of the smaller terrapins and land tortoises have quite modest clutches (under 10), while the curious flexible-shelled *Malacochersus tornieri* produces only a single egg at a laying. Among other reptiles, crocodilians and the big pythons are good layers, though they probably only breed once a year. Clutch size varies between 15 and 88 in the American alligator, and between 25 and 95 (average about 60) in the Nile crocodile [119, 304]. Both the Indian and reticulated pythons have been known to lay over 100 eggs, though the usual number is considerably less. The maximum number of young attributed to the viviparous anaconda, the world's biggest snake, is only 42 [333]. These performances have been matched or excelled by some of the smaller species such as the American water snakes *Natrix cyclopion* and *N. sipedon* (maximum records of about 100 young), but in general clutches or litters of 6 to 30 are much more common [304, 468]. A full grown female grass snake (*Natrix natrix*) lays 30–40 eggs or even more, while young mothers may produce less than 10; as in other reptiles, individuals which have only just reached sexual maturity tend to be less prolific. The smooth snake (*Coronella austriaca*) has 4–15 young, the adder 6–20 [395]. Quite small egg clutches or litters of some 2–8 are produced by the burrowing blind-snakes (Typhlopidae and Leptotyphlopidae).

Lizards seem on the whole to be less prolific than snakes. Only a few species such as the bigger monitors have more than 30 offspring; the maximum figure of 60 eggs laid by *Varanus niloticus* is the largest which I have found quoted for lizards [165]. Figures for the English species which are probably fairly representative of smaller lizards are as follows: slow-worm (*Anguis*), 4–22; common lizard (*Lacerta vivipara*), 4–14; sand lizard (*L. agilis*), 6–13. The majority of geckos produce only one or two eggs at a time, and in the viviparous cordy-lids or zonures the litter seldom exceeds 4 in number [165]. In the case of some species, such as geckos and green anolis lizards, the small size of the clutch may be compensated for by the fact that breeding occurs over a considerable part of the year. It is possible that there is an inverse relationship between the clutch or litter size and the frequency of breeding, and it would be interesting to know whether this was true for individual species like the adder and some turtles, which reproduce more often in the warmer than in the colder parts of their range. In understanding an animal's life-history one needs to know not only the number of offspring which it produces at a time, but also how often it breeds. The product of these two factors gives the best indication of its true reproductive potential.

Nests, babies and parents

The reproductive habits of sea turtles provide a saga of reptilian pertinacity which has fascinated many naturalists. The green turtle (*Chelonia mydas*) is the species which has been most thoroughly studied, because of its economic importance. Archie Carr of the University of Florida and Tom Harrisson and J. R. Hendrickson in Borneo and Malaya have devoted years of painstaking research to its breeding and migrations, while another ambitious study project has been started by Robert Bustard [85] in northern Australia. The following description is based mainly on the publications by Carr and his collaborators which deal with the green turtles of Tortuguero, on the Caribbean coast of Costa Rica [91–94].

The green turtle is the only reptile certainly known to migrate for long distances and deserves an honourable place among the ranks of animal navigators. Its voyages have been studied by marking experiments in which tags of durable material are attached to one of the paddles. As the breeding season approaches these turtles leave the waters where their seaweed food is plentiful and travel, sometimes for distances of 3218 kilometres (2000 miles) to breeding grounds such as the Tortuguero beaches. Other individuals, marked after nesting on Ascension Island in the south Atlantic were later found on the coast of Brazil, about 2254 kilometres (1400 miles) away. How they find their way is a mystery and experiments are now being conducted in which the reptiles are fitted with tiny radio transmitters so that they can be tracked along their route.

Each summer large numbers of green turtles of both sexes appear offshore at the breeding ground. The males remain in the sea while the females are laying their eggs; in fact the former hardly ever come on land at all. It is one of the most curious features of green turtle reproduction that mating seems to take place only in the vicinity of the nesting beach, and either shortly before or shortly after the female lays her eggs. Some of the nesting females bear obvious scars of recent nuptial embrace made by the claws of the males on the front of their shells. The sperm which the female receives is presumably used to fertilise clutches of eggs which will be layed later in the breeding season; it could even be stored up for the next breeding season two or three years later.

The females usually come ashore to lay in the late evening and before leaving the water the turtle may ground for a few minutes in the shallows, testing the submerged sand with her snout and then gazing at the beach in an appraising fashion. She may then swim away to choose another spot, but if the prospect appears suitable she crawls ashore, leaving a broad track in the sand which might have been made by a miniature tank. She journeys inland for 46 metres (50 yards) or so, going well above the high water mark and often into the zone of beach vegetation. After a little preliminary exploration she settles down and begins to dig her nest.

First of all she digs a body pit 1·2 to 2 metres wide and half a metre deep, throwing out the sand with all four paddles and rotating her whole body slowly at the same time (Plate 58). This pit apparently serves to conceal the turtle while she lays her eggs. The female then excavates a smaller flask-shaped cavity in the floor of the pit (figure 129); this is the chamber in which the eggs are actually deposited. This egg chamber is dug out by the rear paddles only, working in rhythmic alternation to scoop out the sand, and goes down as deep as a paddle can reach. When it has been completed the turtle protrudes her tail into the neck of the chamber and begins to lay, the eggs dropping out of her cloaca in ones and twos at intervals of every few seconds. Eventually a clutch of about a hundred is produced, and this just about fills the egg chamber (Plate 58).

After laying the female beings the laborious task of concealing her nest, a precaution which may well have considerable survival value

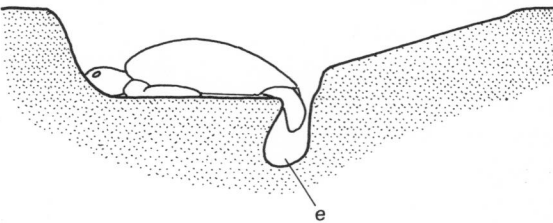

Figure 129   Nest excavation of green turtle, in profile. The turtle is in the main pit, about to lay into the egg chamber (**e**). After Hendrickson [216].

for her offspring. First of all she carefully fills in the egg chamber with her hind paddles, and then uses her front ones to cover up the pit and obscure the whole site, thrashing and throwing up the sand for several feet all round. The process of digging the nest may take about an hour, the laying of the eggs takes some twenty minutes, and the filling in perhaps half an hour more. Finally, late at night or in the early hours of the morning the turtle abandons her now well concealed nest, turns abruptly and crawls back to the sea. About a fortnight later she will return to the beach to lay again, continuing to do so at similar intervals until the end of the breeding season. She hardly feeds during all this time, and indeed there is little if any food for her at the nesting shore.

The buccaneering literature of the seventeenth century contains many references to turtles and it is fascinating to see how much William Dampier and his predecessors knew about these animals which they greatly prized as food. I have taken the following account (which obviously refers to the green turtle) from a book, first published in 1678, by the Dutch buccaneer John Esquemeling; a full reference to this work, with its quaint subtitle, is given in the bibliography [157].

These creatures have certain customary places whither they repair every year to lay their eggs. The chief of these places are the three islands called Caymanes, situated in the latitude of twenty degrees and fifteen minutes North, being at the distance of five and forty leagues from the Isle of Cuba, on the Northern side thereof.

It is a thing much deserving consideration how the tortoises can find out these islands. For the greatest part of them come from the Gulf of Honduras, distant thence the whole space of one hundred and fifty leagues. Certain it is, that many times the ships, having lost their latitude through the darkness of the weather, have steered their course only by the noise of the tortoises swimming that way, and have arrived at those isles. When their season of hatching is past they retire towards the Island of Cuba, where are many good places that afford them food. But while they are at the Islands of Caymanes, they eat very little or nothing.

It is possible that some of the other species of sea turtles – and some sea snakes too – are also migratory, but their life-histories are less well documented. The procedure for nesting and egg-laying, however, is basically similar in all marine chelonians; this is true even for the leatherback (Dermochelys) (Plate 57) which is zoologically very distinct from the others. It is almost as if the various members of these very conservative groups had found out long ago that there was one best way of conducting operations and had stuck to it ever since [94].

Since hundreds of turtles may nest on the same area of beach one might imagine that the different species with their similar habits would compete with each other for space in the regions where their distributions overlap. It seems, however, that this is largely avoided by discrepancies in the precise location and timing of reproduction. Thus, the loggerhead nests chiefly along the margins of the tropics beyond the main breeding ranges of the other genera. In the Caribbean the nesting areas of the other forms coincide, but the leather-backs usually nest earliest in the year, the hawksbills next, and the green turtles last. The hawksbill seem to be less gregarious in its nesting habits than the other species.

Turtles are among the many animals which base their technique of race-survival on the production of very large numbers of eggs, and accept the risk of a high pre-natal and infant mortality. Turtle conservationists have pointed out that predation by man on the adults seems to be a greater danger to the species than harvesting the eggs, since many of the hatchlings would in any case have never reached maturity. Thus the green turtle is much harder pressed in the West Indies where the adults are eaten (see p. 493) than in Malaya where the Muslim peoples seem to have some unwritten taboo against turtle meat and use only the eggs for food [216].

The chance of individual baby turtles surviving seems to depend to a considerable extent on their sheer numbers and on the unconscious effects of group behaviour. In the first place, the metabolic activity of so many eggs in close juxtaposition alters the microclimate of the next, raising its temperature a few degrees above that of the surroundings, and accelerates the rate of development. Secondly, the processes of emergence from the nest and escape to the sea as facilitated by mutual activity and would probably be impossible for an isolated baby to achieve. The scrabbling movements of each new baby which hatches pulls down the sand from the walls and ceiling of the egg chamber so that its floor rises and the other members of the group are able to climb to the surface. The babies may dally on their way down to the sea, exposing themselves unnecessarily to the risk of drying up or being eaten by an enemy. Another baby bumping into a stalled group may stimulate them all to move off abruptly 'like toy turtles wound up and let go together' [93].

Figure 130   Sketch of conditions in one of many field experiments on the orientation of baby green turtles conducted at Tortuguero, Costa Rica by Carr and Ogren [94]. 10 hatchlings, one day old, were released at point **r** at 1928 hours, three-quarter moon high in the south; sky clear. The release point was 72 yards from the sea and separated from it by debris. several low ridges and a mass of bush (**b**) 30 feet long and 4–5 feet high. All turtles had found the correct headings within a minute and reached the sea within 16 minutes after release. The spread of their trails was 2 yards across at the site of the release point and 19 yards at the water.

The incubation period of green turtle eggs is some seven to ten weeks, the hatchlings having carapaces about 5 cm. long. They often emerge from the nest at night, and it is a matter of great interest how they find their way to the sea (Plate 59). Sight is certainly involved, since blindfolded hatchlings scuttle aimlessly about. On the other hand, it is not necessary for the baby turtles to see the sea; they can often find it on a broken terrain with an upward incline and sand-dunes obstructing the ocean vista (figure 130). By the same token they are not dependent on some geotaxic orientation to a downward slope, although this may help to speed their progress. Nor do they depend entirely on some obscure compass sense, since young trans-ported by air across Central America were able to find their way down to the Pacific just as well as they could locate their native Caribbean. The young turtles seem to be attracted by light, moving in the direc-tion where it is brightest, and can be guided towards or away from the sea by playing the beam of a torch on the sand near them [216]. Experiments on adult female turtles show that they find the sea after nesting by moving towards the brightest part of the horizon where there is a broad, unobstructed vista. If one eye is blindfolded they travel along a path which curves towards the side of the other eye and may be unable to reach the water. These turtles, unlike freshwater chelonians, seem to have very poor vision on land and can probably do little more than distinguish areas of relative light and darkness in any given direction [153]. Whether this phototropic orientation plays any

425

part in the navigation of adult turtles when they are migrating across the high seas is unknown.

Despite the effectiveness of these complex adaptations, a sentimentalist cannot help feeling how much better the turtles would have done for themselves if they had followed the example of the ichthyosaurs and sea snakes and learned to produce their young alive. A fully aquatic life is hard to reconcile with the need to lay terrestrial eggs. How many thousands of nesting turtles must have paid for their dedication with their lives since the advent of man; and many nests must have been ravaged by protein-hungry littoral peoples. Now, too, as for millions of years in the past, the emerging young must run the gauntlet of amphibious predators: shore-hunting mammalian carnivores, rapacious birds, monitor lizards, and the fierce ghost crabs (Plate 60) which hunt on many tropical beaches. Even in the water there is no respite, for sharks devour the hatchlings before they reach the comparative safety of the open sea.

The reproductive habits of terrestrial and freshwater chelonians shows curiously close resemblances to those of the marine turtles. Those of the latter suffer to a lesser extent from the same drawbacks, since certain species nest in vast numbers of sandbanks, and expose their eggs and young to similar hazards.

Almost all chelonians bury their eggs in sand or earth, and while they may use their front legs to dig out a shallow nesting pit, the hind pair are always used to excavate the real egg chamber. This is even true for the gopher tortoises whose front feet are highly modified for digging burrows in the desert. The habit of moistening the nest with urine has been observed in many species, and the European terrapin (*Emys orbicularis*) will sometimes interrupt her egg-laying in hot weather, returning to the water to drink and thus replenish her cloacal bladders in which the fluid is stored. This expedient renders the soil easier to work, and perhaps is also useful to preserve the eggs from desiccation.

Crocodilians also make nests for their eggs near the edge of the water. The American alligator constructs hers in a most complicated fashion [331]. First she clears a patch of ground about 2·4 metres (8 feet) and 3 metres long by biting off and crushing down the vegetation. She then piles up the broken plants with her jaws and body into a compact mound and hollows out the middle of it with her hind feet, revolving her whole length at the same time. This hollow is then apparently filled in with mud and more plant debris, and another one is excavated in the same place; in this the eggs, some fifteen to eighty in number, are laid. The female covers the eggs with material from the edge of the nest and then with fresh mud and water plants which she brings from the water with her mouth. Finally she smooths the nest down with her body, and crawls round and round it, moulding it into a smooth conical shape hillock up to nearly a metre in height. The whole procedure may take two to three days. Fermentation of the nest material raises the temperature and incubates the eggs.

Other species such as the estuarine crocodile *(Crocodylus porosus)* and certain caimans also make nests out of vegetation mixed with mud, but an alternative method used by the Nile and American crocodiles is to bury the eggs in a sandbank; Carr has described his excitement at finding the remains of nests and eggs of three reptiles, the hawksbill turtle, the American crocodile and a big tree iguana on the same stretch of Caribbean beach [90].

The nesting of the Nile crocodile has been described by Cott, to whom we are indebted for so much information about this impressive reptile [119]. The nests are usually made in sandy or pebbly ground, close to trees or some other source of shade, although they may be 180 metres (nearly 200 yards) or more from the water. In regions where they are not molested, large numbers of crocodiles will nest communally in the same area, rather like turtles, but this is unusual in modern times when a crocodile is seldom allowed to live a peaceful life. The nest (Plate 63) is dug with the feet to a depth of about 61 cm. (2 ft.) if possible and the eggs are covered over.

Although the reproduction of crocodiles seems to repeat the same mistake as that of turtles, its shortcomings may to some extent be offset by the provision of such maternal care as a large and formidable mother can provide. Throughout the incubation period, female alligators and Nile crocodiles remain sitting on top of, or lurking in the close vicinity of the nest (Plate 62), guarding it against intruders and taking little if any food. It is uncertain how many other crocodilian species look after their eggs in this way; the American crocodile is said to leave her nest unprotected.

There is some disagreement as to just how aggressively the duty of guarding is conducted. Female alligators have apparently been known to attack or at least threaten people who have ventured near their nests, although these attacks are easy to evade. On the other hand, Cott believes that in the Nile crocodile, guarding is mainly passive; many of the females which he observed on their nests were in an

almost torpid state. It is reasonable to suppose that the mere presence
of the mother acts as a deterrent to monitor lizards and other predators which do in fact speedily rifle nests if the females leaves them
for a short period. Such protection is, of course, useless against man,
and the crocodiles' breeding habits are as vulnerable to human mis-
chief as those of turtles.

When the time of hatching (Plate 64) approaches the young Nile
crocodiles croak, and this apparently acts as a signal to the mother to
free them from the nest by lying upon it and wriggling in such a way
that the sand is pushed away. It would otherwise be very difficult for
the young to escape unaided, since the 30 cm. (1 ft.) or so of sand which
covers the top tier of eggs becomes baked so hard by the sun that
one can only expose them by chipping with a knife. The mother may
even continue to look after her young when these have emerged from
the nest, and there are apparently reliable accounts of her escorting
them to and in the water like a duck, and driving storks and other
predators away. Nevertheless, many baby crocodiles are eaten by
large birds and fish, monitors, turtles and older crocodiles[※].

Colbert [106] describes the fossil nests of the Cretaceous horned
dinosaur *Protoceratops* which were discovered in association with
adult skeletons in Mongolia. The eggs, each about 20 cms. (8 in.)
long, are arranged in concentric circles, as if the mother had turned
around several times to deposit them in expanding circles within a
crater that she had made in the sand. Eighteen eggs were found in the
largest cluster, but there may originally have been many more.
Similar remains have been discovered in France. It is not surprising
that the habit of nesting should have become well developed in
reptiles of the archosaurian lineage such as crocodiles and dinosaurs,
since other members of this group gave rise to the birds.

The great majority of oviparious lizards and snakes hardly deserve
the name of nest-builders and exhibit virtually no maternal care.
They lay their eggs in sheltered positions, under stones and logs, in
crevices or among piles of rotting vegetation, and show no further
interest in them. The grass snake in England, for example, often lays
its eggs in a manure or compost heap where the heat of fermentation
accelerates embryonic development. A few species, such as the Nile
monitor in Natal, habitually lay in termite mounds, which make
excellent natural incubators, maintaining a fairly high and equable
temperature [121].

Many other lizards, and also the tuatara, dig a hole for their eggs and cover it over. The Bengal monitor makes a deep goblet-shaped egg-chamber something like that of turtles, and then scrapes down the earth with her snout and front legs until the nest is hidden. She also excavates several additional pits over or near the nest which may have the object of misleading predators; similar 'false nests' are also made by some chelonians. The flap-necked chamaeleon (*Chamaeleo dilepis*) digs an oblique tunnel with her hind legs to a depth great enough to contain her body, and after laying her eggs in it fills it in with tamped-down earth; one specimen was seen to scatter dry grass and twigs over the filled-in nest.

It is well known that the females of several North American skinks of the genus *Eumeces* and of the limbless anguid lizard *Ophisaurus* brood their eggs by curling around or among them (Plate 61), and that the former will threaten mice and other small creatures which approach the nest. An interesting study of the brooding habits of *Eumeces laticeps* and *E. fasciatus* has been made by Noble and Mason [299]. They observed that when the female returned to the eggs after a short absence she would lick and turn them, occasionally lifting one in her mouth to a new position. She would also gather up any of her eggs which had been scattered and would even appropriate eggs laid by other individuals of either species in nests under bark or moss nearby.

Tests were carried out to determine whether females would brood eggs of other kinds of lizards, and it was found that those of *Ophisaurus* and *Sceloporus* were rejected, as also were eggs of *Eumeces* which had been treated with varnish, and egg models made of wax. Apparently egg-recognition depends mainly on the tongue-Jacobson's organ sense, since removal of the tongue tips prevented the female from finding her eggs. On the other hand, a blindfolded individual could find and brood eggs even when these were removed to another site. Noble and Mason believed that *Eumeces* is able to incubate its eggs as well as brooding them by basking in the sun and then warming them with her body. Some doubt on this point has been expressed by more recent observers. The brooding of *Ophisaurus* seems to have no thermoregulatory function except perhaps in so far as it may involve shifting the eggs nearer to or further from the surface of the ground [438].

An even more remarkable exhibition of maternal care has been reported by Evans [16c] in another species of skink, *Eumeces obsoletus*. Besides licking and turning her eggs regularly, the parent helps the partly hatched baby to escape from the egg by rubbing it with her head, body or feet, so stimulating it to wriggle free from the shell. She retains her interest in her young for at least ten days after hatching and periodically grooms them by licking their cloacal regions.

Female snakes of quite a few species brood their eggs by coiling round them; presumably this protects them from chilling draughts and from the attention of predators, and may possibly warm them up a little if the snake has just come out of the sun. Brooding is also practised, however, by certain subterranean forms such as *Leptoty-lops*. The big pythons are renowned for their brooding habits, which have often been observed in captivity [333]. For weeks on end the mother will remain coiled around her mound of eggs, only leaving them at rare intervals.

It was discovered more than a hundred years ago in the Jardin des Plantes in Paris, that the temperature between the coils of a brooding Indian python was some 11–17°C above that of the air in the cage. This and subsequent observations have led many people to believe that the brooding female temporarily becomes a warm-blooded or endothermic creature. It is probable, however, that in some of these earlier observations, the high temperature measured within the coils was primarily due not to active heat production by the snake, but to absorption of heat from the ground on which it was resting. Of the six or more species of pythons which have acquired the brooding habit, only the Indian python is now known on good evidence to be a true incubator. Reliable modern observations show that one individual of this species was able to maintain a coil temperature of about 32°C even when the substratum temperature fell as low as 26°. Many people who have watched an Indian python brooding her eggs have noticed her coils contracting spasmodically at intervals of some ten to twenty times a minute. It has been found that these contractions become more frequent when the temperature of the substratum is reduced, suggesting that the energy generated in this way helps to maintain the python's warmth.

Stories such as Kipling's *Rikki-Tikki-Tavi* of cobras guarding their eggs are not entirely fictitious, and two species of these reptiles are known to carry parental responsibility further than is usual among snakes. Malcolm Smith has described the domestic behaviour of a pair of Indian cobras *(Naja naja)* in the Bellevue Zoo at Manchester [393]. The snakes cooperated in making a nest by burrowing into a pile of earth which had been provided until their noses met in the middle, where they formed a cavity large enough to contain them both. The female laid her eggs in this chamber and remained guarding them throughout the incubation period. She would leave her eggs for an hour or two each day to drink and lie about; sometimes she fed. In her absence the male snake kept guard.

Oliver [305] has written a remarkable account of the reproduction of the king cobra Ophiophagus or Hamadryas hannah, which contains a quite touching photograph of the male 'kissing' the back of the female's head with his tongue (figure 126 E). For two years running in the New York Zoological Park the 3·96 metre (13 ft.) female built a nest for her eggs out of sand and a litter of bamboo stalks and dried magnolia leaves which had been put in the cage. She piled up this material with a coil of her body, using it like a hook, and repeatedly crawled away from the nest to drag in more loose vegetation. Eventually she made an egg-chamber in the middle of the nest by coiling tightly and revolving her body; after laying, she covered the eggs with leaves and remained coiled on top of the heap. It is interesting that she made no attempt to strike when the eggs were removed for artificial incubation. There are many reports of the aggressive behaviour of this snake in the wild, especially of females guarding their eggs, but some of these may be exaggerations.

The king cobra seems to be the only snake known to construct a nest out of vegetation. The male, unlike the male of the Indian species, does not appear to cooperate in the task, and indeed the female drove off her cage-mate who had fathered the eggs with jabs of her head, if he approached the nest too closely while it was under construction.

There is little evidence for maternal care among viviparous reptiles. A south African skink (Mabuya trivittata) however, has been observed to assist the escape of her babies from the membranous embryonic coverings in which they were born by tearing these with her jaws [361]. Female night lizards (Xantusia vigilis) are also known to expedite the birth of young as they struggle free from her cloaca by nipping them and so provoking them to more violent efforts. She may then pull out the embryonic membranes and eat them [390]. This habit of eating the placenta or 'afterbirth' is well known in certain mammals and has even been reported among primitive human communities, but seems unusual in reptiles.

The young of viviparous reptiles sometimes remain close to the mother for a little while after they are born and if threatened they

431

might conceivably hide beneath her body. Such behaviour, together with the discovery of large embryos inside snakes which have been killed, may be responsible for the stories that adders and rattlesnakes shelter their young by swallowing them in time of danger.

Chapter 10

Embryonic Development, Chromosomes and Parthenogenesis

Embryonic development

MOST reptiles lay their eggs, as has been described, but others retain them internally and bear their young alive. One might imagine that the eggs of the two groups would be very unlike each other, as the eggs of birds are unlike the tiny eggs of mammals, but this is not the case. Apart from the reduction of the shell which takes place in viviparous forms, the eggs of all reptiles are much alike and also show a close resemblance to those of birds. In fact the general mode of embryonic development in reptiles and birds is essentially similar, and emphasises the close zoological relationship between the two classes.

The largest known reptilian eggs are those of a long-necked quadrupedal dinosaur called *Hypselosaurus*, which have been found fossilised in late Cretaceous deposits in the south of France [106]. They seem to have been about 25 cm (10 in.) in their longest diameter; this is less than the largest birds' eggs, those of the extinct *Aepyornis* of Madagascar, which sometimes measured over 37 cm. The smallest eggs laid by modern reptiles are about 6 mm long. Some representative average dimensions and other particulars are given below for a few oviparous species; even within a single clutch, however, the eggs may vary considerably in size. They also take up moisture from their surroundings so that eggs with a pliable shell may swell considerably in the course of incubation.

Thus, during their 10–11 weeks of incubation, ten eggs laid by a king cobra increased by an average of about 66 per cent in weight, 8 per cent in length and 26 per cent in width.

Eggs may be round, as in marine and some freshwater turtles, or more or less oval as in the majority of other reptiles; they are often elongated with rounded ends, and in a few species they are aberrant in shape (figure 131). In colour they are whitish or yellowish, though the eggs of the leathery turtle sometimes have greenish flecks. There

433

	Species	Av. size	Shape	Shell
[89]	*Dermochelys coriacea* (leathery turtle)	57 × 55 mm. c. 2·2 in.	nearly round	soft
[89]	*Chelonia mydas* (green turtle)	48 mm. 1·9 in. or more	round	soft
[301]	*Testudo graeca* (common 'Greek' tortoise)	38 × 32 mm. 1·5 × 1·25 in.	oval	hard
[42]	*Crocodylus niloticus*	75 × 50 mm.*	oval	hard
[383]	*Sphenodon punctatus* (tuatara)	3 × 2 in. 33 mm. long**	oval	parchment
[433]	*Sphaerodactylus macrolepis* (a tiny West Indian gecko of 2 in. adult length)	6 × 4·5 mm. 0·25 × 0·2 in.	oval	hard (? soft when laid)
[395]	*Lacerta agilis* (sand lizard)	14 × 9 mm.*	oval	parchment
[53]	*Heloderma suspectum* (Gila monster)	71 × 36 mm. 2·8 × 1·5 in.	oval	parchment
[394]	*Varanus salvator* (water monitor)	70 × 40 mm. 2·8 × 1·6 in.	oval	parchment
[333]	*Python molurus* (Indian python)	96 × 58 mm. 3·8 × 2·3 in. (may be over 4 in.)	oval	parchment
[305]	*Ophiophagus hannah* (king cobra)	60 × 34 mm.* 2·3 × 1·3 in.	oval	parchment
[395]	*Natrix natrix* (grass snake)	28 × 18 mm.* 1·1 × 0·7 in.	oval oval	parchment

*newlaid.   **end of incubation

seems to be no indication of cryptic colouration such as many birds' eggs possess, and since most reptiles bury or hide their eggs, such colour could have little purpose.

The shell is well developed in all oviparous reptiles. It is secreted by glands in the oviduct, and usually has a fibrous structure; the alternate layers of fibres may be arranged so as to run at right angles to each other. These fibres, especially those in the outer layers, are impregnated to varying degrees according to species with calcium salts; eggs that are well calcified are hard and brittle like those of birds. Hard eggshells of this type are produced by terrestrial and some freshwater chelonians, by crocodilians, but among the Squamata only by the majority of geckos. Minute pores have been described in the egg-shells of crocodiles and some terrapins; pores are not obvious in the eggs of some land tortoises although these eggs are not completely impermeable to water [471]. Since many tortoises lay their eggs in comparatively arid surroundings, their embryos need to conserve all the water-supply which is initially provided in the

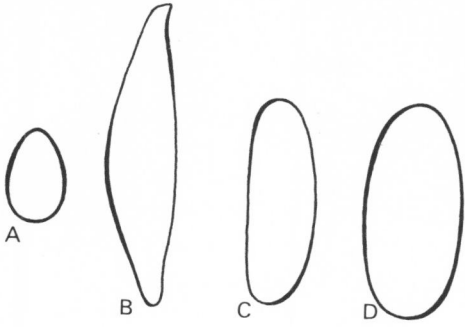

Figure 131 Eggs of agamid lizards. A, *Draco volans*, × 1⅛: B, *Calotes jubatus*, × 1. C, *Calotes cristatellus*, × 1. D, *Japalura ornata*, × 2¼. After de Rooij, N. (1915) *The Reptiles of the Indo-Australian Archipelago*. Leiden, E. J. Brill.

egg. The egg-shells of many turtles are quite thinly calcified and feel soft and rubbery; those of the tuatara, of lizards (other than geckos) and of snakes have a tough, parchment-like or leathery consistency and are often indented by contact with other eggs or solid objects in the neighbourhood. Gecko eggs are said to be quite soft when laid but harden after exposure to the air; this would explain how the tiny sphaerodactyl geckos are able to lay eggs of such relatively large size. In many species of reptile the shells of the freshly laid eggs are coated with a sticky material; this makes them adhere in clusters, or in the case of most geckos, in pairs which may themselves be attached to the under surface of a stone or the side of a crevice.

Laboratory experiments have shown that the eggs of certain Philippine geckos can survive exposure to salinity for periods of up to eleven days, much longer than the survival period of the parchment-shelled eggs of a species of skink from the same region. Such resistance may enable gecko eggs to endure long journeys on logs and other flotsam across the sea, and hence facilitate dispersal of the species [73].

Beneath the calcified egg-shell there may be one or more shell membranes. In crocodiles there is an air space at one end of the egg, but such a space has not been described in other reptiles, though it is present in birds' eggs. The eggs of both Chelonia and Crocodilia contain a substantial quantity of egg-white or albumen which is secreted, like the shell and shell membranes, by glands in the oviduct. Its function, by analogy with birds, is to provide a reserve of water and a little food material, and also perhaps to support and protect the yolk and embryo. In the hen's egg the latter are actually suspended by twisted fibrous strands covered by albumen known as chalazae. These appear to be absent in all reptile eggs and it is perhaps because

435

of this that disturbance of the eggs during incubation may lead to damage and death of the embryos. Generally speaking, reptiles do not turn their eggs; the maternally inclined skink *Eumeces* and possibly other species which brood, are exceptions. Albumen is sometimes stated to be quite or almost absent from the eggs of lizards and snakes; a small quantity of thin glairy fluid will ooze from a lizard egg if this is punctured, however; it seems likely that this is a weak solution of albumen, but further studies on the nature of the fluids in reptilian eggs would be most welcome.

The yolk is of course the main source of food for the embryo and this is true not only for egg-laying reptiles but also for the majority of viviparous species (p. 447). It is contained in a thin-walled bag called the yolk-sac which is attached by a narrow stalk to the alimentary tract of the embryo, entering the body at the umbilicus (figure 132, p. 439). Yolk consists mainly of fat and protein combined (lipoproteins); these substances are present in the form of spherical droplets which can be seen under the microscope, and in greater detail, under the electron microscope [36]. In birds, and probably in reptiles also, this material is manufactured in the liver of the mother and is conveyed to her ovaries in the blood-stream, where it is reconstituted in the egg-cell. Unlike the shell and albumen, the yolk therefore is formed before the egg is shed from the ovary.

In some species the mother appears to have another source of yolk material on which she can draw to stock up her eggs. This is a pair of organs known as the fat bodies – masses of fat covered by peritoneal membrane which project into the hinder part of the body-cavity in the neighbourhood of the kidneys and gonads. These fat bodies are best developed in reptiles which inhabit temperate zones and in some species are bigger in the females than in the males. Studies on *Uta* lizards [424] suggest that they have a specific function associated with yolk formation. These north American iguanids lay several clutches of eggs each summer and their fat bodies become greatly depleted at the time when the yolk of the first clutch is being laid down at the end of the winter. Experimental removal of the fat bodies retards the formation of the yolk and causes some of the ovarian follicles to degenerate. The fat bodies are of little importance, however, in the formation of later egg clutches; their main function is to allow the lizard to start egg-laying early in the season, before she can find abundant supplies of food.

In other reptiles, such as the adder, the fat bodies do not seem to be drawn on for yolk formation in this way, and only become exhausted after starvation or at the end of pregnancy. Neither are they used up during hibernation, when the metabolic rate of a reptile is, in any case, very low [441]. Perhaps they come in useful as a safety reserve of food when the animal has just emerged from its winter retreat, or in other times of dietary hardship.

After the egg has been fertilised the embryo begins to feed on its yolk, and this, like the food eaten by the adult, is broken down by digestive juices or enzymes. In the chick embryo the yolk is partly digested within the yolk-sac and carried by the vitelline blood vessels to the embryo where the digestive process is completed. It is probable, though not yet certainly known, that the reptile embryo digests its yolk in the same way.

The bulk of the yolk is used up during the course of embryonic life. The yolk-sac and any left-over yolk which it contains may be discarded when the young hatches or is born; the sac breaks off near the point where its stalk enters the umbilicus. This takes place in many species, including the viviparous lizard and the grass snake. In many other reptiles and in birds, however, the remaining yolk, sometimes quite a substantial amount, is withdrawn along with the yolk-sac into the body of the young through the umbilicus. It is uncertain whether it is only drawn in as far as the body cavity and is digested outside the intestine as it is in the embryo, or passes right into the gut itself and is digested like ordinary food.

Withdrawal of the yolk just before birth has been described in a number of lizards including the sand lizard *(Lacerta agilis)*, in snakes such as the adder and copperhead [162], and in crocodilians. The amount of yolk in the body of the new-born copperhead may amount to some 14–29 per cent of the total weight of the snake; it seems to disappear within about a fortnight. In the Nile crocodile on the other hand, traces of the yolk have been found six months after hatching [see 119]. Such yolk may constitute a useful reserve of food during the early part of post-natal life.

As well as protein and fat, the yolk also contains calcium, phosphorus and other minerals which are utilised during later embryonic life for the ossification of the skeleton. It would seem, however, that in the leathery and loggerhead turtles this supply of calcium is inadequate, for the hatchling contains nearly five times as much calcium as was present in the yolk and albumen at the time of laying [386]. It is believed that the additional calcium is obtained from the egg-shell, as in birds, even though the shell of these turtles is comparatively lightly calcified as compared with that of certain other reptiles. The precise way in which the calcium is taken up from the egg-shell is unknown; probably it is absorbed through the shell membrane by the chorio-allantois (p. 440).

A rather different state of affairs has been found in all the Squamata studied. Here the yolk is extremely rich in calcium, so much so that excessive quantities of it may in some cases be stored in the endolymphatic sacs of the embryo (p. 376). In these reptiles there is no evidence that calcium is obtained from any source besides the yolk — either from the shell in oviparous forms or through the placenta in some viviparous ones such as the adder, at least. This generalisation appears to hold true even for geckos which mostly lay hard-shelled eggs.

Owing to the huge size of the yolk only a small part of the egg-cell is able to divide after fertilisation. As a result of the earliest cell divisions a small whitish germinal disc or blastoderm is formed which stands out against the yellow yolk. The eggs begin to pass down the oviducts while the blastoderm is being formed, and in the slow-worm and perhaps other species also they rotate in an anti-clockwise direction during their passage; finally they assume a position in which the embryos are generally uppermost (ie nearest the back of the mother) while the yolky side of the egg faces towards the belly [342].

Quite rapidly, by complex processes of cell division and migration, the single-layered blastoderm is converted into an embryo with front and hind ends, and consisting of three primary germ layers, the ectoderm, encoderm and mesoderm. A red network of tiny blood vessels soon appears in a ring round the embryo, and probably give the first indication to a person who is not used to studying embryos that the egg is fertile. A little later the heart can be seen as a tiny pulsing spot, and blood-vessels develop inside the embryo itself.

Three extra-embryonic membranes in addition to the yolk-sac, the chorion, amnion and allantois, arise quite early in development and play a most important part in ante-natal life (figure 132). The chorion, which consists of ectoderm covered by mesoderm, lies just beneath the shell and its membranes; it comes into contact with both the yolk-sac and the allantois. The amnion lies more deeply inside the egg and is made up of a thin layer of ectoderm covered with mesoderm. It becomes a sac filled with fluid which encloses the embryo in a

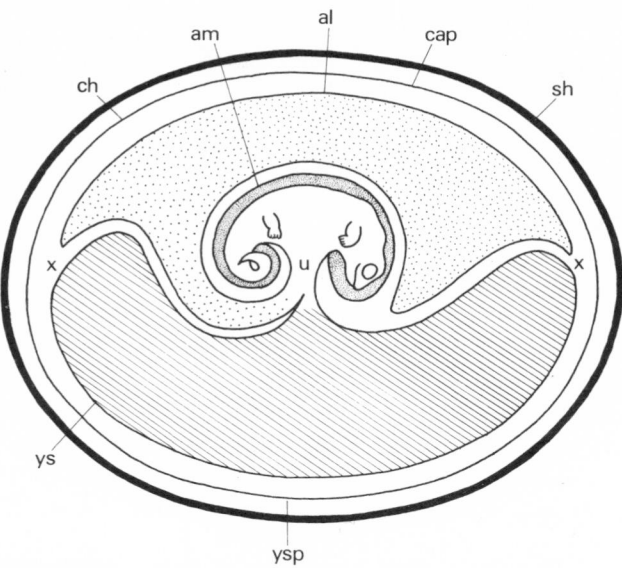

Figure 132 Simplified diagram showing extra-embryonic membranes of a reptile during the later stages of embryonic life. Actually, there may be one or more shell-membranes between the shell and the chorion, while the inner surface of the chorion and the outer surfaces of the amnion, allantois and yolk-sac are each covered with a layer of extra-embryonic mesoderm. Owing to fusion of these adjacent mesodermal layers, an amnio-chorion and a chorio-allantois are formed. The chorion and yolk-sac may also fuse in places, and in viviparous forms where the shell is reduced, a placental area may be established at either the chorio-allantoic or chorion-yolk-sac sites, or at both. In some lizards (and perhaps in reptiles generally), the edges of the allantois acquire a more complex relationship with the yolk-sac than is shown, and appear to fuse with it at the regions marked **x**.

al, allantois, outer layer (allantoic cavity stippled). **am**, amnion (amniotic cavity darkly stippled). **cap**, site of chorio-allantoic placenta in viviparous forms. **ch**, chorion. **sh**, egg-shell. **u**, umbilical cord. **ys**, yolk-sac (yolk shown by slanting lines). **ysp**, site of yolk-sac placenta in viviparous forms.

little pond, reproducing in a way the aquatic environment of larval amphibian ancestors. Muscle fibres develop within its mesoderm and these rock the embryo slightly and keep the amniotic fluid circulating.

The allantois is another sac formed of endoderm covered by mesoderm. It grows out from the hinder end of the alimentary canal, behind the region where the yolk-sac stalk is attached. Its own stalk and that of the yolk-sac may become fused together where they

439

emerge from the umbilicus to form an umbilical cord. This cord is basically similar to that of mammals, except that in these animals the yolk-sac and its stalk usually degenerate quite early in embryonic life. The allantoic sac soon enlarges to fill much of the space between the chorion and amnion, and its outer layer fuses with the chorion, the attached parts of the two membranes with their intervening extra-embryonic mesoderm being collectively known as the chorioallan-tois (figure 136, p. 450; Plate 67).

The allantois has two main functions. Its cavity acts as a storage tank for some of the nitrogenous excreta of the embryo, especially of the fairly insoluble substance uric acid. Other excretory products such as urea may be stored in the albumen and yolk-sac. The chorio-allantois also acts as a kind of embryonic lung, for it is richly supplied with blood vessels and can take up oxygen and give off carbon dioxide through the porous walls of the shell, against which it is pressed. In viviparous reptiles both chorio-allantois and yolk-sac may participate in the formation of a placenta (p. 449).

The amnion, chorion and chorio-allantois are left behind in the shell when the young reptile emerges from its egg and breaks its umbilical cord. The umbilical scar may remain visible on the belly of the young – near the middle of the plastron in chelonians – for some months, but eventually disappears instead of persisting like the human navel.

The amniote egg with its hard or leathery shell and built-in food-supply needs little from its surroundings except air and moisture; even the latter is probably unnecessary in some cases. It must have been one of the main 'improvements' which the reptiles were able to make on the typical amphibian way of life, with its primitive com-pulsion to breed in the water. We know that such eggs were being laid as long ago as the lower Permian, for a fine fossil of one about 59 mm. long has been discovered in Texas.

Romer [357] has made the interesting suggestion that the amniote egg preceded the adult in its adaptation to terrestrial life, and that the first reptiles lived mainly in the water but laid their eggs on land in the fashion of present-day turtles. Later on, of course, these self-sufficient eggs became indispensable for the more terrestrially inclined groups of reptiles when they moved away from the water and became the first vertebrate colonists of arid uplands and deserts.

So far as one can judge from fossil remains, many of the better-known early reptiles were still more or less aquatic, like their amphibian forbears. They lived in times when the climate fluctuated seasonally between severe drought and flooding; there is evidence for this in the geological record of the later Palaeozoic. Under such conditions aquatic spawn and tadpoles would be in danger of drying up or being washed away into deep inhospitable waters. Terrestrial eggs laid in a secure place above high water mark would have had a better chance of survival, both from climatic hazards and from the attention of predators which at that time might not have been very numerous on land. Evidence for or against this attractive theory may be forthcoming when we know more about the mode of life of the most ancient reptiles of the Upper Carboniferous. Some of these creatures seem to have been terrestrial rather than amphibious in habits [see 96].

During the later phases of embryonic, or as some would call it, foetal life the various organs are formed. The general shape of the body alters rapidly. The branchial grooves which correspond with the gill clefts of fishes appear and then disappear, merging into the surrounding tissues. The trunk lengthens and the tail curls up; in the

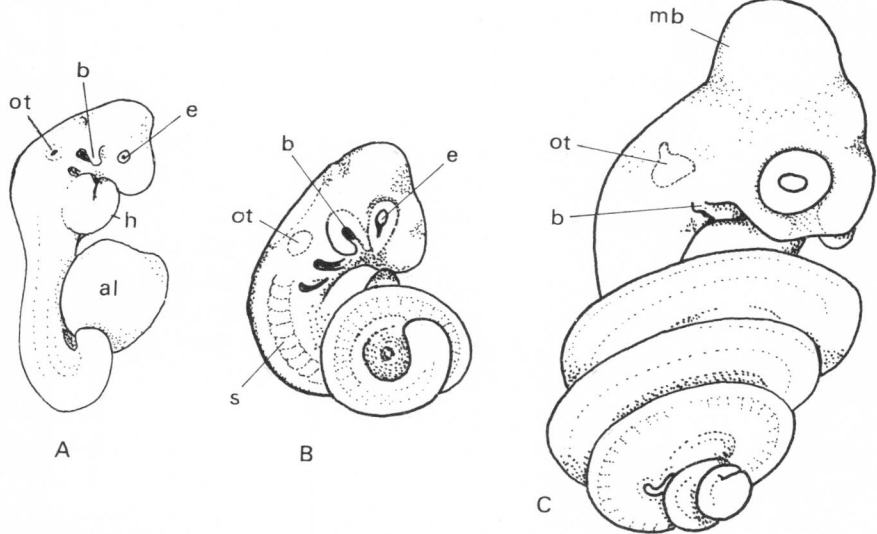

Figure 133   Three embryonic stages of the garter snake, *Thamnophis sirtalis*. After Zehr [474]. A. The trunk has begun to coil. Zehr stage 18. × 10. B. Two trunk coils. Stage 20. × 19. C. $5\frac{1}{2}$ to $6\frac{1}{4}$ trunk coils. Stage 26. × 9.

al, allantois (not shown in B and C). **b**, branchial arch region. **e**, eye. **h**, heart. **mb**, mid-brain prominence. **ot**, otocyst. **s**, somites.

441

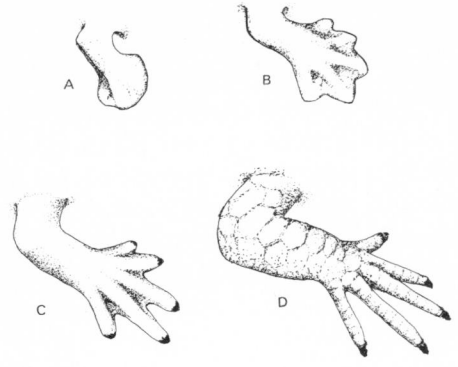

Figure 134   Stages in the development of the fore limbs in *Lacerta vivipara*. After Dufaure and Hubert [146].
A. Paddle-like stage, but with upper arm and forearm differentiated.
Dufaure and Hubert stage 33. ×13. B. Digits differentiating Stage 34. ×13. C. Digits still slightly webbed, claws forming. Stage 36. ×10. D. Digits well differentiated. Stage 38–39. ×8.

case of snake embryos, the whole body becomes coiled in a tight spiral (figure 133).

Limb buds grow out like paddles from the sides of the body and later transform themselves into front and hind legs with hands and feet and separate digits (figure 134). These buds may appear transiently in forms such as the slow-worm, even though the adult is more or less limbless. It is interesting that the vestigial limb buds of *Anguis* lack the little apical cap or crest at their tips which appears in more typical vertebrates; in these the apical cap is believed to play an important part in stimulating the further growth and differentiation of the limb tissues [343]. No limb buds have yet been discovered in snakes, although they must exist in species such as pythons which normally possess vestigial hind limbs (p. 99).

The scales develop comparatively late in embryonic life and those on the head appear more tardily than those over the body. Pigment first becomes visible in the eyes and then around the parietal or 'pineal' eye of lizards, where it shows up very strikingly through the skin of the head. The pigment in the skin appears last.

The embryo lizard or snake develops a special instrument, the egg-tooth, with which it can finally cut its way out of the egg-shell. This tooth is attached to the tip of the premaxillary bone in the midline. In structure it is essentially like the ordinary teeth, but is bigger and curves forwards, projecting in front of the snout when it erupts from the gum shortly before hatching. Its edge is flattened, and razorsharp (figure 135). Geckos are unique in normally possessing two egg-teeth side by side instead of a single one, but paired egg-teeth have been reported as an abnormality in embryos of other species [397].

An egg-tooth is present in all, or almost all viviparous forms, though it is often small (as in *Lacerta vivipara*) or rudimentary. The egg-tooth of the adder (figure 135 C) points backwards instead of forwards and would appear quite ineffective, even for tearing the embryonic membranes; this task is accomplished by jabs of the snout. The mere existence of such a tooth, however vestigial, in such reptiles is convincing evidence that egg-laying rather than viviparity was the primitive method of reproduction.

The embryos of chelonians, crocodilians and birds have no true egg-tooth but they do possess a structure called the egg-caruncle which performs the same function. This caruncle is formed from a horny thickening of the epidermis at the tip of the snout (figure 135 D, E), and like the egg-tooth is shed shortly after hatching.

It is interesting that the egg-laying monotreme mammals (platypus and echidna) possess a large egg-caruncle supported by a nodule of bone, the *os carunculi*, and a small egg-tooth as well, though the latter may not be functional [218]. The tuatara has a horny caruncle but no egg-tooth, and this is surprising since in most respects *Sphenodon* is much closer to lizards than it is to turtles or crocodiles.

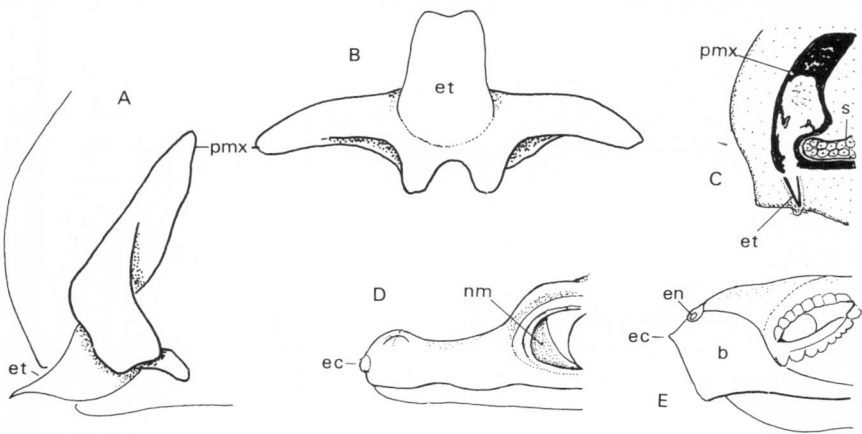

Figure 135 Egg-teeth and caruncles. A, B. Egg-tooth and premaxilla of late embryo grass snake (*Natrix natrix*), A seen from left side; B, from below, × 31. After Smith *et al.* [397]. C. Longitudinal section through egg-tooth of late embryo of adder (*Vipera berus*), showing its backward inclination. × 12. D, E. Egg-caruncle of D, late embryo of *Crocodylus niloticus* (× 3); E, of ridley turtle (*Lepidochelys olivacea*). × 2·2.

b, beak. **ec**, egg-caruncle. **en**, external nostril. **et**, egg-tooth. **nm**, nictitating membrane. **pmx**, premaxilla. **s**, front of nasal septum.

443

The incubation period of eggs, from the time of fertilisation to that of hatching, is exceedingly variable. Some oviparous species do not lay their eggs until the embryos are quite advanced, and in these the incubation period may be very short, only two or three weeks. In many reptiles, however, for instance the grass snake in England, the green turtle in the Caribbean, and the Nile crocodile, the period ranges between about six and twelve weeks. This is also quite a usual range for the gestation period in live-bearing species. Generally speaking all the embryos in a clutch of eggs are at about the same stage of development and hatch or are born around the same time. Occasionally, however, eggs laid at the same time and incubated together hatch in early and late batches, possibly owing to some genetic difference which determines the rate of development [233]. Even among a clutch of embryos inside a viviparous reptile one can exceptionally find the odd individual which is more or less advanced than the rest. In some cases, however, delayed hatching may perhaps be due to the full-time 'embryos' remaining inactive inside their eggs, as if reluctant to emerge.

For any given species, either oviparous or viviparous, the incubation or gestation period depends to a large extent on the temperature and is accelerated by heat. It has been estimated that in the viviparous garter snake *Thamnophis sirtalis* an increase of 1°C in the average temperature during gestation brings the date of birth four and a half days earlier. Gestation in this snake may vary from 87 days in an exceptionally hot summer to 116 days in an unusually cold one [46].

It is possible that during a particularly cold season, or perhaps after an autumn mating, the embryos may not be able to complete their development in the normal time, but can remain alive in their eggs or within the body of their hibernating mother until the following season. Here it is the whole embryo which is being stored, as it were, and not just the sperm as previously described. It is uncertain whether this embryonic hibernation ever occurs successfully in British reptiles, but it has been reported in some North American turtles [304] and actually appears to be the normal procedure with the tuatara in New Zealand. This creature regularly lays its eggs from October to December and the young hatch in the following year after an incubation period of thirteen or fourteen months, perhaps the longest known in any reptile [383].

Atlases which show annotated pictures of embryos at various stages of development have been prepared for several species of reptiles, including the alligator, viviparous lizard, garter snake and snapping turtle [146, 345, 470a, 474]. These 'normal tables' as they are called, are very helpful to embryologists who wish to indicate a particular stage which they are describing. Indeed, they are especially important to the student of reptilian embryos which do not develop at a constant rate under natural conditions, and cannot be staged, like chick embryos, from simply knowing the date on which they were laid [*].

During the last century embryology was mainly concerned with descriptions of dead specimens cut into sections and mounted on slides for examination under the microscope. Nowadays, however, one also wants to observe and carry out experiments on living embryos as an aid to understanding the processes of development. Unfortunately reptiles do not breed readily in captivity and it may be necessary to collect large numbers of eggs and incubate them artificially. For various reasons it is sometimes easier to obtain un-laid eggs by killing the mother, or even to induce premature egg-laying by injecting her with hormone preparations of the posterior lobe of the pituitary gland which bring on contractions of the oviduct. Such techniques have recently been used to study the earliest stages of development in oviparous reptiles (turtles) whose eggs are norm-ally too advanced at the time of laying to be suitable [see 426, 470].

Similar but more elaborate methods have also been applied to the investigation of viviparous species. A great advance in this work was made in 1956 when Maurice Panigel [309] showed that embryos of the viviparous lizard would develop after being removed from the female and placed in small dishes lined with gauze moistened in saline. They will often hatch from their membranous eggs and can be reared like normal young (Plate 67). Embryos of the slow-worm can also be explanted but they seem to have a closer physiological rela-tionship with their mother and more elaborate techniques of culture are necessary to keep them in good health.

It is possible to operate on embryos treated in this way, removing parts of the limbs and tail, and even much of the head. This last, heroic operation has been performed in order to study the effect of pituitary gland deprivation or development. Sometimes the results of experiments are obscured by post-operative complications. For example, it is very difficult to decide whether the tail of embryo lizards is able to regenerate like that of the adult. If one cuts the tail off through a hole in the egg, which it is not difficult to do, the stump usually becomes constricted by a ring-like adhesion derived from the amnion and allantois. This may contract around the stump and cause a part of it to fall off just in front of the site of the original experimental injury. The results of this kind of 'self-amputation' (which is not followed by regeneration) are very hard to interpret [74].

The rate of development of explanted reptile embryos, like that of eggs or young developing normally within the mother, can be retarded or accelerated by varying the temperature. Embryos of *Lacerta vivipara* which have reached fairly late stages can be stored without harm at about 10°C for up to a fortnight, during which they undergo virtually no development; they can then be transferred to warmer surroundings and will develop normally. Temperatures of about 28°C seem to be most suitable for embryos of this species, but for those of tropical reptiles much greater heat may be desirable. It has been shown that cultures of both embryonic and adult cells of certain Australian lizards will grow best at 37·5°C., but it is not yet known whether entire living embryos would withstand this treatment [411].

We have watched the behaviour of explanted embryos of *Lacerta vivipara* through their thin transparent shells and chorio-allantoic membranes. They begin to move quite spontaneously when they are at about the stage of a five-day chick embryo. In the earliest movements the trunk bends from side to side owing to contraction of the back muscles. This simple type of movement occurs even in early turtle embryos, before the shell develops and makes the body rigid. A few days later, activity spreads to the head, limbs and tail and increases progressively in frequency and vehemence. It can now also be elicited as a reflex response if the embryo is lightly touched or pinched through its membranes. None of these embryonic movements, however, appear to be coordinated in the sense that they foreshadow the type of movements made by the newborn lizard, as for example in walking or swimming. A little while before the time of birth the embryo again becomes practically quiescent and then there is a final burst of activity which leads to the creature rupturing its membranes with its snout and emerging from its egg [223].

I have noticed a rather similar state of affairs in late embryos of the grass snake *(Natrix natrix)* after removal from their eggs. Although the little snakes, which were well pigmented and about 15 cm long, could bend separate parts of their bodies, they seemed quite unable to transmit the serpentine wave down their lengths in the manner necessary for crawling or swimming. It was only just before they were ready to hatch that locomotion on land or in the water became possible.

446

Young reptiles often feed within a few hours of birth or hatching; they seem to have developed all the necessary reflex responses which the adult needs for survival, and generally speaking are quite able to fend for themselves. It is therefore surprising that the behaviour pattern of the embryo seems to bear so little relation to that exhibited by the new-born young. It would be interesting to know whether this apparently sudden change in behaviour is correlated with changes in the nervous system.

In both behaviour and appearance the baby reptile is almost a miniature replica of its parents. It does not play like a kitten or a puppy, and it is uncertain how far learning by experience is important in its life. It may change later on in colour, and there may be slight alterations in the relative proportions of its body. Its habits may also undergo some minor readjustment as it gets bigger, becomes less vulnerable to minor predators and is itself able to tackle larger prey. By and large, however, the only dramatic change in its life will centre on the maturation of its glandular system and the awakening of sexual activity.

The development of reptiles, like that of other animals, may occasionally go wrong so that the young appear with some congenital malformation [see 365]. The formation of Siamese twins, with two individuals partly or completely joined is fairly common, and snakes with two heads have been known to naturalists since the days of Aristotle. Double-headed lizards and turtles are also quite frequently reported; sometimes the heads are almost fused into one.

Other abnormalities include cleft lip and palate in lizards and snakes (Plate 69), which is anatomically remarkably similar to the well-known human affliction. Reduction of the eyes to tiny vestiges buried beneath the skin, shortening of the upper jaw, protrusion of the viscera through a deficiency of the body wall, and absence of one of the limbs has all been described.

These defects may depend on some faulty genetic constitution of the embryo. In other cases they may be produced by unfavourable conditions of the environment, especially in egg-laying species. It has been shown experimentally that drastic alteration of the incubation temperature during the earlier stages of embryonic life may produce congenital malformations in hatchling turtles [470].

Although all chelonians and crocodilians lay eggs, a very substantial number of lizards and snakes bear their young alive (Plates 66, 71). The distribution of viviparity among the various families and genera of Squamata seems curiously haphazard and bears only a fitful relationship to zoological affinity. Among the bigger families of lizards there are only a few, such as the Agamidae and Varanidae, in which all members practise the same mode of reproduction – in these instances, egg-laying. In many families either viviparity or oviparity predominates, but there is generally at least one odd genus or species which fails to conform. The New Zealand geckos of the genera *Hoplodactylus and Naultinus,* the iguanid genus *Phrynosoma* and the lacertid species *Lacerta vivipara* are examples of viviparous forms which belong to predominantly oviparous groups. Some members of the subfamily Laticaudinae are exceptional among sea snakes in laying eggs, but this is perhaps not surprising since they are less thoroughly adapted to aquatic life than their relatives. Some idea of the distribution of the two methods of reproduction among Squamata generally may be gained from the synopsis of living reptiles in Chapter 13.

As a matter of fact, the distinction between oviparity and viviparity in Squamata is not a very fundamental one. Certain oviparous species may retain their eggs for longer periods than others, especially when suitable facilities for laying are not available; it may even happen exceptionally that an individual will give birth to living young. Nevertheless, it is uncertain whether any reptiles fluctuate between oviparity and viviparity under normal circumstances. Pope [333] states that the royal python *(P. regius)* of West Africa has been accredited with both methods of reproduction.

The viviparous lizard is another problematical case. Its young, like those of many other viviparous reptiles, are normally born within their thin-shelled eggs, and escape from these while they are being expelled from the mother, or shortly afterwards. Sometimes, however, the babies remain within their membranous eggs for several days before they hatch. Over forty years ago, some sixty lizard eggs with quite tough, parchment-like shells were found under a stone in the Pyrenees at an altitude of 610 metres (2000 ft). Some of these hatched and were identified as *Lacerta vivipara*. The large number of eggs pointed to communal laying by several females and it was claimed that in this region the lizard had reverted to the more primitive habit of egg-laying. Unfortunately this observation has never been repeated, either in the field or in captivity. Nevertheless, one may be justified in regarding this species as being only marginally viviparous, since as we have seen, its eggs will develop after removal from the mother under suitable laboratory conditions [309].

Turtles may also retain their eggs if they are kept under conditions unsuitable for laying, but no instances of live birth in this group seem to have been reported. In some cases the eggs may erode the oviducts and enter the body cavity where they will presumably die and perhaps eventually be absorbed. However, this does not necessarily have any serious effect upon the mother. Ectopic embryos have also been found in the body-cavity of viviparous species.

Viviparity in reptiles has certain advantages over egg-laying. Protected inside a mobile and possibly venomous parent, the eggs are less likely to fall victim to predators. They are also less exposed to the hazards of physical circumstance: the danger of becoming too moist, which renders eggs liable to fungal infection, or of drying up. Furthermore, by basking in the sun or by sheltering from extremes of heat and cold, the mother unconsciously selects the range of temperature most suitable for herself, and presumably also for the development of her unborn young. Weekes [446] has pointed out that the majority of reptiles which live at altitudes of 915 to 1220 metres (3000–4000 ft.) or more are viviparous, and this seems to be the general rule for all species, such as *Lacerta vivipara* and *Vipera berus* which inhabit regions where the climate is really severe (p. 42).

The simplest stage in the evolution of viviparity in Squamata may be envisaged as very much like the state of affairs in *Lacerta vivipara*. Owing to some change in the mechanism for provoking labour, the eggs can be retained inside the mother instead of being expelled before the embryos have completed their development. The eggshell, no longer needed for protection against injury and dessication, disappears although there is still a thin, shell membrane. Inevitably, there will be interchange of water and gases between embryo and mother through the egg-coverings and wall of the oviduct. The chorio-allantois, now the principal egg-covering, is therefore still carrying out its original function under different circumstances; it exchanges material with the maternal blood-system instead of with the outside world through pores in the tough egg-shell. We therefore have the beginnings of a placenta, an organ which is characteristic of mammals and which consists essentially of adjacent modified areas of embryonic and maternal tissues which allow interchange of substances between them.

The placenta of *Lacerta vivipara* is, however, of extremely primitive type and allows little transfer of substances other than water and

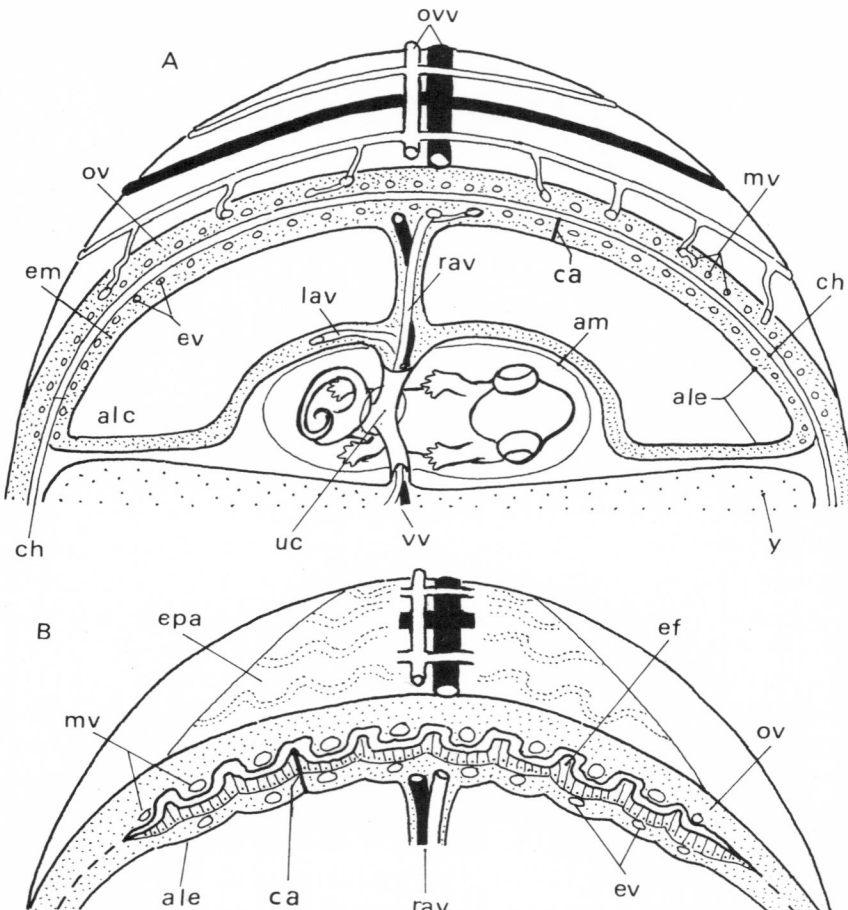

Figure 136 Diagrams showing chorio-allantoic placentation in lizards, as seen in transverse section through the oviduct and embryonic membranes. Based partly· on Weekes, H. C. (1930) *Proc. Linn. Soc. N.S. Wales*, **55** 550. A shows the simplest condition where the embryonic and maternal tissues are close together and well supplied with blood-vessels, but there is no specialisation of their adjacent surfaces. The narrow gap between them may be occupied by a thin shell membrane which is not shown. In many lizards the right allantoic artery and vein pass across the allantoic cavity as shown, while the left vessels pass round the inner wall of the allantois. B shows the most advanced condition, as seen in the skink *Chalcides chalcides*. Both embryonic and maternal tissues are thrown into interlocking folds in the main placental area which is elliptical in shape. At the sides of the placenta the line of apposition between the embryonic tissues (chorion) and the oviduct lining is shown in broken lines. Various conditions intermediate between A and B are found in many lizards and snakes.

450

alc, allantoic cavity. **ale**, allantoic endoderm. **am**, amnion. **ca**, chorio-allantois (thickness shown by thick black lines). **ch**, chorion (ectoderm). **ef**, embryonic fold, formed of enlarged chorion cells. **em**, extra-embryonic mesoderm between chorion and allantois. **epa**, elliptical placental area. **ev**, embryonic blood-vessels (capillaries). **lav**, left allantoic (umbilical) vessels (only artery shown). **mv**, maternal blood-vessels (capillaries). **ov**, oviduct (cut wall). **ovv**, main vessels of oviduct running along its dorsal surface, with transverse branches (arteries white, veins black). **rav**, right allantoic (umbilical) vessels. **uc**, umbilical cord emerging from amnion and forking into allantoic and vitelline (yolk-sac) branches. **vv**, vitelline vessels. **y**, yolk.

gases. Panigel found that salts of sodium, phosphorus and iodine, labelled by being rendered radioactive and injected into the pregnant female, reached the embryos only in minute quantities. All the food required by the embryo is present in its yolk so that it can develop successfully outside the mother when placed in suitably moist and aerated conditions.

The next stage involves the loss of the shell membranes altogether (or their extreme reduction) and a thinning out of the maternal tissues so that the two sets of blood vessels are brought into still closer proximity (figure 136). In some cases the maternal capillaries are raised up into tiny folds. Two separate placental areas, one based on the chorio-allantois and the other on the yolk-sac, are usually established. Placental conditions of this general type have been found in many viviparous reptiles such as the New Zealand geckos of the genus *Hoplodactylus*, the night lizards *(Xantusia)*, some skinks (eg certain species of *Chalcides, Egernia, Lygosoma* and *Tiliqua)*, and among snakes in the Australian elapid *Denisonia* and probably in *Vipera berus*, some sea snakes and some species of *Natrix* and *Thamnophis* [22, 446]. Such placentae may not be recognisable by naked-eye inspection of the embryonic membranes and oviduct.

The physiology of these placentae has been little studied, but it has been suggested that the yolk-sac placenta is chiefly important in helping the embryo to obtain water from the maternal tissues, while the chorio-allantois continues to function mainly as a lung though it may also have some slight nutritional role. It has been shown experimentally that sodium and iodine isotopes will pass across the chorioallantoic placental barrier from mother to embryo in certain viviparous species of *Natrix* [113], and there is evidence for some transfer of amino-acids in *Thamnophis* [101].

In the most advanced type of reptilian placenta the blood-supply of the more important, chorio-allantoic placenta becomes further increased, and it can be recognised by the naked eye as a distinct elliptical area beneath the main longitudinal blood-vessels of the oviduct. Moreover, the oviduct lining is thrown into well-marked folds which interlock with folds of the chorio-allantois, thus considerably increasing the area of contact (figure 136). The yolk now tends to become reduced, though not to the same extent as in mammals; some food (in the form of amino-acids, for example) is probably transferred from the mother reptile to her embryos and it is possible that some of the latters' excretory products pass in the opposite direction. Chorio-allantoic placentae of this highly developed type have been described in the European skink *Chalcides chalcides* [=*C. tridactylus*], whose small-yolked eggs only measure 3 mm., in diameter at the time of ovulation, and in the Australian skinks *Lygosoma weekesae* and *L. entrecasteauxi* [446]. In all probability further examples will be discovered.

Viviparity in reptiles thus shows all gradations between a state of affairs where the mother does little more than act as a mobile incubator for her unborn young, to one in which she probably supplies the embryo with a fair amount of food to supplement its inadequate yolk. Some workers like to use the term ovoviviparity* for the first condition in order to distinguish it from the more truly viviparous state of reptiles which possess an advanced and structurally specialised placenta. Since there are many intermediate types it seems unwise to try and draw such a hard and fast distinction; I prefer to call all live-bearing reptiles viviparous, and have done so throughout this book.

It is a pity that much of the important work on placentation in reptiles was done before 1940 and has never really been assimilated by mammalian embryologists. Further studies, particularly with a physiological bias, would be of great interest. Viviparity and placentation must have evolved independently in Squamata and mammals. Nevertheless, as Bauchot has pointed out in a review [22], these reproductive adaptations appear to be basically similar in the two groups; they have probably arisen from a similar type of oviparity involving the production of large-yolked, amniote eggs.

* The term ovoviviparity was probably first used to distinguish the reproduction of live-bearing reptiles in general, whose eggs are typically large and yolky, from that in mammals whose eggs are virtually devoid of yolk, so that the embryo is entirely dependent on placental nutrition. Used in this original sense the term has something to be said for it.

The chromosomes

Inside the nucleus of every cell are a number of threadlike or punctate structures known as chromosomes which occur in pairs. They carry the genes which are responsible for the transmission of hereditary characters, and are made up of nucleic acids and proteins. The main nucleic acid is desoxyribonucleic acid or DNA; the quantity of this material in the red cell nucleus of the green turtle has been estimated at about 5×10^{-9} mgm. [457].

Chromosomes are normally visible only when the cell is in the process of division. At this time each chromosome is seen to be double; the duplicates separate so that one goes to each daughter nucleus. In the formation of mature germ cells, however, the process is more complicated and involves what is called a reduction division. The final result is that the sperm or egg has only half the number of chromosomes of the cells elsewhere in the body. At fertilisation this half (or haploid) number is restored to the full or diploid number characteristic of the body cells in general.

The chromosome complement or karyotype varies greatly within and among the different animal groups, and may have some bearing on their zoological relationships. In reptiles the chromosomes vary in size, some being large (macrochromosomes), others minute (micro-chromosomes), while others again may be of intermediate size. Further, they may have a J or V-like shape (metacentric chromosomes), or resemble rods (acrocentric types) or dots. It is thought that during the course of evolution of new species the chromosome complex has in some cases been altered as the result of the fusion of two rod-like chromosomes to form a single V-shaped one, or that the latter may have divided to give two rods. Consequently a 'fundamental number' of chromosomes can be calculated for each species by counting two for each of the Vs (ie one for each arm of the V), and one for each rod or dot-like type. This is generally abbreviated to N.F. *(nombre fondamental)* after the usage of Robert Matthey [276], the Swiss zoologist who developed the idea.

Among reptiles the highest chromosome numbers are found in Chelonia where the N.F. ranges from 54 to 70, including 4–8 V-shaped metacentrics. The Nile crocodile has an N.F. of 38, while in the American alligator and spectacled caiman the figure is 42 [221]. In both chelonians and crocodilians the chromosomes intergrade in size so that there is no sharp distinction between the macro and micro types.

453

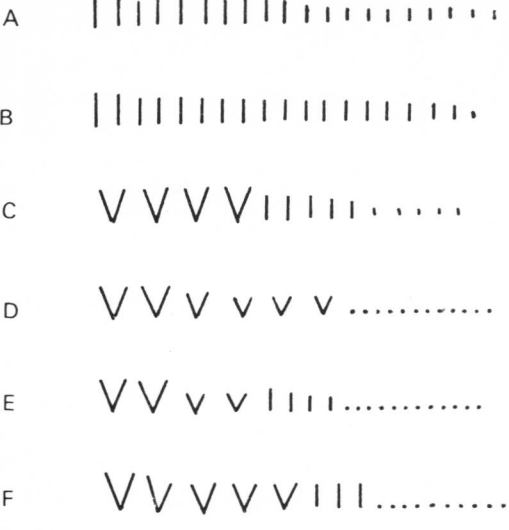

Figure 137 Diagrams showing haploid chromosome complements of Squamata. Formulae in text give diploid (double) numbers. A–E after White [457], based on Matthey [276]. A. *Tarentola mauritanica* ('complexe geckonoïde'). B. Most lacertids. C. Skink, *Chalcides chalcides*. (B and C, 'complexe scincolacertoïde'). D. *Anolis carolinensis*. E. *Varanus gouldii*. (D and E, 'complexe iguanoïde'). F. 'Basic' snake complement, as in *Vipera berus* and *Natrix natrix*.

Matthey's analysis of lepidosaurian chromosomes is of general interest to herpetologists. Many of these reptiles possess chromosomes of three types; V-shaped metacentrics which are usually fairly large, rod-like types of varying sizes, and a series of dot-like types which are often very much smaller than the rest. The karyotype of any species is often expressed as a formula in which $2N$ = the total diploid number; V = the number of metacentrics; I = the number of rods; m = the number of dot-like microchromosomes, and N.F. = the 'fundamental number'. Thus, in *Sphenodon* the formula is $2N=36$; $V=12$; $I=18$; $m=6$; N.F. $=48$. This last is the characteristic fundamental number of lizards, apart from geckos.

Matthey recognised three main groups of lizards on the basis of their karyotypes (figure 137). The 'complexe geckonoïde' contains the family Gekkonidae alone; the chromosomes of pygopods, the other members of the infraorder Gekkota, do not seem to have been studied. The chromosomes show no sharp distinction between large and small types and consist mainly or entirely of rods of graded size. The N.F. ranges from 32 to 46 in the species investigated.

The 'complexe scinco-lacertoïde' comprises the Scincidae and Lacertidae which are both placed in the infraorder Scincomorpha of conventional classification (p. 532). In the lacertids there appear, typically, to be 36 rod-like macrochromosomes and 2 'micros'; it is

454

possible that some 'micros' have been lost by fusion (see Table). In the skinks there are 4–10 large Vs and a big series of rods of varying sizes.

The remaining group, the 'complexe iguanoïde', is very large and contains the other main families of lizards which have not yet been mentioned, irrespective of their position in orthodox classification. The karyotype usually consists of V-shaped metacentrics, often of different sizes, rods (acrocentrics), and a series of dot-like micro-chromosomes. The N.F. is 46 or 48 in the great majority of species examined. Formulae of some representative forms taken from Matthey are given in the table below. Figures in brackets for the N.F. of three species show further corrections made to allow for possible fusions or losses of microchromosomes.

Family	Species	2N	V	I	m	N.F.	
		See p. 454 for abbreviations					
	COMPLEXE GECKONOÏDE						
Gekkonidae	*Tarentola mauritanica*	42	0	42	0	42	
	COMPLEXE IGUANOÏDE						
Agamidae	*Agama stellio*	36	12	0	24	48	
Chamaelonidae	*Chamaeleo vulgaris*	24	12	0	12	36	(48)
Iguanidae	*Anolis carolinensis*	36	12	0	24	48	
Anguidae	*Anguis fragilis*	44	4	16	24	48	
Varanidae	*Varanus gouldii*	40	8	8	24	48	
Helodermatidae	*Heloderma suspectum*	38	10	4	24	48	
Amphisbaenidae	*Trogonophis wiegmanni*	36	12	0	24	48	
Amphisbaenidae	*Rhineura floridana*	46	2	44	0	48	
Teiidae	*Tupinambis teguixin*	36	10	2	24	46	
	COMPLEXE SCINCO-LACERTOÏDE						
Lacertidae	*Lacerta viridis*	38	0	36	2	38	(50)
Scincidae	*Scincus officinalis*	32	4	28	0	36	(48)

The snakes are perhaps a more closely knit group than the lizards and their chromosome complements have been regarded as less variable. Recent studies [see 77] indicate a greater diversity than was previously recognised; nevertheless, an appreciable number of species belonging to various families and including the primitive burrower *Leptotyphlops phillipsi*, have an identical karyotype of $2N=36$; $10V \times 6I + 20m$; N.F.$=46$; this has been regarded as the basic ophidian formula [434]. The colubrid *Clelia occipitolutea* has the largest number of chromosomes, with a formula of $2N=50$; 14 macros$+36$ m.

Sex chromosomes Generally speaking, the two members of each pair of chromosomes are identical. In many vertebrates, including mammals, however, one or other sex has a pair of unequal 'sex chromosomes' among the others, designated X and Y; in the opposite sex the members of the corresponding pair are alike and are designated XX. The sex of the offspring depends on whether, after the restitution of the diploid number of chromosomes which occurs at fertilisation, the egg has the XX or XY complement. In mammals the sex chromosomes of the male have the XY and those of the female the XX arrangement. In many (perhaps all) birds, and also in a number of species of colubrid and viperid snakes the opposite condition has been demonstrated, the male having the equal pair and the female the unequal one. In these snakes the XX chromosome of the male and the X of the female are of the V-shaped metacentric type and form or belong to the fourth pair. The Y chromosome of the female is smaller and acrocentric. In other reptiles studied, however, including certain chelonians, crocodilians, lizards and boid snakes, no difference in the chromosomes of the two sexes can be recognised. It is possible that in such cases sex determination depends on certain individual genes rather than on whole chromosomes [287; see W. Becak in 77].

Parthenogenesis

It has been established that certain Caucasian rock lizards of the *Lacerta saxicola* group have populations which consist entirely of females which reproduce by parthenogenesis ('virgin birth') [125]. This has been convincingly demonstrated and there seems little possibility of sperm storage or delayed fertilisation confusing the issue. Some of these lizards are represented in different parts of their range by bisexual and parthenogenetic species which interbreed in border territory. The hybrid offspring are sterile females with reduced ovaries and oviducts.

Normally, the eggs laid by parthenogenetic females only give rise to females; sometimes, however, the embryos are identifiable as males, but these almost invariably develop malformations and die before hatching. Apart from a very occasional hermaphrodite, only the females reach maturity.

It has been suggested that parthenogenetic strains of animals are most liable to arise under conditions of climatic hardship, such as may have occurred in the Caucasus during the Pleistocene glaciations. At such times natural selection may have favoured unisexual reproduction in the lizards, since the parthenogenetic females produce greater numbers of eggs than normal females, and the incubation period of these eggs is shorter. Nevertheless, one may suppose that such advantages would in the long run be cancelled out by reduction in the potentiality for genetic variation which bisexual reproduction confers.

Parthenogenesis is also believed to occur in certain North American whiptail lizards *(Cnemidophorus)* of the family Teiidae [259], and is suspected in certain geckos. It is likely that this method of reproduction is more widespread among reptiles than has been realised. It has been reported in turkeys bred on experimental poultry farms, where a few mature individuals (males in this case) have been raised from eggs which have never been fertilised by a cock *.

The genetics of these parthenogenetic lizards are very interesting. One might expect that the cells of the female *Lacerta saxicola* would show the single or haploid number of chromosomes normally found in mature unfertilised eggs. In fact, however, they possess the diploid number (2N) of 38 like the forms which reproduce in the normal bisexual fashion. It appears that when the eggs are maturing in the ovaries of the parthenogenetic females they undergo a reduction division in the normal way. They then begin a second cell division, but this is never completed. The egg-cell nuclei, each containing the haploid number of chromosomes, fuse again instead of passing into respective daughter cells, and consequently the diploid set of chromosomes is formed. The sterile female hybrids which arise from the occasional crossing of parthenogenetic females with normal males are triploid, with a chromosome complement of 3N=57. This is the natural result of fertilisation of a parthenogenetic diploid egg-cell (complement 2N=38) by a normal haploid sperm (N=19). One of the parthenogenetic species of *Cnemidophorus* is also diploid, but others are triploid; unlike the triploid rock lizards *(Lacerta saxicola)*, however, these females can reproduce parthenogenetically in turn.

Chapter 11

Growth, Age and Regeneration

Growth

Overall patterns of growth THE GREAT majority of vertebrates tend to get bigger as they get older; this increase in size is fastest when they are embryos and young animals and slows down after the onset of sexual maturity, the stage in life when they are able to breed. In mammals such as man, growth is virtually complete quite soon after maturity and at a fairly well-defined age. In reptiles, however, growth ends less abruptly and may continue for a relatively much longer period after maturity has been reached; a reptile may grow nearly twice as big before it dies as it was at the time of its first successful mating. Nevertheless, one has the impression that many species of reptile, particularly the smaller kinds, show a similar type of limited or determinate growth pattern as the mammals, and that they ultimately stop getting any bigger after a certain age or size has been attained.

There is some direct evidence for this idea. Fitch [162] studied a sample of copperhead snakes *(Agkistrodon contortrix)* which were marked individually, liberated and recaptured for measurement at successive intervals. He found that a few specimens had not grown significantly after substantial periods and concluded that some of these were old adults which had virtually stopped growing. Legler [249] obtained similar results in his study of the box turtle *(Terrapene ornata)* which increases only a little in size after it has reached an age of about twelve years. After this there may be irregular bursts of intermittent growth, but even these probably cease entirely when the animal is between 15 and 20 years old and has a shell length of 12·7 to 15·2 cm. (5 to 6 in.).

Circumstantial evidence can also be brought to bear on the problem. If a certain species has the power of lifelong growth one would expect that in any population some of the older members would be considerably larger than the rest. If, on the other hand, growth stops long before the potential life-span is run, the size range of mature individuals is likely to be smaller and the maximum size limit fairly well defined. We know that this is so for mammals, and it also seems to be true in many reptiles such as the smaller chelonians and lizards, where all the adults are much of a size and giants are seldom if ever encountered.

It is probable, however, that in certain reptiles at least, growth can go on, though at a diminishing rate, throughout the life of the individual. The occasional discovery of individuals much above the average for their species in size is strong circumstantial evidence for this idea, though it is hard to prove (or disprove) by direct methods. The existence of giant pythons is well known and comparatively enormous individuals of the smaller kinds of snakes are sometimes found. Mature specimens of the grass snake *(Natrix natrix)*, for instance, are generally between 60 and 102 cm. in length; individuals of much over 102 cm. (40 in.) are fairly uncommon in England today, but at least four grass snakes of over 150 cm. (including one of 175 cm. (5 ft. 9 in.) have been recorded [395]. Similarly outsized specimens of the bigger chelonians and crocodilians turn up from time to time.

It is possible that these giant individuals may have some genetic or glandular abnormality; no investigation of this seems to have been made. It is much more likely, however, that sheer longevity is involved. These giants are probably very old beasts which have been lucky enough to escape the usually hazards of their kind for an exceptionally long period; they are becoming increasingly rare as their haunts are encroached upon by expanding human populations. It must be added, however, that some very long-lived reptiles such as the box turtles, tuatara and slow-worm never appear to grow above a fixed adult size, so that sheer longevity cannot be the only factor involved.

The differences between the growth patterns of mammals and reptiles are sometimes ascribed to differences in the method of skeletal growth. In both groups the greater part of the skeleton is first formed of cartilage, which is subsequently converted into bone by the process of ossification. The main part or shaft of each bone ossifies first, and in mammals, smaller secondary centres of ossification develop later at its ends or epiphyses (figure 138 D). A zone of cartilage remains for a time between the main (primary) and secondary

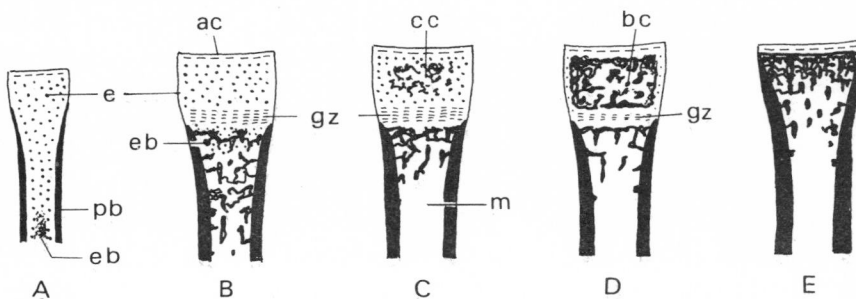

Figure 138   Diagrams illustrating bone growth and epiphysial structure in reptiles. The figures show longitudinal sections through one end and part of the shaft of a long bone such as the tibia. A. Bone in later embryonic life. Most of the shaft of the 'bone' and its ends or epiphyses are composed of cartilage (stippled). A shell of bone (black) is being laid down around the shaft beneath its connective tissue covering (perichondrium) which is not shown. There is also some internal (endochondral) ossification towards the middle of the shaft. B. Condition in chelonians and crocodilians, at least before they reach full maturity. The shaft is well ossified with a shell of periosteal (originally perichondral) bone and an internal meshwork of bone which was originally laid down endochondrally, replacing the cartilage of the shaft and surrounding the marrow spaces. The epiphysis is cartilaginous and has a cap of specialised articular cartilage. Between epiphysis and shaft is a growth zone of flattened cartilage cells arranged in columns which may disappear with age but perhaps in some forms (? crocodiles) persists through-out life, allowing continuous though diminishing growth in length. The bone grows in thickness by addition to the outer surface of the periosteal shell, the inner surface being correspondingly absorbed. C. Condition in immature *Sphenodon* and immature lizards. A secondary centre of calcified cartilage has formed in the epiphysis; in some small lizards this may never ossify. The growth zone is still active. D. Condition in many lizards approaching maximum size. The secondary centre has become ossified, as in mammals. The growth zone is still present but is becoming exhausted and in most cases will eventually disappear. In varanids, however, it may persist throughout life. These lizards are unusual among reptiles in that their epiphyses are nourished by blood vessels carried through the cartilage in a system of canals. E. Condition where bone has reached its full size and is entirely ossified except for its cap of articular cartilage. The growth zone has disappeared and the epiphysis has become ossified either by extension of the bone of the shaft or by fusion of the bony shaft with the bony secondary centre. The marrow cavity of the shaft and epiphysis have become continuous and (as in C and D) much of the internal bony network has disappeared.

ac, articular cartilage. **bc**, bony secondary centre. **cc**, cartilaginous secondary centre (calcified). **e**, epiphysis (entirely cartilaginous in A and B). **eb**, endochond-ral (internal) bone. **gz**, growth zone. **m**, marrow cavity. **pb**, perichondral bony shell.

460

centres, and the cartilage cells retain the capacity for growth while the animal is young, so that the bone can increase in length. At maturity, however, the growth cartilage also becomes ossified and the main and secondary centres fuse to form a single bony mass (figure 138 E). When this occurs, as it does in many at the age of 18–21, no further increase in the length of the bone can take place.

R. W. Haines [208] has shown that in many lizards secondary centres of ossification also develop in outlying parts of some of the bones, and since these usually unite with the main centre in time growth must cease entirely, as it does in mammals. The same effect is probably produced in *Sphenodon* and certain other (mostly small) lizards, where the secondary centres are calcified, but not actually ossified ※ This may be one of the reasons why giant individuals of most saurian species are not encountered. The one group of lizards in which the occurrence of occasional giants is well known is the monitor family (Varanidae), many of which normally reach a large size. It is interesting that although these lizards do possess bony secondary centres these are said never to unite completely with the rest of the bone. I have examined the skull of a gigantic example of the African monitor *Varanus exanthematicus* which measured nearly 13 cm. from snout to occipital condyle (Plate 16). This lizard was probably well over 122 cm. (4 ft.) in length, the size of a normal full-grown specimen. Yet the ossified secondary centre at the upper end of the quadrate bone had not yet fused with the shaft and there may still have been the possibility of further growth.

A more primitive condition is found in chelonians, snakes and crocodilians, where the ends of the bones do not develop secondary centres of ossification but remain cartilaginous throughout life. There is therefore no definite mechanism for bringing bone growth to an abrupt halt. In species with limited growth such as the box turtle the growth cartilage presumably becomes inactive after a certain age. In others, however, especially in the bigger forms such as sea turtles, pythons and crocodiles, its activity may perhaps be continued indefinitely, so that if the animal lives long enough it will slowly grow into a giant.

Growth rates The growth rates of reptiles are probably a good deal more irregular than those of mammals. There may be great variations in the size of the new-born young from a single litter. Fitch found that copperhead snakes born in captivity varied from 16·0 to 26·4 cm. in

461

length, and from 7·1 to 14·9 gms. in weight. Such differences became even greater in early post-natal life, depending upon the young snakes' ability to find prey and on various environmental factors.

The influence of the environment on growth, especially during early life, is also shown by Legler's study of the box turtle. In a good summer the eggs hatch at least a couple of months before the young turtles hibernate, so that they have time to get enough food to promote considerable growth. In a bad season, however, hatching is delayed, and the young, which may remain in the nest throughout the winter, hardly have time to feed or to grow significantly. Turtles which had a good start in their season of hatching usually maintained their rapid growth for a year or two; a few of these favoured animals actually reached adult size three or four years earlier than the average.

Legler also found that some years were more favourable to growth than others, and that these fluctuations were related to temperature, rainfall, and the abundance of grasshoppers which form a major food item of the box turtle. It seems fair to assume that in reptiles generally, the climate may influence growth in the following ways – by accelerating or retarding the incubation time of the eggs, or the gestation period in the case of viviparous species; by regulating the overall amount of time which the animal spends in an active state on its business of hunting and feeding, and by its effects on the available supplies of plant or animal food.

Under good conditions many reptiles, even the larger and more long-lived species, grow surprisingly quickly during early life. Carr [89] mentions a loggerhead turtle *(Caretta caretta)* which grew from a hatchling to a weight of about 36 kilograms (kg.) or 80 lb in four and a half years, and a giant tortoise from the Galapagos which increased in weight from 13 to 163 kg. (29 to 360 lb) in seven years. The American alligator, which is about 20 cm. (8 in.) long at hatching, may grow at the rate of over 30·5 cm. (1 ft.) a year for its first three years of life; after this period it is about 137 cm. (4½ ft.) long. Even up to nine years, growth must be quite rapid for alligators of this age measure from 213 to 270 cm. (7 to nearly 9 ft.) (figure 139).

The measurements made by Pope [333] of his docile pet python 'Sylvia' must give us one of the most complete growth records available for any individual reptile in captivity. 'Sylvia' was a few months old and about 107 cm. (3½ ft.) long when she was first measured in February 1946. In February 1947 she measured over 183 cm. (6 ft.) and weighed 2·9 kg (6 lb. 6 oz.). At the end of February

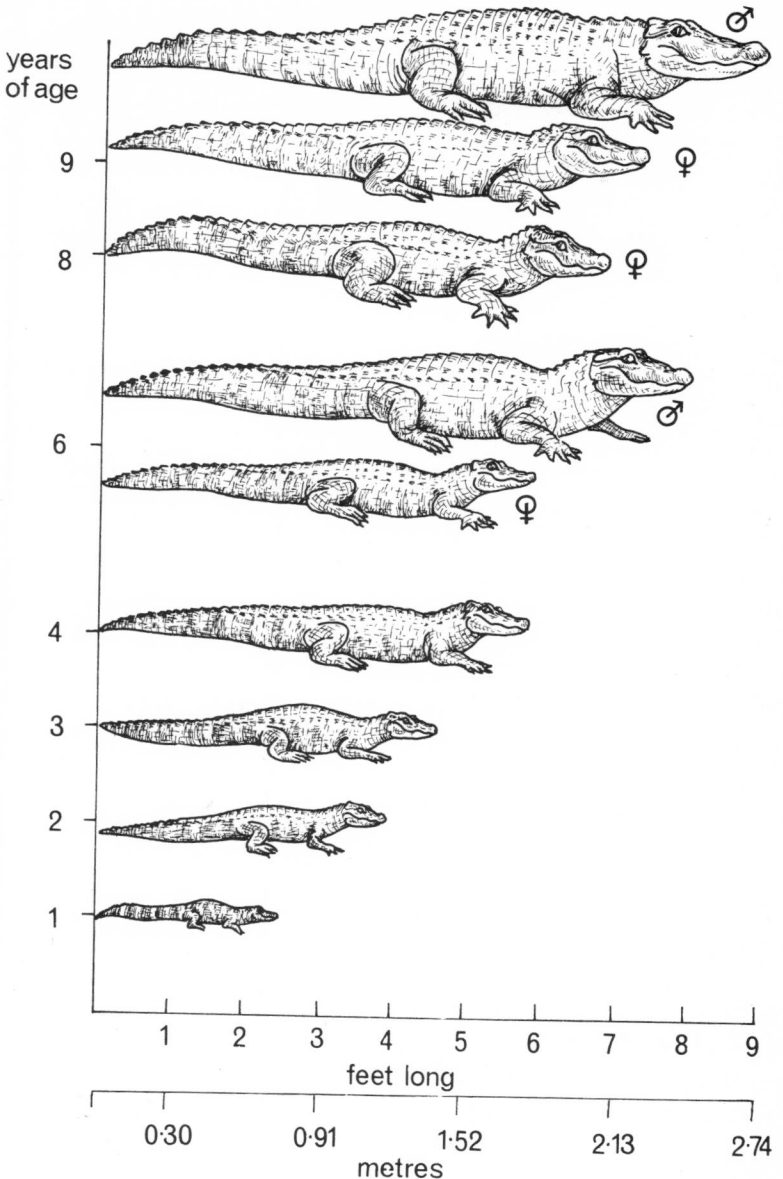

years
of age

9

8

6

4

3

2

1

1   2   3   4   5   6   7   8   9

feet long

0·30   0·91   1·52   2·13   2·74

metres

Figure 139   Growth of *Alligator mississippiensis* in Louisiana. After Oliver, J. A.
(Copyright 1955) *The Natural History of North American Amphibians and Reptiles.*
Princetown, New Jersey, D. Van Nostrand Company Inc. Based on data from
E. A. McIlhenny.

1948 her statistics were 290 cm. (9½ ft.) and 14 kg. (31 lb). This python was therefore growing at an average rate of about 91 cm. (3 ft.) a year, 7·6 cm. (3 in.) a month or 1·8 cm. (0·7 in.) a week. After this period, when 'Sylvia' was rather more than two years old and was probably reaching sexual maturity, her growth slowed down very considerably, and during her remaining twelve recorded years of life she only grew about another 107 cm. Her final length is given as 396 cm. (13 ft.), with a weight of 31·75 kg (70 lb). Whether this snake would have grown so quickly if she had had to fend for herself in the wild is open to question; as the pet of a herpetologist she may have received unusually favoured treatment *.

Growth rates of the smaller reptiles are also quite impressive. Figures given by Smith [395] for the British species show that the young of the common lizard *(Lacerta vivipara)* may grow from a total length (including tail) of 37–47 mm. to one of 108 mm. after about 12 months. *Agama* lizards in West Africa almost double their length within six months of hatching [213]. Legler found that box turtles increased in length by about 68 per cent on average in their first year of life, and by 28·6 per cent and 18 per cent in their second and third years respectively. After this growth slowed down from a 13·3 per cent increase in the fourth year to one of 3 per cent in the fourteenth. These figures were based on measurements of the length of the plastron, which is often used as a convenient index in chelonian growth studies.

It is a strange fact that the growth rates of turtles, like those of some invertebrates, seem to be increased if they are subjected to a moderate rise in the intensity of the gravitational field. Young red-eared terrapins *(Pseudemys scripta elegans)* which were placed in centrifuges for five weeks and subjected to a field five times as strong as the normal pull of gravity were found to grow about twice as fast as control specimens in carapace length. The animals were only removed from the centifuge for about 20 minutes each day, for feeding, and for a few hours once a week for measurement [141].

Sex and growth The state of sexual maturity can be determined by examining the ovaries or testes to see whether ripe eggs or sperm are being produced. In reptiles generally the onset of maturity is more strictly related to size than age, and as we have mentioned, the sizes even of young from the same litter may vary considerably, depending upon environmental and other factors. Despite these variations it has been possible to work out an average figure for the breeding age of many species. The green anolis lizard *(Anolis carolinensis)*, for example, is able to reproduce within less than year of hatching [304]. Other small lizards such as the common lizard *(Lacerta vivipara)*, the sand lizard *(L. agilis)* and the common *Agama agama* of West Africa reach maturity within two years or less, and many snakes, including the big pythons, within two to five years. In northern Europe, however, the grass snake *(Natrix natrix)* and adder *(Vipera berus)* take some three to five years before they are ready to breed. The hawksbill turtle *(Eretmochelys imbricata)* and the red-eared terrapin *(Pseudemys scripta)* may mature at around three years; the box turtle seems to mature rather late, between eight to eleven years of age on average, though some individuals do so when they are several years younger.

Crocodilians also seem to begin their sex lives rather later than most other reptiles. The American alligator, one of the more rapidly growing species, matures when it is about six years old and 1·8 metres (6 ft.) or more in length. Cott [119] believes that the Nile crocodile does not generally breed until it is 2·44 to 3·05 metres (8 to 10 ft.) long and probably about 20 years old. The interesting work of Dawbin [130] on the tuatara *(Sphenodon)* shows that this archaic creature is one of the most slow-growing of reptiles and probably requires at least twenty years to attain the age of reproduction.

In some reptiles the growth pattern differs according to the sex of the individual, at least during the earlier years of life. In the box turtle, for instance, the males grow faster than the females to begin with and reach sexual maturity two or three years earlier. In both the agama lizard and the copperhead snake the male is also said to have the faster rate of growth when young. The growth rates of juveniles, however, are not necessarily a guide to the final adult size. Female box turtles ultimately grow bigger on average than the males, though in the copperhead and *Agama* the reverse is true.

Adult size range The sizes of animals, particularly the maximum size which any species may reach, have a curious interest which perhaps exceeds their scientific importance. So far as reptiles are concerned such figures may not be easy to obtain, quite apart from the logical difficulty of setting a maximum limit for a species in which growth may theoretically continue throughout life. James A. Oliver has discussed the problem in his book *Snakes in fact and fiction* [306],

465

where he assesses the reported dimensions of various giant snakes; his remarks are of course equally applicable to other reptiles such as crocodiles. Three rather different kinds of information have to be considered.

The only totally reliable data are those derived from specimens in collections which can be checked by anyone who wishes to do so. A stuffed specimen or a complete mounted skeleton is irrefutable evidence, but such preparations of really large reptiles are rare in even the best museums; the big stuffed crocodiles in the exhibition gallery of the British Museum (Natural History) are only about 4 metres (13 ft.) long. Although giant reptiles are seldom killed under circumstances where their preservation *in toto* is a practicable possibility, remains of them such as skulls are less difficult to bring home as objective evidence of size. If a series of measurements of smaller individuals are available, it may be possible to calculate the total dimensions of the animal with a fair degree of accuracy.

Evidence of a reasonably authentic type can be obtained from field records made by naturalists and hunters. Here one may be guided, perhaps not always correctly, by circumstantial considerations. A clear-cut statement 'measured with a steel tape', or 'measured between two pegs' carries conviction. One may also be influenced by individual reputation. An observation by a famous naturalist, or indeed by anyone who is known to have received some scientific education is usually given more weight than one by some less favoured person. In fact most of the size records for large reptiles which have been generally accepted belong to this category. For instance, the maximum size of 7·01 metres (23 ft.) usually quoted for the Orinoco crocodile *(Crocodylus intermedius)* [373] rests on a personal measurement made over a hundred years ago by the famous scientific traveller, Baron Alexander von Humboldt.

It should be added, however, that measurements of the skin of snakes, and perhaps also of crocodiles, removed from the body, give notoriously exaggerated figures. Benedict [37] cites the case of an Indian python which was carefully measured at death and found to be 247 cm. long. Its skin after removal had stretched to 297 cm., an increase of about 20 per cent.

Finally there is evidence of a different type based on estimates couched in terms such as 'about as long as our canoe', or 'the crocodile was so big that one of my bearers could hardly jump over it'. Such evidence should be treated with reserve, but may yet be worthy of consideration. As every fisherman knows, the biggest ones are always the ones which get away, and one may hope that there are remote corners of the world where anacondas and crocodiles, larger than any yet recorded, are still lurking undisturbed.

The dimensions of the smallest and largest species of reptiles given in the following account are irrespective of sex, which in the case of giant specimens killed in out of the way places is seldom ascertained. Apart from the crocodilians, the majority of present-day reptiles are animals of small or modest size, ranging from about 15 cm. to 2 metres in length. It is quite possible that ever since the origin of reptiles, far back in the Upper Carboniferous, the smaller species have outnumbered the larger ones. Owing to the fragility of their bones, however, they are less likely to be preserved as fossils than forms such as the giant dinosaurs, the remains of which are more familiar to palaeontologists.

Few chelonians are much less than 15 cm. (6 in.) in shell-length, and the Madagascar spider tortoise *(Pyxis arachnoides)* and certain American mud terrapins *(Kinosternon)* with shell-lengths of 10 to 15 cm. are among the smallest species. The biggest living chelonian is certainly the leathery turtle *(Dermochelys coriacea)* which may occasionally reach a shell-length of 152 to 183 cm. (5 to 6 ft.) over its curvature, a width of 274 cm. (9 ft.) across the front paddles, and a weight of over 544 kilograms (1200 lb). Two other species of sea turtle, the loggerhead *(Caretta caretta)* and the green turtle *(Chelonia mydas)* may approach the leatherback in size with shell-lengths of 122 cm. (4 ft.) and weights of 227 kg. (about 500 lb). That much bigger specimens *have* existed is evident from the fact that Carr [89] has the skull of an Australian loggerhead in his collection which is about 28 cm. (11 in.) wide; the monster to which this belonged may have weighed over 454 kg. (1000 lb). These figures are presumably near the maximum growth potential and are far above the average size; today a loggerhead with a shell-length of 91 cm. (3 ft.) and a weight of 136 kg. (300 lb) is quite a big one. Uncontrolled fisheries are no doubt responsible for the scarcity of giant turtles today.

The alligator snapper *(Macroclemys temmincki)* of the southern USA is perhaps the most bulky freshwater chelonian, although some of the large soft-shelled turtles of India and Africa *(Chitra* and *Trionyx)* may exceed it in length. *Chitra* may measure over 80 cm. (31½ in.) from the front to the back of its leathery 'shell' or dorsal disc, whereas the biggest *Macroclemys* probably does not much exceed

467

72 cm. (28 in.) in shell-length, with a weight of about 91 kg. (200 lb). A specimen from Kansas with the quite exceptional weight of 183 kg. (403 lb) has, however, been reported; such reports illustrate the extreme difficulty of defining a strict maximum size limit for many of the bigger kinds of reptiles.

Of the land tortoises, the giant species *Testudo* [= *Geochelone*] gigantea from Aldabra and other islands in the Indian Ocean, and *T. elephantopus* from the Galapagos Is. are the only really large extant forms; perhaps the biggest known Aldabra tortoise had a straight shell-length of 1·4 metres (55 in.), measured 1·70 metres (67½ in.) over the curve and weighed 254 kg. (560 lb) [178]. A few mainland species such as *T. denticulata* of South America are of substantial size with shells about 61 cm. (2 ft.) long. As with most of the other groups of reptiles, however, the biggest chelonians are extinct. *Archelon* of the Upper Cretaceous was probably the largest marine turtle of all time, with a shell 3·05 metres (10 ft.) or more in length, while the terrestrial *Testudo atlas* from the Lower Pliocene of India had an immense domed carapace about 2·44 metres (8 ft.) long.

The lizards are the reptiles which have, *par excellence,* specialised for small size and agility. The smallest species are probably certain geckos of the American and West Indian genus *Sphaerodactylus;* several species may be under 5 cm. (2 in.) in total length when full grown [433]. These tiny geckos are comparable with new-born common lizards *(Lacerta vivipara),* which commonly weigh around 0·2 gm. Very small species are also found in certain other families such as the skinks and chamaeleons; some of the dwarf chamaeleons such as *Brookesia* and *Rhampholeon* from Africa and Madagascar are under 7·6 cm. in length.

The Komodo dragon *(Varanus komodoensis)* has been generally regarded as the largest existing lizard and reaches a length of at least 3 metres (10 ft.) and a weight of 163 kg. (360 lb). It is found only on the small island of Komodo to the east of Java and on one or two neighbouring islands. Worrell [467] states, however, that the little-known Salvador's monitor *(V. salvadorii)* is a longer though more slender beast and probably reaches 4·6 metres (15 ft.); it is known locally as the 'tree-climbing crocodile'. At least four other monitors occasionally approach or exceed a length of 2 metres (6½ ft.); these are the Nile monitor *(Varanus niloticus)*, the water monitor *(V. salvator)* of South-East Asia, and from Australia the lace monitor *(V. varius)* (Plate 4) and the perentie *(V. giganteus)*. Most of the remaining species (over thirty) in the family grow between about 90 cm. and 1·8 metres, but there are dwarf Australian forms which are under 60 cm. (2 ft.) in length (Plate 5). A fossil monitor *(Megalania)* from quite recent (Pleistocene) deposits in Australia may have been about twice as big as the Komodo dragon. This in turn was dwarfed by some of the mosasaurs (figure 2, p. 23), a group of marine lizards from the upper Cretaceous closely related to the monitors, which grew over 9 metres (30 ft.).

Certain other families of present-day lizards contain members of very substantial size. Among the Iguanidae, the common species *(Iguana iguana)* may be at least 1·5 metres (5 ft.) long, and there are others such as the rhinoceros iguana of Haiti *(Metopoceros cornutus)* and both the marine and terrestrial Galapagos types *(Amblyrhynchus cristatus* and *Conolophus subcristatus)*, which reach a length of about 1·2 metres (4 ft.). This is also the order of size attained by the biggest agamids such as the sailed dragon *(Lophura amboinensis)* from the East Indies, the water dragon *(Physignathus leseueri)* from Australia, and by the biggest teiids, the tegu *(Tupinambis teguixin)* of southern America and the caiman lizards *(Dracaena)* of the Guianas and Paraguay. The biggest limbless lizard is probably the European glass 'snake', *Ophisaurus apodus,* a relative of the slow-worm, which grows about 1·2 metres long.

The smallest snakes are probably certain blind burrowing species which belong to the families Typhlopidae and Leptotyphlopidae (p. 536), and may not exceed 15 cm. (6 in.) in length. The largest are certainly to be found in the family Boidae, which includes the pythons and the anaconda. Oliver [306] concludes that at least five species may reach or exceed 6·1 metres (20 ft.). The maximum lengths which are reasonably well substantiated – and which are, of course, greatly above the average lengths – are as follows: reticulated python *(Python reticulatus)* of South-East Asia, 10 metres (33 ft.); African python *(P. sebae)*, 9·7 metres (32 ft.); Indian python *(P. molurus)*, 6·1 metres (20 ft.); amethystine python *(Liasis amethystinus)* of northern Australia, at least 6·7 metres (22 ft.). The boa constrictor *(Constrictor constrictor)*, widely distributed in America from Mexico to northern Argentina, is not known to exceed 5·63 metres (18½ ft.); most individuals are a good deal smaller.

The dimensions of the huge anaconda *(Eunectes murinus)* of southern America have proved very difficult to ascertain. Stories of anacondas of much over 12·2 metres (40 ft.) can probably be dis-

469

counted but there is firm evidence that this species reaches 9·1 metres (30 ft.) and two records of about 11·3 metres (37 ft.) can be accepted as probable. One of these last was made about 1944 by a petroleum geologist in Colombia with a steel tape; the snake had been shot but later recovered sufficiently to make its escape. Both the anaconda and the Indian python are bulky snakes and tend to weigh more, length for length, than the other giant species. A reticulated python of 8·68 metres (28½ ft.) has been recorded as weighing at least 145 kg. (320 lb) [333].

Remains of some very big primitive snakes related to boas, such as *Madtsoia,* from South America, and *Gigantophis,* from Egypt, have been found in Eocene deposits, 60 to 70 million years old; the length of *Gigantophis* has been estimated at 15 to 18 metres (50 to 60 ft.), but it has been suggested that this figure, based on remains of the vertebral column, is too high. The reticulated python and anaconda of today may well be as large as any snakes which have existed in the past.

The king cobra *(Ophiophagus hannah)* of India and South-East Asia is certainly the longest poisonous snake of the present day, reaching a maximum length of 5·58 metres (18 ft. 4 in.). Two other slender, agile members of the elapid family, the black mamba *(Dendroaspis polylepis)* of Africa and the taipan *(Oxyuranus scutel-latus)* of nothern Australia may grow to 4·27 metres (14 ft.) and to over 3·05 metres (10 ft.) respectively. The biggest sea snakes (Hydro-phiidae) may be about 2·44 metres (8 ft.) long, a size regrettably inferior to that of the legendary sea serpent. Of the pit-vipers (Crotalinae), the bushmaster *(Lachesis muta)* from tropical America reaches 3·05 to 3·36 metres (10 to 11 ft.), while the diamond-back rattlesnakes *(Crotalus atrox* and *C. adamanteus)* may be the heaviest and bulkiest of the poisonous species, though they do not exceed 2·43 metres (8 ft.) in length. The Indian rat snake *(Ptyas mucosus)* and the indigo snake *(Drymarchon corais)* of North America with maximum respective lengths of nearly 3·65 metres (12 ft.) and 3·05 metres (10 ft.) are certainly among the biggest of the non-poisonous colubrid species.

Crocodilians are the giants among modern reptiles, although all but the largest individuals may be surpassed in weight by huge specimens of the leathery turtle. Of the 25 or so species, only two, the dwarf caiman *(Paleosuchus palpebrosus)* from the Amazon basin, and the dwarf crocodile *(Osteolaemus osborni)* from the Congo are normally under 1·22 metres (4 ft.) in length. Maximum sizes quoted for the larger species [373] on the basis of field records are as follows: American alligator *(A. mississippiensis)*, 5·84 metres (19 ft. 2 in.); Nile crocodile *(Crocodylus niloticus)*, about 6·7 metres (22 ft.); Indian gharial *(Gavialis gangeticus)*, 6·55 metres (21½ ft.); American and Orinoco crocodiles *(Crocodylus acutus* and *C. intermedius)*, 7·01 metres (23 ft.). Many of these records go back to the nineteenth century, when big crocodilians of all kinds were a good deal commoner than they are now; today the average adult sizes fall short of these figures by about 3·05 metres (10 ft.). The weights of large crocodilians are not often recorded, but that of a 1·98 metre (6½ ft.) American alligator is given as 24·5 kilograms (about 54 lb).

The estuarine crocodile *(C. porosus)* has occasionally been reported to grow larger than any other species. There is, for example, the skull of a huge individual in the Harvard Museum of Comparative Zoology which was killed at Jala Jala in the Philippines in the early nineteenth century. This animal was alleged to have been about 8·84 metres (29 ft.) long and to have measured 3·35 metres (11 ft.) round the body behind the front legs [15]. Another very large skull in the exhibition gallery of the British Museum (Natural History) is stated to have come from an individual 10·06 metres (33 ft) long which was killed in Bengal in 1840. Are these figures likely to have been correct?

At least two ways of calculating the length of a crocodile from measurements of its skull have been proposed. A simple method, applied to the estuarine species, allows 30·5 cm. (12 in.) of crocodile for every 2·54 cm. (1 in.) of the lower jaw which carries teeth [137]. I have found this a rather rough and ready guide. Another method which has been substantiated by fuller numerical data was originally suggested by K. P. Schmidt [373]. He found that in most species of crocodile the length of the head (or skull) in the dorsal midline from the tip of the snout to the back of the occiput (supraoccipital bone) was about one-seventh the total length of the animal. This ratio is borne out by a magnificent series of unpublished measurements made on 87 Nile crocodiles from East Africa by Dr Hugh Cott. The animals varied between 40·6 cm. (16 in.) and 4·71 metres (15 ft. 5 in.) in total length, and throughout this range of size and age the proportion of head length to total length remained fairly constant at around 1:7·5. There was, however, some individual variation, the occasional specimen having a relatively longer or shorter head than the average.

471

Figures published by H. Wermuth [447], and other measurements which Cott and I have made on museum specimens, show that these proportions are fairly similar in other crocodilians, including species such as the alligator where the snout is relatively broader than in most crocodiles; the very long-snouted Indian gharial departs from the usual range with a ratio of about 1:5. In some species there is a definite tendency for the skull itself to become relatively broader with age, and it is possible that the whole head becomes shorter in proportion to total length in gigantic specimens, giving a ratio of 1:8 or even more. Little evidence for this trend is indicated, however, in Cott's sample of animals in the 3·66 to 4·57 metre (12 to 15 ft.) range.

Judged by these criteria the dimensions of these two great estuarine crocodiles must have fallen far short of those originally claimed. The skull of the Harvard specimen has been photographed alongside a yard rule and appears to measure about 76·2 cm. (30 in.) from snout to occiput. Mr Benjamin Shreve of the Museum of Comparative Zoology at Harvard has been kind enough to send me accurate measurements of this skull. He finds its length to be only 66 cm., or about 26 inches; the lower jaw measures 84·4 cm. (about 33 in.). The photograph must therefore give an exaggerated impression of size, unless there can have been some past mistake in the specimen's identity. If one makes the generous assumption that the figure of 66 cm. was $\frac{1}{9}$ of the crocodile's total length (to allow for a possible change in relative proportions) the beast could only have been about 5·94 metres (19$\frac{1}{2}$ ft.) long.

The skull in the exhibition gallery of the British Museum is a little larger, measuring 71·1 cm. (28 in.) from snout to occiput; each side of the lower jaw measures about 91·4 cm. (3 ft.) and some half of this length carries teeth. The crocodile could hardly have exceeded 6·4 metres (21 ft.), and if assessed on the basis of a 1:7·5 ratio would only have been 5·33 metres (17$\frac{1}{2}$ ft.) long. A slightly bigger skull of an American crocodile in the American Museum of Natural History has been described in a paper dealing with crocodilian osteology [289]; it measured 73·5 cm. (28·7 in.) but no indication of the original size of its possessor is stated, perhaps wisely.

The skulls of these three crocodiles may well be the longest taken from living species (apart, perhaps, from long-snouted gharials) which are preserved in collections anywhere in the world. Cott's 4·71 metre (15 ft. 5 in.) Nile crocodile with a snout to occiput length of 62 cm. (24·4 in.) could be the largest of which accurate overall measurements are available. It is hard to reconcile these facts with the existence of so many apparently authentic field records of crocodiles of over 6·1 metres (20 ft.), and one is driven to the conclusion that the skulls of these giants can seldom if ever have been salvaged.

The relatively modest proportions of even the biggest modern crocodiles are emphasised by comparison with the life-size cast of the skull of the giant Cretaceous crocodile *Phobosuchus* in the British Museum. This measures about 152 cm. (5 ft.) from snout to occiput, with a lower jaw of about 183 cm. (6 ft.); it is therefore more than double the length of the skull of the biggest estuarine crocodile. *Phobosuchus* had a massive, broad snout and the total length of the creature has been estimated, generously though not impossibly, at 13·72 metres (45 ft.) or more.

Differential growth and neoteny Growth is not only a matter of increase in overall size; different parts of an animal may grow at different rates at different times in its life-history. For example, in young crocodilians the snout (in front of the orbits) is shorter by comparison with the rest of the head than it is in the adult; in the late embryo the relative shortness of the snout is even more striking (Plate 54). This suggests that growth of the snout is at first rather slow as compared with that of the cranium, but that later on the trend is reversed and the growth of the snout catches up with and eventually surpasses that of the back part of the skull. In this way the broad stumpy proportions of the late embryo or hatchling are changed into the longer-snouted shape of the adult.

Such differential growth rates are partly controlled by heredity. It is possible to see how slight alterations in their pattern, acting cumulatively from one generation to the next, may help to produce new species. Among a population of crocodiles, for instance, differential growth of the head may alter in such a way that the snout tends to become longer and narrower. Such a change might conceivably be of survival value in a particular environment; it might make it easier for the animal to catch some kind of small fish which abounded at the time. In this way natural selection, acting on variations of this kind, might transform a broad-snouted alligator-like species into a gharial-like one with a long narrow snout. The progressive reduction and loss of the limbs that we find in certain groups of lizards could have come about in the same kind of way. This is certainly one of the mechanisms of evolution.

Another kind of differential growth which has attracted attention is the tendency for certain features of the embryo and juvenile to persist into adult life. This is very widespread among vertebrates, particularly the tailed amphibians; the phenomenon is generally known as neoteny or paedomorphosis. The most famous example is the overgrown axolotl tadpole of the salamander *Ambystoma,* which never loses its external gills or fully ossifies its skeleton. No such dramatic cases of neoteny are known among reptiles, and indeed, the idea of neoteny occurring in this group at all is a fairly new one. However, some zoologists in Australia [410] have suggested that rather subtle forms of neoteny can be seen among lizards. In certain geckos and agamids, for example, the structure and proportions of parts of the skull remain throughout life very much like those of the hatchlings; the retention of these baby features distinguishes them from other related species. It is likely that future studies will bring to light other examples and will emphasise the part that neoteny and differential growth has played in reptilian evolution.

Age

The longevity of animals is also of both popular and scientific interest, and may be as difficult to determine as the maximum size which they attain. On the whole, animals kept under good conditions in captivity tend to live longer than they would in the wild, since they are protected from many obvious dangers and may receive skilled treatment for their ailments. It is uncertain how far this generalisation can be applied to reptiles, which are not the easiest creatures to keep in confinement. As we have seen, the sporadic occurrence of giant individuals suggests that with a good deal of luck a big turtle, crocodile or python can achieve an exceptionally long, healthy life under natural conditions. The fact that these animals do not have to face the dangers of losing their teeth, as old mammals do, no doubt improves their actuarial prospects.

It is also true however, that some individual reptiles have survived for very long periods in captivity and it is upon such recorded examples that estimates of potential life-span must mainly rest. Biologists interested in aging have reason to be grateful for the labours of Major Stanley Flower, who devoted many years to the tracing and careful scrutiny of longevity records from Zoological Gardens and private sources all over the world. Many of Flower's observations have been collected by Alex Comfort in his book on aging [112], a mine of information on all matters connected with the growth and aging of animals.

As everyone knows, tortoises are among the longest lived of all animals and for some species a life-span of 200 years might well be possible. The highest record generally accepted, however, is 152 years for one of the giant tortoises of the Indian Ocean islands (*Testudo gigantea*). This individual, which is sometimes referred to as 'Marion's Tortoise', was obtained by the French explorer Marion de Fresne in the Seychelle Is. in the year 1766. It was taken to Mauritius and died in 1918 as the result of falling through a gun emplacement in the garden of the artillery barracks where it was kept. Since this tortoise seems to have been more or less adult when it was captured it may have lived for a total of about 180 years; it was blind and perhaps senile when it met with its fatal accident [376].

Ages of considerably more than a century have been claimed for several other giant tortoises, but their records seem to be less satisfactorily authenticated. For example, the case of the fairly recently living specimen on St Helena which is supposed to have shared its exile there with Napoleon is not believed by Carr [89] to withstand critical scrutiny. Some of the smaller kinds of tortoises appear to be potentially almost as long-lived as the giant ones. The Noël-Humes [301] mention a Greek tortoise of at least 115 years; American box turtles (*Terrapene*) of well over 100 have been reported, but some of the records, based on individuals captured in the wild with dates marked on their shells, are open to question. A European pond tortoise (*Emys orbicularis*) has lived to at least 70 years, and an alligator snapper (*Macroclemys temmincki*) to at least 58 [304].

It is possible that crocodiles are as long-lived as chelonians; Cott suggests on the basis of growth curves that a 5.49 metre (18 ft.) Nile crocodile might be 100 years old, while a specimen of 6.1 metres (20 ft.) could be well into its second century. However, 56 years seems to be the longest recorded life of a crocodilian (American alligator) in captivity. Oliver [304] mentions a pair of alligators in the Dresden Zoo which were said to have bred when they were at least 40 years old.

Lizards and snakes seldom live for more than 20 years in confinement, and figures of 29 for an anaconda (*Eunectes murinus*) and 20 for a Gila monster (*Heloderma suspectum*) perhaps represent the usual maximum. The slow-worm (*Anguis*), however, is either exceptionally long-lived or, more probably, is exceptionally good at adjusting itself to captivity. A specimen is known to have lived for 54 years in the Zoological Museum in Copenhagen, achieving by far the longest recorded life of any lizard [395]. Field studies on some of the smaller species, such as *Anolis carolinensis,* show that in the wild the life expectation, as judged by the recapture of marked individuals, is only a year or so; however, individuals may survive for several years in captivity. Chamaeleons, on the other hand, are notoriously short-lived in zoos; it has been suggested that their high mortality is due to ignorance of their dietary needs or other physiological requirements.

Dawbin [130] has suggested that the tuatara is probably one of the longest-living reptiles, perhaps being good for as much as a century. This view is based on growth studies of wild populations; the longest recorded life for a captive individual is about 25 years.

It would be very desirable if we could find some reliable index of the age of a reptile apart from its size. In many chelonians a possible indication is given by the presence of lines or rings around the laminae of the shell (Plate 74). These rings are caused by interruptions in the rate of deposition of new horny material around the edges of the lamina. In species which live in temperate climes one ring should be formed each year, corresponding with the period of hibernation, when growth ceases. In cross section each ring appears as a wrinkle or groove; the inner slope of the groove corresponds with the stoppage of growth in the winter, the outer slope with the resumption of growth in the spring. It should therefore be quite easy to determine the age of the animal in years by simply counting the growth rings.

Unfortunately, there are complicating factors. Minor interruptions of growth due to temporary activity, food shortage and other physiological stresses also produce rings, although these are usually less marked than the major rings associated with seasonal hibernation. A ring has even been observed on the laminae of a hatchling tortoise, suggesting that such fluctuations of growth may take place during embryonic life. Furthermore, the more superficial and older layers of the lamina are shed or worn away in time, so that the older rings disappear. In some species which do not hibernate the major rings are not formed at all, or are too poorly marked to be discernable.

Nevertheless, and despite the scepticism of some writers, it would seem that growth rings are a valuable guide to the age of the younger individuals of some species, especially when they are still undergoing regular growth. In older animals, however, the growth rings become increasingly difficult to interpret. The study of minor growth rings may also provide useful information about growth conditions during individual years, for example, the occurrence of temporary food shortage or spells of unseasonable weather.

These growth rings on the chelonian shell are obviously comparable with the rings formed round some tree trunks and fish scales, and it is not unreasonable to search for other possible indications of seasonal growth. The series of bands which can be seen around the ends of certain bones, such as the femur in chelonians and the ectopterygoid in snakes has been interpreted in the same light. Griffiths [203] has concluded, however, that although these bands are clearly related to the growth pattern they are formed too irregularly to be used as accurate indicators of age. He suggests that in both tropical and temperate species the ossification and growth of bones takes place in intermittent bursts rather than by regular increment, and that it is unlikely that any fixed number of bands would be formed per year.

Regeneration

New tails So far we have been considering growth and age in as much as they affect the animal as a whole, or, in the case of differential growth, the way in which the proportions of the animal alter during its life-span. There are, however, other types of growth, such as those involved in the healing of wounds and in the regeneration of parts of the body which have been lost. The borderline between repair and regeneration is sometimes difficult to draw. It is hard to classify such processes as the renewal of the outer layers of the epidermis (p. 289) and the replacement of teeth (p. 177), while the remarkable annual shedding and renewal of the antlers in deer falls into a category of its own. For practical purposes, however, the term regeneration can be restricted to the replacement of fairly large or complicated organs which have been lost as the result of injury. Reptiles are the highest vertebrates which possess any substantial powers of regeneration in the sense defined. They are, however, considerably less well endowed in this respect than the Amphibia, and their capacity extends only to a few organs such as the tail, the limbs, and in the case of chelonians, the shell. Furthermore, the tails and limbs which they regenerate do not ever seem to be perfect replicas of the original.

The power of tail regeneration is found in many lizards, in the tuatara, and apparently in certain crocodilians. Caimans have been reported to produce new tails covered with smooth horny skin and containing a core of cartilage; one of these reached a length of 21·5 cm [452].

In lizards the ability to grow a new tail is usually associated with a facility for shedding the old one by autotomy through predetermined planes of weakness; this is a valuable method of defence (p. 499). The process of regeneration seems to be much the same in *Sphenodon* and in all the species of lizards in which it has been observed. It makes little difference whether the original injury was due to autotomy through one of the natural fracture planes or to experimental amputation with a knife or scissors. Some workers believe that regeneration is prevented or delayed if the cut is made between two fracture planes, and therefore between two adjacent vertebrae instead of through a vertebra near the normal autotomy site. So far as geckos and lacertids are concerned, the level of amputation hardly seems to affect the regenerative process, although it is possible that its onset may be slightly retarded if the cut is made through the intervertebral region. It has been shown in lacertids, however, that if the skin at the edges of the wound is closed by a suture, regeneration will fail to occur. Amputation of the tails of *Lacerta* embryos in their eggs is sometimes followed by the appearance of small regenerative outgrowths; if the operation is performed shortly before hatching a regenerate similar to that of the adult is nearly always formed. My own original belief that the embryonic tail is unable to regenerate is possibly incorrect, for it was based on specimens in which the effect of the experimental operation had been obscured by interference from the injured embryonic membranes [74].

After a part of the tail has been broken or cut off, the raw tip of the stump is soon covered by a scab formed from clotted blood and dead tissue; beneath this regeneration begins and its progress can be followed by microscopic examination of specimens taken at successive periods after injury. One of the first changes to be seen is the growth of new epidermis across the surface of the wound and underneath the scab, which then falls off. In geckos a portion of the remaining fragment of the autotomised vertebra is separated from the rest by the action of cells known as osteoclasts which are responsible for the absorption of bone, and comes away with the scab [451]. It is quite likely that this rather curious process occurs soon after autotomy in other types of lizard as well, although I have found little evidence for it in *Lacerta vivipara*. .

The new epidermis soon builds up to form a thick layer of cells which covers the tip of the tail stump like a cap (figure 140). This apical cap, as it is called, can be seen as the smooth cone of dark coloured skin which appears over the tip of the broken tail of a gecko or a lacertid a week or two after injury (Plate 73). Many pigment

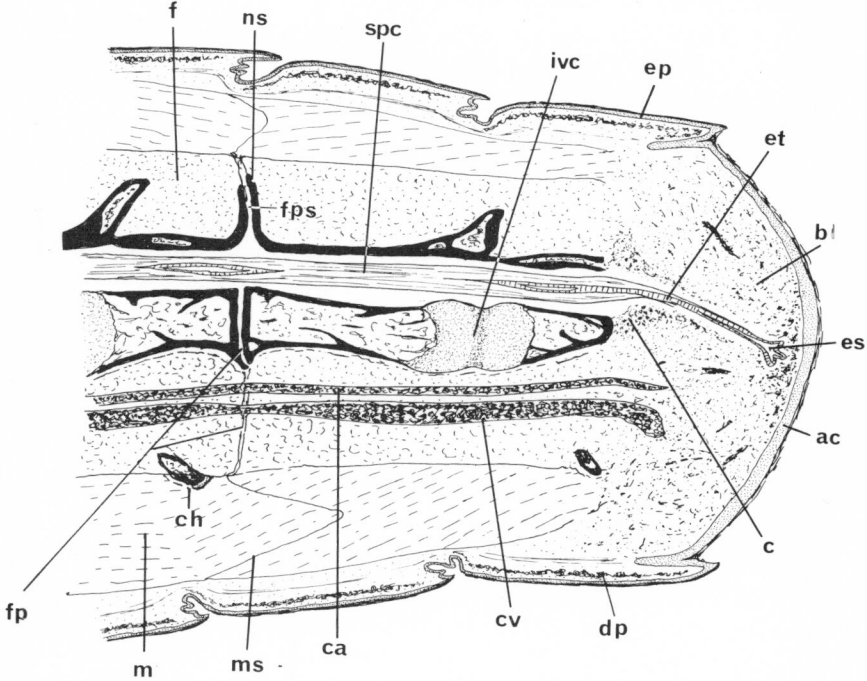

Figure 140   Longitudinal section through regenerating tail stump of lizard (*Lacerta vivipara*) shortly after end of latent period (2–3 weeks after autotomy). An apical cap and ependymal tube have formed and the blastema is well developed. ×17.

ac, apical cap. av, autotomised portion of vertebra. bl. blastema. c, condensation of cells around ependymal tube. ca, caudal artery. can, canal of spinal cord and ependymal tube. ch, chevron. ct, cartilage tube. cv, caudal vein. dp, dermal pigment. es, ependymal sac. ep, normal epidermis. et, ependymal tube. f, fat band. fp, fracture plane through vertebral centrum and fat band. fps, fracture plane through anterior neural spine. is, immature regenerating scales. ivc, intervertebral cartilage. m, segmental muscles of tail. ms, connective tissue septum (myoseptum). ns, anterior neural spine. rm, regenerated muscle. s, mature regenerated scales. spc, spinal cord.

cells appear in and beneath the epidermis, and give it a characteristic brown colour.

Microscopic study of the apical cap shows that by the end of a week after autotomy several interesting differences from the normal skin have appeared. For instance, the cells of the stratum germinativum and stratum intermedium are more numerous and are separated from each other by wide intercellular spaces. These contain scavenger-type cells known as macrophages which seem to have wandered in from the deeper tissues, perhaps to remove debris. There is no organised layer of dermis such as is present in normal skin, and the membrane which normally separates the epidermis from the dermis beneath it appears under the electron microscope to be perforated by large holes. The epidermal cells bulge inwards through these holes like blisters (Plate 44) and these eventually become pinched off from the epidermis altogether, and appear to pass into the deeper tissues. It is therefore possible that the epidermis is actively engaged in passing substances of some kind into the mesenchyme of the early regenerate. Electron microscope study also shows that the apical cap epidermis has a rich nerve-supply, although this is difficult to make out under the light microscope.

Another important feature of early regeneration which can be seen in *Lacerta* a few days after autotomy is the outgrowth of a slender tube from the broken end of the spinal cord (figure 140). It is derived mainly from the ependymal membrane which lines the cavities of the central nervous system and is called the ependymal tube. Its tip becomes closed off and dilated to form a small sac. The other tissues around the ependymal sac and beneath the apical cap then undergo a curious transformation. They lose their identities and revert to a condition like that of embryonic tissue. What were previously fibres of muscle or connective tissue, for instance, change into a mass of embryo-type cells which is called mesenchyme or blastema. The development of the blastema is really vital to the whole process of regeneration, for nearly all the tissues of the new tail are going to be produced from it. As the cells of the blastema multiply they also differentiate. The first new structure formed is a hollow cylinder of cartilage which surrounds the ependymal tube. A little later new muscle fibres appear, and later still (in *Lacerta*) the fat layer is differentiated from the mesenchyme around the cartilage (figure 141).

The scales are among the last of the new tissues to arise; they are formed first at the base of the regenerate and then spread back to-

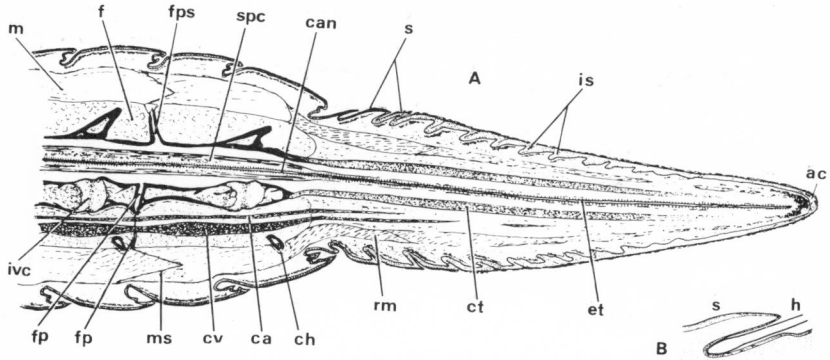

Figure 141 A. Longitudinal section through tail regenerate of *Lacerta vivipara*, some weeks after autotomy. ×9. Abbreviations as for figure 140. The difference in the antero-posterior lengths of successive scale rows is not always obvious, even in sectioned material. It can be seen, however, that the three normal scales in front of the regenerate at the top show the sequence long-short-long and that the fracture planes roughly coincide with the back edges of the long scales (see p. 502). B. Section through tail skin of a mammal (desman) showing scales (**s**) and hair (**h**).

wards its tip. Each new scale begins as a slanting ingrowth of the epidermis into the deeper tissues which develops a sheet of keratin (p. 287) down its middle. The ingrowth then splits so that one side of it is converted into the inner surface of one scale, while the other side of it forms the outer surface of the next, as shown in figure 141. In the slow-worm *(Anguis)* the osteoderms are also regenerated beneath the scales [75], and this probably occurs in other lizards which possess these little bony plates beneath their epidermis.

It is interesting that the scales of the regenerate develop in a different way from those in the normal lizard embryo [75]; in the latter they first appear as a series of bumps on the surface and not from epidermal ingrowths. In fact regenerating scales look more like mammalian hairs than embryonic lizard scales. The resemblance is particularly striking if one compares a section of the regenerate with one of the tail skin of a mammal such as a desman *(Myogale)* which possesses both hairs and scales. The meaning of this resemblance is quite mysterious, but one can see from figure 141 B why some people have suggested that the hairs of mammals evolved from the proliferation of cells in the hinge regions between the adjacent scales of their reptilian ancestors.

Occasionally, regeneration may go wrong and double or even

481

triple new tails are produced. In many kinds of lizards, however, a mature regenerate appears superficially like the original tail though it is usually possible to distinguish it if one looks hard enough. The scales are often abnormal in colour or arrangement, and tend to be smaller than normal scales. In some forms such as the Madeira wall lizard *(Lacerta dugesii)* over 90 per cent of the original tail length is regained in time, if one adds the length of the stump and that of the regenerate together; whether a regrown tail can ever be longer than the old one is not known.

In internal structure even the oldest regenerate differs in a number of ways from the original, and has been described as a 'jerry-built' affair [465]. Its skeleton remains as an unsegmented cylinder of cartilage which may become calcified but never develops into separate bony vertebrae. The spinal cord is represented by the tube of ependyma with its outer covering of meninges. Some nerve fibres are also regenerated outside the ependyma, but nothing like the full thickness of nervous tissue found in the original spinal cord is regained. The greater part of the regenerate's nerve supply is derived, not from the cord but from the last two or three pairs of spinal nerves above the level of the injury; from these many new nerve fibres grow back into the regenerate, and supply its various tissues. In some species the muscles acquire a segmental arrangement rather like that of the original, but the blocks of fibres are not so regularly arranged or so clearly separated from each other by partitions or connective tissue. The new tail is less flexible than the old one with its jointed vertebral column, but does have some power of independent movement and bends from side to side when it is cut off from the lizard. Since the regenerate has no fracture planes it does not undergo autotomy; if it is seized by a predator it often breaks off at its junction with the original stump. If, however, the new tail is broken through its substance or amputated, it will regenerate again and there seems to be no limit to the number of times that regeneration in the same individual can occur.

Various experiments have been carried out in an attempt to analyse the causes of regeneration. At first it was believed that the downgrowth of new nerve fibres around the ependymal tube was primarily responsible for initiating the process; the presence of nerve fibres in sufficient quantities near the site of the wound has been shown to be necessary for the regeneration of limbs, both in lizards and amphibians. Later work suggests, however, that so far as the lizard tail is concerned, it is the ependymal tube itself which mainly stimulates the production of new tissue, especially of the cartilage cylinder. If, for example, portions of the ependymal tube are removed from their normal positions and transplanted elsewhere in the tail, the formation of small accessory tails will result [389].

The speed of tail regeneration seems to vary a good deal, even among individuals of the same species. It is certainly accelerated by raising the temperature, so long as this remains within the range of the lizard's tolerance. It may be slowed down if the creature does not get enough to eat; it possibly depends also on the activity of the endocrine glands which control physiological rhythms such as the reproductive and skin-shedding cycles. There is some evidence that regeneration is retarded after successive autotomies in which the original tail is progressively whittled away. The effects of such experiments may be hard to interpret, however, since the rate of growth is also affected by the level of autotomy. It tends to rise when larger portions of tail are lost, as if the appendage was 'trying harder' to regain its original length. Since a second autotomy through the original stump must be at a higher level than the first, its possible retarding effect may be cancelled out by the fact that more original tissue is removed.

After any autotomy or amputation there is a latent period of one to two weeks (or more) before the regenerate begins to grow obviously in length. During this time the scab is shed, and the initial blastema and apical cap are formed. After this the regenerate begins to lengthen quite quickly and continues to do so for several weeks, its growth rate falling off gradually as the original overall tail length is approached. The highest rate which I have encountered in lizards was seen in certain specimens of *Lacerta dugesii*, where the new tail grew at a rate of 2·6 mm. a day throughout the fifth week after autotomy [75]. The average rate among the group of lizards used in the experiment was considerably lower than this, about 1·3 mm. a day (figure 142). These animals were all kept at a temperature of around 28°C. Rates of 1–2 mm. per day have been recorded in other lacertids.

Not enough is known about the comparative regenerative capacities of different kinds of lizards, and most studies of regeneration have been made on geckos, lacertids, certain skinks, and on the iguanid *Anolis;* these are all rather good at growing new tails. There are few accounts of regeneration in the larger species, but its results can be quite impressive. The finest regenerate I have ever seen belonged to

483

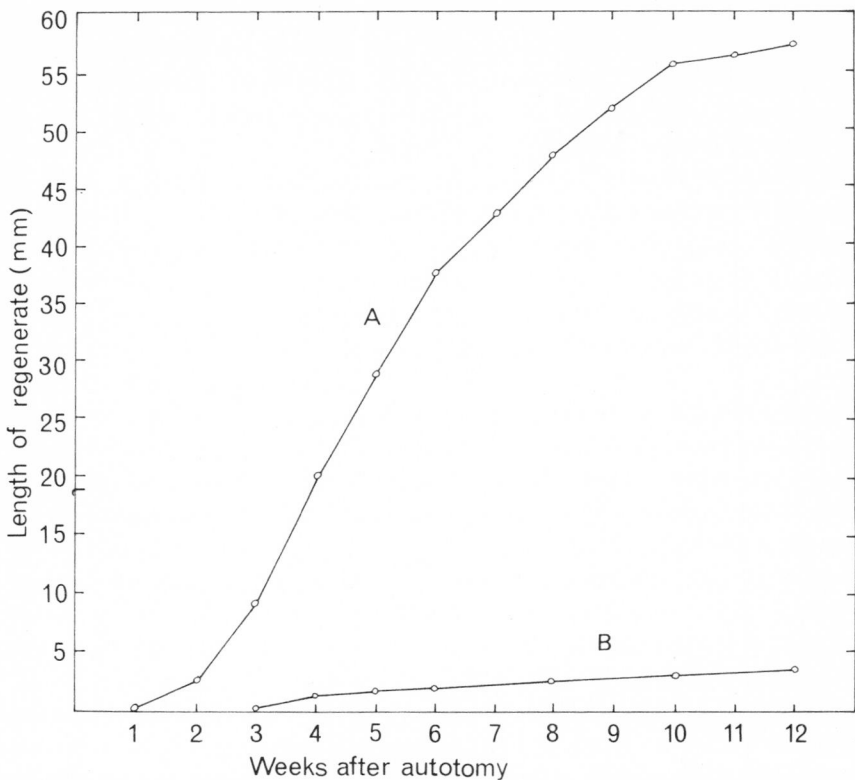

Figure 142   Graph showing growth rates of lizard tail regenerates. After Bryant and Bellairs [75]. A. Average growth of tail in 10 specimens of *Lacerta dugesii* after autotomy through previously undamaged tail. B. Fastest growth observed in slow-worm (*Anguis fragilis*) kept at 27°C.

a tegu lizard *(Tupinambis)* which was perched on the shoulder of a lady visiting the pet department of Harrods famous store in London. It had at some time lost about two-thirds of its tail, and the new growth was some 20 cm. (8 in.) long and nearly 2·5 cm. across its base. Most of the lizards which lack fracture planes, such as monitors, appear to have little, if any power of regeneration.

A few species such as *Anguis fragilis* are well known as poor regenerators. The best regenerate grown by one of a group of slow-worms used in our experiments measured only 4 mm. after three months (figure 142) and 5 mm. after five months. This individual had been kept at an average temperature of 27°C – higher than that which the reptile would have probably enjoyed in the wild during an English

484

summer. Slow-worms never seem able to produce more than a conical stump of one to two cm. in length, and amounting to perhaps 10 or 15 per cent of the portion lost. Even this might take several years to grow under natural conditions, allowing for six-monthly periods of quiescence during hibernation. Despite its very slow growth rate, however, the structure and mode of formation of the slow-worm's regenerate is essentially similar to that of other lizards. A comparable rate is found in the related footless lizard *Anniella* from California [283], and one would like to know more about the state of affairs in the alligator lizards *(Gerrhonotus)* and the glass-lizards *(Ophisaurus)* which also belong to the family Anguidae.

Regeneration of other organs If the leg of a lizard is cut or bitten off it usually heals and does not regenerate except in so far as new scales are eventually formed by the skin which covers the wound. Occasionally, however, quite a substantial regenerate is produced, though it probably takes a long time to grow. This has been described in lacertids, and in certain iguanids and skinks, and seems to happen more often with the hind limbs than the front ones. The new append-age is abnormal in appearance, being conical or tapering, in which case it may look like a short tail (figure 143); sometimes it is hooked at the tip. It usually contains new bone or cartilage when mature, but does not ever seem to differentiate proper hands and feet with separate digits like the regenerated limbs of newts. Despite its imperfect character such a regenerate may be of some service to the lizard, increasing the length of the stump and providing a lever or prop which may help in walking.

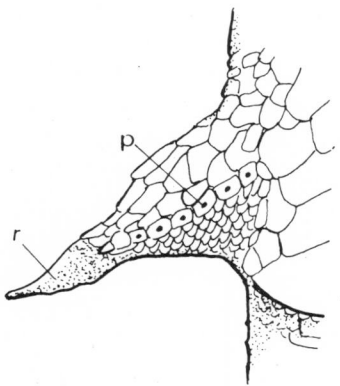

Figure 143   Right hind limb of lizard (*Lacerta vivipara*) from below showing tapering regenerate (**r**) and femoral pores (**p**). This specimen was caught in the wild; the original injury had probably involved the lower thigh, just above the knee. After Poyntz, S. V. and Bellairs, A. d'A. (1965) *Br. J. Herpet.* **3** 204.

Limb regenerates of this type can be consistently produced in laboratory experiments. Marcus Singer and his colleagues have shown that the hind limb of *Anolis* will regenerate after amputation through the thigh if the nerve-supply to the stump is artificially augmented by diverting the sciatic nerve of the opposite side to it. These ingenious experiments show that nerve-fibres play an important part in provoking regeneration, possibly by secreting some substance which stimulates cell division. Unless the number of fibres present near the wound is sufficient, regeneration will not take place [475]. Other experiments have also suggested that regeneration is more likely to occur if the area of the wound is very large. Possibly it is only after they have suffered extensive jagged wounds that lizards are able to regenerate their limbs in the wild, but it is not yet understood why this should be such an infrequent and haphazard occurrence.

The practice of amputating the digits of lizards has long been used by herpetologists for the purpose of identifying individuals, either in field studies of populations or where groups of animals are kept together in the laboratory. The general impression that such digits do not usually regenerate has recently been confirmed in experiments on *Lacerta dugesii* and *L. vivipara* by S. V. Bryant and myself[*]. Shortly after amputation, however, the wound undergoes changes which are not at all unlike those seen after autotomy of the tail. A kind of apical cap is formed and in some cases a small conical protruberance is built up. Only a limited amount of blastema is produced, however, and the wound soon heals over, while the cut digital bone or phalanx becomes invested with a kind of sleeve of cartilage. This tendency to form masses of cartilage around bones which have been injured can also be seen in the stumps of amputated limbs and seems to be a characteristic reaction of the reptilian skeleton to serious damage.

Chelonians and crocodiles seem unable to produce even the apologies for new limbs which have been reported in lizards, but the chelonian shell has a considerable capacity for regeneration. Legler examined many box turtles with shells in the process of repairing damage. After a severe injury death of both horny and bony layers of the affected region takes place. The healthy epidermis around the wound then grows in beneath the dead bone which eventually sloughs away; the new epidermis then keratinises and new bone is formed beneath it. Areas amounting to about a third of the shell may be replaced within a year or two in this way. The remains of a box turtle *(Terrapene carolina)* found in a museum have been described, in which an entire new bony carapace had apparently been regenerated. The greater part of the original bony shell (devoid of horny plates) was still adhering to the outside of the new one, although it seemed likely that the former would in time have been broken off and shed if the animal had survived. Unfortunately, nothing is known of the history of this very interesting specimen [391].

In parts of the Caribbean and elsewhere turtle hunters have for centuries followed the cruel practice of roasting off the horny laminae – the material of tortoiseshell – from the hawksbill turtle *(Eretmochelys imbricata)*. The still living animals are then returned to the sea in the belief that they will eventually regenerate a new horny carapace. There has been some scientific discussion as to whether this is in fact possible. The general view seems to be that turtles treated this way are unlikely to live in the wild for very long and would be vulnerable to such hazards as shark attack. If the turtle did survive, however, it is possible that some regeneration would occur, provided that the living matrix of the basal cell layer of shell epidermis was not too severely damaged. The whole problem of shell regeneration and repair in Chelonia is wide open for study by any biologist who has the patience to wait a year or more for the result of his experiments.

Chapter 12

Enemies and Defence

Enemies and allies

ALL ANIMALS have enemies. Some of these are large enemies which slay them in open combat by means of superior weapons and eat them, or in some other way exploit the products of their dead bodies. They also have small enemies in the form of micro-organisms and larger multicellular parasites which may kill them in a more insidious way. In a more sophisticated sense, they are subjected to the enmity of other individuals of their own or different species which compete with them for food or living room as motorists in a crowded city have to queue for petrol or compete for parking space.

Almost any animal with carnivorous tendencies is a potential predator on tiny reptiles, such as geckos and very small snakes, which share its habitat. Some of the more formidable invertebrates such as scorpions, giant centipedes and spiders, and the fierce, spider-like arachnids known as solpugids kill and eat lizards if they get the chance. Marauding columns of driver and safari ants will consume piecemeal any animal which cannot quickly take flight, and are said occasionally to kill large pythons when these are immobilised by a recent heavy meal. The herpetologist Arthur Loveridge [260] has given a vivid account of the invasion of his house in East Africa by an army of the driver ant *Dorylus nigricans*. After devouring a variety of the insects, rats and other animals which live in houses in the tropics, the ants attacked some young crocodiles kept in a vivarium. One crocodile was thrashing about in a pan of water, the edges of which were lined with ants; these hurled themselves on the reptile whenever its struggles brought it close to the side. Another crocodile and a chamaeleon were consumed down to the bones. Captive tortoises were also attacked, but the Bell's box tortoises *(Kinixys belliana)* were practically immune since their armour-plated forelegs, when drawn in, protected the head almost completely. Loveridge

488

adds that the burrowing snakes *(Typhlops)* which feed on ants and termites and are sometimes found in their nests may be protected by their close-grained shiny scales from the bites and stings of these insects.

Aquatic and amphibious reptiles must sometimes fall a victim to predatory fish such as pike and may also be eaten by large frogs. Some reptiles are eaten by other reptiles, even of their own species, but this subject is dealt with from the other end of the food chain, as it were, in the chapter on the food and feeding methods of reptiles (p. 116). Birds such as shrikes, crows, storks, hornbills and hawks will all eat reptiles of various kinds, and in England the buzzard *(Buteo buteo)* is said to prey on the adder. The secretary bird *(Sagittarius)*, a kind of large cursorial hawk found in Africa, is renowned as an enemy of snakes which it kills with blows from its long scaly legs. It is doubtful, however, whether this voracious bird deliberately selects snakes as a major item in its diet. It feeds on a variety of prey, and frogs, lizards, tortoises, small birds and mammals, as well as snakes, have been taken from its stomach.

Many mammals such as baboons, lemurs, hedgehogs and pigs, as well as true Carnivora, must include reptiles in their diet from time to time. Jaguars and lions have been known to kill big caimans and crocodiles, though it could well be that under different circumstances they might themselves fall victims to these reptiles. Mongooses *(Herpestes,* etc.) are well known enemies of reptiles, destroying the smaller snakes and lizards as well as the eggs and young of turtles and crocodiles. These little mammals are indiscriminate predators and the catastrophic effect of their introduction to the West Indies on the local lizards, birds and small mammals is well known.

In fights with poisonous snakes the mongoose relies mainly on its agility and on its long fur, which when fluffed up gives some protection against a bite. There is also evidence that it has some measure of immunity. It is interesting that a high natural immunity of the African mongoose has only been demonstrated against the venom of cobras and other elapid snakes, and that the mongoose and its ally, the meerkat are nearly or quite as susceptible to puff adder venom as other mammals of comparable size [100]. It should be added, however, that some of these conclusions are based on early immunological studies and might well benefit from critical re-examination.

The European hedgehog *(Erinaceus)* is another mammal which sometimes feeds on reptiles, including adders. When attacking an adder the hedgehog erects the long bristles on its forehead and repeatedly bites the snake until it succumbs. As a rule the hedgehog's spines effectively prevent retaliation but even if it does get bitten it rarely dies, probably because it also has some natural immunity.

There are few examples of reptiles benefiting from the activities of other organisms, except in so far as all species are dependent on others for food, or participate in complex ecological systems which help to provide a favourable environment. The growth of algae on the shells of certain freshwater turtles is an instance of commensalism which may perhaps confer some advantage on the reptile in terms of concealment. Gopher tortoises, the tuatara and some lizards and snakes inhabit burrows made by birds or rodents, and sometimes share them with these animals. Unfortunately, the picturesque idea that tuatara and petrel live together like human flat-mates and regularly occupy sleeping chambers which open from the right and left of a communal burrow is now known to be erroneous. The association seems to depend only on the tuatara's predilection for an underground den, and it sometimes feeds on the petrel chicks [383]. Some subterranean reptiles such as amphisbaenids and blind snakes frequent the nests of ants or termites, while other species find these insect dwellings convenient incubators for their eggs (p. 428).

A more interesting example of mutual aid is the famous association between water birds and crocodiles which was described in the fifth century BC by Herodotus and has recently been confirmed by Cott. The spur-winged plover *(Hoplopterus spinosus)*, the sandpiper *(Actictis hypoleucos)* and the water dikkop *(Burhinus vermiculatus)* habitually frequent basking crocodiles and apparently warn them of approaching danger by their cries and fluttering; Cott describes the crocodiles stampeding into the water in response to the birds' alarm signal. The plover and sandpiper perform another service for they probably remove leeches and other parasites from the crocodiles' skin and even from the mucosa of the gaping jaws. Basking turtles are sometimes attended in a similar fashion, and crabs have been seen to remove ticks from the marine iguana [25]. Cott adds that the water dikkop often makes its nest close to a crocodile which is guarding her own eggs and suggests that the bird may gain some protection from egg-eating enemies [119].

Relationship with man Many people have a strong aversion to reptiles, especially snakes, and this is often attributed to a deep-rooted instinct inherited from primeval forbears. The majority of mammals seem to be unafraid of these creatures, however, at least if they have had no previous acquaintance with them. Mice and rats given to captive snakes as food will run heedlessly over their bodies until they are attacked, and will sometimes even kill the snakes as vivarium keepers have discovered to their cost. My cat was unperturbed by close proximity with a 1·22 metre (4 ft.) king snake and a 1·7 metre python, though he regarded them with watchful interest. Monkeys and apes, on the other hand, are usually enraged or alarmed at the sight of a live snake or, as Darwin discovered, even of a stuffed one; a painted model snake made out of rubber tubing may evoke the same response.

According to some recent work, rhesus monkeys which have been reared in captivity react much less intensely to snakes than individuals caught as adults in the wild; this difference suggests that their attitude owes something to early environment, perhaps to learning from experience or example. Some American psychologists have shown that very young human children have no fear of snakes, but often begin to acquire it before they have reached the age of four; it is uncertain whether this is due to the emergence of some previously latent instinct or to the example of elders. In their book *Men and Snakes* [290], Ramona and Desmond Morris describe the results of a poll taken of the opinions of nearly twelve thousand children on their attitudes to various animals. Snakes easily top the list as the most disliked inmates of the London Zoo. It is gratifying to herpetologists, however, that a few select children (0·9 per cent of the boys in the sample, and 0·3 per cent of the girls) said that the snake was the animal they liked the best.

Human dealings with reptiles often reflect an ambivalent attitude of fear mixed with veneration, or at least with respect. Crocodiles and even turtles are revered in parts of the East, and there are, of course, countless examples of serpent-worship. Even in the twentieth century, serpent-handling Christian sects have flourished in the hillbilly regions of the USA. Their devotees were accustomed to praise the Lord with rattlesnakes and copperheads draped around them, until the occurrence of fatalities led to the legal prohibition of this form of worship.

Reptiles have been put to many more material human uses. They are used for dissection in the teaching of zoology at universities, and to a limited extent, for biological and medical research, especially on snake venoms. There is some demand for lizards, snakes and small alligators as pets, and tortoises, the most popular of reptiles, often suffer from man's good intentions. The wholesale importation, frequently under very poor conditions, of baby tortoises from North Africa and of North American species such as the red-eared terrapin (*Pseudemys scripta elegans*) could have a serious effect on local populations. It is sad that most of these baby chelonians soon die in captivity, since special care is needed to rear them. Legislation to restrict this traffic should be welcomed so long as it remains possible for bona-fide vivarium keepers and zoologists to obtain the few specimens which they need.

Men eat reptiles in many parts of the world [230, 231]; among the most highly esteemed are turtles, crocodiles, iguanas, monitors and pythons. Such creatures are eaten not only by the bushmen and aboriginals of southern Africa and Australia but by members of more advanced communities. Lizards and snakes are a popular item of food among the Hong Kong Chinese and the carcasses of these reptiles are used to fortify local wines. Canned rattlesnake is sold in the USA, while terrapins, especially those of the diamond-back group (*Malaclemys*) are served at fashionable restaurants. The skin, fat and other organs of various reptiles have been used as folk cures for many types of complaint [240].

The giant tortoises of the Galapagos and Indian Ocean islands (*Testudo elephantopus* and *T. gigantea*) afford a sadly typical example of the fate of animals with a limited distribution which have the misfortune to be a ready source of human food. William Dampier, one of the most famous and certainly the most literate of the buccaneers, described the Galapagos tortoises as 'extraordinarily large and fat, and so sweet that no pullet eats more pleasantly'. Since these animals would survive on board ship for long periods, they were carried off in vast numbers during the seventeenth and eighteenth centuries until many of their island races were exterminated [25]. Although colonies survive on some of the Galapagos today [154], giant tortoises are now only found in large numbers on the Aldabra islands in the Indian Ocean, where their total population has been estimated at some 33,000 [189]. The continued existence of these harmless and impressive reptiles will be a challenge to human enlightenment; it is a sad commentary on our affairs that the threat to build a military base on Aldabra has only been averted by a recent economic crisis in Britain.

Of all reptiles, the green turtle *(Chelonia mydas)* has been the most thoroughly exploited as a source of human food. This huge reptile is found throughout the warmer seas all over the world and breeds, or used to breed, in many localities in the Caribbean and the Indian and Pacific Oceans. The excellence of its flesh has been attributed to its almost exclusively herbivorous habits. The 'calipee' and 'calipash', the West Indian names for the unossified portions of the plastron and of the carapace and backbone, are particularly relished, while soup, made from the whole turtle has figured as a traditional item at city banquets. The eggs of this and of other marine turtles are also eaten, especially by coastal natives of the East, who seldom take the flesh of the adults.

Parsons, in his book *The Green Turtle and Man* [318], describes the turtle fisheries throughout the world, and a curious method of capturing the reptiles with the aid of sucking-fish, which is used in such widely separate areas as the Caribbean, East Africa, North Australia and the South China Sea. The sucking-fish *(Remora)* normally adheres to turtles and other large sea beasts by means of a sucker derived from the modified dorsal fin. The turtle-fisher tethers the fish to his boat by a line round its tail, and throws it overboard when a turtle is sighted. With a little luck the fish soon adheres to the turtle and the fisherman then does his best to induce one or two more fish to stick to it as well. If the turtle has to be played with only one sucker-fish on it, it has a 75 per cent chance of escape, and this is reduced to about 20 per cent with two fish. With three fish clinging to it, it very seldom gets away. This method, which is sometimes also used for the capture of other species of turtle, and of manatee, was first described by Christopher Columbus. It is not surprising that by this and other more conventional means of fishing the green turtle has been brought close to extinction in many parts of its range.

Many people who do not normally eat reptiles are glad to use tortoiseshell products, or the choice leather derived from the skin of various species. The overlapping horny laminae of the carapace of the hawksbill turtle *(Eretmochelys imbricata)* are the source of tortoiseshell, or 'carey' as it is known in the Caribbean trade. In addition to its wide use in such articles as hair-brushes, spectacle frames and jewellery, this material has been employed in a most attractive way as an inlay for furniture in conjunction with brass. The technique was first developed in France during the seventeenth century by André Charles Boulle whose name is still attached to this style of work. One might imagine that the replacement of tortoiseshell by plastic substitutes would have relieved the pressure on the hawksbill turtle, but Archie Carr, the great authority on turtles, wrote in 1963 [90] that the demand for the genuine article had been revived and that substantial quantities of carey were being exported from the West Indies.

Reptile leathers are both handsome and durable, and command high prices. Today (1968) a good handbag made of crocodile hide may cost £60 to £100 in a London store. Reptile skins are sometimes used in other items of clothing and I possess a tie from Hong Kong made from the skin of a monocled Chinese cobra. Monitors *(Varnus)* are the principal source of commercial lizard skin, while snakeleathers are obtained from boas and pythons and from some of the smaller species as well. The hides of certain freshwater snakes *(Acrochordus)* from Indonesia, with their distinctive granular scales, are said to make particularly fine leather and are known in the trade as 'Karung'; in Japan, the skins of sea snakes are apparently popular [312].

The greatest demand is probably for crocodile hide, especially for the skin of the belly which is more serviceable than the rest since it lacks bony scutes. In the past, alligator skins were much used, but these reptiles now enjoy legal protection in many parts of their depleted range. Cott, who has studied the exploitation of the Nile crocodile in Uganda, states that it has been practically wiped out in many places where it was once abundant. In 1954, 60,000 crocodiles were killed in East Africa alone. This reptile is particularly vulnerable to hunters who operate at night from boats, since the iridescent reflecting layer (tapetum) of the crocodile's retina shows up conspicuously in the beam of a torch. Once located, the animal is killed by a short-range blast from a shotgun and the carcass dragged aboard.

Undoubtedly the greatest destruction of reptile life occurs as an incidental by-product of human activity, as our senselessly proliferating species encroaches on the natural habitats of wild animals. Building programmes, clearing of land for agricultural and military purposes, and the use of insecticides, to some of which reptiles are highly susceptible, have had devastating effects on wild life. Motor roads are another menace to turtles and snakes in places such as the southern states of North America. The reptiles are attracted to the road by the warmth of its surface and readily become traffic casualities.

One need hardly emphasise the importance of animal conservation for material as well as for sentimental, or at least emotional, reasons.

The virtual extermination of any species, even one which like the crocodile is liable to prey on man and his food animals, may have unforeseen repercussions on the local ecology. Cott found that in most of the regions which he studied the fish which formed the principal prey of the Nile crocodile belonged to species which were of little value as human food. However, the crocodiles killed otters and many predatory fish which are seldom eaten by man; hence their destruction might well in the long run prove harmful rather than beneficial to fisheries.

The value of national parks and nature reserves as a tourist attraction bringing in a substantial revenue is now widely recognised. Many people who live far from the wild places of the earth find the sight of fine animals in their natural surroundings a tremendously thrilling and satisfying experience. Reptiles such as crocodiles, pythons and monitors are spectacular and photogenic, and no film on tropical wildlife is complete without a sequence of crocodiles sliding in dozens down a river bank.

Moreover, once the survival of animal populations has been assured it is possible to exploit them for man's needs in a reasonable fashion, cropping a quota of mature individuals without damaging the reproductive potential. Reptile leathers are perhaps a marginal amenity to human society, but the potential food value of the green turtle is indisputable. In recent years Archie Carr in America and his fellow turtle biologists in the far East and Australia have developed effective techniques of conservation which can be applied not only to the green turtle but to other species such as the leatherback. Eggs are collected wholesale from the nesting beaches and placed in hatcheries [91, 216, 318]. The young turtles are then carried out to sea in a boat and liberated at night over a wide area. A proportion of them are also tagged in the hope of subsequent recovery. These measures not only eliminate the most vulnerable phase of the turtles' life-history (p. 426) by reducing the risk of predation, but also provide valuable information on the growth and movements of the young. Let us hope that these admirable projects will play their part in establishing conservation as a major feature in the political programme of all countries. Unless those who walk in the corridors of power soon come to realise that the husbandry of the world's natural resources and the limitation of human numbers are among the few material problems which really matter, the future of mankind is likely to be a bleak one.

Methods of defence

Reptiles, like other animals, have evolved various means of defence against their enemies, some rather crude, but others of a most refined character. The teeth and jaws of bigger reptiles can naturally be used for defence as well as predation, while the claws, though seldom deliberately used as weapons, may inflict severe scratches on an aggressor.

Lashing with the tail is another technique which can be used for defence as well as attack. Although no modern reptile has a caudal armament as formidable as the huge bony spikes of stegosaurian dinosaurs, the tails of crocodilians are fringed with hard projecting scutes, while those of lizards such as *Uromastyx* and *Cordylus* are furnished with spines.

The big monitors are among the most accomplished exponents of caudal defence and use their smooth but hard tails like whips. When at bay these lizards adopt a characteristic defence posture, with the throat inflated, the rear end of the body raised slightly from the ground on the hind legs and the tail doubled back in readiness to strike. The blow is often delivered with some accuracy and may be powerful enough to damage the eye of an attacking dog. The harm which a 1·5 metre monitor can inflict with its tail on a trousered human leg, however, is not very alarming.

Rattlesnakes adopt a curious technique when threatened by king snakes *(Lampropeltis)* which sometimes kill and eat them. Instead of rattling, the rattler places his head on the ground and arches the middle of his body, using the raised loop to deliver a vigorous slapping blow. This defence reaction is given only to king snakes (and perhaps occasionally to skunks, which are also snake-eaters); it is not elicited by other kinds of snakes such as boas which do not prey on their fellows. C. M. Bogert [47] found that a rattler would even behave in this way when confronted with a colour variant of the king snake which it had never seen, since it came from a different geographical area. Further experiments showed conclusively that it was the smell of the king snake which provoked the response (p. 370), perceived by the organ of Jacobson.

Armour plating has served many animals well in their struggle for survival, although creatures which have come to depend on it seldom show much evolutionary enterprise in other directions. The Chelonia are so well protected by their shells that they have hardly bothered to develop other methods of defence, though some of the larger species can behave more aggressively if aroused. The giant tortoises of Aldabra Island *(Testudo gigantea)* hiss and withdraw into their shells when threatened, despite the fact that until the advent of man they must have been free from natural enemies for countless generations [189]. If a limb of one of these huge tortoises is grasped it will try to trap its aggressor beneath the edge of its shell, revolving its whole body so that the enemy has to let go or be injured. Some of the other larger chelonians such as the snappers, the soft-shelled turtles and the marine loggerhead will lunge and snap viciously when molested; the shell has actually undergone reduction in the first two of these types of predatory turtle.

Lizards such as the zonures *(Cordylus;* Plate 47), and the horned iguanids *(Phrynosoma;* Plate 20) and agamids *(Moloch;* Plate 47), derive protection from their armament of long spines which would stick in the throat of a would-be predator. Spines and claws may also be used together to wedge the lizard in a rocky crevice so firmly that it is impossible to dislodge, especially when it inflates its body with air. This method of defence is employed by various kinds of lizards including zonures and *Uromastyx*. The flexible-shelled tortoise *Malacochersus*, though devoid of spines, is able to resist its foes in a similar fashion. Crocodiles are unusual among specialised carnivores in being heavily armoured, at least on the back; their tough horny and bony scutes must often protect them from retaliation by their larger victims, and though probably ineffective against a modern rifle, are alleged to have turned many a musket ball.

The Squamata have evolved many more refined methods of defence such as bluff, concealment, chemical warfare, and discarding portions of the tail. The poison-fang, one of the most sophisticated weapons developed by any vertebrate animals, and its long-range defensive use by spitting cobras is described in Chapter 5, p. 184, which deals with the venom apparatus of snakes.

Emission of noxious substances The possibilities of chemical warfare have been exploited by various animals ranging from termites to skunks, and have been utilised in defence by a number of reptiles. Snakes, apart from certain cobras, do not spit poison from their mouths, but some otherwise harmless colubrids of the genera *Natrix* and *Macropisthodon* have nucho-dorsal glands which exude their irritating secretions on to the skin of the back (figure 89, p. 286).

It is likely that they are primarily concerned with defence like the skin glands of toads, and will deter an animal from holding the snake in its mouth.

The spiny little horned lizards (Phrynosoma) are able to squirt drops of blood from their eyes for several feet, and although the properties of this fluid have not been fully investigated, there is a little evidence that it may irritate the eyes of an agressor. The blood is apparently ejected by the sudden rupture of small vessels in the nictitating membrane, which is remarkably thin. The underlying mechanism is similar to that employed by other lizards to swell the head and break the old 'skin' before moulting and depends upon constriction of certain blood vessels (p. 290). The dwarf boas of the genus Tropidophis have a curious habit of spitting or dribbling blood from the mouth when alarmed, but the significance of this is not understood [312].

Some Australian geckos of the genus Diplodactylus are able to emit a sticky, strong-smelling substance from the soft, spiny tubercles on the tail, or in the case of one species which does not have spines, from the caudal skin [82]. This material is apparently derived from sub-epidermal lymph vessels, and reaches the outside under pressure through rupture of the epidermis. It can be ejected for a foot or so and forms cobweb-like filaments which are difficult to remove. The tail can be directed towards an enemy so that the fluid can be aimed with some accuracy. It is interesting that these lizards seem to be less prone to lose their tails by autotomy than other kinds of geckos.

When seized many reptiles void their excreta, both solid and liquid, and since these may become smeared over the face of an attacker it is probable that the nasty habit has some value in defence. It is said to be used, as a last resort, by the Nile monitor [121].

Snakes possess in the base of the tail a pair of large glands known as the anal glands or anal sacs which open near the cloacal orifice (figure 128, p. 416). In some species such as the grass snake (Natrix natrix) the secretions of these glands, added to the faecal dejecta, produce a particularly foul-smelling material which may well have a repellant effect. The characteristic and lingering odour of a freshly caught grass snake is familiar to all who have had dealings with these otherwise attractive reptiles; fortunately they soon become accustomed to handling and cease to produce it. The cottonmouth (Agkistrodon piscivorus) can spray its musky anal gland secretion for a metre or so by switching its tail from side to side [80]. It is probable that the anal glands of snakes have some other significance besides defence (see p. 406) since in some species such as the adder *(Vipera berus)* the secretion is almost odourless to man and is not voided when the creature is caught. They show seasonal changes related to the cycle of sexual activity and are larger in females than in males. Like many epidermal glands found in reptiles they are of the holocrine type, producing their secretion by cellular breakdown [175, 395, 441].

Autotomy Some animals are able to shed parts of themselves such as limbs or tails when they are seized or threatened by predators, and this is known as autotomy (self-mutilation). It is essentially a means of defence; the broken-off part is expendable, its owner escapes, and since these animals usually have the capacity for regeneration the loss is eventually made good.

The tuatara, lizards and a very few snakes [see 220] are the only living reptiles with the power of autotomy; this is confined to the tail which has predetermined planes of weakness through which breakage can occur with the minimum of damage. Such fracture planes were also present in the Lower Permian stem reptile *Captorhinus* [356] and in some primitive fossil lepidosaurs, so that the power of autotomy must have been evolved at an early stage in reptilian history. Many lizards have no autotomy mechanism, however, and among these are forms which use their tails for some special purpose such as defence (as in monitors) or prehension (as in chamaelons).

The value of autotomy is obvious to anyone who has tried to catch lizards in the wild; the large number of individuals with regenerated tails found in any natural population is its best recommendation. Broken-off tails have also been recovered from the stomachs of predators. The violent writhing of the tail fragment, which may continue for many minutes, serves to divert the aggressor while the lizard runs away to safety. In some species the bright colour of the tail, which contrasts with that of the body, probably adds to the distracting effect.

Autotomy is to a large extent an active process, involving muscular contraction. The ease with which it can be elicited varies considerably in different species, the majority of geckos being particularly good autotomisers. Generally speaking, lizards of any kind which are warm, active and wild are more liable to shed their tails than cold sluggish individuals, or ones which have become accustomed to handling in captivity. In the Australian gecko *Gehyra variegata,* however, the tail is shed more readily at low temperatures around 4°C, a peculiarity which may help it escape from enemies which steal upon it in the chill of night [86].

As a rule autotomy is only provoked when some part of the tail is grasped or pinned down; the caudal muscles then go into violent spasm which causes the tail to be broken through a little way in front of the point of seizure. Instances are known, however, of frightened lizards shedding their tails before being actually touched by an enemy; this may occur in *Gehyra variegata* while it is in cold torpor. The tail of a dead or anaesthetised lizard can, of course, be pulled off by mechanical force; as in autotomy the break usually takes place at one of the special fracture planes which are naturally the regions of greatest fragility. The direction in which the force is applied may also have some bearing on the matter, and I have noticed that the tail of the slow-worm can be broken much more easily by bending in the vertical than in the lateral plane.

The anatomy of the fracture planes is complicated and interesting [159, 465]. As a rule they pass through and not between the caudal vertebrae. In most lizards there is a fracture plane in each caudal vertebra except for the first few at the tail base. Consequently breakage can occur through any part of the tail behind the basal region; since this is near the cloaca and contains the hemipenes in the male damage to it would clearly be undesirable. A rather different arrangement is found, however, in a few geckos such as the Australian *Nephrurus laevis,* which have flat leaf-shaped tails separated from the basal region by a constriction. Here there are only two or three fracture planes which involve the vertebrae of the constricted part, and the whole of the tail behind this is lost when autotomy takes place *.

The fracture plane is essentially a split in the body or centrum of the vertebra (figures 140, 141, 144). In lacertids and many geckos it lies slightly in front of the middle of the vertebra, but in other forms such as the glass lizard *Ophisaurus ventralis* and the slow-worm *(Anguis)* the split is quite close to the front of the vertebra. In many lizards it passes just behind the transverse processes and extends upwards through the neural arch on each side into the anterior neural spine. In some, however, it runs through the transverse process; in some iguanids where there are two transverse processes on each side it passes between them (figure 144) [159]. On the under surface of the centrum the edges of the split are raised up to form conspicuous bony lips or ridges which may be visible in fossil material.

The fracture planes involve the soft structures of the tail as well as its skeleton. The connective tissue at the edges of the vertebral split continues outwards towards the skin as a fibrous sheet or septum through which cleavage takes place (figure 141). The septum passes through the layer of fatty tissue which surrounds the vertebrae, and then through the tail muscles, dividing them into a series of blocks or

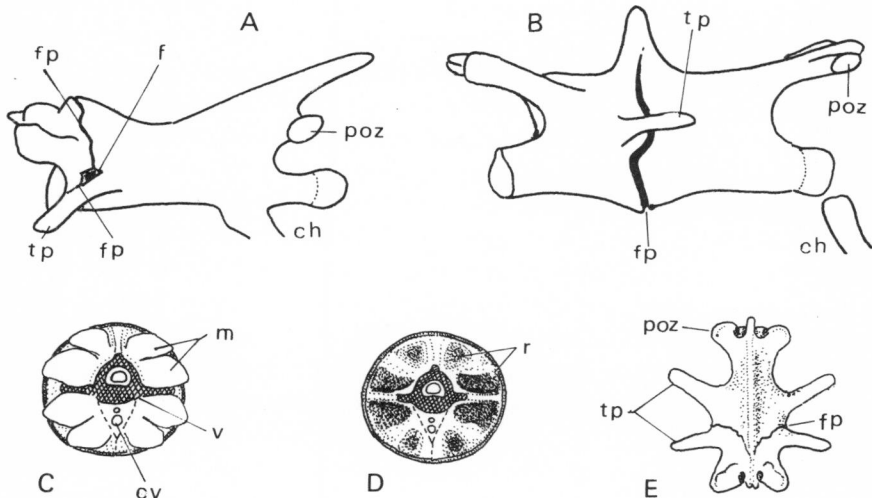

Figure 144   Adaptations to autotomy in lizards. A, B. Caudal vertebrae of A, slow-worm (*Anguis fragilis*) and B, common lizard (*Lacerta vivipara*) seen from left side, showing fracture planes, through transverse process in A and behind it in B. ×9 and 19. Modified from Pratt, C. W. M. (1946) J. Anat. **80** 184. C. Surface of autotomised tail fragment of *Anguis* showing eight projecting tongues of muscle detached from their connective tissue septa, and broken vertebra with larger, posterior portion of transverse process. ×2·5. D. Surface of tail stump of *Anguis* after autotomy showing recesses for muscle tongues and vertebra with smaller, anterior portion of broken transverse process. E. Caudal vertebra of desert iguana (*Dipsosaurus dorsalis*) from above. This lizard has two pairs of transverse processes and the fracture plane passes between them. ×2·5. After Etheridge [159].

ch, chevron (upper part only shown). **cv**, caudal blood vessels. **f**, foramen in transverse process, continuous with fracture plane. **fp**, fracture plane. **m**, projecting tongues of muscle. **poz**, postzygapophysis. **r**, recess for muscle. **tp**, transverse process. **v**, autotomised vertebra with spinal cord and transverse process.

segments. Along the sides of the tail each of these muscle blocks is firmly fixed behind to the transverse process of the vertebra; in front, however, it is attached only to the fibrous fracture plane and not to the bone. When the tail is grasped, the muscles a few segments in front of the point of seizure contract violently, pulling the tail to one side and throwing a great strain on the region of the vertebral split and the fibrous fracture plane so that these are ruptured. When this has occurred the corresponding muscles on the opposite side contract so that the whole of the tail is broken through. It will be seen from figure 144 that the fibrous septum is disposed in such a way that tongues of muscle project from the front of the broken-off tail-piece; cavities corresponding with them can be seen on the end of the stump. The reason why normal movement of the tail does not result in autotomy is that the bending is distributed over the region of several vertebra and muscle segments; the strain imposed on the individual fracture planes is therefore less severe.

Modifications are also found in certain tail structures which are not actually divided by the fracture plane. The spinal cord is constricted opposite the level of each vertebral split. Woodland [465], who gave a detailed account of the autotomy mechanism in the gecko *Hemidactylus*, described an interesting modification of the caudal blood vessels which prevents undue loss of blood. The main tail artery possesses a series of circular sphincter muscles, one in front of each fracture plane, which are thought to contract when the tail is broken. The caudal vein is also constricted in the region of each vertebral split. These features are perhaps also present in *Lacerta*, but seem to be less well developed.

The plane of fracture is also related to the arrangement of the caudal scales, although this differs considerably in the various kinds of lizards. In lacertids the scales are arranged in transverse rows round the circumference of the tail in such a way that each plane passes between every second row. In *Lacerta vivipara* the scales of successive rows tend to alternate slightly in length, a row of shorter scales being followed by a row of longer ones in some cases at least. In normal autotomy the break occurs behind one of the longer scale rows, (see figure 141), but it may be possible to amputate the tail between fracture planes by cutting behind a shorter scale row. This has been of some interest in experimental work.

Studies of development show that the fracture planes conform with the primitive segmental pattern of the tail during embryonic life, each plane separating adjacent segments of muscle and fat. The vertebrae in the embryo come to lie between the adjacent muscle segments instead of opposite them, and this explains why the fracture planes pass through instead of between the vertebrae. However, the full development of these planes is not completed until after the time of birth or hatching; the embryo has no need to practise autotomy.

It is possible that a few lizards have a different type of fracture mechanism. In the agamid *Goniocephalus cristatus*, for example, the planes of weakness are said to lie between adjacent vertebrae, as in certain salamanders with the power of autotomy. Some skinks and geckos, such as *Geckolephis* from Madagascar, practise a curious variant of self-mutilation and shed large portions of the skin from the body if they are seized. Apparently the denuded area is soon covered by the growth of new skin [280].

Threat and bluff Many animals react to situations of stress and danger in a seemingly aggressive fashion; they assume postures or utter sounds which to the human observer convey the idea of menace. Some instances of this kind of behaviour may have been misinterpreted by naturalists, especially since in some reptiles much the same kind of aggressive display may be directed towards sexual rivals as to enemies of another species. Nevertheless, it is fair to assume that in the majority of cases a timely show of threat or bluff may have a definite survival value as a deterrent. Enemies may be frightened off or kept at bay until escape is possible, or perhaps merely baffled until they lose interest by devices such as shamming dead. Many examples of this kind of thing are to be found among reptiles, and are described in the books by Cott, Mertens and Parker [118, 280, 312].

Crocodilians and certain chelonians may open their jaws and hiss loudly when disturbed. The big alligator snapper *(Macroclemys)* dilates the opening of its windpipe (glottis) as it gapes its jaws, and the white lining membrane so displayed contrasts with the dark interior of the mouth in a striking and perhaps threatening fashion. By and large, however, such reptiles have little need for special types of warning behaviour, at least once they have reached a certain size. Their bulk, ferocity or armour is an adequate defence against most natural enemies. Many methods of threat and bluff are used, however, by the lizards and snakes and may be of service to even deadly species which can back up a show of ill-temper with a venomous bite. The slender bodies of these animals are quite fragile and it can be of little satisfaction to a badly hurt snake that its attacker will be the first to die!

The frill of the big Australian agamid *Chlamydosaurus* (Plate 46) is one of the best examples of a warning device, though possibly it may also be used in sexual rivalry display and possibly plays some part in temperature control. When cornered this 2–3 foot lizard rears up to face its aggressor and suddenly erects its frill which may be 25 cm. (nearly 10 in.) across and almost hides the body. In some specimens the frill is brightly coloured with blotches of pink and white. The disconcerting effect is enhanced by gaping of the mouth which has a conspicuous pinkish-yellow lining, and by vigorous hissing and lashing of the tail. In the last resort the lizard springs forward at its enemy and tries to bite. The beard-like ruff of *Amphibolurus barbatus* and the spiny flaps of skin on the neck of the sand agama *Phrynocephalus mystaceus* (figure 97, p. 312) are employed in a similar fashion; in the latter species they become pink in colour when erected owing to dilatation of blood vessels, and when the jaws are simultaneously gaped the appearance is of one huge, ferocious mouth.

A striking example of defensive display has been described in the curious helmeted lizard *Corythophanes cristatus*, an iguanid from British Honduras [129]. When confronted by a snake it compresses its body, rises on its front legs, lowers its head and expands its nuchal crest and throat-fan. The whole effect is to exaggerate the height of the animal, particularly of the head which is converted into a high, thin disc and presented sideways on to its enemy (figure 145); sometimes the head is slowly bobbed at the end of the display. If threatened by a human hand the lizard will lunge forward with open jaws and bite fiercely if actually seized, but this behaviour was not observed in any of the experiments where a snake was used as a threat stimulus.

A cobra in classic pose, with its neck reared up and hood spread is an impressive sight which may well frighten off many potential foes (Plate 39). It is perhaps disappointing that the king cobra, the longest of all poisonous snakes, should have a relatively less well-developed hood than some of the smaller species. In the African black-necked cobra *(Naja nigricollis)* the imposing effect of the hood is enhanced by a broad dark band which stands out conspicuously against the whitish colour of the rest of the front of the neck. The Indian cobra *(Naja naja)* and its Chinese variant have striking

Figure 145 Defence posture of iguanid lizard *Corythophanes cristatus.* Based on photo in Davis [129].

markings on their hoods also, in the form of a spectacle-like, or monocle-like pattern (figure 149, p. 515); it is curious, however, that these should be on the back, not the front of the neck, and are therefore invisible when the cobra faces its foe.

Many other snakes flatten or inflate their necks when alarmed, though they do not possess the elongated and freely movable neck ribs (Plate 76) which give the cobra's hood its impressive spread. The harmless Asiatic colubrids of the genus *Macropisthodon* rear up in cobra style, and the acrid secretion of their nucho-dorsal glands is discharged on to the skin as the neck is flattened. Some snakes, such as the rear-fanged boomslang *(Dispholidus typus)* (figure 146) and the bird snakes *(Thelotornis)* inflate the trachea when annoyed, exposing areas of conspicuously coloured skin at the stretched hinges of the scales.

Hissing, often combined with gaping of the mouth (Plate 77) and inflation of the neck or body, is a common defensive gambit in reptiles generally, not only in formidable species such as snapping turtles, alligators, puff adders and monitors but also in chamaeleons and other virtually harmless forms. With its well-developed system of air sacs communicating with the lungs, a chamaeleon can blow itself out to look much bigger than it really is, and when it turns its gaping jaws on an aggressor it presents quite an intimidating appearance.

The North American bull snake *(Pituophis catenifer)* and the hog-nosed snakes *(Heterodon)* are further examples of innocuous reptiles which try to look fierce by swelling, coiling and weaving their bodies and making sham strikes with their heads. The bull

505

snake is renowned for the loud blowing noise it is able to make; this has been compared, probably with exaggeration, to the bellow of a bull. Its larynx, unlike that of most snakes, is provided with an epiglottis, a narrow flap of tissue in front of the glottis or windpipe opening, which probably increases the sound of the hiss as the snake expels air from its windpipe. Some species, such as the hog-nosed snake, will finally sham dead if their bluff is called, lying inert and belly uppermost with the jaws open and the tongue protruding (Plate 78). English grass snakes *(Natrix natrix)* sometimes behave in this way, rapidly coming to 'life' again and moving off when they are left alone.

Another peculiar habit practised by quite a number of snakes from widely separate groups is to wave or strike with the tail which is made to mimic the movements of the head. In such reptiles the underside of the tail is often brightly coloured and in some species bears a conspicuous eye-like spot. During the display the proper head is hidden under the coils; this may puzzle an enemy as to which is the biting

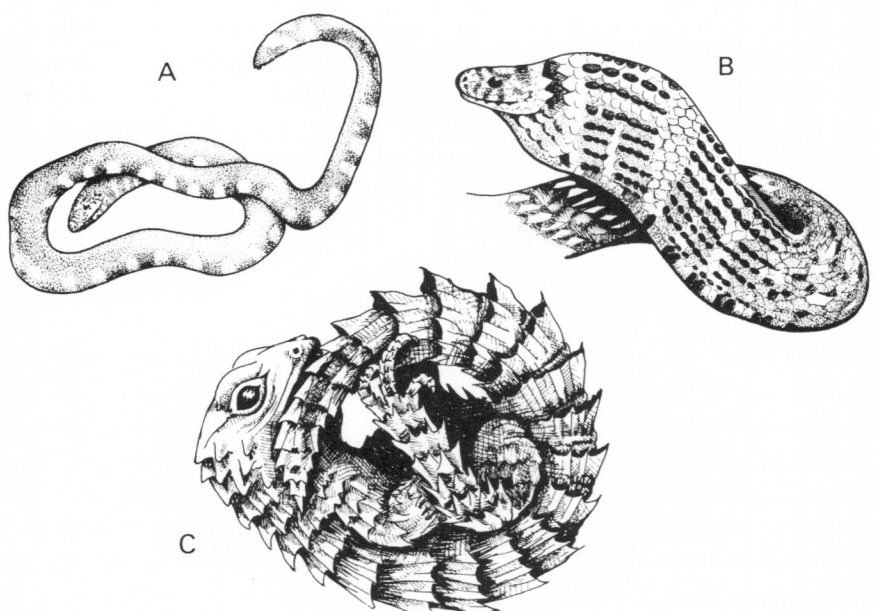

Figure 146   Defensive and warning behaviour in reptiles. Based on illustrations in Mertens [280] and Rose [361]. A. Pipe snake *(Cylindrophis rufus)* hiding its head and waving its tail in the air. B. Boomslang *(Dispholidus typus)* inflating its throat. C. Armadillo lizard *(Cordylus cataphractus)* with tail in mouth.

end of the snake. Species which behave like this include the beautiful and highly venomous coral snakes of America and Asia *(Micrurus* and *Maticora)* and the Malayan pipe snake *(Cylindrophis)*, a primitive, harmless form (figure 146).

Various other kinds of postural defence are used by certain lizards. The hard, spiny zonure *Cordylus cataphractus* of South Africa rolls itself into a ring with its tail held tightly in its jaws, a ruse which has earned it the name of the armadillo lizard (figure 146). The North American alligator lizards *(Gerrhonotus)* protect themselves by encircling a branch and then grasping the tail with the jaws, and the African monitor *Varanus exanthematicus* is alleged to sham dead with its body looped and one of its hind legs in its mouth. Many snakes such as the West African royal python *(P. regius)* coil up into a tight ball when alarmed. The object of these manoeuvres is presumably to render the reptile more difficult to drag away and swallow.

Although the hiss is the characteristic vocal expression of reptilian displeasure, threatening noises of various other kinds are made by certain species. Some rough-scaled vipers such as the highly poisonous *Echis carinatus* throw their bodies into concentric circles, and by moving adjacent coils in opposite directions are able to rub their sides together and produce a loud rasping sound. This habit is apparently mimicked by some of the harmless African egg-eating snakes *(Dasypeltis)* which also resemble the vipers in appearance. The curious geckos of the genus *Teratoscincus,* found in desert regions from Persia to China, can stridulate in a rather similar fashion, by rasping together the enlarged scales on the upper surface of the tail. At one time it was thought that the function of the noise was to attract grasshoppers. It has also been suggested that it is made as a kind of group display; the laryngeal sounds made by many other geckos very probably has some social significance. More recent workers believe, however, that the stridulation is a form of threat. It can be maintained for a while by the violent bending and unbending of a freshly autotomised tail. The specialised scales which make the noise are reproduced very perfectly in the regenerate, so that if *Teratoscincus* loses its tail it is only temporarily deprived of its power of sound production [450]. A final and rather droll method of producing offensive sounds is used by one of the American coral snakes *(Micruroides euryxanthus)* and the harmless hook-nosed snake *(Gyalopium canum)* which make repeated popping noises by expelling air from the cloaca [312].

A number of snakes have acquired the habit of vibrating the tip of the tail very rapidly, which will produce a rustling sound among dead leaves. This behaviour must have arisen independently in different groups, since it occurs in the non-poisonous pine and bull snakes *(Pituophis)* which are celebrated for their elaborate threat display, as well as in certain pit-vipers, including the largest of all, the dreaded bushmaster *(Lachesis muta)*. In some of these snakes the tail terminates in a specialised horn-like scale which is perhaps a kind of precursor of the rattlesnakes' rattle.

Laurence Klauber has devoted many pages of his great book on rattlesnakes to the uses of the rattle, and to its structure and method of growth which are described here on p. 316. The first printed accounts of the rattle were given by a few scholarly spirits who followed in the wake of the Spanish conquistadors and the early Portugese colonists of Brazil – much as the first studies of Indian reptiles were made nearly 200 years later by doctors and army officers who helped to found the British Empire. Thus, one finds statements made in the late sixteenth and early seventeenth centuries that the rattle sounds whenever the snake moves (incorrect), that the rattle is sounded furiously when the snake is angry, and that passersby avoid it when they hear it (definitely along the right lines). Many of these remarks probably refer to the deadly tropical rattlesnake or cascabel *(Crotalus durissus)*, the only species which is found south of Mexico and which ranges throughout much of South America.

Among the numerous later theories which have been advanced about the use of the rattle, the following are worth a mention: that it is sounded as a signal to other rattlesnakes for assistance, or as a mating call, and that it attracts or fascinates prey; the tail movements of certain other snakes genuinely appear to have the latter function (p. 122). There is little direct evidence for any of these ideas, and the first two have generally been discounted on the assumption that snakes have little if any power of perceiving airborne sounds and hence cannot hear each others' rattles. Although no one seems to have been able to demonstrate that the behaviour of snakes is influenced by such sounds, the widely held view that they are virtually deaf has been shaken by some fairly recent experimental work (p. 384). It is now known that the ears of some snakes respond physiologically to low notes, which are in fact within the range of those produced by the rattlesnake's rattle, perhaps between 128 and 135 cycles per second. This work was done on colubrids and not on rattlesnakes, and it does not necessarily prove that snakes react in their behaviour to airborne sounds of this frequency. Nevertheless, it would be as well to preserve an open mind on the matter, until the possible role of hearing in the life of snakes has been investigated much more critically.

It is now generally accepted that an important use of the rattle is to warn intruders to keep their distance, whatever other functions it may possibly have. The rattlesnake insignia shown on certain flags used by the American Navy during the war of independence with the motto 'Don't tread on me', just about sums the matter up. If the first sound of the rattle fails to achieve its object the snake often assumes a most menacing posture, with the front of its body reared up, the neck looped and the head poised ready to strike. At the same time, the tongue with the tips spread wide is alternately pointed upwards and downwards, while the snake puffs out its body and then exhales, hissing violently. Such behaviour is likely to frighten off any carnivore which is not an experienced rattlesnake killer, as well as large ungulates such as cattle which might inadvertently trample on the reptile. Many human beings have been saved from serious injury by heeding the rattlesnake's warning which under optimal conditions may be audible thirty yards away. The sound made by certain species with small rattle such as *Sistrurus miliarius*, the pigmy rattler, may however, only carry two or three yards. The effects of the rattle were often attributed to divine providence by early writers, but unhappily this is not always reliable; the occasional, ill-bred specimen will strike first and rattle afterwards.

The sound made by the rattle is perhaps best described as a dry whirring hiss which has been compared with that of a small steam jet and resembles the stridulation of certain cicadas. Its character is much the same in all species, though its intensity varies with the size of the snake and the length of the rattle, a string of six to eight segments giving the best performance. It is muffled by damp, as for instance when the snake has been in the water. The rattling can be maintained for a long time, possibly for over an hour, but captive individuals which are accustomed to visitors rattle less readily and less persistently than snakes which have been freshly taken from the wild. The speed of vibration of the rattle depends to a large extent on temperature, though both speed and amplitude tend to increase if the snake is thoroughly annoyed. An average speed, registered at 25°C (77°F), is around 60 cycles a second; each cycle is a complete to and fro movement. At 40°C (104°F) it is increased to nearly 100 cycles [240]. The difference between the rattle rate and the note produced is perhaps accounted for by the number of impacts between the different lobes per cycle.

Concealment Concealment by artful devices of colour, shape and posture is one of the most effective and widely used methods of defence in the animal kingdom. It may, of course, be equally useful in attack, for the camouflage which enables an animal to hide from its foes may serve a predator equally well as it lies in ambush or stalks its victims. Hugh Cott in his book [118] on adaptive colouration cites countless examples of the ways in which animals make themselves inconspicuous by the use of what is called cryptic colouration. He shows how the principles involved in the concealment of a fish or a snake can be applied to the problems of hiding ships and guns; his specialised knowledge and experience as a naturalist were put to good use during the second world war when he served as a camouflage specialist in the army.

The evolution of cryptic colouration is not difficult to envisage. In any population of reptiles there are wide variations of shade and pattern. Individuals which move by chance into surroundings where their colours are particularly appropriate, or which by good luck begin their lives there, will have greater chances of survival than those less fortunately endowed. The probable effects of such selection are seen in certain populations which inhabit environments where special colours predominate. For instance, there are extensive tracts of snow-white gypsum dunes known as the White Sands in New Mexico. These are inhabited by a race of earless lizards *(Holbrookia maculata ruthveni)* which are almost white in colour, so that they become almost invisible against their natural background [390]. In neighbouring areas the landscape is made up of black lava rock, and the lizards and snakes which live there are very much darker than individuals of the same species which live in 'normally coloured' regions elsewhere [250].

Perhaps the simplest type of cryptic colouration is seen in animals of a fairly uniform colour which resembles that of the surroundings, or of natural objects such as logs or rocks which they contain. The sombre hues of mature crocodilians and of many freshwater chelonians provide examples of this type of relatively homogeneous colouration; so also do the many species of lizards and snakes in which

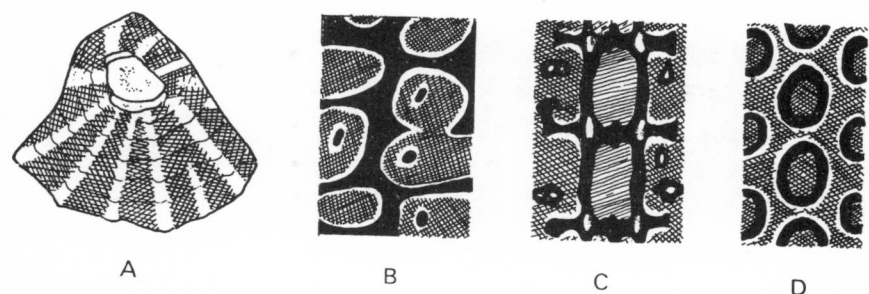

Figure 147 Disruptive patterns of reptiles. A. Lateral horny plate (lamina) from carapace of Indian starred tortoise, *Testudo* [= *Geochelone*] *elegans*. The yellow and brown pattern on the humpy shell makes this tortoise very difficult to see in its grassy jungle habitat. B–D. Dorsal patterns of snakes. B, West African royal python (*P. regius*). C, boa (*Constrictor constrictor*). D, *Vipera russelli*. After Cott [118].

green is the predominant colour, effectively concealing the animal against its background of vegetation.

Few reptiles are completely uniform in colour, however, although as we have seen, one hue frequently predominates. It is common for the dorsal surface of the animal to be a different shade from the under surface, and in aquatic reptiles this arrangement may have a cryptic function, as it does in many fishes. In some sea snakes, for example, this principle of obliterative shading is clearly evident, though it is often combined with patterns of bars and blotches. The dark-coloured back of the snake is inconspicuous when viewed from above against the blue-green of the waves; the lighter belly is hard to see from below against the illuminated background of the surface.

A great many reptiles show a type of colouration known as disruptive. The outline of the body is broken by patterns of blotches or bands which blend very well with the creatures' natural surroundings of leaves or stones, although they are often quite conspicuous in captivity. Such patterns are common among snakes; the dark zigzag along the back of the adder and the beautiful chestnut and beige mottlings of the boa constrictor are good examples (figure 147). The reticulated markings on the shells of some tortoises and the spots on the back of some soft-shelled turtles which lurk on the bottom of a pool among shingle or mud probably have the same effect. Disruptive colouration of the most subtle type is shown by the bark geckos (*Uroplatus*) whose dull greyish markings, like those of certain moths, harmonise perfectly with a tree trunk. In these reptiles the

511

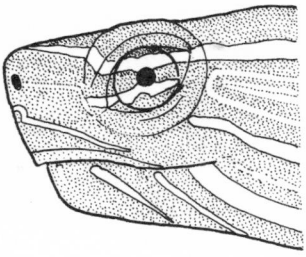

Figure 148   Head of painted
terrapin (*Chrysemys picta*)
with disruptive yellow bands
passing across head, including
the eyelids and iris, thus helping to conceal the eye. After
Walls [444].

cryptic effect is enhanced by the presence of scaly fringes along the
sides of the jaws, flanks and tail which break up the outline still further.
In some reptiles, such as the terrapin *Chrysemys* (figure 148) the
difficulty of concealing the eye is overcome by means of longitudinal
stripes down the head which cross the conjunctiva and iris without
interruption and break up the circular outline of this conspicuous
organ.

The colours of many reptiles change with age, and such changes
sometimes appear to have adaptive significance. Young crocodilians
and monitor lizards, for instance, are much more brightly coloured
than the adults, having light yellowish bars or spots upon the body
and tail. Such markings are very suitable for concealment among
rushes at the water's edge where the young mostly dwell, but are no
longer so useful when the animal grows bigger and seeks less sheltered
habitats.

The physiology of colour change in reptiles has already been
described (p. 299). It seems unlikely that such a complicated mechanism would have been evolved if it was not of some value to the
animal, and one tends to imagine that its primary object is for concealment. The fact that it may serve other purposes such as display (p.
398) and temperature control (p. 225) would not unduly disturb
adherents of this view. Yet the evidence is by no means clear-cut and
we have seen that many of the responses of chamaeleons and *Anolis*
lizards, for instance the pallor they assume at night, are most unlikely
to be useful for concealment.

In fact, the apparently simple question as to how far chamaeleons,
the most accomplished of all reptiles at colour change, can adapt
their colour to their surroundings has proved extremely difficult to
answer, and very divergent views on the matter have been expressed
by reputable naturalists. It seems clear that a chamaeleon does not
necessarily match its colour to its background; one may see a pre-

dominantly green individual on a brown twig and vice versa, at least in captivity. Many artificial backgrounds would in any case be quite beyond its colour range.

A much better case could be put up for the idea that the chamaeleon can blend its colour to its surroundings, especially in nature. Cott, a firm believer in the protective value of colour change, wrote [118] 'No one who has not searched for species like *Chamaeleon dilepis* ... can realise how marvellously these creatures harmonise with, and melt into, the medley of foliage where they have their home, and where they are relatively secure from every eye'. E. M. Stephenson [see 409] also believed that the colours of the dwarf Cape chamaeleon *(Lophosaura)* gave it admirable protection among its natural foliage, and I can confirm this from personal experience when trying to find these animals among the bushes on the campus of the University of Stellenbosch. Sceptics, on the other hand, have pointed out that the predominantly green to brown colour range of most chamaeleons is bound to conform with many types of natural arboreal background so that by chance alone it will probably become inconspicuous.

In considering the significance of colour change, and indeed of other types of seemingly protective colouration, one must bear in mind that the sensory equipment of predators may be very different from our own, which depends so largely on visual discrimination by daylight. Many mammalian predators are nocturnal, more or less colour-blind and hunt chiefly by smell, while snakes are probably colour-blind also. It is possible that green and brown look much alike to these animals so that a brown lizard among green leaves may not seem so conspicuous to them as it does to us. On the other hand, such animals may be able to discriminate pattern and shade so that obliterative shading and disruptive markings are likely to be of great value in concealment, even though the actual colours are less significant. Furthermore, diurnal birds of prey are thought to have good colour vision, and these must be among the more important enemies of small tree-living reptiles such as chamaeleons.

The present evidence on the adaptive nature of colour change in reptiles seems to justify a compromise view. Although the responses of the animal appear to be automatic or involuntary and are not always appropriate to the surroundings it does not follow that they are without value in its life. Reactions to heat and stress may play a part in temperature control and display, while the reaction to light will help to evoke a disruptive pattern, concealing the animal while it is sitting among shifting foliage. It is characteristic of modern zoology that we should know much more about the behaviour of animals in the laboratory than in the wild; the naturalist who tries to follow the literature on colour change may feel that it was time the data were reassessed in the light of controlled field experiments on animals in their natural surroundings.

In many reptiles the cryptic effect of colour is increased by peculiarities of shape and posture. There can be little doubt about the concealment value of the chamaeleon's shape and behaviour. With its arched back, laterally compressed body and slender, twig-like limbs this slow-moving reptile can under suitable conditions look remarkably like a big leaf; the resemblance is particularly strong in certain dwarf forms *(Rhampholeon)* which sway from side to side as if they were blown by the wind. In other arboreal lizards such as *Corythophanes,* the casqued head, irregular outline and habit of 'freezing' motionless for long periods is also effective in concealment. The green tree snakes *Oxybelis* (Plate 77) and *Ahaetulla,* which may be 1·22 metres (4 ft.) long but only as thick as a fountain-pen, are further examples of such camouflage. Their extraordinary slenderness and the way in which they lie stretched out across the branches of jungle trees make them very difficult to distinguish from lianas.

Warning colouration and mimicry Concealment is not the only defensive function which colours can perform. Since the time of Darwin it has been recognised that poisonous or unpalatable animals are often very brightly coloured and conspicuous, and it is believed that they have the function of warning off foes which learn by experience not to attack creatures which show them. The display of such colours may be combined with other types of threat behaviour, and their sudden 'flashing' by inflation of the neck skin as in snakes like the boomslang, or by the erection of frills or ruffs as in certain lizards, has already been mentioned.

Other reptiles have permanent and striking hues of black and white, or some shade of red, which have often been regarded as examples of warning or 'aposematic' colouration. The Gila monster *(Heloderma suspectum),* one of the only two species of poisonous lizard, with its beaded scales of black and salmon pink or orange is a typical case (Plate 33). It has been suggested, however, that while the colours of this nocturnal reptile may show up very strikingly against the artificial background of a well-lit vivarium, they are far less conspicuous in nature and may really be examples of cryptic colouration of a disruptive type [53]. Similar markings are present in small harmless lizards such as the banded gecko *(Coleonyx variegatus;* Plate 73) which live in the same places, and render them very difficult to see by moonlight against a background of semi-desert containing pink-veined granitic rocks. It is possible, however, that the colouration of the Gila monster has a dual purpose, and while primarily cryptic in function, may act as a warning to any creature which encounters this formidable lizard by day in the open.

There are in many warm parts of the world certain species of elapid snakes which are beautifully marked with contrasting bands of black, yellow and red. Such reptiles, poisonous but usually unaggressive in habit, are universally known as coral snakes; *Micrurus* and *Micruroides* are American genera, *Aspidelaps* is found in Africa, *Maticora* and *Callophis* in Asia, and *Brachyurophis* in Australia. Most of them are quite small although the Brazilian *Micrurus spixi* grows to five feet.

In some regions where coral snakes occur there are various harmless species, often called false coral snakes, which have very similar markings (figure 149). There may be differences in detail; for instance, in the false coral snakes of the USA the coloured bands do not extend completely round the ventral scales, and each black band is followed by a red or yellow one in alternation. In the true coral snakes such as *Micrurus fulvius,* on the other hand, the black and red bands are separated by narrow yellow ones. In some of the tropical forms,

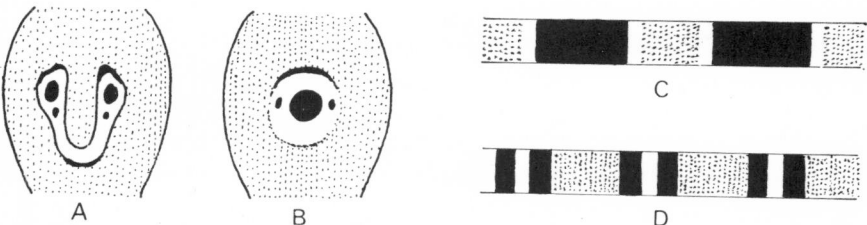

Figure 149   A, B, markings on back of hood of Indian cobra *(Naja naja)*. A shows the 'typical' spectacled variety, B one of the monocled types which are commonest in the eastern parts of the species' range such as Thailand and China. Hood patterns are very variable and there may be subsidiary markings. C, D, patterns of two coral snakes in bands of yellow (unshaded), red (stippled) and black. C. represents the common venomous coral snake *(Micrurus fulvius)* of the USA, D the harmless *Lampropeltis doliata annulata* of the south-eastern USA. This species is generally known as the ringed king snake or milk snake.

however, the patterns of the venomous and harmless species may be almost identical. The non-poisonous coral snakes belong to a variety of groups. Thus the South American species *Anilius scytale* (Plate 8) is a primitive snake with persistent rudiments of the pelvis; this handsome creature has alternate rings of red and black, but no yellow markings. Most of the other harmless types are colubrids of different kinds, such as the ringed king snake *(Lampropeltis doliata annulata)* of North America.

It is likely enough that the bright colours of poisonous coral snakes have a warning function and inhibit predators which might otherwise be deceived by their docility. The majority of human casualties have resulted from people carrying them about to show off their beautiful markings and gentle nature. Even though these snakes are crepuscular secretive in habits they must occasionally be surprised in broad daylight, and it is then that their deterrent colouration might come in most useful.

Many herpetologists have attributed the markings of the harmless coral snakes to mimicry of the same kind as that exhibited by many harmless insects and spiders for wasps and stinging ants. Others, however, prefer to believe that, as in the Gila monster, the colours of all coral snakes serve a cryptic rather than a warning function. They suggest that these have arisen by parallel evolution in harmless and venomous species alike, which live under similar conditions. This is another fascinating problem which can only be solved by some kind of field experiment in which the reactions of a predator to a harmless mimic and venomous 'model' are put to critical test.

Diseases

I have little personal knowledge of diseases in reptiles, a most complex and recondite topic with a substantial but scattered literature [see 281, 346]. One can obtain some idea of the ailments from which reptiles suffer by reading the interesting pathologists' reports published each year by the Zoological Society of London on the animals which die in the Menagerie.

Among the more important bacterial diseases are the oral canker or 'mouth rot' seen in captive snakes and apparently caused by species of *Pseudomonas* and *Pasteurella*, and various forms of septicaemia due to *Aeromonas* or *Proteus* bacilli transmitted by mites. Tuberculosis, produced by various strains of *Mycobacterium*, is also known.

Fungal diseases are less common in reptiles than amphibians, but sores of fungal character sometimes develop around the eyes of captive terrapins.

The majority of infectious diseases which have been reliably described are produced by Protozoa or larger, multicellular parasites. *Entamoeba invadens*, for example, is an intestinal parasite of amphibians and reptiles and causes liver abscesses; it is morphologically indistinguishable from *E. histolytica*, the agent of human amoebic dysentery, but no cases of transmission from 'herptile' to man have been reported. Plasmodia and trypanosomes similar to those which cause malaria and sleeping sickness have been obtained from the blood of reptiles and are carried by flies and other biting insects whose mouthparts can penetrate the hinges of the scales or the oral mucosa [327]. *Trypanosoma grayi*, found in crocodiles, is carried by the infamous tsetse fly, *Glossina palpalis*, which also sucks the blood of domestic animals, but it seems to be uncertain whether crocodiles act as a natural reservoir for mammalian sleeping sickness.

Reptiles harbour their share of the ubiquitous parasitic worms; flat, round, hooked and tape. Ticks and mites of various kinds are often found upon them and infestations with mites (*Ophionyssus*) are particularly feared by vivarium keepers, since these arthropods transmit bacterial diseases which may be speedily fatal. Treatment by painting the reptiles with paraffin oil, or rubbing them with certain proprietary powders such as the American silica-aerogel 'Dri-Die' are generally recommended. Captive *Uta* lizards have been observed to hunt for mites on each other's bodies, and eat them.

Perhaps the most remarkable reptilian parasites are the curious 'lung-worms' or lingulatids. Although they look like worms they are actually degenerate arachnids which live inside the lungs (and sometimes other cavities) of tropical reptiles. Only in a few species has it been possible to determine the life-cycle, and some forms probably complete their whole development inside a single reptilian host. Others, such as *Porocephalus crotali*, however, may pass their larval stages inside mice and amphibians, and become adult inside their rattlesnake predators. The role of biting flies in the transmission of blood parasites has been mentioned; other types of fly are known to lay their eggs in the cloacal region of chelonians, or in wounds elsewhere on the body of a reptile. Subsequent maggot infestations (myiasis) may do considerable damage to the neighbouring tissues.

Certain other diseases, not necessarily due to infective organisms,

may be briefly mentioned. Degenerative arterial diseases of athero-
matous type such as affect mammals including man, have been described in reptiles which have spent long periods in captivity.
Tumours, both of non-malignant and malignant or invasive kind
occur quite frequently and include epithelial cancer (carcinoma),
cancer derived from pigmented tissues (melanoma) and tumours of
bone and cartilage. Skin growths (papillomata) are not uncommon,
and vivarium keepers are familiar with the unsightly pigmented and
highly keratinised warts often found on wild and captive green
lizards. The rough, nodular 'tree-bark' tumours described in sand
and eyed lizards may be exaggerations of the same condition. These
skin growths are perhaps brought on by infections of some kind,
possibly transmitted by mites, but their cause is still uncertain.

Reptiles are unimportant as a source of zoonoses: diseases such
as rabies which can be transmitted from animals to man. Tortoises,
however, can harbour *Salmonella* bacilli which are responsible for
certain types of human dysentery, and an outbreak of this disease
among children some years ago was doubtfully attributed to playing
with tortoise pets. Exceptional cases of people being infected by
porocephali which are normally found as parasites in reptiles have
been reported. Such infections probably result from a diet of un-
cooked reptilian flesh or from drinking water soiled with reptilian
excreta [209].

Immunity

Comparatively little is known about the cellular and chemical
defences which reptiles are able to summon to protect their bodies
from injury and disease, but it is evident that they are basically
similar to those in other higher vertebrates.

As we have seen (p. 213), the mechanism of chemical immunity
depends largely on the ability of the animal to form antibodies in
response to the introduction of certain foreign substances (antigens)
into its blood or tissues. This mechanism is certainly present in
reptiles, which form antibodies against the venom, and under
experimental conditions against the blood of other species.

Quite a lot of work has been done on the reactions of snakes to
snake venoms, and it is generally agreed that venomous animals have
a high resistance to their own personal venom and to that of other
individuals, such as members of the same species, which are genetic-

ally close to them. The idea that they manufacture 'antidotes' against their own poison is supported by experiments on the Gila monster whose bite is usually fatal to small animals such as mice. If, however, samples of the venom are mixed with the lizard's blood serum or with extracts from its liver and then injected into mice, these animals are unaffected. The serum or liver extract has a protective function, presumably by virtue of the antibodies which it contains [427].

While many observations on snakes suggest a similar type of 'auto-immunity', it would appear that their resistance is not absolute, and some contradictory findings have been reported. The copperhead seems actually to be more susceptible to venom of its own kind than to that of other crotalines. At least one case is known where a rattlesnake which accidentally bit itself in the tail died after 27 hours. In other cases of self-inflicted injury no ill-effects have been observed, and many of the older stories of rattlesnakes committing suicide when in a tight place by burying their fangs in their own flesh are certainly unreliable. Rattlesnakes may certainly die after being bitten by other individuals of the same species, or after they have been injected experimentally with large doses of venom. On the other hand, they not infrequently recover, as do snakes of unrelated species, and indeed victims of snake-bite generally. The non-poisonous king snakes, which sometimes constrict and eat rattlesnakes, are said to be partly immune to their venom and have survived doses of it which would have more than sufficed to kill mammals of equivalent weight [240]. Reptiles in general seem, however, to be more resistant to venom of all kinds than warm-blooded animals, and so many variable factors are involved in this kind of work that the results are not easy to assess. For example, the development of immunity in 'cold-blooded' animals depends to some extent on temperature and is delayed or suppressed by cold [217].

It is possible to use immunological reactions in the study of biochemical affinities between different groups of animals, since both serum (a preparation of cell-free blood deprived of its clotting properties) and blood cells contain antigens and evoke the antibody response. If a laboratory rabbit, for example, is injected with serum prepared from the blood of another species of animal, its own serum will come to contain antibodies which neutralise or precipitate further samples of the serum of that species. The same reaction may occur if this specifically sensitised rabbit serum is then mixed with serum from a fairly closely related species, but to a lesser extent. If serum from a more distantly related animal is used such a cross reaction may not occur at all. The degree of reactivity is correlated with the closeness of the zoological affinity between the two species tested.

Such tests have shown that the sea snake *Lapemis* is serologically closer to the cobra than to a colubrid or a rattlesnake, and that the pigmy rattlesnake *(Sistrurus)* is closer to other rattlesnakes than to the cottonmouth moccasin *(Agkistrodon piscivorus)*, another type of pit-viper. It is interesting that the alligator is serologically closer to chelonians *(Chelydra)* than to lizards *(Varanus)* or snakes *(Coluber)*; the zoological relationship suggested here is very doubtful [104].

Another type of immunity reaction occurs between the red blood cells of one species or strain of animals and the serum of another. This forms the basis for classifying human blood into various groups, the red cells of each being incompatible with the serum of the others so that when mixed they become agglutinated or clumped together. Rather similar blood group systems have been found among various chelonian species and may in some cases be related to differences in geographical distribution. The blood of two population samples of the painted terrapin *(Chrysemys picta)* living 121 kilometres (75 miles) apart could be distinguished by such tests [170].

Studies of immunity reactions, like those of other biochemical properties of the blood (p. 248), have naturally been applied to other groups of animals and to other tissues such as the albumen of birds' eggs. Although they may throw only indirect light on mechanisms of immunological defence, they offer great possibilities for investigating degrees of zoological affinity, both between and within different species and larger groups. They provide a useful supplement to conventional methods employed in classification such as comparing scale colours and patterns or counting the numbers of teeth; they might theoretically supersede these old-fashioned techniques in the systematics of the future. In the meanwhile some immunological findings appear formidably complicated and emphasise the uniqueness of the individual. It has been shown that the red cells of every member of a sample of 24 specimens of the tortoise *Testudo hermanni* were immunologically distinguishable from those of the rest [170]!

Research during the last few years, mainly on birds and mammals, has shown that the development of immune responses depends in some way on the organs which make up the lymphoid system.

These consist of lymph nodes in various parts of the body, such as those which swell up in the human neck when the tonsils are infected, the tonsils themselves, the spleen, and the thymus, present in neck or thorax, and in birds a kind of cloacal tonsil called the bursa of Fabricius. These organs lies in the path of lymphatic vessels which permeate the body and eventually communicate with the system of veins. They contain masses of lymphocytes, small rounded cells with large nuclei, which are also found in the bone marrow. Apart from the spleen they characteristically grow smaller with age.

It is suggested that the avian bursa and perhaps the tonsils are involved in the development of the type of immunity we have been considering which depends on the presence of circulating antibodies. The thymus, on the other hand, is believed to be concerned with a rather different type of immunity which is responsible for the rejection of skin grafts taken from other individuals. Normally it is seldom possible to graft successfully tissues from one adult vertebrate to another, even of the same species, although this difficulty does not apply to embryos. The rejection of skin grafts was demonstrated in *Anolis* lizards as long ago as 1924, and it was found that the grafted material was completely destroyed after 60–90 days, leaving the area covered by thin scaleless integument [277].

The lymphoid system of reptiles is represented by occasional nodes in the posterior part of the intestine, by tonsils in the lining of the pharynx, and by multiple thymus bodies in the neck (figure 86, p. 266) [1]. In lizards and snakes there are usually two pairs of these bodies on each side not far from the thyroid gland; in chelonians there is only a single elongated pair. In crocodiles, young specimens at least, the thymus forms a long thin strand of tissue running the length of the neck on each side, much as in birds. No organ corresponding with the avian bursa has been identified.

Experimental work on the thymus and other lymphoid tissues in reptiles, amphibians and fish is now being carried out by R. A. Good and his collaborators in the USA [198]. This work should provide valuable information on the evolution of immunological responses and will be an important contribution to the infant science of comparative pathology.

Chapter 13

Classification of Living Reptiles

MANY classifications of reptiles have been proposed. I have largely followed the system used by Romer who has accomplished the tremendous task of enumerating all the known genera of reptiles, living and extinct, together with their synonyms. My lists of genera and their geographical distribution have been compiled with little alteration from Romer's *Osteology* [356], to which I should like to render enthusiastic acknowledgement. The remarks which I have made about the various groups are intended only as a general guide, and not as a full synopsis of diagnostic characters. Fossil forms are not included, except that I have indicated the antiquity of the orders and suborders, and the relationships of some of the extinct groups to modern forms.

This classification is a conservative one in many ways, but is biased towards 'lumping' rather than 'splitting'. For instance, the three groups of primitive burrowing snakes which have usually been regarded as families – the Aniliidae, Uropeltidae and Xenopeltidae – are given only subfamilial ranks, although this procedure is open to criticism [143]. Classification is to a large extent a matter of taste and judgement, and I would rate convenience very high as a criterion of the merit of any system used. Any reasonable reduction in the number of familial (or other) names which students may have to learn has much to be said for it. With such considerations in mind I have retained the traditional classification of the geckos and colubrid snakes, unwieldy groups though these, especially the latter, may be. I have also refrained from the temptation to raise the amphisbaenids to the status of another suborder of the Squamata. I have reduced the family Anniellidae, represented by a single genus of burrowing North American lizards, to a subfamily of the Anguidae. For this step I am personally responsible and Dr Romer cannot be blamed for it.

With a certain lack of consistency I have deviated from recent trends in retaining the land tortoises (Testudinidae) and sea snakes

(Hydrophiidae) in the status of families rather than subfamilies. Although this may not be justified on morphological grounds it does give recognition to the distinctiveness of their ways of life, and can, I think, be defended on grounds of sheer convenience. I have followed Underwood [434] in giving the three principal groups of living snakes infraordinal status, and in classifying *Acrochordus* and allied oriental water snakes as a family of the infraorder Henophidia, along with other primitive families such as the Boidae. I have not used the super-family unit in the classification of the snakes though its employment might in some cases be justified.

The numbered references placed alongside certain groups indicate important recent publications which deal with their classification; I have naturally taken cognisance of these, although I have not neces-sarily followed all the views expressed in them. Synonyms and English or vernacular names are given for some of the better known forms.

Synoptic classification (denotes extinct group)

Class Reptilia
Subclass Anapsida (chelonians, *cotylosaurs)
  Order Chelonia [= Testudinata] (tortoises, terrapins, turtles)
    Suborder Cryptodira
      Superfamily Testudinoidea
        Family Dermatemydidae
        Family Chelydridae
          Subfamily Chelydrinae (snappers)
          Subfamily Staurotypinae
          Subfamily Kinosterninae (mud and musk turtles)
        Family Emydidae
          Subfamily Platysterninae
          Subfamily Emydinae (contains 'typical' terrapins)
        Family Testudinidae (tortoises)
      Superfamily Chelonioidea
        Family Cheloniidae (sea turtles except leatherback)
      Superfamily Dermochelyoidea
        Family Dermochelyidae [= Sphargidae] (leatherback)
      Superfamily Carettochelyoidea
        Family Carettochelyidae
      Superfamily Trionychoidea
        Family Trionychidae (soft-shelled turtles)

Suborder Pleurodira (side-necked turtles)
  Family Pelomedusidae
  Family Chelyidae (contains snake-necked turtles, matamata etc)
Subclass Lepidosauria (*Sphenodon,* Squamata,*eosuchians, *rhynchosaurs, *mosasaurs, etc)
Order Rhynchocephalia
  Family Sphenodontidae (tuatara)
Order Squamata (lizards and snakes)
  Suborder Sauria [= Lacertilia] (lizards)
    Infraorder Iguania
      Family Iguanidae (iguanas, basilisks; earless, horned, collared lizards, etc)
      Family Agamidae (agamas, Australian 'dragons', etc)
      Family Chamaeleonidae (chamaeleons)
    Infraorder Gekkota
      Family Gekkonidae (geckos)
      Family Pygopodidae (Australian snake-like lizards)
    Infraorder Scincomorpha
      Family Xantusiidae (night lizards, etc)
      Family Teiidae (tegus, caiman lizards, ameivas, etc)
      Family Scincidae (including Anelytropsidae and Feyliniidae of other authors) (skinks)
      Family Lacertidae
      Family Cordylidae [= Zonuridae]
        Subfamily Cordylinae (zonures)
        Subfamily Gerrhosaurinae (plated lizards)
    Infraorder Diploglossa
    Superfamily Anguoidea
      Family Anguidae
        Subfamily Diploglossinae
        Subfamily Gerrhonotinae (alligator lizards)
        Subfamily Anguinae (slow-worm)
        Subfamily Anniellinae
      Family Xenosauridae
        Subfamily Xenosaurinae
        Subfamily Shinisaurinae
Superfamily Platynota [= Varanoidea] (includes *mosasaurs)
  Family Helodermatidae (Gila monster, escorpión)

Family Lanthanotidae ('earless monitor')
Family Varanidae (monitors)
Infraorder Amphisbaenia
Family Amphisbaenidae (amphisbaenids or worm-lizards)
  Subfamily Amphisbaeninae
  Subfamily Trogonophinae
Suborder Serpentes [= Ophidia] (snakes)
Infraorder Scolecophidia
Family Typhlopidae (blind snakes or worm-snakes)
Family Leptotyphlopidae [= Glauconiidae] (blind snakes or thread snakes)
Infraorder Henophidia
Family Aniliidae [= Ilysiidae]
  Subfamily Aniliinae (pipe-snakes, etc)
  Subfamily Uropeltinae (rough-tails)
  Subfamily Xenopeltinae (sunbeam snake)
Family Boidae
  Subfamily Pythoninae (pythons)
  Subfamily Boinae (boas, anaconda)
  Subfamily Erycinae (sand boas, etc)
  Subfamily Bolyerinae (boas from Mauritius: Round Island only)
Family Acrochordidae
Infraorder Caenophidia ('higher' snakes)
Family Colubridae
  Subfamily Colubrinae (includes harmless aglyphs such as grass snake, and back-fanged forms such as boomslang)
  Subfamily Dasypeltinae (egg-eaters)
  Subfamily Xenoderminae
  Subfamily Pareinae
  Subfamily Dipsadinae
  Subfamily Homalopsinae (back-fanged oriental water snakes)
Family Elapidae (cobras, kraits, mambas, tiger snake, taipan, etc)
Family Hydrophiidae (sea snakes)
Family Viperidae
  Subfamily Viperinae (Old World vipers/adders)
  Subfamily Crotalinae (rattlesnakes and other pit-vipers)

Subclass Archosauria (crocodilians, *thecodonts, *phytosaurs, *dinosaurs, *pterosaurs)
    Order Crocodilia [= Loricata = Emydosauria]
      Suborder Eusuchia
        Family Crocodylidae
          Subfamily Crocodylinae (crocodiles, Malayan gharial)
          Subfamily Alligatorinae (alligators, caimans)
          Subfamily Gavialinae (Indian gharial)

Detailed classification of living forms

The particulars of geographical distribution are in some cases approximate. The abbreviations are as follows.

Af., Africa south of the Sahara. As., Asia. Aus., Australasia. C.As., Central Asia. E.As., East Asia, mainly China. E.I., East Indies including southern Malaya, Borneo and Indonesia. Eu., Europe. Mad., Madagascar. N.Af., Africa north of and including the Sahara. N.Am., North America including Mexico. N.Z., New Zealand. Pac., Pacific islands. Phil., Philippines. S.Am., southern America including Central America (south of Mexico). S.As., southern Asia including India and Ceylon, Burma, the Indo-Chinese region and in some cases, southern China. W. As., western Asia including Arabia, Persia, West Pakistan etc. W.I., West Indies.

SUBCLASS ANAPSIDA

Order CHELONIA [89, 337, 448]

Since Upper Trias. Despite rigid basic pattern the 240 or so living species show quite a wide radiation into terrestrial, freshwater and marine forms with a range of dietary habits. Skull technically anapsid but generally with emargination of temporal region; akinetic. Jaws toothless with horny beak. Shell usually formed of epidermal scutes or laminae and bony plates and incorporating ribs which lie external to limb girdles. Clavicles and interclavicle incorporated into plastron; sternum absent. Trunk vertebrae reduced in number and typically anchylosed to carapace. Cloacal opening oval or longitudinal. Male has single median penis.

    Suborder CRYPTODIRA. Since Lower Cretaceous. Neck retracted in vertical bend. Pelvis not anchylosed to shell. Contains majority of living forms.

Superfamily Testudinoidea
Family DERMATEMYIDIDAE

A single large, thoroughly aquatic form, *Dermatemys*, S.Am.

Family CHELYDRIDAE

Subfamily Chelydrinae. Large predatory turtles with reduced plastron, from North America. Head big and non-retractile. *Chelydra* (*C. serpentina*, snapper) – *Macroclemys* [= *Macrochelys*] (*M. temmincki*, alligator snapper, one of the largest freshwater turtles).

Subfamily Staurotypinae. *Claudius*, S.Am. – *Staurotypus*. S.Am.

Subfamily Kinosterninae. Plastron with two hinges. *Kinosternon*, N.Am., S.Am. (mud turtles) – *Sternotherus*, N.Am. (musk turtles).

Family EMYDIDAE

Subfamily Platysterninae. A single form, *Platysternon*, the big-headed turtle with a flat shell, ranging from Burma to S. China.

Subfamily Emydinae. Contains the majority of the smaller terrapins and some quite large forms. *Annamemys*, S.As. – *Batagur*, S.As., E.I. – *Callagur*, E.I. – *Chinemys*, E.As. – *Chrysemys*, N.Am. (*C. picta*, painted terrapin) – *Clemmys*, N.Am., Eu., N.Af., W.As., E.As. – *Cuora*, S.As., E.As., E.I. – *Cyclemys*, S.As. – *Deirochelys*, N.Am. – *Emydoidea* [= *Emys* in part], N.Am. – *Emys*, Eu., N.Af., W.As. (*E. orbicularis*, European pond terrapin) – *Geoclemys*, S.As. – *Geoemyda*, N.Am., S.Am., W.I., S.As., E.As., E.I. – *Graptemys*, N.Am. (map terrapins) – *Hardella*, S.As. – *Hieremys*, S.As. – *Kachuga* S.As. – *Malaclemys*, N.Am. (diamond-back terrapins) – *Malayemys*, S.As., E.I. – *Morenia*, S.As. – *Notochelys*, S.As., E.I. – *Ocadia*, E.As. – *Orlitia*, E.I. – *Pseudemys*, N.Am., S.Am., W.I. (*P. scripta elegans*, red-eared terrapin) – *Siebenrockiella*, S.As., E.I. *Terrapene* [= *Cistudo*] N.Am. (box turtles).

Family TESTUDINIDAE

Land tortoises with (usually) domed shells and strong unwebbed claws. *Gopherus*, N.Am. (gopher and desert tortoises) – *Homopus*, Af. – *Kinixys*, Af. – *Malacochersus*, Af. (flexible shelled tortoise) – *Pyxis*, Mad. – *Testudo* [= *Geochelone* for most forms outside Mediterranean area], N.Af., Af., W.As., S.As., Eu., S.Am. (*T. graeca*, common European or spur-thighed tortoise; *T. elephantopus*, Galapagos gaint; *T. gigantea*, Aldabra giant).

Superfamily Chelonioidea
Family CHELONIIDAE

Contains all living sea turtles except *Dermochelys*. Limbs paddle-shaped with one or two claws. Little if any temporal emargination.

Plastron reduced and pleural plates generally deficient peripherally. The genera have an almost world-wide distribution throughout the warmer seas. *Caretta* (*C. caretta*, loggerhead) – *Chelonia* (*C. mydas*, green turtle; *C. depressa*, flatback turtle) – *Eretmochelys* (*E. imbricata*, hawksbill) – *Lepidochelys* (ridleys; two species are generally recognised, *L. kempi*, the North Atlantic ridley or Kemp's loggerhead, and the Pacific ridley, *L. olivacea*, also found in the Indian Ocean and South Atlantic).

Superfamily Dermochelyoidea
Family DERMOCHELYIDAE [= SPHARGIDAE]
A single living form, *Dermochelys* [= *Sphargis*] *coriacea* (leathery turtle). Limbs paddle-shaped. No temporal emargination of skull. Horny shell absent; bony shell composed mainly of small plates.

Superfamily Carettochelyoidea
Family CARETTOCHELYIDAE
The only freshwater turtle with paddle-shaped limbs. Horny shell absent. *Carettochelys*, New Guinea.

Superfamily Trionychoidea
Family TRIONYCHIDAE
Flattened soft-shelled turtles without horny shell; bony shell reduced. Nostrils drawn out into a proboscis. Highly adapted for aquatic life in fresh waters. *Chitra*, S.As. – *Cyclanorbis*, Af. – *Cycloderma*, Af. – *Lissemys*, S.As. – *Pelochelys*, S.As. – *Trionyx* [= *Amyda*], N.Am., S.As., N.Af., Af.

Suborder PLEURODIRA. Since Cretaceous. Neck withdrawn sideways. Pubis and ischium fused with plastron, ilium attached to carapace. All members aquatic, living forms confined to southern hemisphere.

Family PELOMEDUSIDAE
Pelomedusa, Af. – *Pelusios*, Af. – *Podocnemis*, S.Am., Mad.

Family CHELYIDAE
Batrachemys, S.Am. – *Chelodina*, Aus., (snake-necked turtles) – *Chelus* [= *Chelys*], S.Am. (*C. fimbriatus*, matamata) – *Emydura*, Aus. – *Hydromedusa*, S.Am. – *Mesoclemmys*, S.Am. – *Phrynops*, S.Am. – *Platemys*, S.Am. – *Pseudemydura*, Aus.

SUBCLASS LEPIDOSAURIA

Order RHYNCHOCEPHALIA
Since Lower or Middle Trias. Complete diapsid skull; usually a

beak-like development of the premaxilla. Vertebrae amphicoelous.

Family SPHENODONTIDAE

Beak only slightly developed. Quadrate fixed, kinesis doubtful. Gastralia present. Cloacal opening transverse, no copulatory organ. A single living form, *Sphenodon punctatus* [= *Hatteria punctata*] (tuatara) from coastal islets off New Zealand.

Order SQUAMATA

Skull modified diapsid, usually streptostylic and kinetic. Organ of Jacobson usually well developed. Cloacal opening transverse. Paired hemipenes in male.

Suborder SAURIA (lizards). Since Upper Trias [88, 165, 265, 390, 394]. A most versatile group numbering about 360 living genera and 3000 species. Upper temporal and postorbital arches typically present (except as stated below); upper temporal fossa sometimes closed by bony expansions. Epipterygoid rod-like. Teeth usually pleurodont, sometimes present on palate. Tendency in many families to lose limbs and lengthen body.

Infraorder Iguania

Family IGUANIDAE

A predominantly New World family of active, four-legged diurnal lizards, desert-living, arboreal or amphibious in habits. Some iguanas grow to 1·2 metres (4 ft.) or more. Vision is the predominant sense, as in other Iguania, and many species have bright colours and appendages such as crests and throat-fans; some can change colour. Difference in appearance between male and female sometimes marked. Pterygoids sometimes toothed. Osteoderms usually absent. Parasternum and autotomy planes in tail vertebrae sometimes present. Tongue broad, scarcely or not at all notched. Nearly all oviparous.

Amblyrhynchus (*A. cristatus*, Galapagos sea iguana) – *Anisolepis*, S.Am. – *Anolis*, N.Am., S.Am., W.I. (anoles, an enormous genus) – *Aptycholaemus*, S.Am. – *Audantia*, Haiti – *Basiliscus*, S.Am. (basilisks) – *Brachylophus* (Fiji iguana) – *Callisaurus*, N.Am. – *Chalarodon*, Mad. – *Chamaeleolis*, W.I. – *Chamaelinorops*, Haiti – *Conolophus* (*C. subcristatus*, Galapagos land iguana) – *Corythophanes*, S.Am. (helmeted lizards) – *Crotaphytus*, N.Am. (collared lizards) – *Ctenoblepharys*, S.Am. – *Ctenosaura*, N.Am., S.Am. (ground iguanas) – *Cyclura*, W.I. (ground iguana) – *Deiroptyx*, W.I. – *Diaphoranolis*, S.Am. – *Dipsosaurus*, N.Am., (desert iguana) – *Enyalioides*, S.Am. – *Enyalius*, S.Am. – *Hispaniolus*, W.I. – *Holbrookia*, N.Am. (earless lizards) – *Hoplocercus*, S.Am. – *Iguana*, N.Am., S.Am. – *Laemanctus*,

S.Am. – *Leiocephalus*, S.Am. – *Leiosaurus*, S.Am. – *Liolaemus*, S.Am. – *Mariguana*, S.Am. – *Morunasaurus*, S.Am. – *Norops*, S.Am., W.I. – *Oplurus* (Madagascar iguana) – *Phenacosaurus*, S.Am. – *Phrynosaura*, S.Am. – *Phrynosoma*, N.Am., S.Am. (horned lizards) – *Phymaturus*, S.Am. – *Plica*, S.Am. – *Polychroides*, S.Am. – *Polychrus*, S.Am. – *Proctoretus*, S.Am. – *Sator*, N.Am. – *Sauromalus*, N.Am. (chuckwalla) – *Sceloporus*, N.Am., S.Am. (spiny lizards) – *Stenocercus*, S.Am. – *Strobilurus*, S. Am. – *Tropidodactylus*, S.Am., W.I. – *Tropidurus*, S.Am., (Galapagos) – *Uma*, N.Am. *Uracentron*, S.Am. – *Uranoscodon*, S.Am. – *Urostrophus*, S.Am. – *Uta*, N.Am. – *Xiphocercus*, W.I. – *Metopoceros* [=*Cyclura*].

Family AGAMIDAE

Old World counterparts of the Iguanidae, but distinguished from the latter by acrodont teeth (except often at front of jaw); palate toothless. No osteoderms; no parasternum. No autotomy planes. No limbless forms. Tongue broad, with or without slight notch. Oviparous. Known as 'dragons' in Australia where there are many genera.

Agama, N.Af., Af., W.As., Eu. – *Amphibolurus*, Aus. (*A. barbatus*, bearded lizard) – *Aphaniotis*, S.As., E.I. – *Aporoscelis*, Af., ? W.As. – *Calotes*, S.As., E.I. – *Ceratophora*, S.As. – *Chelosania*, Aus. – *Chlamydosaurus*, Aus. (frilled lizard) – *Cophotis*, S.As., E.I. – *Dendragama*, E.I. – *Diporiphora*, Aus. – *Draco*, S.As., E.I. (flying lizards) – *Goniocephalus*, S.As., E.I., Aus., Phil., Pac. – *Harpesaurus*, E.I. – *Hylagama*, E.I. – *Japalura*, S.As., E.I. – *Leiolepis*, S.As., E.I. – *Lophocalotes*, E.I. – *Lophura*, E.I. – *Lyriocephalus*, S.As. – *Mictopholis*, S.As. – *Moloch*, Aus. (thorny devil) – *Oriocalotes*, S.As. – *Otocryptis*, S.As. – *Phoxophrys*, S.As., E.I. – *Phrynocephalus*, W.As. – *Physignathus*, E.I., Aus. (water dragon) – *Psammophilus*, S.As. – *Ptyctolaemus*, S.As. – *Salea*, S.As. – *Sitana*, S.As. – *Thaumatorhynchus*, E.I. – *Tympanocryptis*, Aus. – *Uromastyx*, N.Af., W.As. (spiny-tailed lizards).

Family CHAMAELEONIDAE

Highly specialised arboreal lizards, probably of agamid descent. Skull usually adorned with casque; horns and other appendages sometimes present. Streptostylic but akinetic; epipterygoid reduced. Teeth acrodont. Palate toothless. Clavicles and interclavicle vestigial or absent. Parasternum well developed. Osteoderms usually absent. Feet with opposable digits. Organ of Jacobson rudimentary or absent. Tongue modified for capture of prey. Tail prehensile, no autotomy. Marked power of colour change. Mostly oviparous.

Brookesia, Mad. – *Chamaeleo*, Eur., S.As., N.Af., Af. – *Evoluticauda*, Mad. – *Leandria*, Mad. – *Lophosaura*, Af. – *Rhampholeon*, Af.

Infraorder Gekkota [= Nyctisauria]

Family GEKKONIDAE [430]

A very large family of small lizards found in warm countries throughout the world, prone to introduction in ships, fruit cargoes etc. Head and body usually flattened. Temporal and postorbital arches absent. Palate toothless. Parasternum sometimes present. Digits often modified for climbing, sometimes for movement over sand. Cloacal bones and sacs often present. Vertebrae amphicoelous in most forms, autotomy planes present in tail. Eyelids generally fused to form spectacle. Tongue broad, with very slight notch. Scales generally small and granular. Osteoderms usually absent. Almost all oviparous, laying hard-shelled eggs*.

Aelurascalabotes, S.As., E.I. – *Afroedura*, Af. – *Agamura*, W.As. – *Ailuronyx*, Mad. – *Alsophylax*, W.As., N.Af., Eu. – *Ancylodactylus*, Af. – *Aristelliger*, W.I. – *Bavayia*, E.I. – *Blaesodactylus*, Mad. – *Bogertia*, S.Am. – *Briba*, S.Am. – *Calodactylodes*, S.As. – *Carphodactylus*, Aus. – *Ceramodactylus*, W.As. – *Chondrodactylus*, Af. – *Cnemaspis*, Af., S.As., E.I. – *Coleodactylus*, S.Am. – *Coleonyx*, N.Am., S.Am., (*C. variegatus*, banded gecko) – *Colopus*, Af. – *Cosymbotus*, S.As. – *Crossobamon*, C.As. – *Diplodactylus*, Mad., Af., Aus. – *Dravidogecko*, S.As. – *Ebenavia*, Mad. – *Eublepharis*, S.As. – *Eurydactylus*, Pac. – *Geckolephis*, Mad. – *Geckonia*, Af. – *Gehyra*, S.As., Aus., Pac. – *Gekko*, S.As., E.I., (*G. gecko*, tokay) – *Gonatodes*, S.Am., W.I. – *Gymnodactylus*, S.As., E.I., S.Am., N.Af., Eu., Pac. – *Hemidactylus*, S.As., E.I., S.Am., W.I., Af., Eu., Pac. – *Hemiphyllodactylus*, S.As., E.I., Pac. – *Hemitheconyx*, N.Af. – *Heteronota*, Aus. – *Holodactylus*, N.Af. – *Homonota*, S.Am. – *Homopholis*, Af., Mad. – *Hoplodactylus*, N.Z. – *Lepidoblepharis*, S.Am. – *Lepidodactylus*, S.As., E.I., Pac. – *Lucasius*, Aus. – *Luperosaurus*, Phil. – *Lygodactylus*, Af., Mad. – *Microgecko*, W.As. – *Naultinus*, N.Z. – *Nephrurus*, Aus. – *Oedura*, Aus. – *Pachydactylus*, Af. – *Palmatogecko*, Af. – *Paragehyra*, Mad. – *Perochirus*, Phil., Pac. – *Phelsuma*, Mad. – *Phyllodactylus*, Eu., Af., Aus., W.As., S.As., N.Am., S.Am., W.I. – *Phyllopezus*, S.Am. – *Phyllurus*, Aus. – *Pristurus*, N.Af., W.As. – *Pseudogekko*, Phil. – *Pseudogonatodes*, S.Am. – *Pseudothecadactylus*, Aus. – *Ptenopus*, Af. – *Ptychozoon*, S.As., E.I. (flying geckos) – *Ptyodactylus*, N.Af., W.As. – *Quedenfeldtia*, Af. – *Rhacodactylus*,

531

Aus., Pac. – *Rhoptropella*, Af. – *Rhoftropus*, Af. – *Rhynchoedura*, Aus. – *Saurodactylus*, N.Af. – *Sphaerodactylus*, S.Am., W.I. – *Stenodactylus*, N.Af., W.As. – *Tarentola*, Eu., N.Af., S.As. – *Teratoscincus*, W.As. – *Thecadactylus*, S.A., W.I. – *Tropiocalotes*, N.Af., W.As. – *Uroplatus*, Mad. (bark geckos).

Family PYGOPODIDAE

A small Australasian group of snake-like lizards, surface-dwellers or burrowers. Temporal and postorbital arches absent. Palate toothless. Osteoderms absent. Spectacle covering eye. Tongue notched.

Aprasia – Delma – Lialis – Ophidiocephalus – Ophioseps – Pletholax – Pygopus.

Infraorder Scincomorpha [= Leptoglossa]

Family XANTUSIIDAE

A small New World family of secretive, superficially gecko-like forms with normal limbs. Upper temporal fossa closed. Palate toothless. No parasternum. Osteoderms probably absent. Autotomy? Spectacle over eye. Tongue short, barely notched. *Xantusia* is viviparous with well-developed placenta.

Cricosaura, W.I. – *Gaigeia*, N.Am. – *Lepidophyma*, S.Am. – *Xantusia*, N.Am. (night lizards).

Family TEIIDAE

A New World family containing some very large forms such as the tegus and some very small ones such as the 9 cm. ($3\frac{1}{2}$ in.) *Leposoma*, an inhabitant of the jungle floor. In genera marked with asterisk (eg *Bachia*) the body is snake-like and the limbs reduced. Upper temporal arch present (except possibly in snake-like forms). No osteoderms. Palate usually toothless. Parasternum usually absent but well developed in *Bachia*. Autotomy planes present in some genera at least. Tongue forked, and long and protrusible in *Tupinambis*. Mostly oviparous.

Alopoglossus, S.Am. – *Ameiva*, S.Am. – *Anadia*, S.Am. – *Argalia*, S.Am. – *Arthrosaura*, S.Am. – (?*) *Arthroseps*, S.Am. – *Bachia*, S.Am. – *Callopistes*, S.Am. – *Cercosaura*, S.Am. – *Cnemidophorus*, N.Am., S.Am. (race-runners) – *Colobodactylus*, S.Am. – *Colobosaura*, S.Am. – *Coloptychon*, S.Am. – *Crocodilurus*, S.Am. – *Dicrodon*, S.Am. – *Dracaena*, S.Am. (caiman lizards) – *Echinosaura*, S.Am. – *Ecpleopus*, S.Am. – *Elaphrosaura*, S.Am. – *Euspondylus*, S.Am. – *Gymnophthalmus*, S.Am., W.I. – *Heterodactylus*, S.Am. – *Iphisa*, S.Am. – *Kentropyx*, S.Am. – *Leposoma*, S.Am. – *Macropholidus*,

S.Am. – *Microblepharus*, S.Am. – *Neusticurus*, S.Am. – *Ophiognomon*, S.Am. – *Pantodactylus*, S.Am. – *Pholidobolus*, S.Am. – *Placosoma*, S.Am. – *Prionodactylus*, S.Am. – *Proctoporus*, S.Am., W.I. – *Ptychoglossus*, S.Am. – *Scolecosaurus*, S.Am., W.I. – *Stenolepis*, S.Am. – *Teius*, S.Am. – *Tretioscincus*, S.Am – *Tupinambis*, S.Am., W.I. (tegu lizards).

Family SCINCIDAE (skinks), including Anelytropsidae and Feyliniidae of other authors, two small groups of limbless burrowers.

A large and cosmopolitan family, mostly living on or beneath the ground. Upper temporal fossa often closed in, upper temporal and postorbital arch reduced or absent in burrowers. The numerous genera in which some or all species have reduced limbs are marked with an asterisk; in some cases this is difficult to discover from the literature. Parasternum usually present. Well developed osteoderms on head and body. Pterygoid teeth sometimes present. Eyelids fused to form spectacle in some cases. Autotomy planes usually present. Tongue fairly broad, slightly notched. Oviparous and many viviparous species, some with well-developed placentation.

Ablepharus, Eu., Af., S.As., E.I., Aus., Pac. – *Acontias*, Af., Mad. – *Acontophiops*, Af. – *Anelytropsis*, N.Am. – *Anguinicephalus*, S.As. – *Ateuchosaurus*, E.As. *Barkudia*, S.As. – *Brachymeles*, Phil. – *Chalcides*, Eu., N.Af., W.As. – *Chalcidoseps*, S.As., – ?*Cophoscincopus*, Af. – *Corucia*. Pac. – *Cryptoposcincus*, Mad. – *Dasia*, S.As., E.I. – *Egernia*, Aus. – *Emoia*, E.I., Aus., Pac. – *Eumeces*, N.Am., S.As., W.As., N.Af. – *Feylinia*, Af. – *Fitzsimonsia*, Af. – *Grandidierina*, Mad. – *Hemiergis*, Aus. – *Hemisphaeriodon*, Aus. – *Insulasaurus*, As. – *Leiolopisma*, S.As., E.As., E.I., Aus., N.Z., N.Am., S.Am., Af. – *Lygosoma*, S.As., E.As., E.I., Aus., Af. – *Mabuya*, Af., S.As., E.I., S.Am., W.I. – *Macroscincus*, Cape Verde I. – *Melanoseps*, Af. – *Neoseps*, N.Am. – *Nessia*, S.As. – *Ophiomorus*, Eu., W.As. – *Ophioscincus*, S.As., Aus. – *Otosaurus*, Phil. – ?*Paracontias*, Mad. – ?*Pseudacontias*, Mad. – *Pygomeles*, Mad. – *Rhodona*, E.I., Aus. – *Riopa*, Af., S.As., E.I., Aus., Pac. – *Ristella*, S.As. – *Scelotes*, Af., Mad. – *Scincus*, N.Af., W.As. – ?*Scolecoseps*, Af. – *Sepsophis*, S.As. – *Tiliqua*, E.I., Aus. (*T. scincoides*, blue-tongue skink; *Tiliqua* [= *Trachysaurus*] *rugosus*, stumpy-tailed lizard) – *Tribolonotus*, E.I. – *Tropidophorus*, S.As., E.I., Aus. – *Typhlosaurus*, Af. – *Typhlacontias*, Af. – *Voeltzkowia*, Mad.

?Family DIBAMIDAE

One burrowing limbless form, *Dibamus*, S.As. Systematic position

533

doubtful; differs from burrowing skinks in lacking osteoderms.

Family LACERTIDAE

Generalised Old World family paralleling the Teiidae in some respects but without limbless forms. Upper temporal fossa often reduced or closed. Pterygoids often with teeth. Parasternum absent. Autotomy planes present. Osteoderms often present on head only. Tongue fairly long, forked at tip. Nearly all oviparous.

Acanthodactylus, Eu., W.As., N.Af. – *Algyroides*, Eu., N.Af. – *Aporosaura*, Af. – *Bedriagaia*, Af. – *Cabrita*, S.As. – *Eremias*, Eu., C.As., W.As., Af. – *Gastropholis*, Af. – *Holaspis*, Af. – *Ichnotropis*, Af. – *Lacerta*, Eu., W.As., N.Af. (*L. vivipara*, viviparous lizard; *L. agilis*, sand; *L. viridis*, green; *L. muralis*, wall; *L. lepida*, eyed.) – *Latastia*, N.Af., W.As. – *Nucras*, Af. – *Ophisops*, Eu., N.Af., W.As. – *Philochortus*, Af. – *Platyplacopus*, E.As. – *Poromera*, Af. – *Psammodromus*, Eu., N.Af. – *Takydromus*, S.As., E.As. – *Tropidosaura*, Af.

Family CORDYLIDAE [= ZONURIDAE], and including GERRHOSAURIDAE of many authors.

African lizards, previously placed in two distinct families but probably related [265]. Upper temporal opening reduced or closed. Palatal teeth present in Gerrhosaurinae. Osteoderms on head, often on body. Parasternum usually absent. Autotomy planes sometimes absent. Some forms with reduced limbs (*). Tongue short, hardly notched. Cordylinae mostly viviparous.

Subfamily Gerrhosaurinae (plated lizards). *Cordylosaurus* – *Gerrhosaurus* – *Paratetradactylus* – *Tetradactylus* – *Tracheloptychus*, Mad. – *Zonosaurus*, Mad.

Subfamily Cordylinae [= Zonurinae]. The limbed forms are often heavily armoured with spiny scales. *Chamaesaura* – *Cordylus* (zonures) – *Platysaurus* – *Pseudocordylus*.

Infraorder Diploglossa [265]

Superfamily Anguoidea

Family ANGUIDAE including ANNIELLIDAE of other authors.

A small family of Old and New World lizards, with and *without limbs. Upper temporal arch and postorbital arch present, or as in *Anniella*, absent. Upper temporal fossa sometimes nearly closed. Palatal teeth present or absent. No parasternum. Osteoderms usually present. Tongue fairly long, forked tip. Autotomy planes present. Oviparous or viviparous.

Subfamily Diploglossinae. Tropical America and West Indies. *Diploglossus* – *Ophiodes* – *Sauresia* – *Wetmorena*.

Subfamily Gerrhonotinae. *Gerrhonotus*, N.Am., S.Am. (alligator lizards) – *Ophisaurus*, Eu., S.As., E.As., N.Af., N.Am. (glass lizards or 'glass snakes').

Subfamily Anguinae. *Anguis*, Eu., N.Af., W.As. (slow-worm).

Sufamily Anniellinae. A single genus, *Anniella*, N.Am. Similar to *Anguis* in many ways but more specialised for burrowing, and with osteoderms less well developed.

Family XENOSAURIDAE

Incompletely known forms with well-developed limbs; probably related to Anguidae, but with reduced osteoderms. *Shinisaurus* has pterygoid teeth.

Subfamily Shinisaurinae. *Shinisaurus*, E.As. (Chinese crocodile lizard, a 38 cm. (15-in.), amphibious form)

Subfamily Xenosaurinae. *Xenosaurus*, S.Am.

Superfamily Platynota [= Varanoidea]

Contains Cretaceous mosasaurs and their allies as well as monitors and other existing forms.

Family HELODERMATIDAE [53]

Upper temporal arch absent, postorbital arch present. Poison fangs in lower jaw. Teeth on pterygoids and palatines. Osteoderms on head and body. No parasternum, no autotomy. Tongue fairly long, forked and protrusible. Oviparous.

Heloderma, N.Am. (*H. suspectum*, Gila monster; *H. horridum*, Mexican heloderm or escorpion).

Family LANTHANOTIDAE [265, 431]

A single form, *Lanthanotus borneensis*, the earless monitor of Borneo, a platynotid with a long body and short limbs. Upper temporal arch absent, postorbital arch present. Teeth on palatines and pterygoids. Osteoderms present. No autotomy. Tongue quite long with forked tip.

Family VARANIDAE (monitors; in Australia, goannas).

A single genus of Old World and Australasian lizards, some very large, with predatory habits. Upper temporal arch present; postorbital arch just incomplete. Palate toothless. No parasternum. Osteoderms generally reduced or absent. No autotomy. Tongue long, forked, highly protrusible. Oviparous.

Varanus, N.Af., Af., S.As., E.I., Aus. (*V. salvator*, water monitor, S.As., E.I.; *V. giganteus*, perentie, Aus.; *V. komodoensis*, Komodo dragon, E.I.).

Infraorder Amphisbaenia [= Annulata]

Family AMPHISNAENIDAE (worm-lizards) [51, 180 *].

A successful group of worm-like burrowers with reduced eyes found mainly in the warmer parts of America and Africa. The skull is massive, without arches, and probably mesokinetic; epipterygoid is generally absent. Interorbital septum absent or very low; anterior 'sphenoid' region of skull strongly ossified. Palate toothless. Middle ear highly modified. Well developed median premaxillary tooth. Limbs absent except in *Bipes* which has front pair only. No parasternum; no osteoderms. Autotomy planes in some forms at least. Scales arranged in rings around the body. This isolated group is given the status of a suborder and divided into families rather than subfamilies by some workers.

Subfamily Amphisbaeninae. Dentition pleurodont. *Amphisbaena*, S.Am., W.I. – *Ancylocranium*, Af. – *Anopsibaena* [= *Anops*], S.Am. – *Aulura*, S.Am. – *Baikia*, Af. – *Bipes*, N.Am. – *Blanus*, Eu., N.Af., W.As. – *Bronia*, S.Am. – *Cadea*, W.I. – *Chirindia*, Af. – *Cynisca*, Af. – *Diphalus*, W.I. – *Geocalamus*, Af. – *Leposternum*, S.Am. – *Loveridgea*, Af. – *Mesobaena*, S.Am. – *Monopeltis*, *Af*. – *Rhineura*, N.Am. – *Tomuropeltis*, Af. – *Zygaspis*, Af.

Subfamily Trogonophinae. Dentition acrodont. *Agamodon*, Af., W.As. – *Diplometopon*, W.As. – *Pachycalamus*, Socotra – *Trogonophis*, N.Af.

Suborder SERPENTES [166, 204, 219, 394, 434, 468]. Certainly known since Upper Cretaceous but probably older. Over 385 living genera and nearly 3000 species. Both temporal arches absent, orbito-temporal part of skull rigid, formed by downgrowths of frontals, parietals, etc. No interorbital septum or epipterygoid. Streptostylic with highly kinetic upper jaw; halves of lower jaw usually separate. All bones of palate except ectopterygoid usually toothed. Eyelids fused to form spectacle. Middle ear cavity and Eustachian tubes absent. Tongue long, forked, highly protrusible. Body elongated with 160 – 400 vertebrae, bearing additional articular facets (zygosphenes and zygantra). Usually no obvious traces of limbs. Usually a single row of enlarged ventral scales. Left lung reduced or absent.

Infraorder Scolecophidia [256]

Family TYPHLOPIDAE (blind or worm-snakes)

A successful group of burrowers (over 180 species) with rudimentary eyes, lacking enlarged ventral scales. Generally considered aberrant and not closely related to main line of ophidian descent, though alternative suggestion has been made [434]. Retaining some primitive features such as pelvic vestiges and coronoid bone. Maxilla toothed, movable and generally transverse in position. Dentary generally toothless, premaxilla and palate toothless. Halves of lower jaw quite firmly united. At least some species oviparous.

Subfamily Typhlopinae. *Typhlophis*, S.Am. – *Typhlops*, Eu., S.As., Af., S.Am., W.I., Aus.

Subfamily Anomalepinae, S.Am. *Anomalepids* – *Helminthophis* – *Liotyphlops*.

Family LEPTOTYPHLOPIDAE [= GLAUCONIIDAE] (blind snakes, worm-snakes or thread-snakes)

Burrowing snakes superficially like Typhlopidae, but usually more slender and with important anatomical differences. Maxilla quite firmly attached to skull; coronoid present. Teeth on dentary only. Well-developed pelvic vestiges.

Leptotyphlops [= *Glauconia*], N.Am., S.Am., W.I., Af., W. As.

Infraorder Henophidia

Family ANILIIDAE [= ILYSIIDAE] and including UROPEL-TIDAE and XENOPELTIDAE of many authors

Burrowing snakes or secretive snakes of less aberrant type than the Scolecophidia and perhaps not far from the main line of descent. *Dinilysia* of the Upper Cretaceous, probably related to this family, is perhaps the most significant snake fossil known and has quite a well-preserved skull. Living forms have the upper jaw quite firmly attached to the skull; the quadrate is short, the coronoid is usually present and the premaxilla is sometimes toothed. Pelvic vestiges are known in the Aniliinae only. Ventral scales are only slightly enlarged except in *Xenopeltis*, where they are well developed. Left lung sometimes quite large.

Subfamily Aniliinae (pipe-snakes). *Anilius*, S.Am. – *Anomochilus*, E.I. – *Cylindrophis*, S.As., E.I.

Subfamily Uropeltinae (rough-tails). All from S.As. *Melanophidium* – *Platyplecturus* – *Plecturus* – *Pseudotyphlops* – *Rhinophis* – *Teretrurus* – *Uropeltis*

Subfamily Xenopeltinae. *Xenopeltis* (sunbeam snake), S.As., E.I.

Family ACROCHORDIDAE [434]

A small group of water snakes with specialised, granular scales. No pelvis. Ventral scales not enlarged.

Acrochordus (*A. javanicus,* elephant's trunk snake) S.As., E.I., Aus. – *Chersydrus,* S.As., E.I.

Family BOIDAE

Embodies many typical ophidian features such as great mobility of the upper jaw, but also retains some primitive ones such as (generally) pelvic vestiges with projecting spurs, presence of coronoid bone and (often) fairly large left lung. Sensory labial pits present in some forms. Contains small burrowers as well as big constrictors. Split into further subfamilies by some authors.

Subfamily Pythoninae. Mostly Old World and Australasian. Supraorbital bone present. Usually teeth on premaxilla. Mostly oviparous.

Aspidites, Aus. – *Bothrochilus,* E.I. – *Calabaria,* Af. – *Chondropython,* Aus. – *Liasis,* E.I., Aus. (*L. amethystinus,* amethystine python) – *Loxocemus,* (dwarf Mexican python, sometimes placed in distinct subfamily) – *Python,* Af., S.As., E.I. (*P. molurus,* Indian; *P. reticulatus,* reticulated, S.As., E.I.; *P. regius,* royal, Af.; *P. sebae,* African rock; *P. curtus,* blood, E.I.; *Python* [= *Morelia*] *spilotes/ argus,* carpet snake, Aus.).

Subfamily Boinae. New World and Madagascar. No supraorbital bone. No teeth on premaxilla. Mostly viviparous.

Acrantophis, Mad. – *Boa,* N.Am., S.Am. (*Boa* [= *Corallus*] *canina,* green tree boa) – *Constrictor,* N.Am., S.Am., W.I. (*C. constrictor,* boa constrictor) – *Epicrates,* S.Am., W.I. – *Eunectes,* S.Am. (*E. murinus,* anaconda) – *Exiliboa,* N.Am. – *Sanzinia,* Mad. – *Trachyboa,* S.Am. – *Tropidophis,* N.Am., S.Am., W.I. – *Ungaliophis,* S.Am.

Subfamily Erycinae. As Boinae in characters given. Burrowing or secretive. *Charina,* N.Am. – *Enygrus,* E.I., Pac. – *Eryx,* N.Af., W.As. (sand boas) – *Lichanura,* N.Am.

Subfamily Bolyerinae. Mauritius. Maxilla divided into anterior and posterior parts (a remarkable modificatios) and other distinguishing features. *Bolyeria – Casarea.*

Infraorder Caenophidia

Family COLUBRIDAE

A vast assemblage of 'typical' snakes, both aglyphs and opisthoglyphs, split into many smaller groups by Underwood [434]. A few of the better known opisthoglyphs marked with asterisk. See also ※ .

Subfamily Colubrinae. *Abastor,* N.Am. – *Ablabophis,* Af. – *Aeluroglena,* N.Af. – *Agrophis,* E.I. – *Ahaetulla* [=*Dryophis*], S.As. –

538

Alleidophis, S.Am. – *Alluaudina*, Mad. – *Alsophis*, W.I. – *Amastri-dium*, S.Am., W.I. – *Amblyodipsas*, Af. – *Amphiardis*, N.Am. – *Amplorhinus*, Af. – *Anoplohydrus*, E.I. – *Aparallactus*, Af. – *Apostole-pis*, S.Am. – *Aproterodon*, S.Am. – *Arizona*, N.Am. – *Arrhyton*, W.I. – *Aspidura*, Ceylon – *Asthenophis*, N.Af. – *Atractus*, S.Am., W.I. – *Atretium*, S.As. – *Blythia*, S.As. – *Boaedon*, Af. – *Boiga, Af., S.As., E.I., Aus. – *Bothrolycus*, Af. – *Bothrophthalmus*, Af. – *Brachyophis*, N.Af. – *Brachyura*, E.I. – *Calamaria*, S.As., E.I. – *Calamelaps*, Af. – *Calamorhabdium*, E.I. – *Carphophis*, N.Am. – *Cemophora*, N.Am. – *Cercaspis*, S.As. – *Chamaelycus*, Af. – *Chamaetortus*, Af. – *Cherso-dromus*, S.Am. – *Chilomeniscus*, N.Am. – *Chilorhinophis*, Af. – *Chionactis*, N.Am. – *Chironius*, S.Am. – *Chrysopelea, S.As., E.I. – *Clelia*, S.Am. – *Collorhabdium*, As. – *Coluber*, Eu., N.Am., S.Am., S.As., E.I., N.Af (includes many fast-moving, rodent- and lizard-eating species such as *Coluber* [= *Zamenis*], European whip-snake; *C. longissima*, Aesculapian s.; *Coluber* [= *Masticophis*], North American racers, 'black snakes', etc. The synonymy of this genus is confusing) – *Compsophis*, Mad. – *Coniophanes*, N.Am., S.Am. – *Conophis*, S.Am. – *Conopsis*, N.Am., S.Am. – *Contia*, N.Am., S.Am. – *Coronella*, Eu., N.Af., As., (*C. austriaca*, European smooth snake) – *Crotaphopeltis*, Af. – *Cyclagras*, S.Am. – *Cyclocorus*, Phil. – *Darling-tonia*, W.I. – *Dendrelaphis*, S.As., E.I., Aus. – *Dendrophidion*, S.Am. – *Diadophis*, N.Am. – *Diaphorolepis*, S.Am. – *Dimades*, S.Am. – *Dinodon*, S.As., E.As. – *Dipsadoboa*, Af. – *Dipsadoides*, E.I. – *Dipsado-phidium*, Af. – *Dispholidus, Af. (*D. typus*, boomslang) – *Ditypophis*, Socotra – *Drepanoides*, S.Am. – *Dromicodryas*, Mad. – *Dromicus*, S.Am., W.I. – *Dromophis*, Af. – *Dryadophis*, S.Am. – *Drymarchon*, N.An., S.Am. (*D. corais*, indigo snake) – *Drymobius*, N.Am., S.Am. – *Drymoluber*, S.Am. – *Dryocalamus*, S.As. – *Dryophiops*, S.As. – *Duberria*, Af. – *Dugandia*, S.Am. – *Eirenis*, W.As., N.Af. – *Elaphe*, Eu., N.Am., S.Am., S.As., E.I. (*E. quatuorlineata*, European four-lined snake) – *Elapocalamus*, Af. – *Elapoides*, E.I. – *Elapomojus*, S.Am. – *Elapormorphus*, S.Am. – *Enulius*, S.Am. – *Erythrolamprus*, N.Am., S.Am. – *Farancia*, N.Am. – *Ficimia*, N.Am. – *Gastropyxis*, Af. – *Geagras*, N.Am. – *Geodipsas*, Mad. – *Geophis*, S.Am. – *Gly-pholycus*, Af. – *Gonionotus*, Af. – *Gonyophis*, S.As., E.I. – *Grayia*, Af. – *Haldea*, N.Am. – *Haplocercus*, Ceylon – *Haplonodon*, Phil. – *Hapsidophrys*, Af. – *Helicops*, S.Am. – *Helophis*, Af. – *Hemir-hagerrhis*, Af. – *Heterodon*, N.Am. (hog-nosed snakes) – *Heteroliodon*, Mad. – *Heurnia*, E.I., Aus. – *Hologerrhum*, Phil. – *Hormonotus*, Af. –

Hydrablabes, E.I. – *Hydraethiops*, Af. – *Hydromorphus*, S.Am. – *Hydrops*, S.Am. – *Hypoptophis*, Af. – *Hypsiglena*, N.Am., S.Am. – *Hypsirhynchus*, W.I. – *Ialtris*, W.I. – *Idiophis*, Mad. – *Idiopholis*, E.I. – *Iguanognathus*, E.I. – *Imantodes*, S.Am. – *Ithycyphus*, Mad. – *Lampropeltis*, N.Am., S.Am. (king snakes) – *Lamprophis*, Af. – *Langaha*, Mad. – *Leimadophis*, S.Am. – *Leioheterodon*, Mad. – *Leptodeira*, N.Am., S.Am. – *Leptodrymus*, S.Am. – *Leptophis*, S.Am. – *Lepturophis*, E.I. – *Limnophis*, Af. – *Liodytes*, N.Am. – *Liophidium*, Mad. – *Liophis*, S.Am. – *Lycodon*, S.As., E.I. (wolf snakes) – *Lycodryas*, Mad. – *Lycognathophis*, Seychelles – *Lycophidion*, Af. – *Lygophis*, S.Am. – *Lystrophis*, S.Am. – *Lytorhynchus*, N.Af., W.As. – *Macrelaps*, Af. – *Macrocalamus*, S.As. – *Macropisthodon*, S.As., E.I. – *Macroprotodon*, Eu., N.Af. – *Malpolon [= *Coelopeltis*], Eu., N.Af., W.As. – *Manolepis*, N.Am. – *Mehelya*, Af. – *Micrelaps*, Af., W.As. – *Micropisthodon*, Mad. – *Migiurtinophis*, Af. – *Mimophis*, Mad. – *Miodon*, Af. – *Morenoa*, N.Am. – *Natrix*, Eu., N.Am., Af., S.As., E.I., Aus. *(Natrix* =[*Tropidonotus*]*natrix*, European grass snake; *N, maura*, 'viperine' snake, Eu.; *N. sipedon*, American water snake) – *Neusterophis*, Af. – *Ninia*, S.Am. – *Ogmius*, N.Am. – *Oligodon*, S.As., E.I. – *Oophilositum*, Af. – *Opheodrys*, N.Am., S.As., E.I. – *Opisthotrophis*, S.As., E.I. – *Oreocalamus*, E.I. – *Oxybelis*, N.Am., S.Am. – *Oxyrhabdium*, Phil. – *Pararhabdophis*, S.As. – *Pararhadinaea*, Mad. – *Paroxyrhopus*, S.Am. – *Philodryas*, S.Am. – *Philothamnus*, Af. – *Phrydops*, S.Am. – *Phyllorhynchus*, N.Am. – *Pituophis*, N.Am., S.Am. *(P. catenifer,* bull snake) – *Plagiopholis*, S.As. – *Platyinion*, S.Am. – *Pliocercus*, S.Am. – *Poecilopholis*, Af. – *Polemon*, Af. – *Prosymna*, Af. – *Psammodynastes*, S.As., E.I. – *Psammophis, Af., W.As. – *Psammophylax*, Af. – *Pseudablabes*, S.Am. – *Pseudaspis*, Af. – *Pseudoboa*, S.Am., W.I. – *Pseudoboodon*, N.Af. – *Pseudorabdion*, S.As., E.I. – *Pseudotomodon*, S.Am. – *Pseudoxenodon*, S.As., E.I. – *Pseudoxyrhopus*, Mad. – *Pseustes*, S.Am. – *Ptyas*, S.As. *(P. mucosus,* Indian rat snake) – *Ptychophis*, S.Am. – *Pythonodipsas*, Af. – *Rhabdophidium*, E.I. – *Rhabdops*, S.As. – *Rhabdotophis*, Af. – *Rhachidelus*, S.Am. – *Rhadinaea*, N.Am., S.Am. – *Rhamnophis*, Af. – *Rhamphiophis*, Af. – *Rhinobothryum*, S.Am. – *Rhinocalamus*, Af. – *Rhinocheilus*, N.Am., S.Am. – *Rhinostoma*, S.Am. – *Rhynchocalamus*, W.As. – *Rhynchophis*, S.As. – *Salvadora*, N.Am. – *Scaphiodontophis*, S.Am. – *Scaphiophis*, Af. – *Seminatrix*, N.Am. – *Sibynophis*, S.As., E.I., Mad. – *Simophis*, S.Am. – *Siphlophis*, S.Am. – *Sonora*, N.Am. – *Sordellina*, S.Am. – *Spilotes*, S.Am. – *Stegonotus*, E.I., Aus., Phil. – *Stenophis*,

Mad. – *Stenorhina*, S.Am. – *Stilosoma*, N.Am. – *Storeria*, N. Am., S.Am. – *Symphimus*, N.Am. – *Sympholis*, N.Am. – *Synchalinus*, S.Am. – *Tachymenis*, S.Am. – *Tantilla*, N. Am., S.Am. – *Telescopus*, Eu., N.Af., Af., W.As. – *Tetralepis*, E.I. – *Thamnodynastes*, S.Am. – *Thamnophis*, N.Am., S.Am. (garter snakes) – *Thelotornis*, Af. (bird snakes) – *Thermophis*, C.As. – *Thrasops*, Af. – *Tomodon*, S.Am. – *Trachischium*, S.As. – *Tretanorhinus*, S.Am., W.I. – *Trimetopon*, S.Am. – *Trimorphodon*, N.Am., S.Am. – *Tripanurgos*, S.Am. – *Tropidoclonion*, N.Am. – *Tropidodipsas*, S.Am. – *Tropidophidion*, Af. – *Typhlogeophis*, Phil. – *Uromacer*, W.I. – *Uromacerina*, S.Am. – *Urotheca*, S.Am. – *Xenelaphis*, S.As., E.I. – *Xenocalamus*, Af. – *Xenochrophis*, S.As. – *Xenodon*, S.Am. – *Zaocys*, S.As.

Subfamily Dasypeltinae. Egg-eaters with spines on their neck vertebrae and reduced dentition. *Dasypeltis* (African egg-eater) – *Elachistodon* (Asiatic egg-eaters).

Subfamily Xenoderminae. *Achalinus*, E.As. – *Fimbrios*, S.As. – *Stoliczkaia* S.As., E.I. – *Xenodermus*, S.As., E.I. – *Xenopholis*, S.Am. – *Nothopsis*, S.Am.

Subfamily Pareinae [= Amblycephalinae]. Blunt-headed snakes from S.As. and E.I. *Aplopeltura, Pareas.*

Subfamily Dipsadinae. Similar to last but from Central and South America. *Dipsas* (thirst snakes) – *Sibon* – *Sibynomorphus*.

Subfamily *Homalopsinae. Opisthoglyphous water snakes from S.As., E.I., and N.Aus. *Bitia* – *Enhydris* – *Erpeton* [= *Herpeton*] – *Fordonia* – *Gerarda* – *Homalopsis* – *Myron* – *Cantoria* – *Cerberus*.

Family ELAPIDAE

Snakes of colubrid type, but with deeply grooved or canaliculated fangs at front of maxilla. The poisonous snakes of Australia belong to this group; some of these are deadly, but others such as *Vermicella* are only slightly venomous. Mostly oviparous.

Acanthophis, E.I., Aus. (*A. antarcticus*, death adder) – *Apistocalamus*, E.I. – *Aspidelaps*, Af. – *Aspidomorphus*, E.I., Aus. – *Boulengerina*, Af. (fresh-water cobra) – *Brachyaspis*, Aus. – *Brachyurophis*, Aus. – *Bungarus*, S.As., E.I. (*B. caeruleus*, common or blue krait; *B. fasciatus*, banded krait) – *Callophis*, S.As., E.I. – *Demansia*, Aus. – *Dendroaspis*, Af. (*D. polylepis*, black mamba; *D. angusticeps*, green mamba) – *Denisonia*, Aus. – *Elapognathus*, Aus. – *Elaps* (African coral snakes) – *Elapsoidea*, Af. – *Glyphodon*, E.I., Aus. – *Hemachatus*, Af. (*H. haemachatus*, ringhals or spitting cobra) – *Hoplocephalus*, Aus. – *Leptomicrurus*, S.Am. (coral snakes) – *Maticora*, S.As., E.I. (coral

541

snakes) – *Melanelaps*, S.As. – *Micropechis*, S.As. – *Micruroides*, N.Am. (coral snakes) – *Micrurus*, N.Am., S.Am. (coral snakes) – *Naja*, N.Af., Af., S.As., E.I. (*N. naja*, Indian cobra; *N. haje*, Egyptian cobra; *N. nigricollis*, African black-necked cobra; *N. nivea*, Cape cobra) – *Notechis*, Aus. (tiger snake) – *Ogmodon*, Fiji – *Ophiophagus* [= *Hamadryas*], S.As., E.I. (*O. hannah*, king cobra) – *Oxyuranus*, Aus. (*O. scutellatus*, taipan) – *Paranaja*, Af. – *Parapistocalamus*, E.I. – *Pseudapistocalamus*, E.I. – *Pseudechis*, Aus., E.I. – *Pseudohaje*, Af. – *Rhinoplocephalus*, E.I., Aus. – *Rhynchoelaps*, Aus. – *Toxicocalamus*, E.I. – *Tropidechis*, Aus. – *Vermicella*, Aus. (bandy-bandy) – *Walterinnesia*, Af., W.As.

Family HYDROPHIIDAE (sea snakes)

Proteroglyphous snakes of elapid descent with tail and back part of body laterally compressed for swimming. Found mainly in S.As. and E.I., with some forms ranging to Aus. Except for *Pelamis*, most sea snakes inhabit coastal waters, and the large oceans have acted as barriers against their dispersal. Viviparous except for some Laticaudinae which still retain large ventral scales and can crawl on land.

Subfamily Hydrophiinae. *Acalyptophis* – *Astrotia* – *Enhydrina* – *Ephalophis* – *Hydrelaps* – *Hydrophis* – *Kerilia* – *Kolpophis* – *Lapemis* – *Microcephalophis* – *Pelamis* (a truly pelagic and widely distributed form, ranging north to southern Siberia, south to Tasmania, eastwards across the Pacific to Central America, and westwards to East Africa and the Red Sea) – *Praescutata* – *Thalassophis*.

Subfamily Laticaudinae. *Aipysurus* – *Emydocephalus* – *Laticauda*.

Family VIPERIDAE

Solenoglyphs with movable maxilla so that canaliculated fangs are erectile. Absent in Australia. Mostly viviparous.

Subfamily Viperinae. Old World vipers. *Atheris*, Af. – *Atractaspis*, Af., W.As. (mole vipers; perhaps wrongly classified as vipers [244]) – *Azemiops*, S.As. – *Bitis*, Af. (*B. arietans* [= *B. lachesis*], puff adder; *B. gabonica*, Gaboon viper; *B. nasicornis*, nose-horned viper) – *Causus*, Af. (night adders) – *Cerastes*, N.Af. (asps) – *Echis*, N.Af., Af., S.As. (*E. carinatus*, saw-scaled viper) – *Eristocophis*, W.As. – *Pseudocerastes*, W.As. – *Vipera*, Eu., S.As., E.I. (*Vipera* [= *Pelias*] *berus*, common European adder; *Vipera* [= *Daboia*] *russelli*, Russell's viper of India, Ceylon, etc) ∗.

Subfamily Crotalinae. Vipers with sensory pits from New World and Asia. *Agkistrodon* [= *Ancistrodon*], Eu., C.As., E.As., N.Am., S.Am. (*A contortrix*, copperhead, N.Am.; *A piscivorous*, water moccasin or cottonmouth, N.Am.) – *Crotalus*, N.Am., S.Am. (rattlesnakes: *C. adamanteus*, eastern diamond-back; *C. atrox*, western diamond-back; *C. durissus*, tropical rattler or cascabel; *C. horridus*, timber rattlesnake; *C. cerastes*, sidewinder) – *Lachesis*, S.Am. (*L. muta*, bushmaster) – *Sistrurus*, N.Am. (pigmy rattlesnakes) – *Trimeresurus*, S.Am., W.I., S.As., E.As., E.I. (*Trimeresurus* [= *Bothrops* = *Trigonocephalus*] *atrox*, fer-de-lance, N.Am., S.Am., W.I.).

SUBCLASS ARCHOSAURIA

Order CROCODILIA. Since Upper Trias.

Suborder EUSUCHIA. Since Upper Jurassic. Large amphibious reptiles with long jaws; teeth set in bony sockets. Skull diapsid with upper temporal opening reduced. Secondary palate well developed; internal nostrils opening between pterygoids. Clavicles absent. Anterior dorsal ribs two-headed. Gastralia present. Osteoderms well developed. Ventricles of heart completely divided by septum. Male has single median penis. Cloacal opening longitudinal.

Family CROCODYLIDAE

Subfamily Crocodylinae. Snout usually fairly long. Fourth lower tooth fitting into open notch in upper jaw. No osteoderms on belly. *Crocodylus*, N.Am., S.Am., W.I., Af., S.As., Aus., Phil. (*C. acutus*, American; *C. intermedius*, Orinoco; *C. niloticus*, Nile; *C. cataphractus*, West African narrow jawed; *C. porosus*, salt water or estuarine, E. India to N. Australia; *C. palustris*, mugger or Indian marsh; *C. johnstoni*, Australian freshwater) – *Osteolaemus*, Af. (broad-fronted) – *Tomistoma* (false or Malayan gharial).

Subfamily Alligatorinae. Snout variable but often quite broad. Fourth lower tooth fitting into pit in upper jaw. Belly osteoderms absent or present. *Alligator*, N.Am., S.As. (*A. mississippiensis*, American; *A. sinensis*, Chinese) – *Caiman*, S.Am. (*C. niger*, black; *C. sclerops*, spectacled; *C. latirostris*, broad-fronted) – *Paleosuchus*, S.Am. (dwarf caiman).

Subfamily Gavialinae. Snout very long and slender. No osteoderms on belly. *Gavialis*, S.As. (*G. gangeticus*, Indian gharial or gavial).

Bibliography

Some of the books cited have been published by more than one company. Dates quoted in such cases refer to the issue by the publisher whose name is given first.

1 ADAMS, W. E. (1939) The cervical region of the Lacertilia. A critical review of certain aspects of its anatomy. *J. Anat.* **74** 57–71

2 ADRIAN, E. D. (1938) The effect of sound on the ear in reptiles. *J. Physiol. Lond.* **92** 9 P–11 P (Proceedings)

3 AHRENFELDT, R. H. (1955) Two British anatomical studies on American reptiles (1650–1750) II. Edward Tyson: comparative anatomy of the timber rattlesnake. *Herpetologica* **11** 49–69

4 ALBRIGHT, R. G. and NELSON, E. M. (1959) Cranial kinetics of the generalised colubrid snake *Elaphe obsoleta quadrivittata* I. Descriptive morphology. *J. Morph.* **105** 193–240. II. Functional morphology. 241–92

5 ALI, S. M. (1948) Studies on the anatomy of the tail in Sauria and Rhynchocephalia II. *Chameleon zeylanicus* Laurenti. *Proc. Indian Acad. Sci.* **28** 151–65

6 ALTLAND, P. D. and BRACE, K. C. (1962) Red cell life span in the turtle and toad. *Am J. Physiol.* **203** 1188–90

7 ANDERSEN, H. T. (1966) Physiological adaptations in diving vertebrates. *Phys. Rev.* **46** 212–43

8 ANGEL, F. (1950) *Vie et moeurs des serpents.* Paris, Payot

9 ARISTOTLE. Aristotle's history of animals. Translated by R. Cresswell (1891), London, G. Bell & Sons (Bohn's Libraries); Cambridge, Harvard UP

10 ARMSTRONG, J. A., GAMBLE, H. J. and GOLDBY, F. (1953) Observations on the olfactory apparatus and the telencephalon of *Anolis*, a microsmatic lizard. *J. Anat.* **87** 288–307

11 AUFFENBERG, W. (1962) A review of the trunk musculature in the limbless land vertebrates. *Am. Zool.* **2** 183–90

12 AUFFENBERG, W. (1966) The carpus of land tortoises (Testudininae). *Bull. Florida State Mus. biol. Sci.* **10** 159–92

13 BAKER, J. R. (1947) The seasons in a tropical rain-forest. Part 6. Lizards (*Emoia*). *J. Linn. Soc. (Zool.).* **41** 243–7

14 BANNISTER, L. H. (1968) Fine structure of the sensory endings in the vomeronasal organ of the slow-worm *Anguis fragilis. Nature, Lond.* **217** 275–6

15 BARBOUR, T. (n.d.) *Reptiles and amphibians. Their habits and adaptations.* London, G. G. Harrap

16 BARME, M. (1968) Venomous sea snakes (Hydrophiidae). Pp. 285–308 in [77]

17 BARRINGTON, E. J. W. (1963) *An introduction to general and comparative endocrinology.* Oxford, Clarendon Press; NY, Oxford UP

18 BARTHOLOMEW, G.A. and TUCKER, V.A. (1964) Size, body temperature, thermal conductance, oxygen consumption, and heart rate in Australian varanid lizards. *Physiol. Zoöl.* **37** 341–54

19 BARTHOLOMEW, G.A. and LASIEWSKI, R.C. (1965) Heating and cooling rates, heart rate and simulated diving in the Galapagos marine iguana. *Comp. Biochem. Physiol.* **16** 573–82

20 BARTHOLOMEW, G.A., TUCKER, V.A. and LEE, A.K. (1965) Oxygen consumption, thermal conductance, and heart rate in the Australian skink *Tiliqua scincoides. Copeia*, No. 2 169–73

21 BARTLEY, J.A. (1966) A histological and hormonal analysis of physiological and morphological chromatophore responses in the soft-shelled turtle *Trionyx* sp. M.A. thesis, Brown University, Providence, Rhode I., USA.

22 BAUCHOT, R. (1965) La placentation chez les reptiles. *L'année biologique* Ser. 4 **4** 547–75

23 BEACH, F.A. (1944) Responses of captive alligators to auditory stimulation. *Am. Nat.* **78** 481–505

24 BECKER, R.E. and GLENN, W.G. (1967) Differential resistance of mice at various time levels to the lethality of rattlesnake venom (*Crotalus atrox*). *Texas Rep. Biol. Med.* **25** 360–4

25 BEEBE, W. (1924) *Galapagos. World's end.* New York and London, G.P. Putnam's Sons

26 BELKIN, D.A. (1963) Anoxia: tolerance in reptiles. *Science*, N.Y. **139** 492–3

27 BELL, T. (1839) *A history of British reptiles.* London, J. Van Voorst (2nd ed., 1849)

28 BELLAIRS, A.d'A. (1950) Observations on the cranial anatomy of *Anniella*, and a comparison with that of other burrowing lizards. *Proc. zool. Soc. London.* **119** 887–904

29 BELLAIRS, A.d'A. (1965 Cleft palate, microphthalmia and other malformations in embryos of lizards and snakes. *Proc. zool. Soc. Lond.* **144** 239–51

30 BELLAIRS, A.d'A. (1968) *Reptiles.* London, Hutchinson University Library (2nd Ed.)

31 BELLAIRS, A.d'A. and BOYD, J.D. (1950) The lachrymal apparatus in lizards and snakes. – II. The anterior part of the lachrymal duct and its relationship with the palate and with the nasal and vomeronasal organs. *Proc. zool. Soc. Lond.* **120** 269–310

32 BELLAIRS, A.d'A. and CARRINGTON, R. (1966) *The world of reptiles.* London, Chatto & Windus; NY, American Elsevier

33 BELLAIRS, A.d'A. and MILES, A.E.W. (1961) Apparent failure of tooth replacement in monitor lizards. Addendum. *Br. J. Herpet.* **3** No. 1 14–15

34 BELLAIRS, A.d'A. and SHUTE, C.C.D. (1953) Observations on the narial musculature of Crocodilia and its innervation from the sympathetic system. *J. Anat.* **87** 367–78

35 BELLAIRS, A.d'A. and UNDERWOOD, G. (1951) The origin of snakes. *Biol. Rev.* **26** 193–237

36 BELLAIRS, R. (1959) The yolk of the adder (*Vipera berus*). *Br. J. Herpet.* **2** No. 9 155–8

37 BENEDICT, F. G. (1932) *The physiology of large reptiles with special reference to the heat production of snakes, tortoises, lizards and alligators.* Washington, Carnegie Institution

38 BENTLEY, P. J. and SCHMIDT-NIELSEN, K. (1966) Cutaneous water loss in reptiles. *Science, N.Y.* **151** 1547–9

39 BENTLEY, P. J., BRETZ, W. L. and SCHMIDT-NIELSEN, K. (1967) Osmoregulation in the diamond-back terrapin *Malaclemys terrapin centrata. J. exp. Biol.* **46** 161–7

40 BERGMAN, R. A. M. (1962) Die Anatomie der Elapinae. *Z. wiss. Zool.* **167** 291–337

41 BETZ, T. W. (1962) Surgical anesthesia in reptiles, with special reference to the water snake, *Natrix rhombifera. Copeia* No. 2 284–7

42 BIGALKE, R. (1931) Note on the egg of the Nile crocodile (*Crocodylus niloticus*). *Proc. zool. Soc. Lond.* 557–9

43 BISHOP, J. E. (1959) A histological and histochemical study of the kidney tubule of the common garter snake, *Thamnophis sirtalis*, with special reference to the sexual segment in the male. *J. Morph.* **104** 307–58

44 BLAIN, A. W. and CAMPBELL, K. N. (1942) A study of digestive phenomena in snakes with the aid of the Roentgen ray. *Am. J. Roentg.* **48** 229–39

45 BLAIR, W. F. (1960) *The rusty lizard. A population study* [on *Sceloporus olivaceus*] Austin, University of Texas Press

46 BLANCHARD, F. N. and BLANCHARD, F. C. (1941) Factors determining time of birth in the garter snake *Thamnophis sirtalis sirtalis* (Linnaeus). *Pap. Michigan Acad. Sci.* **26** 161–76

47 BOGERT, C. M. (1941) Sensory cues used by rattlesnakes in their recognition of ophidian enemies. *Ann. N. Y. Acad. Sci.* **41** 329–44

48 BOGERT, C. M. (1943) Dentitional phenomena in cobras and other elapids with notes on adaptive modifications of fangs. *Bull. Am. Mus. nat. Hist.* **81** 285–360

49 BOGERT, C. M. (1949) Thermoregulation in reptiles, a factor in evolution. *Evolution* **3** 195–211

50 BOGERT, C. M. (1959) How reptiles regulate their body temperature. *Sci. Amer.* **200** No. 4 105–20

51 BOGERT, C. M. (1964) Amphisbaenids are a taxonomic enigma. *Nat. Hist. N. Y.* **73** No. 7 16–25

52 BOGERT, C. M. and COWLES, R. B. (1947) Results of the Archbold Expeditions. No. 58 Moisture loss in relation to habitat selection in some Floridian reptiles. *Am. Mus. Novit.* No. 1358 1–34

53 BOGERT, C. M. and DEL CAMPO, R. M. (1956) The Gila monster and its allies. The relationships, habits, and behaviour of the lizards of the family Helodermatidae. *Bull. Am. Mus. nat. Hist.* **109** 1–238

54 BOGERT, C. M. and ROTH, V. D. (1966) Ritualistic combat of male gopher snakes, *Pituophis melanoleucus affinis* (Reptilia, Colubridae). *Am. Mus. Novit.* No. 2245 1–27

55 BOJANUS, L. H. (1819) *Anatome testudinis Europaeae* [*Emys*] 2 vols. Vilna

56 BOLK, L. *et al.* (Eds.) (1931–9) *Handbuch der vergleichenden Anatomie der Wirbeltiere.* 6 vols. + index. Berlin & Vienna, Urban & Schwarzenberg

57 BOLTT, R.E. and EWER, R.F. (1964) The functional anatomy of the head of the puff adder, *Bitis arietans* (Merr.). *J. Morph.* **114** 83–106

58 BONIN, J.J. (1965) The eye of *Agamodon anguliceps* Peters (Reptilia, Amphisbaenia). *Copeia,* No. 3 324–31

59 BONS, J. and SAINT GIRONS, H. (1963) Ecologie et cycle sexuel des amphisbeniens du Maroc. *Bull. Soc. Sci. nat. phys. Maroc.* 3ᵉ & 4ᵉ trimestres 117–70

60 BOULENGER, G.A. (1885–7) *Catalogue of the lizards in the British Museum (Natural History).* 3 vols. London; NY, Hafner (reprint)

61 BOULENGER, G.A. (1889) *Catalogue of the Chelonians, Rhynchocephalians and crocodiles in the British Museum (Natural History).* London; NY, Hafner

62 BOULENGER, G.A. (1893–6) *Catalogue of the snakes in the British Museum (Natural History).* 3 vols. London; NY, Hafner (reprint)

63 BOULENGER, G.A. (1913) *The snakes of Europe.* London, Methuen

64 BOYCOTT, B.B., GRAY, E.G. and GUILLERY, R.W. (1961) Synaptic structure and its alteration with environmental temperature: a study by light and electron microscopy of the central nervous system of lizards. *Proc. Roy. Soc.* **154 B** 151–72

65 BOYCOTT, B.B. and GUILLERY, R.W. (1962) Olfactory and visual learning in the red-eared terrapin, *Pseudemys scripta elegans* (Wied.). *J. exp. Biol.* **39** 567–77

66 BRADSHAW, S.D. and MAIN, A.R. (1968) Behavioural attitudes and regulation of temperature in *Amphibolurus* lizards. *J. Zool. Lond.* **154** 193–221

67 BRAGDON, D.E. (1953) A contribution to the surgical anatomy of the water snake, *Natrix sipedon sipedon,* the location of the visceral endocrine organs with reference to ventral scutellation. *Anat. Rec.* **117** 145–61

68 BRAIN, C.K. (1960) Observations on the locomotion of the South-West African adder, *Bitis peringueyi* (Boulenger), with speculations on the origin of sidewinding. *Ann. Transvaal Mus.* **24** 19–24

69 BRATTSTROM, B.H. (1959) The functions of the air sac in snakes. *Herpetologica* **15** 103–4

70 BRATTSTROM, B.H. (1965) Body temperatures of reptiles. *Am. Midl. Nat.* **73** 376–422

71 BREATHNACH, A.S. and POYNTZ, S.V. (1966) Electron microscopy of pigment cells in tail skin of *Lacerta vivipara. J. Anat.* **100** 549–69

72 BROCKMAN, H.L. and KENNEDY, J.P. (1964) The surgical occlusion of the left aortic orifice in *Alligator mississipiensis* Daudin. *J. Surgical Res.* **4** 500–3

73 BROWN, W.C. and ALCALA, A.C. (1957) Viability of lizard eggs exposed to sea water. *Copeia* No. 1 39–41

74 BRYANT, S.V. and BELLAIRS, A.d'A. (1967) Amnio-allantoic constriction bands in lizard embryos and their effects on tail regeneration. *J. Zool., Lond.* **152** 155–61

75 BRYANT, S.V. and BELLAIRS, A.d'A. (1967) Tail regeneration in the lizards *Anguis fragilis* and *Lacerta dugesii. J. Linn. Soc. (Zool.).* **46** 297–305

76 BRYANT, S.V., BREATHNACH, A..S. and BELLAIRS, A.d'A. (1967) Ultrastructure of the epidermis of the lizard (*Lacerta vivipara*) at the resting stage of the sloughing cycle. *J. Zool. Lond.* **152** 209–19

77 BÜCHERL, W., BUCKLEY, E. and DEULOFEU, V. (Eds.) (1968) *Venomous animals*

and their venoms. Vol. I. New York & London, Academic Press. [A multi-author compilation on various topics].

78 BUCKLEY, E.E. and PORGES, N. (Eds.) (1956) *Venoms.* [A symposium] Washington, Publication No. 44 of the American Association for the advancement of science

79 BULLOCK, T.H. and COWLES, R.B. (1952) Physiology of an infrared receptor: the facial pit of pit vipers. *Science, N.Y.* **115** 541–3

80 BURKETT, R.D. (1966) Natural history of cottonmouth moccasin *Agkistrodon piscivorus* (Reptilia). *Univ. Kansas Publs. Mus. nat. Hist.* **17** 435–91

81 BURRAGE, B.R. (1965) Copulation in a pair of *Alligator mississipiensis. Br. J. Herpet.* **3** No. 8 207–8

82 BUSTARD, H.R. (1964) Defensive behaviour shown by Australian geckos, genus *Diplodactylus. Herpetologica* **20** 198–200

83 BUSTARD, H.R. (1965) Observations on the life history and behaviour of *Chamaeleo hohnelii* (Steindachner). *Copeia* No. 4 401–10

84 BUSTARD, H.R. (1965) Observations on Australian geckos. *Herpetologica* **21** 294–302

85 BUSTARD, H.R. (1966) Turtle biology at Heron Island. *Aust. Nat. Hist.* **15** 262–4

86 BUSTARD, H.R. (1967) A mechanism for greater predator survival during cold torpor in gekkonid lizards. *Br. J. Herpet.* **4** No. 1 7–8

87 CALLISON, G. (1967) Intracranial mobility in Kansas mosasaurs. *Univ. Kansa Paleont. Contr.* Paper 26 1–15

88 CAMP, C.L. (1923) Classification of the lizards. *Bull. Am. Mus. nat. Hist.* **48** 289–481

89 CARR, A. (1952) *Handbook of turtles. The turtles of the United States, Canada, and Baja California.* Ithaca, New York, Comstock Publishing Associates, a division of Cornell University Press; London, Constable

90 CARR, A. and THE EDITORS OF LIFE (1963) *The Reptiles.* New York, Time Inc.

91 CARR, A. (1968) *The turtle. A natural history.* London, Cassell; (1967) NY, Natural History Press

92 CARR, A. and GIOVANNOLI, L. (1957) The ecology and migrations of sea turtles. 2. Results of field work in Costa Rica, 1955. *Am. Mus. Novit.* No. 1835 1–32

93 CARR, A. and HIRTH, H. (1961) Social facilitation in green turtle siblings. *Anim. Behav.* **9** 68–70

94 CARR, A. and OGREN, L. (1960) The ecology and migrations of sea turtles, 4. The green turtle in the Caribbean sea. *Bull. Am. Mus. nat. Hist.* **121** 1–48

95 CARRINGTON, R. (1960) *A biography of the sea.* London, Chatto & Windus

96 CARROLL, R.L. (1969) Origin of reptiles. Pp. 1–44 in [184]

97 CHAPMAN, D.S. (1968) The symptomatology, pathology and treatment of the bites of venomous snakes of Central and Southern Africa. Pp. 463–527 in [77]

98 CHAPMAN, S.W. and CONKLIN, R.E. (1935) The lymphatic system of the snake. *J. Morph.* **58** 385–417

99 CHIU, K.W., PHILLIPS, J.G. and MADERSON, P.F.A. (1967) The role of the thyroid in the control of the sloughing cycle in the tokay (*Gekko gecko*, Lacertilia). *J. Endocr.* **39** 463–72

100 CHRISTENSEN, P.A. (1955) *South African snake venoms and antivenoms.* Johannesburg, South African Institute for Medical Research

101 CLARK, H., FLORIO, B. and HUROWITZ, R. (1955) Embryonic growth of *Thamnophis s. sirtalis* in relation to fertilization date and placental function. *Copeia* No. 1 9–13

102 CLAY, W.M. (1935) The occurrence of albinos in a brood of the common water snake, *Natrix sipedon sipedon* (L.). *Copeia* No. 3 115–18

103 CLOUDSLEY-THOMPSON, J.L. (1969) *The zoology of tropical Africa.* London, Weidenfeld & Nicolson (The World Naturalist)

104 COHEN, E. (1955) Immunological studies of the serum proteins of some reptiles. *Biol. Bull.* **109** 394–403

105 COLBERT, E.H. (1946) The Eustachian tubes in the Crocodilia. *Copeia* No. 1 12–14

106 COLBERT, E.H. (1962) *Dinosaurs. Their discovery and their world.* London, Hutchinson

107 COLBERT, E.H. (1965) *The age of reptiles.* London, Weidenfeld & Nicolson (The World Naturalist); NY, Norton

108 COLBERT, E.H., COWLES, R.B. and BOGERT, C.M. (1946) Temperature tolerances in the American alligator and their bearing on the habits, evolution, and extinction of the dinosaurs. *Bull. Am. Mus. nat. Hist.* **86** 327–74

109 COLBERT, E.H. and MOOK, C.C. (1951) The ancestral crocodilian *Protosuchus. Bull. Am. Mus. nat. Hist.* **97** 143–82

110 COLE, C.J. (1966) Femoral glands in lizards: a review. *Herpetologica* **22** 199–206

111 COLLETTE, B.B. (1961) Correlations between ecology and morphology in anoline lizards from Havana, Cuba and Southern Florida. *Bull. Mus. comp. Zool. Harvard* **125** 137–62

112 COMFORT, A. (1964) *Ageing. The biology of senescence.* London, Routledge & Kegan Paul; NY, Holt, Rinehart & Winston

113 CONAWAY, C.H. and FLEMING, W.R. (1960) Placental transmission of Na^{22} and I^{131} in *Natrix. Copeia* No. 1 53–5

114 COOKSON, J.H. (1962) Failure of lizards to learn a simple task. *Br. J. Herpet.* **3** No. 2 40

115 COOPER, J.S. (1965) Tooth replacement in amphibians and reptiles. *Br. J. Herpet.* **3** No. 9 214–18

116 COPE, E.D. (1900) The crocodilians, lizards, and snakes of North America. *Ann. Rpt. U.S. nat. Mus.* (1898)

117 CORTI, A. (1847) *De systemate vasorum Psammosauri grisei* Vindobonae [Vienna], Typis congregationis mechitharisticae

118 COTT, H.B. (1957) *Adaptive coloration in animals.* London, Methuen; NY, Barnes & Noble

119 COTT, H.B. (1961) Scientific results of an enquiry into the ecology and economic status of the Nile crocodile (*Crocodilus niloticus*) in Uganda and Northern Rhodesia. *Trans. zool. Soc. Lond.* **29** 211–356

120 COULSON, R.A. and HERNANDEZ, T. (1964) *Biochemistry of the alligator. A study of metabolism in slow motion.* Baton Rouge, Louisiana State University Press

121 COWLES, R.B. (1930) The life history of *Varanus niloticus* (Linnaeus) as observed in Natal South Africa. *J. Ent. Zool.* **22** 1–31

549

122 COWLES, R.B. and BOGERT, C.M. (1944) A preliminary study of the thermal requirements of desert reptiles. *Bull. Am. Mus. nat. Hist.* **83** 261–96

123 COWLES, R.B. and PHELAN, R.L. (1958) Olfaction in rattlesnakes. *Copeia* No. 2 77–83

124 CUELLAR, O. (1966) Delayed fertilisation in the lizard *Uta stansburiana. Copeia* No. 3 549–52

125 DAREVSKI, I.S. (1966) Natural parthenogenesis in a polymorphic group of Caucasian rock lizards related to *Lacerta saxicola* Eversmann. *J. Ohio herpet. Soc.* **5** 115–52

126 DARLINGTON, P.J. (1948) The geographical distribution of cold-blooded vertebrates. *Quart. Rev. Biol.* **23** 1–26 & 105–23

127 DARWIN, C. (1907) *Journal of researches into the natural history and geology of the countries visited during the voyage round the world of HMS 'Beagle' under command of Captain Fitz Roy, R.N.* London, Murray [1st publ. under slightly different title, 1839]; NY, Dutton

128 DARWIN, C. (1936) *The origin of species by means of natural selection or the preservation of favored races in the struggle for life* and *The descent of man and selection in relation to sex.* London, Penguin Books (The Modern Library) [2 books together: 1st publ. 1859 and 1871]; NY, Athenaum

129 DAVIS, D.D. (1953) Behaviour of the lizard *Corythophanes cristatus. Fieldiana : Zool.* **35** 1–8

130 DAWBIN, W.H. (1962) The tuatara in its natural habitat. *Endeavour* **21** 16–24

131 DAWSON, W.R. and BARTHOLOMEW, G.A. (1958) Metabolic and cardiac responses to temperature in the lizard *Dipsosaurus dorsalis. Physiol. Zoöl.* **31** 100–11

132 de BEER, G.R. (1937) *The development of the vertebrate skull.* Oxford, Clarendon Press

133 DENDY, A. (1910) On the structure, development and morphological interpretation of the pineal organs and adjacent parts of the brain in the tuatara (*Sphenodon punctatus*). *Phil. Trans. Roy. Soc.* **201** 227–331

134 DERANIYAGALA, P.E.P. (1939) *The tetrapod reptiles of Ceylon.* Vol. I Colombo Museum; London, Dulau

135 DERANIYAGALA, P.E.P. (1953) *A colored atlas of some vertebrates from Ceylon.* Vol. 2. *Tetrapod Reptilia.* Ceylon National Museums

136 DERANIYAGALA, P.E.P. *A colored atlas of some vertebrates from Ceylon.* Vol. 3. *Serpentoid Reptilia.* Ceylon National Museums (1955)

137 DERANIYAGALA, R.Y. (1958) Pseudo-combat of the monitor lizard *Varanus bengalensis* (Daudin). *Spol. Zeylanica* **28** 16–18 (of reprint)

138 DESSAUER, H.C. (1967) Molecular approach to snake taxonomy. *Herpetologica* **23** 148–55

139 DITMARS, R.L. (1928) *Reptiles of the world.* New York & London, Macmillan (Copyright 1910)

140 DITMARS, R.L. (1937) *Snakes of the world.* New York, Macmillan (1st publ. 1931)

141 DODGE, C.H. and WUNDER, C.C. (1963) Growth of juvenile red-eared turtles as influenced by gravitational field intensity. *Nature, Lond.* **197** 922–3

142 DOWLING, H.G. (1959) Egg-eating adaptations in the Chinese ratsnake, *Elaphe carinata* Günther. *Copeia* No. 1 68–9

143 DOWLING, H. G. (1959) Classification of the Serpentes: a critical review. *Copeia* No. 1 38–52

144 DOWLING, H. G. and SAVAGE, J. M. (1960) A guide to the snake hemipenis: A survey of basic structure and systematic characteristics. *Zoologica, N. Y.* **45** 17–28

145 DRUMMOND, F. H. (1946) Pharyngeo-oesophageal respiration in the lizard *Trachysaurus rugosus*. *Proc. zool. Soc. Lond.* **116** 225–8

146 DUFAURE, J. P. and HUBERT, J. (1961) Table de développement du lézard vivipare: *Lacerta (Zootoca) vivipara* Jacquin. *Archs. Anat. microsc. Morph. exp.* **50** 309–28

147 DUMÉRIL, A. M. C., BIBRON, G. and DUMÉRIL, A. (1834–54) *Erpétologie générale ou histoire naturelle complète des reptiles*. (10 vols.) Paris, Librairie encyclopédique de Roret

148 DUNSON, W. A. and TAUB, A. M. (1967) Extrarenal salt excretion in sea snakes (*Laticauda*). *Am. J. Physiol.* **213** 975–82

149 EAKIN, R. M., QUAY, W. B. and WESTFALL, J. A. (1961) Cytochemical and cytological studies of the parietal eye of the lizard, *Sceloporus occidentalis*. *Z. Zellforsch. mikrosk. Anat.* **53** 449–70

150 EAKIN, R. M., STEBBINS, R. C. and WILHOFT, D. C. (1959) Effects of parietalectomy and sustained temperature on thyroid of lizard, *Sceloporus occidentalis*. *Proc. Soc. exp. Biol. Med.* **101** 162–4

151 EAKIN, R. M. and WESTFALL, J. A. (1960) Further observations on the fine structure of the parietal eye of lizards. *J. biophys. biochem. Cytol.* **8** 483–99

152 EDMUND, A. G. (1969) Dentition. Pp. 117–200 in [184]

153 EHRENFELD, D. W. (1968) The role of vision in the sea-finding orientation of the green turtle (*Chelonia mydas*). 2. Orientation mechanism and range of spectral sensitivity. *Animal Behaviour* **16** 281–7

154 EIBL-EIBESFELDT, I. (1960) *Galapagos*. Translated from the German by A. H. Brodrick. London, Macgibbon & Kee

155 EL-TOUBI, M. R., KAMAL, A. M. and HAMMOUDA, H. G. (1965) The origin of Ophidia in the light of the developmental study of the skull. *Z. zool. Syst. Evolutionsforsch.* **3** 94–102

156 ERNST, V. and RUIBAL, R. (1966) The structure and development of the digital lamellae of lizards. *J. Morph.* **120** 233–66

157 ESQUEMELING, J. (1911) *The buccaneers of America. A true account of the most remarkable assaults committed of late years upon the coasts of the West Indies by the buccaneers of Jamaica and Tortuga (both English and French). Wherein are contained more especially the unparalleled exploits of Sir Henry Morgan, our English Jamaican hero, who sacked Porto Bello, burnt Panama, etc. By John Esquemeling, one of the buccaneers who was present at these tragedies. Now faithfully rendered into English. With facsimiles of all the original engravings,* etc. London. G. Allen; New York, Macmillan (Dutch ed., Amsterdam, 1678)

158 ESSEX, R. (1927) Studies in reptilian degeneration. *Proc. zool. Soc. Lond.* 879–945

159 ETHERIDGE, R. (1967) Lizard caudal vertebrae. *Copeia* No. 4 699–721

160 EVANS, L. T. (1959) A motion picture study of maternal behaviour of the lizard, *Eumeces obsoletus* Baird & Girard. *Copeia* No. 2 103–10

161 FAYRER, J. (1872) *The Thanatophidia of India, being a description of the venomous snakes of the Indian Peninsula, with an account of the influence of their poison on life and a series of experiments.* London, Churchill

162 FITCH, H. S. (1960) Autecology of the copperhead. *Univ. Kansas Publs. Mus. nat. Hist.* **13** 85–288

163 FITCH, H. S. (1963) Natural history of the racer *Coluber constrictor. Univ. Kansas Publs. Mus. nat. Hist.* **15** 351–468

164 FITCH, H. S. and GREENE, H. W. (1965) Breeding cycle in the ground skink, *Lygosoma laterale. Univ. Kansas Publs. Mus. nat. Hist.* **15** 565–75

165 FITZSIMONS, V. F. (1943) *The lizards of South Africa.* Pretoria, Transvaal Museum

166 FITZSIMONS, V. F. M. (1962) *Snakes of southern Africa.* London, Macdonald

167 FORBES, T. R. (1940) A note on reptilian sex ratios. *Copeia* No. 2 132

168 FOX, W. (1956) Seminal receptacles of snakes. *Anat. Rec.* **124** 519–40

169 FOXON, G. E. H., GRIFFITH, J. and PRICE, M. (1956) The mode of action of the heart of the green lizard, *Lacerta viridis. Proc. zool. Soc. Lond.* **126** 145–57

170 FRAIR, W. (1963) Blood group studies with turtles. *Science, N.Y.* **140** 1412–14

171 FRANKLIN, M. A. (1945) The embryonic appearances of centres of ossification in the bones of snakes. *Copeia* No. 2 68–72

172 FRAZZETTA, T. H. (1962) A functional consideration of cranial kinesis in lizards. *J. Morph.* **111** 287–320

173 FRAZZETTA, T. H. (1966) Studies on the morphology and function of the skull in the Boidae (Serpentes). Part II. Morphology and function of the jaw apparatus in *Python sebae* and *Python molurus. J. Morph.* **118** 217–96

174 GABE, M. and SAINT GIRONS, H. (1964) *Contribution à l'histologie de* Sphenodon punctatus *Gray.* Paris, Centre National de la Recherche Scientifique

175 GABE, M. and SAINT GIRONS, H. (1965) Contribution à la morphologie comparée du cloaque et des glandes épidermoïdes de la région cloacale chez les lépidosauriens. *Mém. Mus. natn. Hist. nat., Paris,* Ser. A. **33** 151–292

176 GABE, M. and SAINT GIRONS, H. (1967) Données histologiques sur le tégument et les glandes épidermoïdes céphaliques des lépidosauriens. *Acta. anàt.* **67** 571–94

177 GADOW, H. (1887) Remarks on the cloaca and on the copulatory organs of the Amniota. *Phil. Trans. Roy. Soc.* **178** 5–37

178 GADOW, H. (1901) *Amphibia and reptiles.* London, Macmillan (The Cambridge Natural History)

179 GANS, C. (1952) The functional morphology of the egg-eating adaptations in the snake genus *Dasypeltis. Zoologica, N.Y.* **37** 209–44

180 GANS, C. (1960) Studies on amphisbaenids (Amphisbaenia, Reptilia) 1. A taxonomic revision of the Trogonophinae, and a functional interpretation of the amphisbaenid adaptive pattern. *Bull. Am. Mus. nat. Hist.* **119** 129–204 [Gans has written later papers on amphisbaenids.]

181 GANS, C. (1961) The feeding mechanism of snakes and its possible evolution. *Am. Zool.* **1** 217–27

182 GANS, C. (1966) Locomotion without limbs. *Nat. Hist. N.Y.* **75** No. 2 10–17; No. 3 36–41

183 GANS, C. (1967) The chameleon. *Nat. Hist. N.Y.* **76** No. 4 52–9

184 GANS, C., BELLAIRS, A. d'A. and PARSONS, T. S. (Eds.) (1969) *Biology of the Reptilia*. Vol. 1. New York & London, Academic Press [A multi-author compilation]

185 GANS, C. and HUGHES, G. M. (1967) The mechanism of lung ventilation in the tortoise *Testudo graeca* Linné. *J. exp. Biol.* **47** 1–20

186 GANS, C. and TAUB, A. M. (1964) Precautions for keeping poisonous snakes in captivity. *Curator* **7** 196–206

187 GASC, J. P. (1966) Les rapports anatomiques du membre pelvien vestigial chez les squamates serpentiformes. I. *Anguis fragilis* (Anguidae, Lacertilia) et *Python sebae* (Boidae, Ophidia). *Bull. Mus. natn. Hist. nat., Paris,* **37** 916–25; **38** 99–110

188 GASC, J. P. (1967) Introduction à l'étude de la musculature axiale des squamates serpentiformes. *Mem. Mus. natn. Hist. nat., Paris,* **48** 69–125

189 GAYMER, R. (1968) The Indian Ocean giant tortoise *Testudo gigantea* on Aldabra. *J. Zool. Lond.* **154** 341–63

190 GEORGE, J. C. and SHAH, R. V. (1956) Comparative morphology of the lung in snakes with remarks on the evolution of the lung in reptiles. *J. Anim. Morph. Physiol.* **3** 1–7

191 GEORGE, J. C. and SHAH, R. V. (1959) The structural basis of the evolution of the respiratory mechanism in Chelonia. *J. Anim. Morph. Physiol.* **6** 1–9

192 GEORGE, J. C. and SHAH, R. V. (1965) Evolution of air sacs in Sauropsida. *J. Anim. Morph. Physiol.* **12** 255–63

193 GIRGIS, S. (1961) Aquatic respiration in the common Nile turtle, *Trionyx triunguis* (Forskal). *Comp. Biochem. Physiol.* **3** 206–17

194 GIRGIS, S. (1961) Observations on the heart in the family Trionychidae. *Bull. Br. Mus. nat. Hist.* **8** 73–107

195 GIRGIS, S. (1962) Anatomical and functional adaptations in the venous system of a diving reptile, *Trionyx triunguis* (Forskal). *Proc. zool. Soc. Lond.* **138** 355–77

196 GOIN, C. J. and GOIN, O. B. (1962) *Introduction to herpetology*. San Francisco & London. W. H. Freeman

197 GOLDBY, F. and GAMBLE, H. J. (1957) The reptilian cerebral hemispheres. *Biol. Rev.* **32** 383–420

198 GOOD, R. A., GABRIELSEN, A., PETERSON, R. D. A., FINSTAD, J. and COOPER, M. D. (1966). The development of the central and peripheral lymphoid tissue: ontogenetic and phylogenetic considerations. In *The thymus: experimental and clinical studies.* (Ed. G. E. W. Wolstenholme and R. Porter). London, Churchill [A symposium]

199 GORBMAN, A. (Ed.) (1959) *Comparative endocrinology*. New York, J. Wiley; London, Chapman & Hall [A symposium]

200 GORMAN, G. C. and DESSAUER, H. C. (1965) Hemoglobin and transferrin electrophoresis and relationships of island populations of *Anolis* lizards. *Science*, N.Y. **150** 1454–5

201 GRAY, J. (1953) *How animals move*. Cambridge University Press

202 GRAY, J. (1968) *Animal locomotion*. London, Weidenfeld & Nicolson (The World Naturalist); NY, Norton

203 GRIFFITHS, I. (1961) Skeletal lamellae as an index of age in heterothermous tetrapods. *Ann. Mag. nat. Hist.* Ser. 13. **4** 449–65

553

204 HAAS, G. (1962) Remarques concernant les relations phylogéniques des diverses familles d'ophidiens fondées sur la différenciation de la musculature mandibulaire. Problemes actuels de paléontologie (Évolution des vertébrés). Colloques internationaux du Centre National de la recherche scientifique. Paris. No. 104 215–41

205 HAAS, G. (1964) Anatomical observations on the head of *Liotyphlops albirostris* (Typhlopidae, Ophidia). *Acta Zool. Stockh.* **45** 1–62

206 HAINES, R.W. (1946) A revision of the movements of the forearm in tetrapods. *J. Anat.* **80** 1–11

207 HAINES, R.W. (1952) The shoulder joint of lizards and the primitive reptilian shoulder mechanism. *J. Anat.* **86** 412–22

208 HAINES, R.W. (1969) Epiphyses and sesamoids. Pp. 81–116 in [184]

209 HALL, Z.M. and WILSON, R.R. (1962) A case for diagnosis. *Br. Med. J.* i 802–3

210 HAMILTON, D.W. (1964) The inner ear of lizards. 1. Gross structure. *J. Morph.* **115** 255–72

211 HAMLETT, G.W.D. (1952) Notes on breeding and reproduction in the lizard *Anolis carolinensis. Copeia* No. 3 183–5

212 HARRIS, V.A. (1963) *The anatomy of the rainbow lizard* Agama agama (*L*). London, Hutchinson Tropical Monographs; NY, Hillary House

213 HARRIS, V.A. (1964) *The life of the rainbow lizard.* London, Hutchinson Tropical Monographs; NY, Hillary House

214 HARRISSON, B. (1961) *Lanthanotus borneensis* – habits and observations. *Sarawak Mus. J.* **10** 286–92

215 HELLMICH, W. (1962) *Reptiles and amphibians of Europe* (English editor A. Leutscher). London, Blandford Press

216 HENDRICKSON, J.R. (1958) The green sea turtle, *Chelonia mydas* (Linn.) in Malaya and Sarawak. *Proc. zool. Soc. Lond.* **130** 455–535

217 HILDEMANN, W.H. (1962) Immunogenetic studies of poikilothermic animals. *Am. Nat.* **96** 195–204

218 HILL, J.P. and de BEER, G.R. (1950) Development of the Monotremata. Part VII. The development and structure of the egg-tooth and the caruncle in the monotremes and on the occurrence of vestiges of the egg-tooth and caruncle in marsupials. *Trans. zool. Soc. Lond.* **26** 503–44

219 HOFFSTETTER, R. (1962) Revue des récentes acquisitions concernant l'histoire et la systématique des Squamates. *Problemes actuels de paléontologie (Évolution des vertébrés).* Colloques internationaux du Centre National de la recherche scientifique. Paris. No. 104 243–79

220 HOFFSTETTER, R. and GASC, J.P. (1969) Vertebrae and ribs of modern reptiles. Pp. 201–310 in [184]

221 HOLLINGSWORTH, M.J. (1957) The metaphase chromosomes of *Crocodilus niloticus. Cytologia* **22** 412–4

222 HOPLEY, C.C. (1882) *Snakes : curiosities and wonders of serpent life.* London, Griffith & Farran: New York, E.P.Dutton

223 HUGHES, A., BRYANT, S.V. and BELLAIRS, A. d'A. (1967) Embryonic behaviour in the lizard, *Lacerta vivipara. J. Zool. Lond.* **153** 139–52

224 HUGHES, G.M. (1965) *Comparative physiology of vertebrate respiration.* London, Heinmann Educational Books; Cambridge, Harvard UP

225 HUNTER, J. *The works of John Hunter, F.R.S., with notes* (Ed. J. F. Palmer) (1835). Vol. 4. London, Longman

226 HUXLEY, T. H. (1864) *Lectures on the elements of comparative anatomy.* London, J. Churchill & Sons

227 HUXLEY, T. H. (1871) *A manual of the anatomy of vertebrated animals.* London, J. & A. Churchill

228 IMPEY, O. R. (1967) Functional aspects of cranial kinetism in the Lacertilia. D. Phil. thesis, University of Oxford

229 INGER, R. F. and GREENBERG, B. (1966) Annual reproductive patterns of lizards from a Bornean rain forest. *Ecology* **47** 1007–21

230 IRVINE, F. R. (1954) Snakes as food for man. *Br. J. Herpet.* **1** No. 10 183–9

231 IRVINE, F. R. (1960) Lizards and crocodiles as food for man. *Br. J. Herpet.* **2** No. 11 197–202

232 JAROS, D. B. (1940) Occlusion of the venom duct of Crotalidae by electrocoagulation: an innovation in operative technique. *Zoologica, N. Y.* **25** 49–51

233 JAYAKAR, S. D. and SPURWAY, H. (1964) Bimodality of laying-hatching times in *Testudo elegans* Schoepff (Chelonia). *Nature, Lond.* **204** 603

234 JOHNSON, R. G. (1955) The adaptive and phylogenetic significance of vertebral form in snakes. *Evolution* **9** 367–88

235 JONES, M. D. G. (1900) Can a cobra eject its venom? *J. Bombay nat. Hist. Soc.* **13** 376

236 KAUFFMAN, E. G. and KESLING, R. V. (1960) An upper Cretaceous ammonite bitten by a mosasaur. *Contr. Mus. Paleont. Univ. Michigan* **15** 193–248

237 KENNEDY, J. P. and BROCKMAN, H. L. (1965) Open heart surgery in *Alligator mississipiensis* Daudin. *Herpetologica* **21** 6–15

238 KELLICOTT, D. S. (1898) *The dissection of the ophidian* [*Heterodon*]. Authorised facsimile reproduction, copyright 1938 by General Biological Supply House, Chicago

239 KIRK, R. L. and HOGBEN, L. (1946) Studies on temperature regulation. II. Amphibia and reptiles. *J. Exp. Biol.* **22** 213–20

240 KLAUBER, L. M. (1956) *Rattlesnakes. Their habits, life histories, and influence on mankind.* 2 vols. Berkeley and Los Angeles. Published for the Zoölogical Society of San Diego by the University of California Press.

241 KNOWLTON, G. F. (1936) Lizard digestion studies. *Herpetologica* **1** 9–10

242 KOCHVA, E. (1960) A quantitative study of venom secretion by *Vipera palaestinae*. *Am J. trop. Med. Hyg.* **9** 381–90

243 KOCHVA, E. and GANS, C. (1967) The structure of the venom gland and secretion of venom in viperid snakes. Pp. 195–203 in *Animal toxins.* Oxford & New York, Pergamon Press [a symposium]

244 KOCHVA, E., SHAYER-WOLLBERG, M. and SOBOL, R. (1967) The special pattern of the venom gland in *Atractaspis* and its bearing on the taxonomic status of the genus. *Copeia*, No. 4 763–72

245 KUBIAK, S. (1963) Vascularisation of the skin in the lizard (*Lacerta agilis* L.). *Studia Soc. Sci. Torun.* **7** 1–12

246 LANGEBARTEL, D. A. (1968) The hyoid and its associated muscles in snakes. Illinois Biological Monographs 38. Urbana, Chicago & London, University of Illinois Press

247 LAWRENCE, D. H. (1932) *Collected poems. Birds, beasts and flowers*. London, Heinemann

248 LEE, J. and KNOWLES, F. G. W. (1965) *Animal hormones*. London, Hutchinson University Library; NY, Hillary House

249 LEGLER, J. M. (1960) Natural history of the ornate box turtle, *Terrapene ornata ornata* Agassiz. *Univ. Kansas Publs. Mus. nat. Hist.* **11** 527–669

250 LEWIS, T. H. (1949) Dark coloration in the reptiles of the Tularosa Malpais, New Mexico. *Copeia* No. 3 181–4

251 LICHT, P. (1967) Thermal adaptation in the enzymes of lizards in relation to preferred body temperatures. Pp. 131–45 in *Molecular mechanisms of temperature adaptation*. American Association for the advancement of science, Washington. [A symposium]

252 LIGHT, P. and BASU, S. L. (1967) Influence of temperature on lizard testes. *Nature, Lond.* **213** 672

253 LICHT, P., DAWSON, W. R., SHOEMAKER, V. H. and MAIN, A. R. (1966) Observations on the thermal relations of western Australian lizards. *Copeia* No. 1 97–110

254 LIGHT, P., HOYER, H. E. and van OORDT, P. G. W. J. (1969) Influence of photoperiod and temperature on testicular recrudescence and body growth in the lizards, *Lacerta sicula* and *Lacerta muralis*. *J. Zool. Lond.* **157** 469–501

255 LISSMANN, H. W. (1950) Rectilinear locomotion in a snake (*Boa occidentalis*). *J. exp. Biol.* **26** 368–79

256 LIST, J. C. (1966) *Comparative osteology of the snake families Typhlopidae and Leptotyphlopidae*. Illinois biological monographs 36. Urbana & London, University of Illinois Press

257 LOCKWOOD, A. P. M. (1963) *Animal body fluids and their regulation*. London, Heinemann; Cambridge, Harvard UP

258 LORENZ, K. (1967) *On aggression*. Translated by M. Latzke. London, Methuen (University Paperback Edition); NY, Harcourt, Brace & World

259 LOWE, C. H. and WRIGHT, J. W. (1966) Evolution of parthenogenetic species of *Cnemidophorus* (whiptail lizards) in western North America. *J. Arizona Acad. Sci.* **4** 81–7

260 LOVERIDGE, A. (1949) *Many happy days I've squandered*. London, R. Hale

261 LÜDICKE, M. (1962–4) Ordnung der Klasse Reptilia, Serpentes. In *Handbuch der Zoologie. Eine Naturgeschichte der Stämme des Tierreiches* [Kükenthal] Vol. 7. Berlin, de Gruyter

262 LYDEKKER, R. (1912) Reptiles, in *Reptiles, Amphibia, Fishes and lower Chordata*. (Ed. J. T. Cunningham) London, Methuen

263 LYNN, W. G. and ULLRICH, M. C. (1950) Experimental production of shell abnormalities in turtles. *Copeia* No. 4 253–62

264 McDOWELL, S. B. (1967) The extracolumella and tympanic cavity of the 'earless' monitor lizard. *Lanthanotus borneensis*. *Copeia* No. 1 154–9

265 McDOWELL, S. B. and BOGERT, C. M. (1954) The systematic position of *Lanthanotus* and the affinities of the anguinomorphan lizards. *Bull. Am. Mus. nat. Hist.* **105** 1–142

266 MACKAY, R. S. (1964) Galapagos tortoise and marine iguana deep body temperatures measured by radio telemetry. *Nature, Lond.* **204** 355–8

267 MADERSON, P. F. A. (1965) Histological changes in the epidermis of snakes during the sloughing cycle. *J. Zool. Lond.* **146** 98–113

268 MADERSON, P. F. A. (1966) Histological changes in the epidermis of the tokay (*Gekko gecko*) during the sloughing cycle. *J. Morph.* **119** 39–50

269 MADERSON, P. F. A. (1966) Some macroscopic and microscopic observations on the foot-pads of the tokay (*Gekko gecko*). *Mem. Hong Kong nat. Hist. Soc.* No. 7 6–10

270 MADERSON, P. F. A. (1968) The epidermal glands of *Lygodactylus* (Gekkonidae, Lacertilia). *Breviora Mus. comp. Zool.* No. 288 1–35

271 MADERSON, P. F. A. (1968) Observations on the epidermis of the tuatara (*Sphenodon punctatus*). *J. Anat.* **103** 311–20

272 MAHENDRA. B. C. (1938) Some remarks on the phylogeny of the Ophidia. *Anat. Anz.* **86** 347–56 [of reprint]

273 MAHENDRA, B. C. (1941) Contributions to the bionomics, anatomy, reproduction and development of the Indian house-gecko, *Hemidactylus flaviviridis* Rüppel, Part II. The problem of locomotion. *Proc. Indian Acad. Sci.* **13** 288–306

274 MAHENDRA, B. C. (1947) As above. Part IV. The respiratory and vocal organs. *Proc. Indian Acad. Sci.* **25** 57–73

275 MARSHALL, A. J. and HOOK, R. (1960) The breeding biology of equatorial vertebrates: reproduction of the lizard *Agama agama lionotus* Boulenger at lat. 0° 01′N. *Proc. zool. Soc. Lond.* **134** 197–205

276 MATTHEY, R. (1949) *Les chromosomes des vertébrés.* Lausanne, Librairie de l'Université F. Rouge

277 MAY, R. M. (1924) Skin grafts in the lizard *Anolis carolinensis. Br. J. exp. Biol.* **1** 539–55

278 MERTENS, R. (1942) Die Familie der Warane (Varanidae). *Abh. Senckenbergischen Naturforsch. Ges.* Part 1: Allgemeines. **462** 1–116. Part 2: Der Schädel. **465** 117–234. Part 3: Taxonomie. **466** 235–391 [Mertens has written many later papers on monitors]

279 MERTENS, R. (1964) Über Reptilienbastarde, III. *Senckenberg. biol.* **45** 33–49

280 MERTENS, R. (1960) *The world of amphibians and reptiles.* Translated by H. W. Parker. London, G. G. Harrap

281 MERTENS, R. (1965) Beiträge zum Thema: Krankheiten der Reptilien. *Zool. Garten* **31** 133–43

282 MERTENS, R. and WERMUTH, H. (1960) *Die Amphibien und Reptilien Europas (Dritte Liste, nach dem Stand von 1 Januar 1960).* Frankfurt am Main, W. Kramer

283 MILLER, C. M. (1944) Ecologic relations and adaptations of the limbless lizards of the genus *Anniella. Ecol. Monogr.* **14** 271–89

284 MILLER, M. R. (1966) The cochlear duct of lizards and snakes. *Am. Zool.* **6** 421–9

285 MILLER, M. R. and KASAHARA, M. (1967) Studies on the cutaneous innervation of lizards. *Proc. Calif. Acad. Sci.* **34** 549–68

286 MINTON, S. A. (1967) Observations on toxicity and antigenic makeup of venoms from juvenile snakes. Pp. 211–22 in *Animal Toxins* (Ed. F. E. Russell and P. R. Saunders) London etc., Pergamon Press [A symposium]

287 MITTWOCH, U. (1967) *Sex chromosomes.* New York & London, Academic Press

557

288 MŁYNARSKI, M. and MADEJ, Z. (1961) The rudimentary limbs in Aniliidae (Serpentes) *Br. J. Herpet.* **3** No. 1 1–6

289 MOOK, C.C. (1921) Skull characters of recent Crocodilia with notes on the affinities of the recent genera. *Bull. Am. Mus. nat. Hist.* **44** 123–268. See also pp. 51–66 on age variations of skull.

290 MORRIS, R. and MORRIS, D. (1965) *Men and snakes.* London, Hutchinson

291 MOSAUER, W. (1932) On the locomotion of snakes. *Science, N.Y.* **76** 583–5

292 MOSELEY, J.M., MATTHEWS, E.W., BREED, R.H., GALANTE, L., TSE, A., and MacINTYRE, I. (1968) The ultimobranchial origin of calcitonin. *Lancet* Jan. 20, 1968 108–10

293 MROSOVSKY, N. (1964) Modification of the diving-in response of the red-eared terrapin. *Pseudemys ornata callirostris. Quart. J. exp. Psychol.* **16** 166–71

294 MROSOVSKY, N. and BOYCOTT, B.B. (1966) Intra- and interspecific differences in phototactic behaviour of freshwater turtles. *Behaviour* **26** 215–27

295 MYERS. C.W. (1967) The hemipenis of an anomalepid snake. *Herpetologica* **23** 235–8

296 NEW, D.A.T. (1966) *The culture of vertebrate embryos.* New York & London, Logos Press (Academic Press)

297 NIKOL'SKII, A.M. (1963–4) *Fauna of Russia and adjacent countries.* 2 vols. Translated by L. & E.Kochva. Israel Program for Scientific Translations. Jerusalem. [1st publ. Petrograd, 1915–16]

298 NOBLE, G.K. (1937) The sense organs involved in the courtship of *Storeria, Thamnophis* and other snakes. *Bull. Am. Mus. nat. Hist.* **73** 673–725

299 NOBLE, G.K. and MASON, E.R. (1933) Experiments on the brooding habits of the lizards *Eumeces* and *Ophisaurus. Am. Mus. Novit.* No. 619 1–29

300 NOBLE, G.K. and SCHMIDT, A. (1937) The structure and function of the facial and labial pits of snakes. *Proc. Am. phil. Soc.* **77** 263–88

301 NOËL-HUME, I. and NOËL-HUME, A. (1954) *Tortoises, Terrapins and Turtles.* London, F.Muller

302 OELRICH, T.M. (1956) The anatomy of the head of *Ctenosaura pectinata* (Iguanidae). *Misc. Publs. Mus. Zool. Univ. Michigan* No. 94 1–122

303 OLIVER, J.A. (1951) 'Gliding' in amphibians and reptiles, with a remark on an arboreal adaptation in the lizard, *Anolis carolinensis carolinensis* Voigt. *Am. Nat.* **85** 171–6

304 OLIVER, J.A. (1955) *The Natural history of North American amphibians and reptiles.* Princeton, etc, D.Van Nostrand

305 OLIVER, J.A. (1956) Reproduction in the king cobra, *Ophiophagus hannah* Cantor. *Zoologica. N.Y.* **41** 145–52

306 OLIVER, J.A. (1963) *Snakes in fact and fiction.* New York, Doubleday, Natural History Library

307 OSTROM, J.H. (1963) Further comments on herbivorous lizards. *Evolution* **17** 368–9

308 OWEN, R. (1866–8) *Comparative anatomy and physiology of vertebrates.* 3 vols. London, Longmans, Green

309 PANIGEL, M. (1956) Contribution à l'étude de l'ovoviviparité chez les reptiles: gestation et parturition chez le lézard vivipare *Zootoca vivipara. Ann. Sci. nat.* **18** 569–668

558

310 PARKER, G.H. (1948) *Animal colour changes and their neurohumours. A survey of investigations* 1910–43. Cambridge University Press

311 PARKER, H.W. (1956) The lizard genus *Aprasia*; its taxonomy and temperature-correlated variation. *Bull. Br. Mus. nat. Hist.* **3** 363–85

312 PARKER, H.W. (1963) *Snakes.* London, R. Hale

313 PARKER, H.W. (1965) *Natural history of snakes.* London, Brit. Mus. (Nat. Hist.)

314 PARKER, W.K. (1883) On the structure and development of the skull in the Crocodilia. *Trans. zool. Soc. Lond.* **11** 263–310 [Parker's other papers on the skull of reptiles are listed in de Beer 132]

315 PARKES, A.S. (Ed.) (1952–66) *Marshall's physiology of reproduction.* 3 vols. (3rd edn.) London, Longmans, Green

316 PARRINGTON, F.R. (1958) The problem of the classification of reptiles. *J. Linn. Soc. Lond. (Zool.).* **44**; *(Bot.).* **56** 99–115

317 PARRINGTON, F.R. (1967) The origins of mammals. Presidential address delivered to Section D (Zoology) on August 31, 1967, at the Leeds meeting of the British Association. *Advancement of Science* Dec. 1967

318 PARSONS, J.J. (1962) *The green turtle and man.* Gainesville, University of Florida Press

319 PARSONS, T.S. (1958) The choanal papillae of the Cheloniidae. *Breviora Mus. Comp. Zool.* No. 85 1–5

320 PARSONS, T.S. (1967) Evolution of the nasal structure in the lower tetrapods. *Am. Zool.* **7** 397–413

321 PEARSON, O.P. (1954) Habits of the lizard *Liolaemus multiformis multiformis* at high altitudes in southern Peru. *Copeia* No. 2 111–16

322 PETERS, J.A. (1964) *Dictionary of herpetology.* New York & London, Hafner

323 PETERSON, E.A. (1966) Hearing in the lizard: some comments on the auditory capacities of a nonmammalian ear. *Herpetologica* **22** 161–71

324 PETTUS, D. (1958) Water relationships in *Natrix sipedon. Copeia* No. 3 207–11

325 PETTUS, D. (1963) Salinity and subspeciation in *Natrix sipedon. Copeia* No. 3 499–504

326 PHISALIX, M. (1922) *Animaux venimeux et venins.* 2 vols. Paris, Masson

327 PIENAAR, U.de V. (1962) *Haematology of some South African reptiles.* Johannesburg, Witwatersrand University Press

328 POOLE, D.F.G. (1957) The formation and properties of the organic matrix of reptilian tooth enamel. *Quart. J. microsc. Sci.* **98** 349–67

329 POOLE, D.F.G. (1961) Notes on tooth replacement in the Nile crocodile *Crocodilus niloticus. Proc. zool. Soc. Lond.* **136** 131–40

330 POPE, C.H. (1941) Copulatory adjustment in snakes. *Field Mus. nat. Hist. Zool. Ser.* **24** 249–52

331 POPE, C.H. (1956) *The reptile world. A natural history of the snakes, lizards, turtles and crocodilians.* London, Routledge & Kegan Paul; NY, Knopf

332 POPE, C.H. (1958) Fatal bite of captive African rear-fanged snake (*Dispholidus*). *Copeia* No. 4 280–2

333 POPE, C.H. (1962) *The giant snakes. The natural history of the boa constrictor, the anaconda, and the largest pythons.* London, Routledge & Kegan Paul; NY, Knopf

334 POPE, C.H. and PERKINS, R.M. (1944) Differences in the patterns of bites of venomous and of harmless snakes. *Archs. Surgery* **49** 331–6

335 PRATT, C. W. M. (1948) The morphology of the ethmoidal region of *Sphenodon* and lizards. *Proc. zool. Soc. Lond.* **118** 171–201

336 PRINGLE, J. A. (1954) The cranial development of certain South African snakes and the relationship of these groups. *Proc. zool. Soc. Lond.* **123** 813–65

337 PRITCHARD, P. C. H. (1967) *Living turtles of the world.* Jersey City, New Jersey, T. F. H. Publications

338 PROCTER, J. B. (1922) A study of the remarkable tortoise, *Testudo loveridgii* Blgr., and the morphogeny of the chelonian carapace. *Proc. zool. Soc. Lond.* 483–526

339 PROSSER, C. L. and BROWN, F. A. (1962) *Comparative animal physiology* (2nd Edn.) Philadelphia & London, W. B. Saunders

340 RATHKE, H. (1839) *Entwicklungsgeschichte der Natter.* Königsberg

341 RAY, J. (1693) *Synopsis methodica animalium quadrupedum et serpentini generis.* London

342 RAYNAUD, A. (1961) Quelques phases du développement des oeufs chez l'orvet (*Anguis fragilis* L.). *Bull. biol. France Belg.* **95** 365–84

343 RAYNAUD, A. (1962) Étude histologique de la structure des ébauches des membres de l'embryon d'orvet (*Anguis fragilis* L.), au cours de leur développement et de leur régression. *C.r. hebd. Seanc. Acad. Sci., Paris* **254** 4505–7

344 REED, C. A. (1957) Non-swimming water turtles in Iraq. *Copeia* No. 1 51

345 REESE, A. M. (1915) *The alligator and its allies.* New York & London, G. P. Putnam's sons.

346 REICHENBACH-KLINKE, H.-H. and ELKAN, E. (1965) *The principal diseases of lower vertebrates.* London & New York, Academic Press

347 REID, H. A. (1968) Snakebite in the tropics. *Br. med. J.* iii 359–62

348 REID, H. A. (1968) Symptomatology, pathology and treatment of land snakebite in India and Southeast Asia. Pp. 611–42 in [77]

349 RICHARDSON, J. and LIVINGSTONE, D. (1962) An attack by a Nile crocodile on a small boat. *Copeia* No. 1 203–4

350 RIDLEY, M. W. and PERCY, R. (1958) The exploitation of sea birds in Seychelles. Colonial Research studies No. 25. London, H.M. Stationery Office

351 ROBINSON, P. L. (1962) Gliding lizards from the Upper Keuper of Great Britain. *Proc. geol. Soc.* No. 1601 137–46

352 ROBINSON, P. L. (1967) The evolution of the Lacertilia. In *Problèmes actuels de paléontologie (Évolution des vertébrés).* Colloques internationaux du Centre National de la recherche scientifique, Paris. No. 163 395–407

353 ROCHON-DUVIGNEAUD, A. (1943) *Les yeux et la vision des vertébrés.* Paris, Masson

354 RODBARD, S. (1948) Body temperature, blood pressure and hypothalamus. *Science, N.Y.* **108** 413–15

355 ROLLINAT, R. (1934) *La vie des reptiles de la France Centrale.* Paris, Librairie Delagrave

356 ROMER, A. S. (1956) *Osteology of the reptiles.* University of Chicago Press

357 ROMER, A. S. (1957) Origin of the amniote egg. *Scient. Monthly* **85** 57–63

358 ROMER, A. S. (1962) *The vertebrate body* (3rd Edn.) Philadelphia & London, Saunders

359 ROMER, A. S. (1966) *Vertebrate paleontology.* (3rd Edn.) University of Chicago

Press. See also *Notes and comments on Vertebrate Paleontology* (1968), University of Chicago Press [a supplementary volume]

360 ROMER, A.S. (1967) Early reptilian evolution re-viewed. *Evolution* **21** 821–33

361 ROSE, W. (1950) *The reptiles and amphibians of southern Africa* Capetown, Maskew Miller

362 ROTH, W.D. and GANS, C. (1960) The luminous organs of *Proctoporus* (Sauria, Reptilia) – re-evaluation. *Breviora Mus. Comp. Zool.* No. 125 1–12

363 RUCKES, H. (1929) Studies in chelonian osteology. Part II. The morphological relationships between the girdles, ribs and carapace. *Ann. N.Y. Acad. Sci.* **31** 81–120

364 RUIBAL, R. and ERNST, V. (1965) The structure of the digital setae of lizards. *J. Morph.* **117** 271–93

365 RUBIN, L., BELLAIRS, A.d'A. and BRYANT, S.V. (1967) Congenital malformations in snakes. *Br. J. Herpet.* 4 No. 1. 12–13

366 RUSSELL, F.E. (1962) Snake venom poisoning. In *Cyclopedia of medicine, surgery and the specialities.* Vol. 2 pp. 199–210. Philadelphia, F.A. Davis

367 RUSSELL, F.E. (1965) Venomous animals and their toxins. Smithsonian report for 1964, 477–87. Smithsonian Institution

368 RUSSELL, F.E. (1965) Snake venom poisoning in children. *Med. Arts Sci.* **19** 142–4

369 RUSSELL, F.E. and SCHARFFENBERG, R.S. (1964) *Bibliography of snake venoms and venomous snakes.* West Covina, California; Bibliographic Associates

370 SAINT GIRONS, H. (1966) Le cycle sexuel des serpents venimeux. *Mem. Inst. Butantan.* Simp. Internac. **33** (1) 105–14

371 SAINT GIRONS, H. (1968) La morphologie comparee des glandes endocrines et la phylogenie des reptiles. *Bijdr. Dierk.* Aflevering **37** 61–79

372 SCHIØTZ, A. and VOLSØE, H. (1959) The gliding flight of *Holsspis guentheri,* a West-African lacertid. *Copeia* No. 3 259–60

373 SCHMIDT, K.P. (1944) Crocodiles. *Fauna* **6** 67–72

374 SCHMIDT, K.P. (1955) Herpetology. In *A century of progress in the natural sciences* – 1853–1953. San Francisco, California Academy of Sciences

375 SCHMIDT, K.P. (1957) Reptiles (except turtles) [in salt water]. *Geol. Soc. Am.* Memoir 67, Vol. 1 1213–16

376 SCHMIDT, K.P. and INGER, R.F. (1957) *Living reptiles of the world.* London, Hamish Hamilton; NY, Doubleday

377 SCHMIDT-NIELSEN, K. (1964) *Desert Animals. Physiological problems of heat and water.* Oxford, Clarendon Press; NY, Oxford UP

378 SCHMIDT-NIELSEN, K., BORUT, A., PING LEE, and CRAWFORD, E.J.R. (1963) Nasal salt excretion and the possible function of the cloaca in water conservation. *Science N.Y.* **142** 1300–1

379 SCHMIDT-NIELSEN, K. and DAWSON, W.R. (1964) Terrestrial animals in dry heat: desert reptiles. In *Handbook of Physiology* Section 4: *Adaptation to the environment.* Washington, D.C. American Physiological Society. [A multiauthor compilation]

380 SCHMIDT-NIELSEN, K. and FANGE, R. (1958) Salt glands in marine reptiles. *Nature Lond.* **182** 783–5

381 SENN, D. G. (1966) Über das optische System im Gehirn squamater Reptilien. *Acta anat.* (Suppl. 52 = 1 ad Vol. 65) 1-87 of reprint

382 SEXTON, O. J. (1964) Differential predation by the lizard, *Anolis carolinensis*, upon unicoloured and polycoloured insects after an interval of no contact. *Animal Behaviour* **12** 101–10

383 SHARELL, R. (1966) *The tuatara, lizards and frogs of New Zealand*. London, Collins; San Francisco, Tri Ocean

384 SHRIVASTAVA, R. K. (1963) The structure and development of the chondrocranium of *Varanus*. *Folia Anat. Japon.* **39** 55–83. Later studies in *J. Morph.*, 1964, **115**, 97–108 and *Morph. Jb.*, 1964, **106** 147–87

385 SHUTE, C. C. D. and BELLAIRS, A. d'A. (1955) The external ear in Crocodilia. *Proc. zool. Soc. Lond.* **124** 741–9

386 SIMKISS, K. (1967) *Calcium in reproductive physiology*. London, Chapman & Hall (Modern Biological Studies); NY, Reinhold

387 SIMONETTA, A. (1956) Organogenesi e significata morfologico del sistema intertimpanico dei Crocodilia. *Arch. Ital. Anat. Embriol.* **61** 335–72

388 SIMONETTA, A. (1963) Cranial kinesis and the morphology of the middle ear: two possibly related features. *Evolution* **17** 580–7

389 SIMPSON, S. B. (1965) Regeneration of the lizard tail. Pp. 431–43 in *Regeneration in animals and related problems*. (Ed. V. Kiortsis & H. A. L. Trampusch) Amsterdam, North-Holland Publishing Co. [A symposium]

390 SMITH, H. M. (1946) *Handbook of lizards. Lizards of the United States and Canada*. Ithaca, N.Y., Comstock; London, Constable

391 SMITH, H. M. (1958) Total regeneration of the carapace in a box turtle. *Turtox News* **36** No. 10 234–8

392 SMITH, H. M. and JAMES, L. F. (1958) The taxonomic significance of cloacal bursae in turtles. *Trans. Kansas Acad. Sci.* **61** 86–96

393 SMITH, M. [A]. (1937) Breeding habits of the Indian cobra. *J. Siam. Soc. nat. Hist. Suppl.* **11** 62–3

394 SMITH, M. A. (1931–43) *The Fauna of British India, Ceylon and Burma, including the whole of the Indo-Chinese sub-region. Reptilia and Amphibia* [The Amphibia are not included]. 3 Vols. London, Taylor & Francis

395 SMITH, M. [A]. (1964) *The British amphibians and reptiles*. London and NY, Collins (The New Naturalist) 3rd. Edn.

396 SMITH, M. A. and BELLAIRS, A. d'A. (1947) The head glands of snakes, with remarks on the evolution of the parotid gland and teeth of the Opisthoglypha. *J. Linn. Soc.* (Zool.) **41** 351–68

397 SMITH, M. A., BELLAIRS, A. d'A. and MILES, A. E. W. (1953) Observations on the premaxillary dentition of snakes with special reference to the egg-tooth. *J. Linn. Soc.* (Zool.) **42** 260–8

398 SNYDER, R. C. (1949) Bipedal locomotion of the lizard *Basiliscus basiliscus*. *Copeia* No. 2 129–37

399 SNYDER, R. C. (1954) The anatomy and function of the pelvic girdle and hindlimb in lizard locomotion. *Am. J. Anat.* **95** 1–46

400 SNYDER, R. C. (1962) Adaptations for bipedal locomotion of lizards. *Am. Zool.* **2** 191–203

401 SOLOMON, J. B. (1965) Development of non-enzymatic proteins in relation to

functional differentiation. Pp. 368–441 in *The biochemistry of animal development*. Ed. R. Weber. London, Academic Press [A symposium]

402 STEBBINS, R. C. (1948) Nasal structure in lizards with reference to olfaction and conditioning of inspired air. *Am. J. Anat.* **83** 183–222

403 STEBBINS, R. C. (1958) An experimental study of the 'third eye' of the tuatara. *Copeia* No. 3 183–90

404 STEBBINS, R. C. (1960) Effects of pinealectomy in the western fence lizard *Sceloporus occidentalis*. *Copeia* No. 4 276–83

405 STEBBINS, R. C. (1961) Body temperature studies in South African lizards. *Koedoe* No. 4 54–67

406 STEBBINS, R. C. (1963) Activity changes in the striped plateau lizard with evidence on influence of the parietal eye. *Copeia* No. 4 681–91

407 STEBBINS, R. C. and BARWICK, R. E. (1968) Radiotelemetric study of thermoregulation in a lace monitor. *Copeia* No. 3 541–7

408 STEBBINS, R. C. and EAKIN, R. M. (1958) The role of the 'third eye' in reptilian behaviour. *Am. Mus. Novit.* No. 1870 1–40

409 STEPHENSON, E. M. and STEWART, C. (1955) *Animal camouflage*. London, A. & C. Black

410 STEPHENSON, N. G. (1960) The comparative osteology of Australian geckos and its bearing on their morphological status. *J. Linn. Soc. (Zool.)* **44** 278–99

411 STEPHENSON, N. G. (1966) Effects of temperature on reptilian and other cells. *J. Embryol. exp. Morph.* 16 455–67

412 STOKELY, P. S. (1947) Limblessness and correlated changes in the girdles of a comparative morphological series of lizards. *Am. Midl. Nat.* **38** 725–54

413 SUZUKI, H. K. (1963) Studies on the osseous system of the slider turtle. *Ann. N.Y. Acad. Sci.* **109** 351–410

414 TAUB, A. M. (1966) Ophidian cephalic glands. *J. Morph.* **118** 529–41

415 TAUB, A. M. (1967) Comparative histological studies on Duvernoy's gland of colubrid snakes. *Bull. Am. Mus. nat. Hist.* **138** 1–50

416 TEMPLETON, J. R. (1966) Responses of the lizard nasal salt gland to chronic hypersalemia. *Comp. Biochem. Physiol.* **18** 563–72

417 Ten CATE, J. (1965) Automatic activity of the locomotor centres of the lumbar cord in lizards. *J. Exp. Biol.* **43** 181–4

418 TERENT'EV. P. V. (1965) *Herpetology. A manual on amphibians and reptiles*. Translated by A. Mercado. Israel Program for Scientific Translations, Jerusalem

419 TERENT'EV, P. V. and CHERNOV, S. A. (1965) *Key to amphibians and reptiles*. Translated by L. Kochva. Israel Program for Scientific Translations, Jerusalem

420 THIÉBLOT, L. (1965) Physiology of the pineal body. In *Progress in brain research*. Vol. 10 (Ed. J. A. Kappers and J. P. Schadé). Pp. 479–88. Amsterdam, London, New York. Elsevier Publishing Coy.

421 THOMAS, R. (1965) The feeding habits of captive amphisbaenids. *Herpetologica* **21** 238

422 THOMSON, J. S. (1932). The anatomy of the tortoise. *Sci. Proc. Roy. Dublin Soc.* **20** 359–461

423 THORSON, T. B. (1968) Body fluid partitioning in Reptilia. *Copeia* No. 3 592–601

424 TINKLE, D. W. (1967) *The life and demography of the side-blotched lizard*, Uta

stansburiana. Ann Arbor, Museum of Zoology, University of Michigan

425 TOERIEN, M.J. (1963) The sound-conducting systems of lizards without tympanic membranes. *Evolution* **17** 540–7

426 TOERIEN, M.J. (1967) Experimental embryology and cranial morphology. *S. Afr. J. Sci.* **63** 278–81

427 TYLER, A. (1956) An auto-antivenin in the Gila monster and its relation to the concept of natural auto-antibodies. Pp. 65–74 in [78]

428 UNDERWOOD, G. (1951) Reptilian retinas. *Nature, Lond.* **167** 183–5

429 UNDERWOOD, G. (1954) On the classification and evolution of geckos. *Proc. zool. Soc. London.* **124** 469–92

430 UNDERWOOD, G. (1955) Classification of geckos. *Nature, Lond.* **175** 1089

431 UNDERWOOD, G. (1957) *Lanthanotus* and the anguinomorphan lizards: a critical review. *Copeia* No. 1 20–30

432 UNDERWOOD, G. (1957) On lizards of the family Pygopodidae. A contribution to the morphology and phylogeny of the Squamata. *J. Morph.* **100** 207–68

433 UNDERWOOD, G. (Foreword 1962) *Reptiles of the eastern Caribbean.* Caribbean Affairs (New Series) No. 1. Dept. of extra-mural studies, University of the West Indies, Jamaica

434 UNDERWOOD, G. (1967) *A contribution to the classification of snakes.* London, Brit. Mus. (Nat. Hist.) [see also interesting review of this book by R. Hoffstetter (1968) *Copeia* No. 1 201–13]

435 UNDERWOOD, G. (1966) On the visual-cell pattern of a homalopsine snake. *J. Anat.* **100** 571–5

436 Van der KLAAUW, C.J. (1948) Size and position of the functional components of the skull. A contribution to the knowledge of the architecture of the skull, based on data in the literature. *Archs. Néerland. Zool.* **9** 1–176. Further instalments, vol. 9, 1951 and 1952

437 VILLELA, G.G. and others (1955) Flavoproteins in the blood plasma of the Brazilian snake *Bothrops jararaca. Arch. Biochem. Biophys.* **56** 270–3

438 VINEGAR, A. (1968) Brooding of the eastern glass lizard, *Ophisaurus ventralis. Bull. S. Calif. Acad. Sci.* **67** 65–8

439 VOGEL, Z. (1964) *Reptiles and amphibians. Their care and behaviour.* Translated and revised by G. Vevers. London, Studio Vista; NY, Viking

440 VOLGYESI, F.A. (1966) *Hypnosis in man and animals.* London, Baillière, Tindall & Cassell; Baltimore, Williams & Wilkins

441 VOLSØE, (1944) Structure and seasonal variation of the male reproductive organs of *Vipera berus* (L.) *Spolia Zool. Mus. Hauniensis* V. Copenhagen. 1–172

442 WALKER, W.F. (1959) Closure of the nostrils in the Atlantic loggerhead and other sea turtles. *Copeia* No. 3 257–9

443 WALL, F. (1921) *Ophidia taprobanica or the Snakes of Ceylon.* Colombo, H.R. Cottle

444 WALLS, G.L. (1942) *The vertebrate eye and its adaptive radiation.* Michigan, Cranbrook Institute of Science, Bulletin No. 19

445 WARING, H. (1963) *Color change mechanisms of cold-blooded vertebrates.* New York & London, Academic Press

446 WEEKES, H.C. (1935) A review of placentation among reptiles with particular

regard to the function and evolution of the placenta. *Proc. zool. Soc. Lond.* 625–46

447 WERMUTH, H. (1964) Das Verhältnis zwischen Kopf-, Kumpf- und Schwanz-länge bei den rezenten Krokodilen. *Senckenberg. biol.* **45** 369–95

448 WERMUTH, H. and MERTENS, R. (1961) *Schildkröten. Krokodile Brückenechsen.* Jena, G. Fischer

449 WERNER, Y. L. (1959) Chromosomes of primitive snakes from Israel. *Bull. Res. Counc. Israel* **8 B** 197–8

450 WERNER, Y. L. (1967) Regeneration of specialised scales in tails of *Teratoscincus* (Reptilia: Gekkonidae). *Senckenberg. biol.* **48** 117–24

451 WERNER, Y. L. (1967) Regeneration of the caudal axial skeleton in a gekkonid lizard (*Hemidactylus*) with particular reference to the 'latent' period. *Acta Zool. Stockh.* **48** 103–25

452 WETTSTEIN, O. von (1931–54) Ordnung der Klasse Reptilia. In *Handbuch der Zoologie* (Kükenthal) Vol. 7. Berlin

453 WEVER, E. G. (1967) Tonal differentiation in the lizard ear. *Laryngoscope* **77** 1962–73

454 WEVER, E. G. and VERNON, J. A. (1960) The problem of hearing in snakes. *J. Auditory Research* **1** 77–83

455 WHIMSTER, I. W. (1965) An experimental approach to the problem of spottiness. *Br. J. Dermatol.* **77** 397–420

456 WHITE, G. (N.d.) *Natural history of Selborne (Antiquities of Selborne)* London & New York. F. Warne. 1st Ed. 1789

457 WHITE, M. J. (1954) *Vertebrate chromosomes. Animal cytology and evolution.* Cambridge University Press

458 WILLIAMS, E. E. (1950) Variation and selection in the cervical central articulations of living turtles. *Bull. Am. Mus. nat. Hist.* **94** 505–62

459 WILLIAMS, E. E. (1959) Gadow's arcualia and the development of tetrapod vertebrae. *Quart. Rev. Biol.* **34** 1–32

460 WILLISTON, S. W. (1914) *Water reptiles of the past and present.* Chicago University Press

461 WILSON, E. O. (1957) Behaviour of the Cuban lizard *Chamaeleolis chamaeleontides* (Duméril and Bibron) in captivity. *Copeia* No. 2 145

462 WILHOFT, D. C. (1965) Sexual cycle of the lizard *Leiolopisma fuscum*, a tropical Australian skink. *J. Morph.* **116** 379–88

463 WILHOFT, D. C. (1958) The effect of temperature on thyroid histology and survival in the lizard, *Sceloporus occidentalis. Copeia* No. 4 265–76

464 WOLFLE, D. L. (1940) A learning experiment with snakes. *Copeia* No. 2 134

465 WOODLAND, W. N. F. (1920) Some observations on caudal autotomy and regeneration in the gecko (*Hemidactylus flaviviridis*, Rüppel), with notes on the tail of *Sphenodon* and *Pygopus. Quart. J. micr. Sci.* **65** 63–100

466 WORRELL, E. (1963) *Reptiles of Australia.* Sydney, London, etc., Angus & Robertson

467 WORRELL, E. (1967) *Australian snakes. Crocodiles. Tortoises, Turtles. Lizards.* Sydney, London etc., Angus & Robertson

468 WRIGHT, A. H. and WRIGHT, A. A. (1957) *Handbook of snakes of the United States and Canada.* 2 vols. Ithaca, N.Y., Comstock; London, Constable. Vol. 3 Bibliography (1962). Ithaca, A. H. and A. A. Wright

469 WYNNE-EDWARDS, V. C. (1962) *Animal dispersion in relation to social behaviour.* London & Edinburgh, Oliver & Boyd; NY, Hafner

470 YNTEMA, C. L. (1964) Procurement and use of turtle embryos for experimental procedures. *Anat. Rec.* **149** 577–86

470a YNTEMA, C. L. (1968) A series of stages in the embryonic development of *Chelydra serpentina. J. Morph.* **125** 219–52

471 YOUNG, J. D. (1950) The structure and some physical properties of the testudinian egg shell. *Proc. zool. Soc. Lond.* **120** 455–69

472 ZANGERL, R. (1953) The vertebrate fauna of the Selma formation of Alabama. Part 3 The turtles of the family Prostegidae. Part 4 The turtles of the family Toxochelyidae. *Fieldiana : Geol. Mem.* **3** 57–277

473 ZANGERL, R. (1969) The turtle shell. Pp. 311–339 in [184]

474 ZEHR, D. R. (1962) Stages in the normal development of the common garter snake *Thamnophis sirtalis sirtalis. Copeia* No. 2 322–9

475 ZIKA, J. and SINGER, M. (1965) The relation between nerve fiber number and limb regenerative capacity in the lizard, *Anolis. Anat. Rec.* **152** 137–40

476 ZIMMERMANN, A. A. and POPE, C. H. (1948) Development and growth of the rattle of rattlesnakes. *Fieldiana, Zool.* **32** 355–413

477 ZOOND, A. (1933) The mechanism of projection of the chamaeleon's tongue. *J. exp. Biol.* **10** 174–85

478 ZUG, G. R. (1966) The penial morphology and relationships of cryptodiran turtles. *Occ. Pap. Mus. Zool. Univ. Michigan* No. 647 1–24

Addenda

References to Addenda are indicated throughout the text of both volumes with an asterisk ⌗. Numbered references cited in the Addenda are to the main bibliography.

Volume I

page 7. E. H. Colbert has written a new book dealing with the history of dinosaurian discovery. *Men and dinosaurs.* (1968). London, Evans.

page 15. Vol. I of *Biology of the Reptilia* appeared in 1969 and is listed in the bibliography [184]. Further volumes are planned.

page 26. The millerosaurs, a group of small Permian reptiles with a single temporal opening, may have been intermediate between cotylosaurs and the early eosuchian lepidosaurs.

page 40. *Eunotosaurus* seems to have been a specialised captorhinomorph which paralleled the Chelonia in many ways. No forms intermediate between it and the undoubted Triassic turtles are known, and if it really was a chelonian ancestor it is strange that there are no signs of a plastron. *See* Cox, C. B. (1969). The problematic Permian reptile *Eunotosaurus. Bull. Brit. Mus. nat. Hist.* **18**: 165–96.

The Triassic chelonians are now classified in a suborder separate from the Amphichelydia and called the Proganochelydia. The genus *Proganochelys* may be synonymous with *Triassochelys* [*see* 96, 473].

page 42. The green turtle (*Chelonia mydas*) has not been definitely recorded on British coasts. *See* Brongersma, L. D. (1967) *British turtles.* British Museum (Natural History) [pamphlet].

page 58. This explanation for the perforated acetabulum may be unsatisfactory; it is possible that the hole has some less obvious mechanical significance.

page 71. When moving over a hard surface crocodilians generally walk with the body off the ground. The sprawling type of gait has been observed, however, when the animal is on a soft substrate or when it is walking on the bottom of a pool.

page 72. *Saltoposuchus* perhaps does not give a fair comparison here, since it seems already to have become definitely specialised for bipedalism. The more primitive thecodont *Euparkeria* provides a better example. Estimates of its limb proportions and of the relationship between the lengths of the hind limb and trunk (another significant dimension in this context) suggests that it could run bipedally on occasions about as well as the modern frilled lizard. Interpretation of the gait of fossil forms from limb proportions is, however, a complex problem and the type of locomotion used by the early thecodonts and the ancestors of crocodiles is still debatable. *See* ATTRIDGE, J. & CHARIG, A.J. (July 1967). Crisis in evolution: the Stormberg series. *Sci. Journal*, 48–54, *and* EWER, R.F. (1965). The anatomy of the thecodont reptile *Euparkeria capensis* Broom. *Phil. Trans. Roy. Soc.* **248**: 379–435.

page 83. Recent observations with the scanning electron microscope which shows stereoscopic views of surfaces, have demonstrated that the spatulae on the digital setae of geckos and anoles have the form of minute cups and probably exert a suctorial action. Release of grip is affected when the lizard extends its digits, rolling them back in such a way that the setae can raise their cups with relative ease. *See* GENNARO, J.F. (1969). The gecko grip. *Nat. Hist. N.Y.* **78**, No. 7: 36–43.

page 94, figure 31. Some workers have reported the interclavicle absent in *Anguis* [412].

page 110. *See also* by GANS, C. (1968). Relative success of divergent pathways in amphisbaenian specialisation. *Am. Nat.* **102**: 345–62, and (1969) Amphisbaenians – reptiles specialised for a burrowing existence. *Endeavour*, **28**: 146–51.

page 119. *Sibon nebulatus*, the species shown in Plate 11, is mainly a slug-eater, and its jaws are relatively unmodified.

page 124. Frazzetta [173] draws attention to some interesting differences between the constricting methods of boid and solubrid snakes.

page 139. The ganglion of the ophthalmic may be separate from that of the other sensory components of the trigeminal nerve.

page 147. I am not so sure about this. The bony external nostrils of the gharial are apparently rather complicated [289]. The narial swelling of the male may perhaps involve the cartilage of the front of the nasal capsule and leave some roughening on the bones.

page 186, 197. The following important review has reached me too late for incorporation in the text. GANS, C. & ELLIOTT, W.B. (1968). Snake venoms: production, injection, action. *Advances in Oral Biology*, 3. New York, Academic Press. The authors deal with the venom apparatus and mechanism of secretion, and with the effects and properties of the venom considered as a biological product. The development of Duvernoy's gland in colubrids is by no means always correlated with the presence of grooved teeth, though fairly large glands are often found in species with enlarged but ungrooved teeth at the back of the maxilla.

M. Gabe and H. Saint Girons have produced an important paper on the salivary glands of lepidosaurs (1969). *Mem. Mus. nat. Hist.* **58**, 1–112.

page 206, 212. An important book, *Poisonous snakes of the World*, a manual for use by US Amphibious Forces, has been issued by the US Dept. of the Navy Bureau of Medicine and Surgery (n.d., but since 1965). It was prepared with the advice of Bogert, Gans, Russell and other authorities, and contains information on venom and snake-bite treatment as well as a comprehensive illustrated synopsis of the venomous snakes. The use of incision and suction is generally recommended in the treatment of bites other than those known to have been inflicted by elapid species. It is suggested, however, that local measures are perhaps of greater value after bites by North American crotalines and small vipers elsewhere than after injuries by large Old World vipers such as the puff adder.

page 221. Considerable discrepancies between body temperatures recorded in the field on the one hand, and in laboratory gradients on the other, have been observed in nocturnal geckos. The temperatures of such reptiles may be quite high during the day when they are in retreat and much lower during the night when they are actively foraging. It is possible therefore that minimal foraging temperatures are more important in determining the distribution of nocturnal species than diurnal preferences, or temperatures elicited in a gradient. Nocturnal forms may even be specifically adapted to activity at low temperatures, as has been suggested in the case of *Sphenodon*. It should also be pointed out that the temperature preferences of any species may be influenced by the individual's physiological state. Thus certain reptiles in captivity are known to select warmer areas after feeding, thereby probably accelerating digestion. The relatively high diurnal temperatures of geckos in retreat may have the same function. *See* BUSTARD, H.R. (1967). Activity cycle and thermoregulation in the Australian gecko *Gehyra variegata. Copeia*, No. 4, 753–8.

page 233 and **Vol. II, p. 408.** Licht *et al.* [254] cite evidence from other workers that the duration of daylight or photoperiod is important in influencing testicular activity in lizards. They found, however, that temperature was the principal environmental factor in the control of testicular cycles in the lacertids which they studied, and that photoperiod was of little, if any importance. They also found evidence for an intrinsic rhythm involving testicular activity.

For discussion of the physiological importance of hibernation in captive reptiles, *see* PEAKER, M. (1969). Some aspects of the thermal requirements of reptiles in captivity. *Int. Zoo Yearbook*, **9**: 3–8. This volume contains many articles of interest to vivarium keepers.

page 244. TEMPLETON, J.R. (1960). Respiration and water loss at the higher temperatures in the desert iguana, *Dipsosaurus dorsalis. Physiol. Zool.* **33**, 136–45.

page 253, 260–262. Recent work shows that shunting of blood between the systemic and pulmonary circulations can occur in reptiles and that the direction of the shunts may vary according to circumstances. Thus, in terrapins (*Pseudemys*) oxygenated blood passes from the left to the right side of the ventricle when the animal is breathing air and is actually recirculated to the lungs. The shunt is reversed, however, when the creature dives and the pulmonary resistance rises; much of the deoxygenated blood which would otherwise go to the pulmonary artery is then distributed to the left systemic arch. A similar type of shunt also occurs in the diving alligator, although here the ventricular septum is complete; blood leaving the right ventricle enters the left aortic arch at the expense of the pulmonary artery. There seems to be no evidence, however, for the shunting of blood across the foramen of Panizza in the reverse to normal direction. *See* WHITE, F.N. (1968). Functional anatomy of the heart in reptiles. *Am. Zool.* **8**: 211–19, *and* (1969). Redistribution of cardiac output in the diving alligator. *Copeia*, No. 3, 567–70.

page 263. It is thought that alligators and crocodiles deliberately swallow stones and that these have a hydrostatic function, acting as ballast. *See* [119] and PEAKER, M. (1969). *Br. J. Herpetol.* **4**, No. 4, 103.

page 264, 265. The small intestine of some snakes at least (e.g. *Natrix*) is remarkably convoluted, whereas in the slow-worm and perhaps in certain other snake-like lizards this part of the gut is relatively straight. So little is known about the anatomy of the alimentary viscera of these reptiles that it is impossible to evaluate the significance of such differences. The biliary passages of a snake are described by SABNIS, J.H. (1967). Anatomy and history of the liver in *Natrix piscator*. *Rev. Roumaine Biol. (Zool.)*, **12**, 233–37.

page 267. The paired nature of the depleted fat body is not apparent in the figure.

page 274. A bad guess! It would seem that respiratory water loss in the reptiles which have been studied is surprisingly high [38].

page 275. See RAYNAUD, A., PIEAU, C., & RAYNAUD, J. (1968). Contribution a l'étude de la formation du cloaque chez l'orvet (*Anguis fragilis* L.). *Mém. Mus. nat. Hist. nat.* **52**, 1–64.

Plate 21. After BUSTARD, H.R. (1968). *Pygopus nigriceps* (Fischer): a lizard mimicking a venomous snake. *Br. J. Herpetol.* **4**, No. 2, 22–4. The display shown in the photo was elicited by the approach of a mouse. The gesture is usually followed by a strike past the intruder with the mouth closed. This and another species of *Pygopus* appear to mimic certain small venomous snakes found in the same areas.

Volume II

page 285. Among land snakes only the Typhlopidae have more than one transverse scale row per body segment, the ratio of segments to scale rows varying between about 1 : 1·5 and 1 : 2·2 [434].

page 291. Pieces of skin from *Anolis* and other lizards continue to produce new epidermal generations in tissue culture. See FLAXMAN, A., MADERSON, P. F. A., SZABÓ, G. & ROTH, S. I. (1968). Control of cell differentiation in lizard epidermis *in vitro*. *Developmental Biol.* **18**, 354–74. This article also contains a survey of recent work on the skin in Squamata, and of the nomenclature of the epidermal layers.

page 295. See SPEARMAN, R. I. C. & RILEY, P. A. (1969). A comparison of the epidermis and pigment cells of the crocodile with those in two lizard species. *Zool. J. Linn. Soc.* **48**, 453–66.

page 300. See HADLEY, M.E. & GOLDMAN, J.M. (1969). Physiological color changes in reptiles. *Am. Zool.* **9**, 489–504. Deals mainly with *Anolis*.

page 342. See MROSOVSKY, N., & SHETTLEWORTH, S.J. (1968). Wavelength preferences and brightness cues in the water finding behaviour of sea turtles. *Behaviour*, **32**, 211–57.

page 347. Strictly speaking, the tapetum belongs either to the retina or the choroid, that of crocodilians being retinal. The tapeta of mammalian carnivores is choroidal and does not contain guanine.

page 418. Underwood [434] is sceptical of this.

page 428. Dr H.B.Cott has continued his studies of the Nile crocodile and is preparing a book on the biology of this species. He has observed still more elaborate types of maternal care than those previously described. Female crocodiles with hatched young, as opposed to those on the nest, are often quite aggressive.

page 435, 531. The egg-shell of a few gecko species is parchment-like. See BUSTARD,

H.R. (1968). The egg-shell of gekkonid lizards: a taxonomic adjunct. *Copeia*, No. 1, 162–4.

page 445. *See also* HUBERT, J., DUFAURE, J.P. & COLLIN, J.P. (1966). Matériaux pour une table de développment de *Vipera aspis* L. I. La période d'organogenèse. *Bull. Soc. Zool. France.* **91**, 779–88.

page 457. *See also* CUELLAR, O. (1968). Additional evidence for true parthenogenesis in lizards of the genus *Cnemidophorus*. *Herpetologica*, **24**, 146–50.

page 459, 461. Dawbin believes that *Sphenodon* may continue to grow in size for a long period [130]. In old specimens the ends of the bones are fully ossified, but it is unknown whether the ossification spreads from the shaft, or whether there is ossification of the calcified secondary centre and subsequent fusion with the shaft [208].

page 464. In *Reptiles round the world* (1957), New York, A.A.Knopf), C.H.Pope graphically illustrates the growth pattern of python 'Sylvia' compared with that of a boy. I have only recently come across this delightful and informative little book.

page 486. *See* BELLAIRS, A.d'A. & BRYANT, S.V. (1968). Effects of amputation of limbs and digits of lacertid lizards. *Anat. Rec.* **161**, 489–96.

page 500. Y.L.Werner (1968) has drawn attention to the reduction of autotomy planes in certain sand-living geckos. *Vie et Milieu*, Ser. C., **19**, 199–222.

page 536. GANS, C. (1967). A check list of recent amphisbaenians (Amphisbaenia, Reptilia). *Bull. Am. Mus. nat. Hist.* **135**, 61–106.

page 538, 542. Underwood [434] adds the following genera to the list of snakes of the subfamily Colubrinae. *Amphiesmoides*, S.As. – *Balanophis*, S.As. – *Dendrolycus*, Af. – *Ditaxodon*, S.Am. – *Eridiphas*, N.Am. – *Gomesophis*, S.Am. – *Madagascarophis*, Mad. – *Myersophis*, Phil. – *Natriciteres*, Af. – *Padangia*, E.I. – *Schmidtophis*, N.Am. – *Tantalophis*, N.Am. To the Elapidae, *Parademansia*, Aus. is added. *Atractaspis* is distinct in many ways from other vipers.

General

BROWN, G.W. (Ed.). (1968). *Desert Biology*. Academic Press. Contains valuable information on reptiles.

Corrections

Plate 21. The sign † should read · to indicate a reference to the Addenda.

Plate 45. The dewlap of *Iguana* has some mobility; in the individual shown it is fully extended.

Plate 65. *For* oviduct of common lizard (*Lacerta vivipara*) ... *read* oviduct of slow-worm (*Anguis fragilis*) ... (× 3).

Index

Page numbers in bold type indicate principal references. Citations in italics indicate the pages of text-figures. An asterisk ⁕ indicates items in Addenda, Vol. II. Only authors' names referred to in the main text are listed in the index.

590